Dance
Kinesiology

DANCE
Kinesiology

SECOND EDITION

SALLY SEVEY FITT

UNIVERSITY OF UTAH

*This work was funded in part by a grant
from the University of Utah Research Committee*

Schirmer
Thomson Learning

Australia • Canada • Mexico • Singapore • Spain • United Kigdom • United States

Figures 2.1; 3.1, 3.4, 3.10, 3.13, 3.15; 4.1, 4.3, 4.7, 4.8; 5.1, 5.3; 6.1, 6.3; 7.1, 7.2, 7.4, 7.6, 7.7, 7.8, 7.9; 8.1, 8.2, 8.3, 8.4, 8.5; 9.1, 9.5, 9.6, 9.8, 9.9; 10.1, 10.2, 10.3, 10.4, 10.9; 11.1, 11.2, 11.3; 12.1, 12.2; 14.1, 14.2, 14.3, 14.4(a), (b), 14.5, 14.6, 14.7. Reprinted by permission from Alexander Spence, *Basic Human Anatomy*. The Benjamin/Cummings Publishing Company, Inc., Menlo Park, CA, 1982.

Figures 3.12, 3.14; 4.2, 4.4, 4.9; 5.5; 6.2, 6.4, 6.5; 9.2, 9.3, 9.7; 10.5, 10.8, 10.10, 10.11; 14(c), (d), (e), From *Kinesiology: Scientific Basis of Human Motion*, 6th ed., by Katharine F. Wells and Kathryn Luttgens. Copyright © 1976 by W.B. Saunders Company. Reprinted by permission of CBS College Publishing.

Figure 7.3. Reprinted with permission of Macmillan Publishing Company from the *Physiology of Exercise*, 2d ed., by David R. Lamb. Copyright © 1984 by David R. Lamb.

Figure 15.1. Reprinted with permission of Macmillan Publishing Company from *Structural Kinesiology* by Jerry N. Barham and Edna R. Wooten. Copyright © 1973 by Macmillan Publishing Company.

Cover photograph: Merce Cunningham Dance Company
© Johan Elbers 1993

Schirmer is an imprint of Wadsworth,
a division of Thomson Learning, Inc.
Thomson Learning™ is a trademark
used herein under license.

Library of Congress Catalog Card Number: 96–32649

Printed in the United States of America

Printing Number
          04 05 06   5 6 7 8 9 0

Library of Congress Cataloging-in-Publication Data
Fitt, Sally Sevey.
    Dance kinesiology / Sally Sevey Fitt.—2nd ed.
        p.   cm.
    Includes bibliographical references and index.
    ISBN 0–02–864507–3
    1. Dance—Physiological aspects.   I. Title.
QP310.D35F58   1996
612.7′6—dc20   96–32649
                                        CIP

This paper meets the requirements of ANSI/NISO Z39.48–1992 (Permanence of Paper).

To Pat Paterson:
who first tried to pound kinesiological concepts into my head before I was ready to understand their importance.

To Valerie V. Hunt:
who, years later, made those concepts alive and practical when I was ready to learn.

To Carol Warner:
whose profound kinesthetic awareness of motion and bodily wisdom challenged the textbooks and inevitably forced me to continue to grow and question.

The Soul of a Dancer

I dance because I must.
I dance because
the thoughts, feelings, and responses
of my life
are best expressed in motion,
because
life is motion
and motion is life.

As I move,
I embrace life
and sing the joyous song
of easeful, expressive movement.

Soaring, twisting, turning
in every possible combination,
I am defined by movement,
and actualized through movement.
I AM, therefore I dance;
I DANCE, therefore I am.
Thus I continue to explore, to grow, to be.

To all those who have danced,
who dance now,
and who will dance in the future
I dedicate this
Second Edition of *Dance Kinesiology.*
May your hearts and souls
dance forever. . . .

(and may this book help your body cooperate)
ssf June 15, 1995

Contents

Preface

For many years, dancers did not concern themselves with a conscious study of the sciences of human motion. The lack of research in the area of dance kinesiology before about 1950 indicates an apparent lack of interest in science and the art of dance. As modern dance moved into institutions of higher education in the 1950s (accompanied in some instances by ballet), some dancers and dance educators became aware of the potential benefits the science of movement had for dance.

Notable early pioneers in the application of movement sciences to dance included Margaret H'Doubler, Mabel Ellsworth Todd, Raoul Gelabert, Lulu Sweigard, and Valerie Hunt. Their early works broke ground for the development of a body of knowledge called *dance kinesiology*. Another indication of the acceptance of movement sciences into the discipline of dance was the formation of the Congress on Research in Dance (CORD), whose publications carried the bulk of dance kinesiology research reports in the early stages of development. Further support for the inclusion of dance kinesiology in the curricula of dance departments was gained through the work of the Council of Dance Administrators (CODA) and their publication of a list of standards for dance programs which included dance kinesiology in the recommended offerings. More recently, the publication of *Kinesiology for Dance*, originally a newsletter and now *Kinesiology and Medicine for Dance*, has extended the literature in the area.

Early publications that related anatomy to the art of the dancer include Celia Sparger's *Anatomy and Ballet*, Raoul Gelabert's *Anatomy for the Dancer*, and Mabel Ellsworth Todd's *The Thinking Body*. More recent publications such as Lulu Sweigard's *Human Movement Potential*, and Daniel Arnheim's *Dance Injuries* focused attention on the need for a developing literature of dance kinesiology. The publication of Kenneth Law's *Physics of Dance* was a valuable addition to the literature. It is hoped that the publication of the Second Edition of *Dance Kinesiology* will continue to contribute to the development of knowledge related to the scientific investigation of dance.

This book is not a simple revision of standard kinesiology texts for physical education and sport. Dance kinesiology is different from sport kinesiology, although some components remain the same. The focus of analysis must shift, along with the change from sport to dance.

Traditionally, kinesiology has been offered to students in physical education curricula and has been taught by sport specialists. The primary objectives of kinesiology have therefore centered on the analysis of sports skills to facilitate systematic improvement. That basic objective does not change when one moves into dance kinesiology, but the focus of analysis does change. For example, a kinesiologist might study the relationship between the relative angle of takeoff and the height of a jump. That kind of biomechanical analysis is most effective when evaluation is measured in objective terms such as time, distance, or scores. However, the evaluation of dance is subjective in nature, not objective. While physical education and sport involve movement for the sake of accomplishing an external goal with a product orientation, dance involves movement for its own sake with a process orientation. The essential fire of dance is unquantifiable. Evaluation of dance is done with the heart and soul, not the tape measure or the stopwatch. These basic differences between sport and dance require a different approach to the analysis of motion. With no objective measures to rely on, dance educators must develop even greater sensitivity than they have exhibited in the past to the specific components of each movement performed.

The primary goals of dance education are different from the goals of physical education. The primary educational objective of dance is to develop a generalized skill level that allows for and encourages versatility in movement. Dance utilizes motion for expression and communication. Sport utilizes motion to prove a player more skilled than other players. Competition is the bedrock of sport. While there certainly may be some level of competition in the dance world, the critical goal remains communication of a sensation, a thought, an emotion, or an experience. These differences between sport and dance are not merely superficial in nature but have a direct effect on the way kinesiology is approached and utilized. For example, analysis of force vectors may not be as appropriate for the dancer as for the athlete.

Analysis of force vectors is important to a baseball pitcher or a discus thrower who seeks to achieve the extremes of accuracy or distance in throwing or tossing. A dancer's projectile is actually the body, and the analysis of force vectors is done internally and automatically. A dancer who does not kinesthetically understand the force vector in landing from a leap will not be a dancer long. Sooner or later the stumbling falls will end the career. The biomechanics of motion are *personal* to the dancer: these are the sensations and responses that come automatically in response to gravity's effect on the weight of the body. Such perceptions are difficult to describe and almost impossible to measure, yet they are essential to dance performance. Thus, the dancer and the teacher of dance frequently resort to imagery to describe and share those perceptions. But imagery is far less precise than the objective measures of excellence that are available to the athlete. Time, distance, and scoring provide specific data for comparative athletic evaluation, and, while good form may certainly be one goal of sport, most athletes are more concerned with results than form. For example, the radical shift in high-jumping technique was brought about by the obvious success of a new technique. Athletics are essentially utilitarian: whatever improves time, distance, or score is acceptable. Dance is essentially idealistic and aesthetic: form and alignment are paramount. Beyond these philosophical differences, there are also physical differences.

Physical education students spend an extended period of time studying the structure and function of the arm and hand. This emphasis is reasonable, since that area of the body is the focus of many of the manipulative skills of sports such as tennis, golf, baseball, and others. Dancers have far less interest in the arm and hand and far more interest in the lower extremity than many athletes. This difference in the areas of the body that receive the greatest emphasis is another distinction between dance kinesiology and sport kinesiology.

Yet another distinction is apparent in the mode of muscular analysis of motion. Onetime muscular analysis, conducted with reference to textbooks or notes in an open-book fashion, may be adequate for physical education because sport skills do not change markedly from day to day. There may be some modifications to accommodate the most recent rule changes, but the basic skills remain fairly constant over time. Modern dancers, however, are constantly being confronted with new movement expectations as they take classes from different teachers and as they are exposed to different choreographic demands. The ever-changing nature of the expectations for the modern dancer make onetime muscular analysis obsolete before it is even completed. Dance is a "sport" where the rules change every day. A few principles remain fairly constant in technique class, such as alignment and "working from the center," but even those principles may be forsaken in a specific performance to achieve a particular effect. Consequently, dancers must be able to analyze motion "on their feet," and this means that they must carry in their heads the information concerning joint action, action of gravity, and resultant muscular action. Memorization of this information is essential to immediate analysis of dance skills in the studio, where demands change so frequently.

Each of these differences between sport and dance points to the need for specialized courses of study in dance kinesiology. The potential benefit to dancers increases in geometric progression when class content is specifically focused on dance.

This book provides a beginning of the body of knowledge of anatomical dance kinesiology. It will be of assistance to dance educators attempting to add specialized dance kinesiology classes to the curricula. Although specifically written for dancers, this book expounds the new approach to kinesiology from a practical and usable standpoint—to increase skill and reduce injury. And this certainly may be of value to coaches, physical education teachers, and athletes. A new emphasis on the role of gravity in the production of human motion may also be of value to sport kinesiologists, who have sometimes neglected the analysis of gravity's role in determining muscular action.

There has long been a need for kinesiology to be taken out of the realm of the abstract and theoretical analyses and placed in the domain of practical movement analysis. In order for this to happen, a new pragmatic approach to kinesiology is needed. What information is essential to physical educators, coaches, and dance educators as they deal with the practical problems encountered in the studio, in the gymnasium, or on the playing field? What information is essential to the athletes and dancers, themselves, as they struggle to increase skill without injuring themselves? The author's experiences in the dance studio and on the playing field, although limited, have played an important role in screening the usual content of kinesiology classes. No component of kinesiology escaped the screening process reflected in the question, "Will this information be useful?" The screening process resulted in the deletion from this book of a number of the "sacred cows" of kinesiology. For example, most of the information on biomechanics has been deleted. Once again, the exclusion does not mean that the author deems the information unimportant. Rather, the concepts of mathematical analysis of motion, epitomized by the analysis of force vectors and the trigonometry of motion, are thought to be much more appropriate for graduate students than for undergraduates.

In this book, all of the examples and illustrations are taken from dance, not sport. The exclusive use of dance examples is intended to formally acknowledge the dancer as a legitimate focus for kinesiological analysis of motion.

Second Edition

When the publisher approached me with the suggestion that I do a second edition, I responded, "Why? How many muscles and bones have changed since the first edition?" However, as I thought about it, a second edition would offer an opportunity to make needed corrections and to expand on sections of the book in areas where the body of knowledge or the interest of dancers has greatly expanded since the first edition.

The first edition of *Dance Kinesiology* was written on a typewriter, not a computer, and "a few" errors slipped through the cracks, despite my efforts to carefully proofread each phase of the work. The second edition allows for the correction of those errors, and for needed revisions and expansion.

The chapter entitled "Tension, Stress, Efficiency, and Relaxation" in the first edition needed considerable revision and expansion, in order to reflect the increased interest of dancers in somatic work. However, my respect for the intensive training of the somatic practitioners is far too great to let me distort the concepts by writing from my limited perspective. Therefore, instead of expanding the discussions myself, I recruited trained practitioners to write about what I perceived to be the most popular of the somatic approaches for dancers: Susan McClain: The Pilates Method™; Mary Bond: Rolfing™; Carol Lessinger: Feldenkrais Method®; Jacque Lynn Bell: Alexander Technique™; Pamela Matt: Ideokinesis; Bonnie

Bainbridge Cohen: Body-Mind Centering™; Peggy Hackney: Bartinieff Fundamentals™; and Madeleine Scott: Laban Movement Analysis.™

> "Ninety-five percent of being smart . . .
> is knowing what you're dumb at."
>> (Anonymous)

I must add that the other 5 percent is knowing people who are smart in the areas where you are dumb. I am sincerely grateful to the contributors to the second edition noted above. Their expert contributions add depth and breadth to the new edition of *Dance Kinesiology*.

Acknowledgments

First and foremost, I must thank my students, who over the years have asked probing and pertinent questions that forced me to continue to grow. Thanks also go to the entire faculty of the Department of Modern Dance at the University of Utah for their continuing support and for their patience as I "disappeared" to do the work on the Second Edition. I am also grateful for the valuable, specific suggestions for revision that I received from a number of people in the field of dance kinesiology, including Anthony Morgan, Dana Appling, Tom Welsh, and Marjorie A. Moore. I must further thank all of the contributors to the Second Edition, who were "smart where I was not," including Jacque Bell, Mary Bond, Bonnie Bainbridge Cohen, Peggy Hackney, Carol Lessinger, Pamela Matt, Madeleine Scott, and Susan McClain-Smith. Their contributions to the Second Edition are valuable additions, and I am grateful for their generous sharing of their expertise.

I had hoped to include chapter sections from Martha Eddy and Silvie Fortin, who made stunning and pertinent presentations at the Somatics and Science Conference in February of 1995. Even though I received great cooperation from both Martha and Silvie; from Ruth and John Solomon, the editors of the issue of *Impulse* covering the conference; and from Linda Bump, the editor of *Impulse* at Human Kinetics Publishers, the logistics and timing simply couldn't coordinate with my dates for submission of the manuscript. Nevertheless, I thank each of the people involved in the attempt to "make it work."

Illustrations are by Mary Scopes; text photography is by Rosalind Newmark.

S. S. F.

The Science of Motion in Support of the Art of Dance

*T*he arts and the sciences often seem to be at odds with each other because of certain assumptions. It is assumed the artist is intuitive, reaching to often untraceable thoughts, feelings, and perceptions about the world. The artist's inspiration frequently comes from an unknown source and is seldom a logical, step-by-step process. In contrast, it is assumed that the scientist is logical and rational, proceeding with careful investigation from one conclusion to the investigation of the next question. The scientist and the artist have frequently viewed each other with misunderstanding and the stereotyped assumptions that have led to the separation of art and science. To the scientist, the artist often appears scatterbrained and illogical. To the artist, the scientist is often rigid and myopic. Both science and art suffer greatly by separation. The most visionary artists and scientists refute such separation as ridiculous and limiting.

It is thought that many artistic processes relate to the functioning of the nondominant hemisphere of the brain, while scientific processes relate to the dominant hemisphere of the brain. Current research in brain function indicates that two hemispheres of the cerebral cortex of the brain have unique functions: one hemisphere guiding the logical, linear, and verbally oriented thought processes and the other guiding the intuitive, nonverbal, and spatially oriented thought processes (Sperry, 1973). The two hemispheres of the brain are connected by the corpus

Note: Parts of the Introduction and Chapter 1 are taken from: Sally S. Fitt, "The Science of Motion in Support of the Art of Dance." In Howell and Barham (eds.), *Proceedings of the VII Commonwealth and International Conference on Sport, Physical Education, Recreation, and Dance. Volume I.* University of Queensland, Brisbane, Australia, 1982.

callosum and, in normal functioning, operate in concert with one another. If we accept the unified yet dualistic function of the human brain as a model, we must realize that normal functioning is not based exclusively on one mode or the other. Rather, the two hemispheres of the brain work together to deal effectively with the challenge of human experience. Further applying this model of human brain function, we see that the scientist must sometimes use the nonlinear, intuitive mode of thought, and the artist must sometimes use the linear, logical mode. It is not the purpose of this section to discuss the research on hemispheric dominance in the brain, even though that scientific information is applicable to the creative process. Rather, hemispheric dominance is cited to serve as a model of synergistic functioning. In optimal functioning, the relationship between the two hemispheres is truly complementary, with each hemisphere contributing to the complex act of processing information. It is such a synergism that merges the science of human motion with the art of dance.

Dance is an expressive art form that relies totally on human movement for communication. Choreography and performance are the two primary avenues of expression in dance. The work of the choreographer is making dances. The work of the dancer is performing those dances with clarity and adherence to the purposes of the choreographer. Each of these two roles is potentially benefited by accurate scientific knowledge of human motion.

The choreographer is a selector. He or she selects movement to express an idea or feeling and also selects dancers to perform the work. The choreographer must be aware of the full range of movement possibilities in order to be able to select the combination of movements that will communicate his or her intent accurately and effectively. Likewise, accurate knowledge of the movement potential of the available dancers allows for effective casting of the dance work. The science of human motion can facilitate the choreographer's selection process.

The dancer is a performer. Dance, as an expressive art form, is totally dependent on the dancer's physical skills. As such, dance holds a unique position in the arts because of the absolutely essential synthesis of art and science. The dancer, in effect, must build and tune his or her instrument (the body) before a truly elegant performance can be achieved. Unfortunately, most dancers are not provided with perfect raw materials. One leg may be longer than the other, the spine may exhibit an abnormal curve, or the foot may provide an uneven base of support for balance. No Stradivarius or Steinway would accept such inferior materials. Yet the dancer has no choice: one body per dancer is the allotment. The dancer must accommodate to the imperfections. Dance, therefore, requires a unique synthesis of the science of human motion with the art of dance. In the past, the synthesis has often been on an unconscious level and somewhat governed by chance. However, when the dancer has access to specific information about the structure and functions of the human body, the synthesis may shift to the conscious level. Conscious awareness of the science of motion can do much to facilitate excellence in performance and prevent injury. The science of human motion provides the dancer with essential information about structure, function, and the achievement of optimal performance. The merging of art and science is essential in dance. Through the rigors of disciplined training, the dancer may attain true freedom of expression. The better the training, the greater the freedom.

The purpose of this book is to present the various scientific tools of movement analysis that support and facilitate the work of the dancer and the choreographer. A cocktail party definition of kinesiology is: "the study of muscles and bones and how they work." While this definition is adequate for laypeople, it is not inclusive enough for the purposes of this book: I wish to clarify what dance kinesiology includes and what it does not include. I do not presume to represent every dance kinesiologist in this presentation, because anyone's particular approach may differ from my own. Instead, I shall identify those elements of kinesiology I have found to be most pertinent to dance.

CHAPTER 1

Domain of Dance Kinesiology

Kinesiological analysis falls into three general categories: *structural* analysis, *biomechanical* analysis, and *neuromuscular* analysis. These three categories form the superstructure for the domain of dance kinesiology. Structural analysis focuses on bony and ligamentous determination of potential action, on restrictions of actions, and on proper alignment. Biomechanical analysis focuses on the physics of motion, application of forces on the lever system, and the resultant possible actions. Neuromuscular analysis focuses on identification of those muscles and groups of muscles that are most efficient in producing a given action. These three components of kinesiological analysis merge to provide information for the dancer and teacher of dance. Understanding the physical variables involved in dance performance allows for more efficient and effective training, prevention of injury, and thus potential extension of the dancer's life as a performer. Some aspects of kinesiology are more valuable to the dancer than others and have determined the content of this book.

Selection of Course Content

For approximately the last thirty years, I have worked with dancers, primarily in modern dance, teaching kinesiology, screening dance injuries, and advising on conditioning techniques. In those years, I have gradually selected the areas of kinesiology that most effectively adapt to modern dance. Certain areas of traditional kinesiology have been deleted from my classes. Other areas have been amplified considerably.

In selecting and evaluating the content of my classes, I have asked myself: How long will it take for the student to learn this? How much immediate- and long-range value does it have for the student? These questions have guided the selection process and have helped me decide what to include and what not to include. Teaching is, at least in part, a process of deciding what to throw away when one is confronted with the time constraints of the academic setting. In my own work with dancers, I have made a number of decisions. I spend no time on the analysis of force vectors, the mathematical analysis of motion, the memorization of the classes of levers, or the scientific terms for the types of joints. I know that, to a traditional kinesiologist, deletion of this information borders on heresy, yet the relative value of knowing and the time required to learn are so unbalanced that, in my opinion, the deletion is justified. Generally, much biomechanical analysis has been deleted and structural and neuromuscular analyses have been amplified. One of my primary objectives is to foster a positive attitude toward understanding the determinants of human movement. Memorization of information that has limited immediate value to the student or dancer does not promote a positive attitude. Analyses of structural and neuromuscular variables are immediately applicable in the dance studio.

Skeletal and Muscular Analysis

Sections II and III focus on skeletal and neuromuscular analysis respectively. The two sections examine:

1. Bony and ligamentous structure, including possible actions, the restrictions of actions, common injuries to those structures, and ideal skeletal alignment.
2. Attachments, paths, and potential actions of the voluntary muscles of the body.
3. Neuromuscular analysis of any action of the human body (without the use of books or notes) by identifying the joint action; the action of gravity; the effective muscle group and the type of contraction (lengthening, shortening or static contraction); and the specific muscles that would be most efficient in the performance of the action.

The last of these three major requirements demands the practical application of information; thus students must develop a clear understanding of the basic information. Dancers must be able to analyze action "on their feet." The information facilitates the wise use of the body in class by giving the student information about the specific muscles being used and the knowledge of how to stretch out these muscles to prevent spasm or undue muscle soreness. Therefore, information on the general structure and function of the skeletal and muscular systems is included. Also included is information on the physiological systems that support human movement. A fundamental understanding of the physiological support systems allows pertinent application in the practical situation. Chapter 14 presents a simplified review of the physiological support systems.

In addition to the general outline above, there are two clusters of information that form critical threads throughout the book. The first is the identification and analysis of individual differences, and the second is the application of the principles of conditioning to dance.

Individual Differences

The information on individual differences in several areas begins in Chapter 2 and weaves throughout the remainder of the book:

1. Muscular imbalances.
2. Differences in skeletal structure that have an effect on performance.
3. Differences in body type (somatotype), including emphasis on the conditioning needs of the ectomorph, the endomorph, and the mesomorph.
4. Differences in natural movement style or movement quality, including analysis of characteristic patterns in the use of time, space, and force.
5. Differences in tension, relaxation, and efficiency.
6. Weight management.
7. Differences in propensity to certain types of injury.

Information on individual differences is absolutely critical for dancers and for future teachers of dance. Traditionally, teachers of dance have been ignorant of the components of individual differences. Having been trained in the same way as their teachers were trained, some teachers of dance have erroneously assumed that each student has the same physical potential as the teacher or as other students: "If I can do it, you should be able to do it."

Chapter 13, on *muscular imbalances,* integrates information from Sections II and III and reviews the implications for dancers.

Knowledge of individual differences in *skeletal structure* can definitely aid teachers and students in the dance studio. For example, it is assumed in many dance classes that every student can achieve 180-degree turnout at the hip joint. However, differences in the anatomical structure of the pelvis—specifically the relative facing and/or depth of the acetabulum (hip socket)—make a 180-degree turnout impossible for some dancers. When demands are placed on all students to achieve that ideal, potentially hazardous compensation must be made. Demanding the same range of motion from every dancer in a class is foolishness. It is my hope that by focusing on structural individual differences, this book may modify some of the traditional and potentially dangerous demands placed on dancers.

My focus on individual differences also includes discussion of *body type* or *somatotype*. While one seldom finds examples of unidimensional body types, the information adds considerably to the student's awareness that there are certain motional propensities that correspond to a given body type. Dancers most frequently fall into the ectomorphic or mesomorphic categories—with a predictable number of combinations—and these two categories demand very different conditioning techniques. The mesomorph's primary conditioning need is for increased flexibility. The ectomorph's primary conditioning needs are for strength, endurance, and reduction of tension. While the conditioning needs for these two body types are so very different, it is not unusual to find ectomorphs and mesomorphs taking the same dance class, which can cause problems for the teacher who tries to meet all students' needs. Further problems occur when an ectomorph student takes a class from a mesomorph, or in the reverse situation. Dancers constantly seem to compare themselves with other dancers. Sometimes the comparison becomes very negative and self-defeating. Understanding the information on somatotype allows the dancer and the teacher of dance to set realistic expectations and further helps them to systematically analyze motional strengths and limitations.

Another area of information on individual differences critical for dancers is *Movement Behavior* (Fitt, 1979; Fitt and Hanson, 1978; Hunt, 1964). Movement Behavior is an Americanization of Rudolph Laban's Effort Analysis (Laban and Lawrence, 1947) and is defined as the systematic analysis of movement style.

> The basic components that are considered in the analysis of Movement Behavior are time, space, and force. Each movement is instigated by a given amount of force, occurs within a given amount of time and occupies a given amount of space. The movements of an individual exhibit a characteristic energy expenditure and can be analyzed by the observation of these components. The observation and analysis of a person's characteristic use of time, space, and force identifies the consistencies and certain variabilities of a person's expenditure of energy and reveals particular capacities and limitations dictated by that style of movement. (Fitt and Hanson, 1978, pp. 17–18)

Thus, Movement Behavior deals with the same elements as Laban's Effort Analysis, but from a slightly different perspective.

Movement Behavior analysis of characteristic *movement style* provides the dancer with a strong information base that relates directly to performance qualities. Movement Behavior also facilitates the casting process when a certain movement quality is called for in a given dance role.

Each person in the profession of movement education is aware, either consciously or unconsciously, of the importance of movement style. A major benefit of Movement Behavior analysis is in bringing this awareness to the conscious level and labeling it. Before the work of Rudolph Laban (1947) and Valerie V. Hunt (1964) the analysis of expressive movement was dependent on such adjectives as *adroit* and *lazy*, which are infused with personal connotations. Systematic analysis of time, space, and force took the personal connotations out of the analytic process.

Another area of information on individual differences is *emphasis on somatics, relaxation, and efficiency.* Efficient motion is one goal of the dancer, superseded only by a strong adherence to the intent that is explicit or implicit in any dance work. Muscular efficiency means achieving the desired effect by using the least amount of physical effort. A certain amount of tension is clearly required, but muscular "overkill" is not desirable. It leads to excessive fatigue and eventually to chronic or traumatic injuries. Dancers and teachers of dance must be conversant with the various body therapies that can contribute to increased efficiency. A description of selected somatic approaches is given in Chapter 17.

Second in the category of individual differences is information on *weight management.* In the real world, fat dancers seldom get jobs. Moreover, fat dancers are more susceptible to injury. Strategies for weight management are given in Chapter 20. The hazards of both overweight and underweight are emphasized.

A final area of individual differences, which is woven throughout the book, is *dance injury.* Propensities for certain types of injuries are discussed in many chapters, and these concepts are brought together in Chapter 18.

Each of these major categories of individual differences (muscular imbalances; skeletal structure; body type; Movement Behavior; tension, relaxation, and efficiency; weight management; and dance injuries) is threaded throughout the book, and each is discussed specifically in a single chapter.

Conditioning for Dancers

Another conceptual thread that appears throughout the book is the information on the conditioning process. Conditioning is the systematic development of movement potential. There are five general categories of conditioning: strength, flexibility, muscular endurance, cardiorespiratory endurance, and neuromuscular coordination. The purposes of conditioning may be corrective, rehabilitative, or developmental, but the principles of conditioning remain the same regardless of the purposes of the conditioning program. Like the information on individual differences, the information on conditioning is presented throughout the book; it is then pulled together in Chapter 19. Implications and content for the chapter on conditioning are drawn from the chapters on muscular imbalances, body types, physiology, relaxation, and dance injury. The "Core Conditioning Program" and the "Mini-Programs" presented in Chapter 19 reflect the general and specific needs of dancers outlined in the preceding chapters.

Objectives of Dance Kinesiology

The objectives of a kinesiology class for dancers can be divided into three general categories: *cognitive* objectives, *affective* objectives, and *practical* objectives. The cognitive objectives outline the critical areas of information. The affective objectives focus on the desired attitudinal changes. The practical objectives emphasize potential studio applications of the information. Tables 1.1, 1.2, and 1.3 present the objectives of dance kinesiology. Figure 1.1, "A Conceptual Model of Dance Kinesiology," shows a complete picture of the domain of dance kinesiology.

To repeat: Affective objectives deal with the critical area of attitudinal change. It has been my experience that dancers, as a group, play down their capabilities and focus on their limitations. This characteristic focus is usually accompanied by a blatant lack of information about how to effectively bring about change. Consequently, the dancer often seems locked into a negative, self-chastising, defeatist cycle which is counterproductive for growth and for the development of high-skill levels. There is, admittedly, a fine line between self-acceptance and self-indulgence. The dancer must be self-acceptant but cannot afford the luxury of self-indulgence.

TABLE 1.1 **Cognitive objectives**

The student of dance kinesiology should demonstrate the following knowledge and understanding.

1. Knowledge of the skeletal structure, bony landmarks, joint action, restrictions of joint actions, proper alignment and its assessment, and individual differences in bone structure.
2. Knowledge of the muscular system, microscopic structure of muscle tissue, variations in muscle structure and function, the mechanism of muscular contraction, muscular attachments, and muscle actions.
3. Knowledge of the role of gravity in determining the type of muscular contraction and the ability to apply that information.
4. Integration of objectives 1, 2, and 3 as demonstrated by analysis of dance movement without the use of books or notes.
5. Knowledge of the general and specific demands of dance on the human body including strength, flexibility, muscular endurance, cardiorespiratory endurance, neuromuscular coordination, tension, and efficiency.
6. Knowledge of techniques to build physical potential and increase efficiency of motion.
7. Knowledge of individual differences that have an impact on dance performance.
8. Knowledge of the types of injury common to dance, as well as preventative measures and treatment modalities.
9. Knowledge of the basic elements of physiological functioning as it supports human movement.

TABLE 1.2 **Affective objectives**

Students should exhibit behaviors that are consistent with the following attitudes.

1. Realistically appraising one's physical capacities and limitations.
2. Realizing that each capacity may also become a limitation if pushed to extremes.
3. Accurately classifying limitations into those which are changeable and those which are not changeable.
4. Being self-acceptant without being self-indulgent.
5. Being willing to take responsibility for one's growth and change.
6. Exhibiting patience; realizing that some changes take longer than others.
7. Becoming increasingly aware of the signals given by the body.

TABLE 1.3 **Practical objectives**

1. To increase awareness of capacities and limitations.
2. To facilitate growth and achieve excellence as fast as possible.
3. To increase muscular efficiency.
4. To prevent injury.
5. To speed up the rehabilitation process when injuries occur.
6. To increase the longevity of the dancer's professional career.

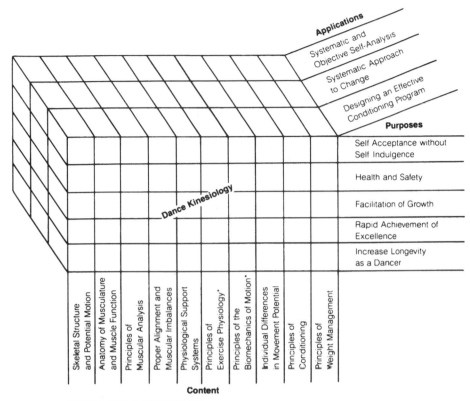

Applications

Systematic and
Objective Self-Analysis

Systematic Approach
to Change

Designing an Effective
Conditioning Program

Purposes

	Self Acceptance without Self Indulgence
	Health and Safety
	Facilitation of Growth
	Rapid Achievement of Excellence
	Increase Longevity as a Dancer

Dance Kinesiology

Skeletal Structure and Potential Motion | Anatomy of Musculature and Muscle Function | Principles of Muscular Analysis | Proper Alignment and Muscular Imbalances | Physiological Support Systems | Principles of Exercise Physiology* | Principles of the Biomechanics of Motion* | Individual Differences in Movement Potential | Principles of Conditioning | Principles of Weight Management

Content

*Covered only minimally in this book.

FIGURE 1.1.   A conceptual model of dance kinesiology: a fusion of content, purposes, and applications

There is a vast difference between saying, "I am naturally inflexible" and saying "I am naturally inflexible and therefore there is no need to try to improve my inflexibility." In dance, self-acceptance is an asset; it allows objective analysis of limitations and distinction between those that can be changed and those that cannot be changed. Self-indulgence forms a basis for defeatism and blocked growth. The affective objectives in Table 1.2 reflect my own perceptions of the needs of dancers. The objectives form a substructure for the presentation of all factual information in my classes.

Each of the practical objectives listed in Table 1.3 may be applied to students of dance, teachers of dance, professional dancers, and choreographers. The objectives remain the same. The only difference is who is using them and whether the desired change is one's own or someone else's.

Figure 1.1 pulls together the objectives listed in Tables 1.1, 1.2, and 1.3 and presents a conceptual model of dance kinesiology. A conceptual model for any discipline must focus on what, why, and how. The *what* is the content or information to be shared. The *why* focuses on the relative value and importance of the information. Finally, the *how* identifies the possible application of the information.

Conclusion

The desperate need for a solid knowledge of dance kinesiology is pointed out to me every time I watch a dance class. I find myself constantly evaluating structural alignment and wincing when a dancer is misaligned, knowing how that misalignment might lead to injury. I find myself analyzing the neuromuscular movement combinations given in the class and mentally noting the particular demands for strength, flexibility, and endurance that are made on the dancers. I find myself seeing stylistic weaknesses of certain dancers and realizing that those limitations can prevent proper performance of certain movement combinations. Furthermore, I am totally delighted when the teacher of the technique class indicates an understanding of the principles of kinesiology and gives specific and knowledgeable information to the students. I am proud of the fact that the guest artists and the regular faculty at the University of Utah use kinesiological references with accuracy and care. Unfortunately, this is not always the case elsewhere. In observing some classes outside the university, I have heard some of the most incredibly distorted concepts presented as fact (such as the notion that the muscles on the back of the thigh, the hamstrings, produce hip flexion). I have been frustrated by a lack of concern for individual differences when the same strength, endurance, and range of motion are demanded of every dancer in the class. I have been terrified when a movement combination was given that actually did damage to the dancer such as driving, weighted bounces done in a grande plié (deep squat) position. I have been enraged when a teacher forcibly pushed a student who was already in a maximal stretch position. In each of these actual instances, observed in various locations outside the university, I have realized the importance of dance kinesiology for both the protection and the development of the dancer. Teachers of dance must learn the principles of dance kinesiology so they can present classes that are challenging and safe. If the teachers are resistant to learning new information, the students must learn to protect themselves.

In my years of work in dance kinesiology, I have found that my classes have two primary effects on students. First, students develop an objective, realistic attitude toward their physical strengths and limitations. Second, the solid knowledge base regarding human movement potential allows students to effectively and efficiently approach the difficult task of building their own instrument and turning limitations into strengths. Providing students with knowledge of the science of human movement, and teaching them to use that information in the dance studio, will increase their artistic potential and their longevity as performers. As students move into the teaching role, their understanding of dance kinesiology, individual differences, and proper conditioning procedures will ensure the safety and rapid growth of their students.

No physical activity calls for greater physical versatility than dance. Because of the range of the demands, no single dancer comes equipped with the "ideal" body to meet all the demands. Each dancer must deal with his or her own technical weaknesses with dedication and self-discipline.

Teachers of dance have for far too long ignored the science of human motion, on the assumption that art and science are separate domains. Given a chance, kinesiology can serve as an essential support for the art of dance by providing the intellectual tools for accurate structural analysis and for the design of efficient and effective conditioning programs. The fire and the passion for the art form can be supported and attained by the application of the science of motion. Just as the right and left hemispheres of the brain work together in processing information, so the science and the art of motion must merge to produce safety and excellence in dance.

The growth of dance kinesiology as a valued component of dance curricula is most heartening. I remember beginning my presentation at the First Conference on Science and Somatics of Dance at Temple University with the statement, "I am truly delighted by the number of professionals attending this conference. Welcome to my soapbox!"

The Skeletal System

CHAPTER *2*

Overview of the Skeletal System

The bone structure (the skeleton) is the architectural support for the human body. Bone tissue is "soft" at birth and hardens (*ossification*) as the skeleton ages. The natural shape and structure of the skeleton can be somewhat affected by stress. At points where muscles pull on the surface of the bone, rough surfaces appear. When the weight is carried unnaturally on the feet, bunions appear. When there is constant stress in one direction at the hip joint, a modification of the shape of the socket can occur. Likewise the shape of the vertebrae can change with continued stress. These changes in the basic structure of the skeleton occur because of stress to a given area. That stress causes irritation and results in the buildup of bony scar tissue at the site of the irritation, thus changing the shape of the bones. Discussion of specific changes common in dance will be presented with the discussion of the pertinent bone structure.

The skeleton (see Figure 2.1) provides only the *potential* for human movement. It is the muscular system that provides the *force* necessary for motion to occur. The potential for motion exists because the skeleton is made up of an intricate series of bones which articulate (join together) with each other at the joints. In other words, movement potential is a direct result of the presence of joints. Moreover, the relative range of motion at each given joint is, in part, a function of the structure of the bones at the point of articulation. At each joint, movement is restricted or limited in some way. At some joints the primary restriction of motion is provided by the bone structure itself. At other joints, the movement is primarily restricted by the ligamentous structure supporting the bony articulation. At still other joints, the primary restriction is muscular. Each joint has a combination of these three restrictions—bony, ligamentous, and muscular—but one type of restriction may predominate.

Individuals vary in their relative mobility at the joints. Some people seem to be "loosely strung together," while others seem to be "tightly strung together." Lay people call extreme joint mobility "double-jointedness," but in fact there is no such phenomenon. The difference in mobility is primarily in the ligamentous structure. The variance is usually in the actual length and the relative density—or a combination of both—of the ligaments surrounding and supporting the joint. Ligaments are the connec-

17

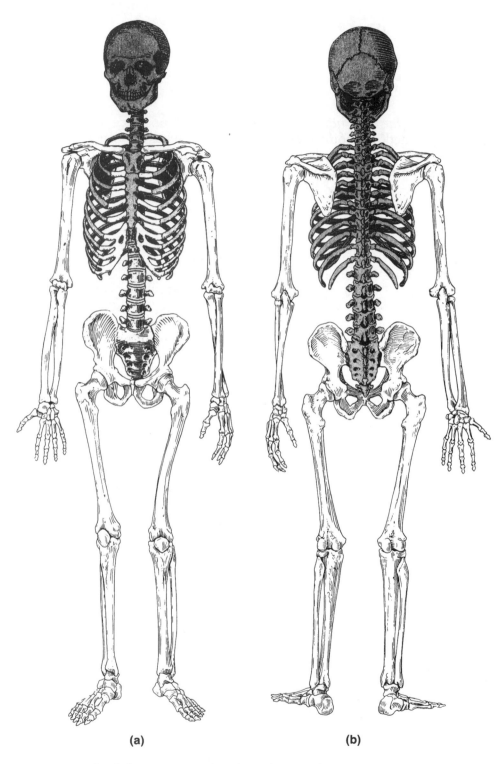

(a)   (b)

FIGURE 2.1.   The skeleton: (*a*) anterior view; (*b*) posterior view

tive tissue that connect bone to bone. Ligaments are pliable, but they are also very tough and inextensible. However, the "loosely strung together" individual seems to be provided with original equipment that allows for greater range of motion. Conversely, the "tightly strung together" individual has more limited range of motion. There is some evidence that these characteristics have some positive correlation to specific body type (see Chapter 15). *One does not wish to stretch a ligament.* Once a ligament has been lengthened, the joint it supports no longer has its original stability. Owing to extreme demands for outward rotation and a high arabesque, dancers sometimes attempt to stretch the restricting ligaments, despite the risks.

While most dancers would be likely to question the need for restrictions of joint actions, there is an essential reason why restrictions are important. *There is an inverse relationship between mobility and stability.*[1] As mobility increases, stability decreases, and vice versa. Dr. Valerie Hunt, in one of her lectures on this concept at the University of California, Los Angeles, spoke of her first study of human anatomy. She related that as a student, she was frustrated by the limited movement of the human body and courageously undertook the task of redesigning the body to maximize its movement potential. In her story, Dr. Hunt talked of the addition of many potential actions in her creative design; her "new" skeleton could have probably done a pirouette without even pivoting the foot. She concluded her story with the statement: "That skeleton could do absolutely anything . . . except stand up."

Both stability and mobility are needed in dance. Extremes in range of motion like a dance "extension" that makes an earring out of the patella are certainly revered. Yet, the dancer is also expected to be able to balance for extended periods of time on a ridiculously small base of support. Consequently, stability is just as essential to the dancer as mobility. Neither by itself is sufficient for excellence in dance. The dancer must be exceedingly mobile and yet still have the stability of a boulder. We all know that dance does not always set realistic expectations for those dedicated enough to devote their lives to the art. The impossible is frequently asked of dancers and often, through blind faith and intense commitment, dancers appear to do the impossible. Doing the impossible, however, sometimes takes a severe toll. One of the purposes of this book is to facilitate more realistic expectations, possibly to extend the longevity of dancers, reduce the number of crippled dancers, and make dance training more efficient.

This book will consistently follow the pattern of starting at the bottom of the body and working up. The rationale for this pattern follows the pattern of all structural analysis: the foundation is of primary importance. If the foundation in a building is faulty, no amount of strengthening the upper stories can correct the essential instability. Many of the misalignments of the knee, hip, spine, and even shoulders can be traced to a chain reaction of compensations that began with a faulty foundation.

1. *Stability* is defined here as the ability to maintain a desired position of a joint over time in performance.

TABLE 2.1   Anatomical Terms

Terms describing location
___

Anterior front
Posterior: back
Lateral: to the side
Medial: toward the middle
Superior: above
Inferior: below
Proximal: usually used in limbs—closer to the center of the body
Distal: farther away from the center of the body (The knee joint is formed by the distal end of
    the femur and the proximal end of the tibia.)
Superficial: muscle layer closest to the skin
Deep: muscle layer closest in to the bone

Terms describing joint action
___

Flexion: decreasing the angle between two levers
Extension: increasing the angle between two levers
Hyperextension: increasing the angle between two levers beyond 180 degrees
Abduction: movement away from the midline of the body
Adduction: movement toward the midline of the body
Rotation: movement around the central axis of a lever
Inward rotation (inversion): rotation of the limbs inward toward the front of the body
Outward rotation (eversion): rotation of the limbs outward, away from the front of the body

Terms used in reference to bone and joint structure
___

Ossification: hardening of bone
Epiphysial line: region of the long bones of the body where growth occurs
Articulation: point(s) at which two or more bones meet to form a joint
Articulating surface: surface of a bone that contacts another bone
Hyaline cartilage: dense cushioning material found on the articulating surface
Synovial membrane: connective tissue encasement around a joint (joint capsule)
Synovial fluid: lubricating fluid secreted by the synovial membrane into the joint capsule
Ligaments: nonelastic connective tissue that connects bone to bone
Tendons: elastic connective tissue that connects muscle to bone
Bursa: tiny fluid-filled sacs that serve as "ball bearings" at the body's high-friction points

Terms used to describe bony landmarks
___

   Indentations or holes:
Fossa: big cavity, depression, or hollow
Fovea: deep pit
Groove: long narrow indentation
Foramen: hole

   Protrusions:
Trochanter: large "chunk" of bone
Tuberosity: medium-sized "chunk"
Tubercle: little "pimple" of bone
Crest: large ridge or border of bone
Line: smaller ridge of bone
Spine: projection of bone
Head: spherical shape beyond a narrow neckline portion of bone—usually at the end of a
    bone
Condyle: big segments of bone, usually at the end of a bone, frequently serving as joint
    articulations.

Section II deals only with the skeletal structure of the body. (Section III returns to the foundation once again and presents the muscular system.) The content of the chapters in Section II is divided as follows:

1. Discussion of the bone structure and bony landmarks for each region.
2. Discussion of the joint structure, actions, and restrictions of actions.
3. Individual differences in bone structure that have particular importance for dancers.
4. Criteria for proper alignment and method of assessment.

Anatomical terminology can be a quagmire if definitions are unclear. For this reason, Table 2.1 presents a list of anatomical terms commonly used.

Planes of Action

A plane is a flat, level surface extending into space. Movement can occur on a plane. For example, put a pencil down on a table, hold one end of the pencil and swing the pencil back and forth (windshield-wiper fashion) on the table, making sure that the whole pencil stays in contact with the table. The pencil is a moving lever on the plane described by the tabletop. Kinesiologists have classified human movement as occurring on three planes: the *sagittal* plane, the *frontal* plane, and the *transverse* plane. Each of these three planes is perpendicular to the two other planes. For clarification, stand in a corner. Stand with your back touching one wall and your right shoulder touching the other wall. Swing your right hand and arm up and down the wall closest to it. Next, slide your left hand and arm up and down the wall closest to it. Finally, keeping your feet in place, turn your whole body to the left, pivoting around your central axis. Any right-angle corner in a room is the meeting of three planes and can serve to loosely represent the three planes of human motion. In this position, the wall (plane) to which your back was pressed is a frontal (or lateral) plane. The other wall (next to your right shoulder) is a sagittal plane. The floor is a transverse plane.

Actually, there are many parallel sagittal planes. One bisects the shoulder joint, one bisects the hip joint, one bisects the spine, and so on. Likewise there are many parallel frontal planes and many parallel transverse planes. Basic movements of flexion, extension, and hyperextension occur on the sagittal plane (see Figure 2.2). Basic movements of abduction and adduction occur on the frontal plane. Rotary movements occur on the transverse plane. Movements to the diagonal involve movements on both the frontal and the sagittal plane (combinations). Of course, movements can be further complicated by adding inward or outward rotation to diagonal movements. Then the movement occurs simultaneously on all three planes. While the concept of planes of action may seem remote to dance at

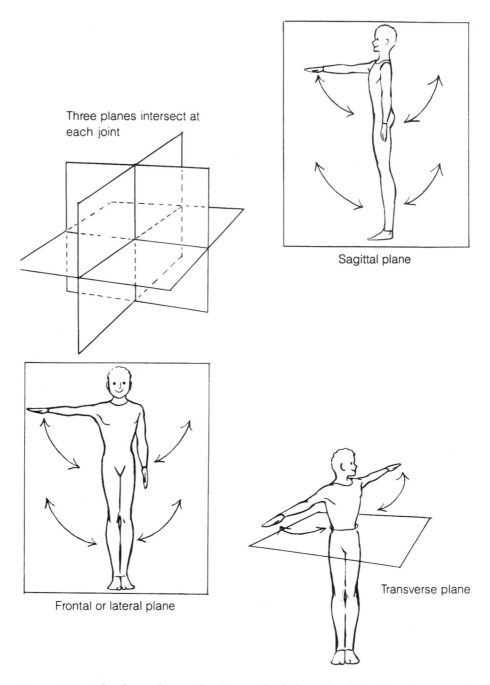

Three planes intersect at each joint

Sagittal plane

Frontal or lateral plane

Transverse plane

FIGURE 2.2.   The three planes of action: sagittal, frontal or lateral, and transverse

this point, it will be most helpful as a reference in later work involving complex movement analysis.

Labeling, Position, and Action

Another introductory concept is the distinction between *position* and *action*. Analysis of human motion also involves the analysis of static positions. Any dancer realizes that the maintenance of a position often requires as much effort as motion through space, or more. Kinesiological analysis must be prepared to make a distinction between maintenance of a position and movement through an arc in space. For this reason, a distinction is made between position and action, and the labeling can sometimes become somewhat confusing. For example, at most joints there is a single position of extension and an infinite number of positions of flexion. The action of extension defines a direction of movement. The action of flexion defines the opposite action or direction of movement. Labeling of positions is quite simple because the names are absolute. However, *labeling of actions is relative to direction.* Any movement toward flexion, even if it is from hyperextension to extension, is called an *action of flexion.* Conversely, any movement toward extension, even if it is from a position of flexion to a position of lesser flexion, is called *extension.* This concept may seem confusing at first, but errors can be avoided if one remembers that *action is defined by direction.* Students in my classes have found the following image helpful in distinguishing position and direction of action. When traveling from Los Angeles to Denver, you are going in an eastward *direction,* even though when you reach Denver your position is considered to be in the west. Likewise, a joint action traveling toward flexion is labeled *flexion* even though it may begin in a position of extension and travel to a position of lesser extension; the *direction of the action is flexion.*

Gravity

Any kinesiological analysis must take into consideration the action of gravity on the human body. Gravity is a constant factor in human movement. We move against it, with it, and we maintain positions by counteracting its effect. Only the astronauts have had the experience of moving in zero gravity. We earthbound creatures must constantly counteract the pull of gravity to be able to move about. Gravity defines the concept of verticality, and the effect of gravity on any mass is to pull it toward the earth on a vertical line from its point of support. For example, a vertical line of gravity passes through the center of the shoulder joint. In a relaxed standing position, the arm naturally hangs down at the side of the body. Gravity maintains that position, and any movement away from that position requires muscular effort against the pull of gravity. If the body's position is changed, the action of gravity on the joint will change according to the new position of the vertical line which passes through the center of the joint. Because the musculature must almost always counteract the action of gravity to produce motion or maintain a position, gravity is an essential consideration in kinesiological analysis.

Gravity and Balance

Balancing any mass on a base of support requires equalization of the weight over the base of support. The larger the base of support, the easier it is to balance on it. The more centered the weight is above the base of support, the easier it is to balance. The lower the center of gravity, the easier it is to balance. These basic principles of balance have a profound effect on all dancers, since they are required to balance a relatively large mass on a very small base of support. For this reason, one of the high priorities for every dancer is "finding center." In dance studios across the country, "finding center" is spoken of as if center were a single point. Actually, the "center of gravity" shifts with every change in position because the distribution of weight changes. Nevertheless, the dancer must be kinesthetically aware of the center of gravity in every movement. Shifting the weight of a body part while retaining balance requires either shifting another body part in the opposite direction or contracting the counterbalancing muscle group. Balancing with the weight centered over the base of support is the most efficient position. That is, it requires the least muscular contraction. Balancing with the weight unevenly distributed requires proportionately greater effort. This is the primary reason for the dancer's concern with alignment and center of gravity. Movement is easier when one is efficiently aligned.

There are three types of balance[2] that deal with different movement conditions. *Stable balance* is when the center of gravity is directly centered over the base of support. *Off-set balance* is when the center of gravity has moved toward the edge of the base of support. Off-set balance is used to initiate locomotor movement or is used to create an effect. *Dynamic balance* is when the center of gravity is actually outside of the base of support. In this situation, locomotion of some kind must occur, for there is no "going back." The weight has been committed to locomotion. While that movement can be directed, it cannot be stopped. Gravity has taken control.

Effect of Gravity on the Standing Position

In a normal standing position, gravity has a considerable effect on each of the joints in the body. We do not stand without effort. The so-called antigravity muscles are constantly in a state of contraction to maintain an upright position. The antigravity muscle groups are those which perform the action opposite to gravity's action on a given joint. Table 2.2 lists the action of gravity on the major weight-bearing joints of the body in a normal

---

2. Stable, off-set, and dynamic balance are concepts developed by Judith Hatcher in her master's thesis at the University of California, Los Angeles, in 1975.

TABLE 2.2 **Action of gravity and antigravity muscle groups for a normal standing position***

Joint	Action of Gravity	Antigravity Muscle Groups
Tarsus	Pronation	Supinators
Ankle	Dorsiflexion	Plantar flexors
Knee	Flexion	Extensors
Hip ·	Flexion, adduction, and inward rotation	Extensors, abductors, and outward rotators
Spine	Flexion	Extensors

*The reader will wish to refer to this table after each of the chapters on specific joints. At this point, before the reader has assimilated the possible actions at the different joints, this information may seem somewhat confusing.

standing position and also lists the muscle groups which maintain an upright position (antigravity muscles).

Standing erect requires constant contraction of all of the antigravity muscles. Even when we are fatigued and feel as if nothing is working, the antigravity muscle groups must be in contraction or we would fall flat on our . . . faces. The specific action of gravity at the joints listed in Table 2.2 needs further explanation.

Gravity is a pronator of the tarsus (rolling to the inside of the foot) in a normal standing position. This is true because of the weight distribution on the foot. The medial side of the foot carries more weight than the lateral side. Consequently, the effect of gravity will be to pull the weight to the medial side, like a canoe tipping to the side that carries the most weight. The presence of more weight on the medial side results in pronation of the tarsus (see Figure 3.8 in Chapter 3). In a normal standing position, gravity will dorsiflex (bend) the ankle joint. Because the line of gravity falls slightly anterior to the ankle bone (malleolus), gravity will dorsiflex the ankle. At the knee, the ideal line of gravity falls slightly posterior to the joint. Therefore gravity will be a flexor of the knee in a normal standing position. The ideal line of gravity falls slightly anterior to the center of the hip joint, and gravity flexes the hip in a normal standing position. The other actions of gravity at the hip joint are related to the action of gravity at the tarsus. As the weight falls medially (because of pronation of the tarsus), adduction and inward rotation of the hip accompany the pronation of the tarsus. At the spine, gravity has an action of flexion in a normal standing position. This is true because of the location of the spinal column in relation to the great percentage of the torso's weight. The spinal column is posterior with the weight of the viscera, and ribs "hung" on the front of the spine, causing gravity's action of flexion.

Please note that, for each joint, care is taken always to say, "in a normal standing position." This may seem unnecessarily repetitious. It is done for a reason. One can never say that gravity has a given effect on a joint without identifying the position of the joint. Gravity pulls on an absolute vertical, and yet the human being moves around that vertical—thereby changing the effect of gravity on the joints. For example, we have stated that gravity is a flexor of the hip in a normal standing position. However, arching the spine and carrying the weight of the torso back behind the base of support would make gravity an extensor of the hip joint. Maintenance of this position would require contraction of the flexors of the hip. The kinesiological analysis of any position or action of the human body must include the analysis of the action of gravity if one wishes to accurately identify the active muscle groups.

Analysis of Joint Position and Action and Analysis of Action of Gravity

Distinction between position and action must be made in every kinesiological analysis. The terms used to indicate a position may or may not agree with the terms to describe an action. For example, the action of plantar flexion of the ankle describes a *direction of action* while a plantar flexed position is a single point in the joint's range of motion. Kinesiological analysis of action involves four steps:

1. Identification of the joint position or action.
2. Analysis of the action of gravity.
3. Determination of the active muscle group (flexors, extensors, etc.) and the type of contraction.
4. Identification of the specific muscles which are active to perform the action or maintain the position.

These four steps in kinesiological analysis must all be completed for accurate analysis. At this point you have the preliminary information necessary to complete steps 1 and 2 of the process. In each of Chapters 3 through 6, you will be given the opportunity to practice these first two steps of analysis, after presentation of the bony structure and possible joint actions.

CHAPTER 3

Foot and Leg

Including toes, tarsus, and ankle joint

The Foot

Bones of the Foot

The foot is a remarkable structure. It is a series of small bones (see Figure 3.1) that together support the weight of the entire body and simultaneously provide the impetus for locomotion. Viewing the skeleton, it seems impossible that a structure as delicate as the foot can support the entire weight of the body. The only way such an incredible feat (pun intentional) is possible is through architectural engineering. The arch is known to be the strongest of structures, and the bones of the foot are arranged in a series of arches which combine to form a dome when the two feet are parallel to each other. The concept of two arches (the longitudinal arch and the transverse arch) is a simplification of the actual structure. Because of the architectural efficiency of the foot, it is possible to support the weight of the body and also give impetus for locomotion. It must be noted here that the most efficient position for giving impetus for locomotion is with the feet facing straight ahead (parallel). The human body is designed for locomotor movement on the sagittal plane. This concept and the resultant difficulties it presents for dancers will be discussed later in the analysis of actions and individual differences.

The foot is divided into three major sections: the phalanges, metatarsals, and tarsals. The five toes are numbered from medial to lateral, one through five. The first toe (the great toe) has two *phalanges*, and all four of the lesser toes have three phalanges. There is one *metatarsal* bone for each of the toes, and these are also numbered one through five. The *tarsals* are as follows. Proximal to the first, second, and third metatarsals are the first, second, and third *cuneiforms*. Lateral to the third cuneiform and proximal to the fourth and fifth metatarsals is the *cuboid*. The *navicular* is proximal to the three cuneiforms and medial to the cuboid. The *talus* is proximal to the navicular and cuboid and superior to the *calcaneous*.

In addition to the names of the bones, there are some major bony landmarks which are fundamental to analyzing the action of the foot. Each metatarsal has two ends. The distal end is called the *head* and the proxi-

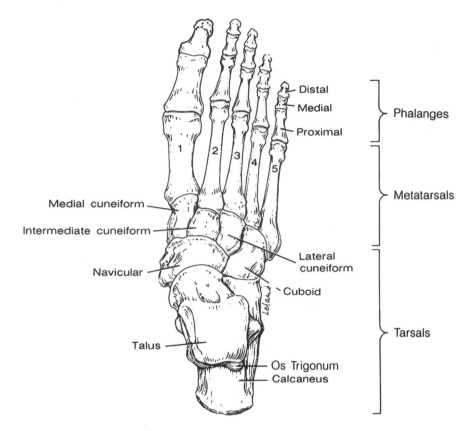

FIGURE 3.1.   Bones of the foot

mal end the *base*. Inferior to the head of the first metatarsal are two *sesamoid* bones which are encased in connective tissue. The most medial aspect of the navicular is a bony protrusion called the *tuberosity of the navicular*. On the lateral aspect of the base of the fifth metatarsal is another bony protrusion called the *tuberosity of the fifth metatarsal*. The most posterior aspect of the calcaneous is called the *tuberosity of the calcaneous*. On the posterior of the talus is a small bony protrusion called the *os trigonum*.[1]

You are encouraged to learn these names immediately, for all of the information on muscle attachments depends on knowledge of these names and landmarks. A good study aid is to find the bony landmarks on your own feet. Learning the names as you identify the landmarks on your own body means that you will carry your "textbook" with you.

Feet and Weight Bearing

In a normal weight-bearing position (parallel), the weight of the body is divided equally between the two feet and further subdivided in weight-

1. Some authorities use the name *os trigonum* only when it is a separate bone.

bearing patterns for each foot. The single foot carries half its weight anteriorly on the ball of the foot (the heads of the five metatarsals) and half posteriorly on the calcaneous (the heel). The first toe (the largest of the five toes) carries half of the lateral/medial distribution of weight; the four lesser toes carry the other half of the weight, with metatarsals two, three, four, and five carrying decreasing amounts of weight. The fifth metatarsal carries the smallest portion of the lateral distribution of weight, and the first carries the most. The great toe is efficiently designed to carry the majority of the weight because it has the largest of the metatarsals. Furthermore, the sesamoid bones, which lie beneath the head of the first metatarsal, provide a shock-absorbing system for that area. To further support the foot, the plantar ligaments on the inferior surface of the foot are assisted by the plantar fascia.[2] The connective tissue structures aid in the support of the domelike structure of the foot. Laxity of the plantar ligaments and fascia combined with weakness of the muscles on the plantar ligaments and fascia combined with weakness of the muscles on the plantar surface of the foot allow the condition known as "flat feet." Although the muscles involved in supporting the dome-like structure of the foot can be strengthened, once the ligaments are stretched, there is no way to reshorten them. When the dancer goes on *relevé* (half toe) or on *pointe*, the medial side of the foot still bears the majority of the weight, but the relative proportion varies depending on individual differences in bone structure which will be discussed later.

Joints of the Foot and Possible Movement

Technically, each articulation of any two or more bones of the foot constitutes a joint. But analysis of action of each of these joints becomes very cumbersome. Therefore the actions of the foot are grouped into two main categories: actions of the toes and actions of the tarsus. The "joint" labeled *toes* includes all of the interphalangeal joints and the phalangeal/metatarsal joints. The *tarsus* "joint" includes all of the actions that occur at the articulations of the seven tarsal bones with each other.

The movements of the toes are mainly restricted to action on the sagittal plane and include flexion, extension, and hyperextension. Gripping the toes (as one would grip the fingers) is called *flexion* of the toes. Extension and hyperextension of the toes in a standing position are executed by raising the toes off the floor. There is one position of extension of the toes but an infinite number of positions of flexion and hyperextension. While there is some degree of abduction and adduction of the toes, these actions are relatively limited; they are produced by the intrinsic muscles of the foot, which are not emphasized in this book. For the purposes of this book, the actions of the toes will be listed as only flexion, extension, and hyperextension.

---

2. *Fascia* is fibrous connective tissue, less elastic than tendons but more elastic than ligaments. Fascia is located in high-stress areas of the body and provides a sheath of connective tissue support and protection.

The actions of the tarsus occur on the frontal and transverse planes. Abduction and adduction are possible, as are inversion and eversion. The muscles that move the tarsus act in such a way that isolated action on only one plane is almost impossible. For this reason, the actions of the tarsus are labeled *pronation* and *supination*. Pronation is the combination of abduction and eversion. Supination is the combination of adduction and inversion. In dance terms, pronation is called *beveling* the foot and supination is called *sickling* the foot. Pronation and supination are the only actions possible at the tarsus. The analysis of positions of the tarsus is made in reference to the *neutral position* of the tarsus. The neutral position is when the central sagittal plane passing through the ankle joint is aligned with the center of gravity of the foot, between the first and second toes. Any position of adduction and inversion is supination. Any position of abduction and eversion is pronation. Any action toward medial is supination, and any action toward lateral is pronation. Figures 3.2 and 3.3 show two positions of the tarsus.

Restrictions of Actions

The primary restrictions of action for the joints of the foot are the ligaments of the foot. Figure 3.4 illustrates the complexity of the ligamentous structure of the foot. Memorization of the names of the ligaments and their location is not essential, but these illustrations point out that the actions of the foot at the toes and at the tarsus are clearly limited by the ligamentous structure.

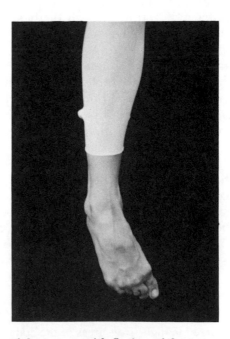

FIGURE 3.2. **Supination of the tarsus, with flexion of the toes, and plantar flexed ankle**

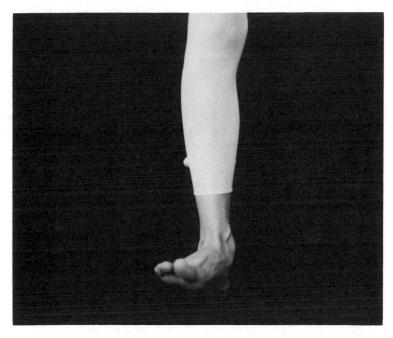

FIGURE 3.3.   Pronation of the tarsus, with toe hyperextension, and dorsiflexion of the ankle

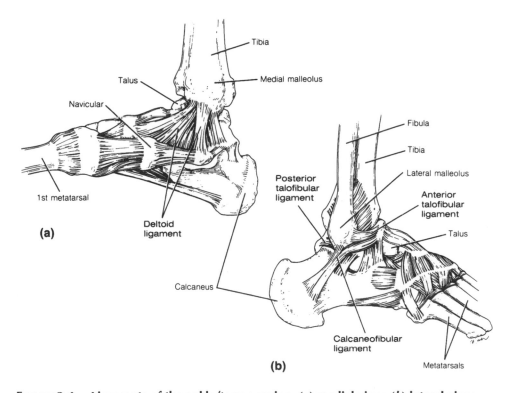

FIGURE 3.4.   Ligaments of the ankle/tarsus region: (*a*) medial view; (*b*) lateral view

Individual Differences in the Foot

Dancers are noted for comparing their bodies with the bodies of other dancers. In many cases, the comparison leads to an unrelenting forcing of a joint structure based on the erroneous assumption that if one body is capable of a certain range of motion, all bodies ought to be able to do the same. The assumption that every human body is identical in movement potential is, very simply, wrong. In the foot, there are some individual differences which are particularly important to dancers. The relative length of bones has an effect on the efficiency of the propulsive mechanism. The relative width of the foot has an effect on balance. The relative length of the ligaments (looseness or tightness) has an effect on both stability and range of motion in the foot. A number of particular differences occur with sufficient frequency to warrant specific discussion of their effect on performance.

RELATIVE LENGTH OF METATARSALS

Modern dancers spend a lot of time on *relevé* or on half toe. Ballet dancers spend a lot of time on *pointe* and on half toe. Consequently, the relative length of the metatarsal bones is of real importance to the dancer. Ideally the first metatarsal will be the longest of the five and the length will gradually decrease as one moves laterally from first to fifth metatarsal. After all, the first toe is designed to bear the most weight, being the biggest and having the sesamoid bones as shock absorbers.

There is a rather common phenomenon called *Morton Short Toe* (named after Dudley Morton, a noted podiatrist). *Morton Short Toe* (sometimes called *Morton Long Toe*) is when the first metatarsal is shorter than the second metatarsal. This causes a shift from the ideal weight-bearing patterns by shifting the weight laterally. This is particularly true in *relevé* or *pointe* work. Accompanying the lateral shift of weight, there is a tendency to supinate (sickle) the tarsus in order to get the four lateral metatarsals on the floor to broaden the base of support (see Figure 3.5). The problem with this particular compensation for *Morton Short Toe* is that it puts the tarsus in a very dangerous position, increasing the likelihood of severe sprains. When a dancer with *Morton Short Toe* corrects the supination by pronating the tarsus to a neutral position, pulling the weight up onto the heads of the first and second metatarsals, the heads of the third, fourth, and fifth metatarsals are not on the floor. This substantially narrows the base of support and makes balance on *relevé* far more difficult. It is possible to "reach down" with the three lateral toes to effectively broaden the base of support, but then the dancer is told not to "grip with the toes." There are exercises to strengthen the pronators which can help dancers stabilize when they have this condition, and they will be presented in the chapter on conditioning. Another problem for the dancer with Morton Short Toe is the stress placed on the head of the second metatarsal, which bears most of the weight in locomotion. There are no sesamoid bones beneath the head of the second metatarsal to buffer the shock of landings. Continued stress on a foot with the Morton Short Toe

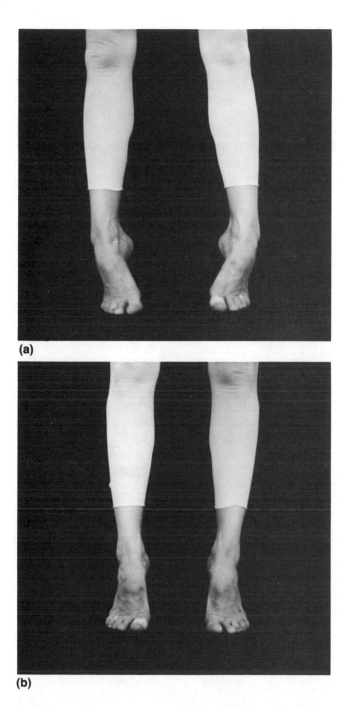

FIGURE 3.5.   Relevé in two positions: (*a*) with supinated tarsus (sickled); (*b*) with neutral tarsus (correct).

will cause buildup of a major callous beneath the head of the second metatarsal. The callous is the body's compensation for the stress on that area. The callous is more pronounced in modern dancers than in ballet dancers because more time is spent on *relevé*, while the female ballet dancer spends more time on *pointe*. Recognizing Morton Short Toe is the first step in making effective compensation for the problems which accompany the bony variance. Figure 3.6 illustrates the assessment for Morton Short Toe.

Another variance of metatarsal length is reflected in the actual length of the foot. The dancer with a longer foot may have an advantage in locomotion because the lever is actually longer, thereby reducing the amount of muscular work required to push off in a walk, jump, leap, or run. Frequently the dancer with a long foot will have smaller calf muscles (actually less muscle bulk) than the dancer with a short foot. This is not a function of improper training, but rather a simple matter of mechanics. The shorter lever requires more muscle.

LENGTH OF THE CALCANEOUS

The calcaneous can also vary in relative length. A short calcaneous will require more muscle bulk to do the same amount of work. A long calcaneous provides a more efficient machine for locomotion. Accurate checking of the length of the calcaneous is difficult and is accomplished most effectively by x-ray. However, there is one simple indication of the relative length of the calcaneous. If heelstraps on shoes or sandals frequently fall down, this indicates that the calcaneous does not protrude posteriorly and

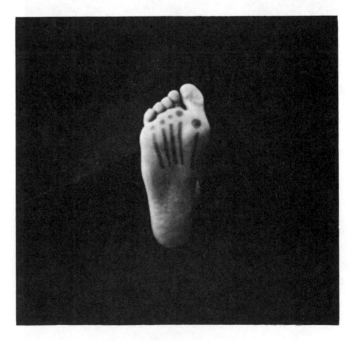

FIGURE 3.6.   **Plantar view of Morton Short Toe**

may be relatively short. Some sources in comparative anatomy indicate that blacks have a tendency toward a longer calcaneous than whites. Those same sources state that Asians have a shorter calcaneous than whites. This variance in calcaneous length could be another explanation for variance in size of the calf muscle and could also provide a partial explanation for individual differences in jumping ability.

LIGAMENTOUS LENGTH

If the ligaments of the foot are short and tight, the individual will be likely to have a strong, stable arch. The stability of the arch can be checked by marking the tuberosity of the navicular of the right foot; by standing on the left foot and holding the right foot off the floor to observe the non-weight-bearing position of the arch; and by putting weight on the right foot and observing whether the arch drops when bearing weight. It is common for "loosely strung together" individuals to have some instability in the arch. This is a disadvantage with actions requiring stability, but an advantage with actions requiring mobility. The "loosely strung together" individual may actually have some possibility for plantar and dorsal flexion in the tarsus region, which is normally nonexistent. This allows for a more "aesthetically pleasing" extended foot. In the dance world, dancers with excessive mobility in the tarsus are frequently said to have "good feet." Yet the student of kinesiology must ask, "Good for what?" The range of motion is there, but what about stability? There are always two sides to the coin: the advantage is one side of the coin and the compensating disadvantage is the other side. Awareness of both sides is essential to the dancer who wishes to increase capacities and reduce limitations. Excessive mobility is a major cause of misalignment; gravity has a more pronounced effect on the mobile structure.

Proper Alignment of the Foot

The ideal alignment of the foot is indicated in the illustration of the bones of the foot (refer back to Figure 3.1). The metatarsals extend straight to the front of the tarsal bones, the phalanges protrude straight out from the metatarsals, and the arch is stable. Deviations from this ideal alignment may occur at the toes, as in the case of hallux valgus (see below), or may occur in the tarsus, with pronated or supinated feet. Ideally the foot should be in the same sagittal plane as the lower leg. This alignment reduces twisting stress (torque) on the knee and reduces the likelihood of sprains and strains.

HALLUX VALGUS

Hallux valgus refers to a misalignment of the first toe (see Figure 3.7). In this condition the two phalanges of the first toe angle off to the lateral side of the foot. In this position the big toe is less efficient for push-off than it is when the phalanges are on the same sagittal plane as the metatarsal (extend straight to the front). Hallux valgus can result from wearing shoes that are too narrow at the time when the bones of the foot are ossifying.

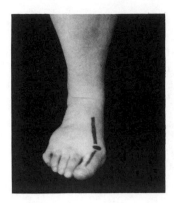

FIGURE 3.7.   **Hallux valgus**

Likewise, hallux valgus might be caused by putting a young girl on *pointe* too soon. Nothing can do greater damage to a young foot than the stress of *pointe* work. The human foot was not designed for work on *pointe*. It is the responsibility of teachers of dance to familiarize themselves with the normal ossification rates and to consider them before asking a child to go on *pointe*. Most authorities agree that ossification of the foot usually occurs sometime around puberty. It is sheer insanity to put a child on *pointe* before the age of twelve, and it may be wise, in some cases, to wait even longer.

ALIGNMENT OF TARSUS

Alignment of the tarsus is as critical for the dancer as any alignment in the body. Proper alignment takes stress off the knees, prevents injuries to the ankle/tarsus region, and ensures more efficient landings and takeoffs. Yet misalignment of the tarsus is one of the most common problems of beginning dancers. In checking the alignment of the tarsus, two approaches may be used. One focuses on the path of the Achilles tendon. In the other, three bony landmarks are used as reference points: the medial aspect of the head of the first metatarsal, the tuberosity of the navicular, and the most medial aspect of the calcaneous (see Figure 3.8). In *ideal alignment of the tarsus,* all three of these bony landmarks fall on the same sagittal plane. Misalignment of the tarsus shows one of the bony landmarks out of line with the other two landmarks. With a *pronated tarsus*, the head of the first metatarsal falls lateral to a line described by the tuberosity of the navicular and the medial aspect of the calcaneous. A *supinated tarsus* will show the head of the first metatarsal medial to the line described by the tuberosity of the navicular and the medial aspect of the calcaneous. (Of course, any two of the bony landmarks can serve as the indicators of the reference line. For example, one could use the medial aspect of the calcaneous and the medial aspect of the head of the first metatarsal as the reference points. Pronation would then be indicated if the tuberosity of the navicular is medial to the line, and supination would be indicated if the tuberosity of the navicular is lateral to the line.)

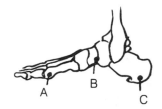

Bony Landmarks
A. Medial aspect of head of
   first metatarsal
B. Tuberosity of the
   navicular
C. Medial aspect of the
   calcaneous

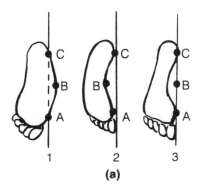

Bony Landmarks As Key to
Assessing Alignment
1. Pronation
2. Supination
3. Ideal alignment

(a)

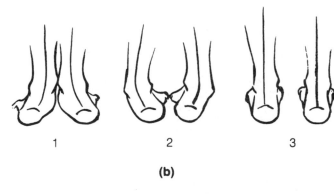

Achilles' Tendon As
Key to Assessing
   Alignment
1. Pronation
2. Supination
3. Ideal alignment

(b)

FIGURE 3.8.   Two methods for assessing alignment of the tarsus: (*a*) using bony landmarks; (*b*) using visual inspection of the Achilles tendon.

Teachers of dance have long warned against pronation and supination
of the tarsus whether they realized it or not. The frequent warning to keep
the knees directly over the toes in *plié* is a protection against the tendency
to pronate the tarsus in *plié* position. Figure 3.9 illustrates the do's and
don'ts of tarsus alignment in *plié*. Beyond the prevention of potential injuries, correction of a pronated tarsus (far more common and more dan-

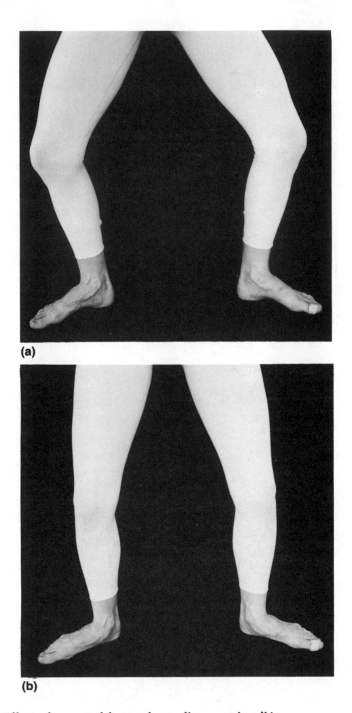

(a)

(b)

FIGURE 3.9.   Effect of pronated feet on knee alignment in *plié*
(*A*) PROPER ALIGNMENT WITH NEUTRAL TARSUS POSITION AND NO TORQUE ON THE KNEES;
(*B*) IMPROPER ALIGNMENT WITH PRONATED FEET CAUSING A ROTARY TORQUE ON THE KNEES.
NOTE: *TORQUE* IMPLIES A TWISTING FORCE THAT IS DANGEROUS TO THE KNEE JOINT.

gerous than a supinated tarsus) can also reduce stress on the bones of the foot. Consistent patterns of pronation at the tarsus, when combined with the dancer's common tendency to walk like a duck (turned out at the hip), can increase the likelihood of bunions on the head of the first metatarsal. Turning the hip out and pronating the tarsus make the last point of contact in locomotion the medial aspect of the head of the first metatarsal. The foot is designed with the phalanges anterior to the metatarsals to take the stress of walking and running. When one pronates and turns out, the toes no longer do their job. The body responds to stress and builds calcium deposits at the point of stress, resulting in a painful bunion. This is only one example of a bunion. Actually, they can occur in many different locations—wherever there is undue stress. *Tailor's bunion* is on the tuberosity of the fifth metatarsal. One cause of stress on that bony landmark is prolonged sitting cross-legged (thus the name *tailor's* bunion). Another possible cause of stress is extreme supination (pigeon-toed). This condition puts excessive stress on the lateral side of the foot in walking and can be another cause of a bunion. Analysis of characteristic movement patterns can usually identify the habitual pattern that is causing the stress. Changing the habit can frequently reduce the irritation of the bunion area. But such a change requires constant effort.

The Lower Leg

The bones of the lower leg are the *tibia* and *fibula*. The tibia is on the medial side and the fibula on the lateral side. The tibia is the larger of the two bones and is the primary weight-bearing bone of the lower leg.

Since the fibula has no role in weight-bearing, and since it has nothing to do with the knee joint, it seems to have a role only in expanding the bone surface of the lower leg for muscle attachments and, inferiorly, forming the lateral completion of the ankle joint. There are three bony landmarks worthy of note on the fibula (see Figure 3.10): the *lateral (or fibular) malleolus*, the *shaft of the fibula*, and the *head of the fibula*.

The tibia has a number of landmarks that must be pointed out. In cross section, the tibia is a triangular-shaped bone with three angles called *borders* and three sides called *surfaces* (see Figure 3.11). Please note that the names of the borders and surfaces follow a logical pattern, reflecting the relative locations. The three borders are the *anterior border* (shin), *medial border*, and *interosseous border*. The surfaces are labeled *medial*, *lateral*, and *posterior*. Memorization is hardly necessary, owing to the logical nature of the labels, except for *interosseous border*, which is not a layperson's term. Between the tibia and the fibula is the interosseous membrane, which serves to increase the surface areas available for the many muscles attached on the bones of the lower leg. On the tibia, in addition to the borders and the surfaces, are other bony landmarks. Two large chunks of bone at the proximal end of the tibia are named, respectively, the *medial condyle* and the *lateral condyle* of the tibia. The *tibial tuberosity* is below the condyles and immediately superior to the upper end of the anterior

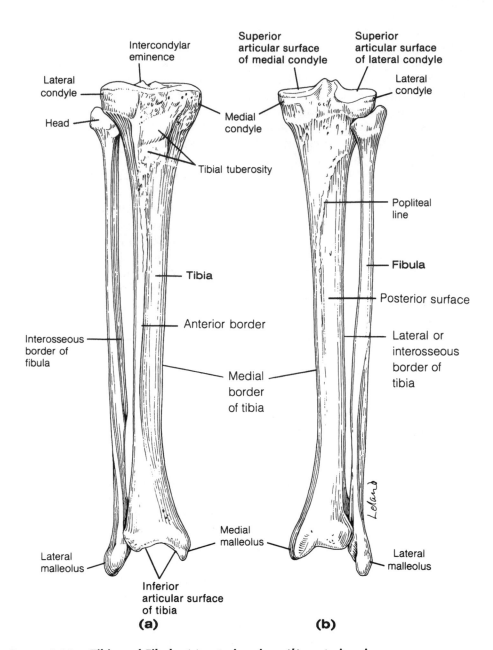

FIGURE 3.10. Tibia and Fibula: (*a*) anterior view; (*b*) posterior view

border. On the most superior aspect of the tibia are the *superior articulating surfaces*, which are very slightly indented. Between the condyles, on the superior surface of the tibia, is the *intercondylar eminence*. At the inferior end of the tibia, extending downward on the medial side, is the *medial (or tibial) malleolus*. The most inferior aspect of the tibia (other than the most inferior point of the malleolus) is the *inferior articulating surface*, which articulates with the talus bone of the tarsus.

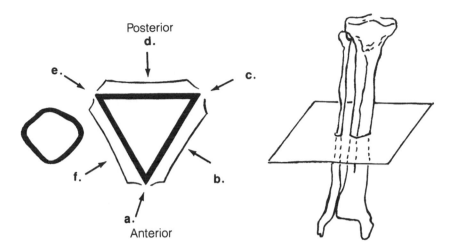

FIGURE 3.11. Cross section of the tibia, showing the labeling for the borders and the surfaces: (*a*) anterior border; (*b*) medial surface; (*c*) medial border; (*d*) posterior surface; (*e*) lateral border (interosseous); (*f*) lateral surface

The Ankle

Ankle Joint

The true ankle joint is formed by the articulation of the talus (one of the bones of the tarsus), the inferior articulating surface of the tibia, the lateral malleolus of the fibula, and the medial malleolus of the tibia (see Figure 3.12). The inferior articulating surface of the tibia articulates with the superior surface of the talus, and the medial and lateral malleoli articulate with the sides of the talus. The bone structure of the ankle provides the major restrictions of actions. The restriction of action is further assisted by the ligaments which hold the bones in place. The two malleoli prevent abduction and adduction of the ankle joint and are also restrictors of any rotary action of the ankle. Having no possibility of motion on the frontal or transverse planes, the ankle joint is restricted to the possible actions of flexion and extension on the sagittal plane. The terms *flexion* and *extension* of the ankle can create serious confusion when one begins to do muscular analysis, because flexion of the ankle goes in one direction and flexion of the toes goes in the opposite direction. (Don't be too worried if that isn't crystal clear at this point. It will become clear when we get to the muscular system.) In order to prevent this possible confusion, the term *flexion* for the ankle is replaced with *dorsiflexion*, and the term *extension* is replaced with *plantar flexion*. There is only one position of plantar flexion (which is at the extreme of the range of extension of the ankle), but there are an infinite number of positions of dorsiflexion. The direction of plantar flexion is toward "planting" the toes into the ground. The direction of dorsiflexion is opposite to plantar flexion, with the dorsal surface (top) of the foot approaching the anterior of the tibia and fibula.

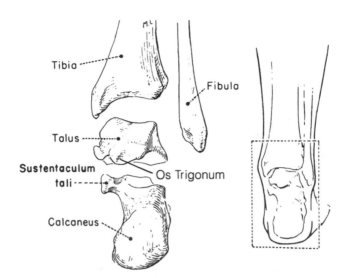

Figure 3.12.   Ankle joint

Individual Differences at the Ankle

In addition to the standard possibility of looseness and tightness, there are two other individual differences in the ankle that can affect range of motion. The os trigonum (review Figure 3.12) on the back of the talus is sometimes larger than normal. When this happens there is a restriction of the range of plantar flexion. Surgery is the only correction for this problem, and that seems a bit extreme for the normal population. However, for dancers, who need the full range of motion at the ankle joint, surgery is sometimes warranted when the os trigonum is oversized. The other bony individual difference that might have an effect on the range of motion at the ankle joint is an *exostosis* (a bony protrusion) on the tibia, just anterior and superior to the anterior portion of the inferior articulating surface. The location of this bony protrusion can serve as a bony restriction of dorsiflexion, but a far more common restriction of dorsiflexion of the ankle is provided by the Achilles tendon. Tightness of the Achilles tendon (attaching the gastrocnemius, soleus, and plantaris muscles to the calcaneus) is the most common restriction of dorsiflexion of the ankle.

Proper alignment of the ankle is reflected in the relative degree of total anterior or posterior leaning of the body. The ankle is properly aligned for a static position when the total body is vertical, not leaning forward or backward. Another consideration in assessing alignment in this region is the relative verticality of the talus. It is possible for the talus to tilt toward the lateral or medial side of the foot. This condition may be congenital or may develop through prolonged stress. If the talus is tipped so the medial side is down, the tendency to pronation of the tarsus will be increased. If the talus is tipped down on the lateral side, the tendency to supination is increased. Since this misalignment is directly due to the shape of the bone, correction is not possible, but strengthening the muscles on the medial and lateral side of the ankle/tarsus may help to prevent injury.

Another bony difference that can affect the dancer's alignment of the foot is tibial torsion. This is a simultaneous bowing and twisting of the tibia and can be observed when a dotted line is drawn down the anterior border of the tibia. When the person with tibial torsion stands in parallel position with the feet together the dotted lines drawn on the two tibias look like parentheses: ( ). Since this condition is an actual bend in the bone, it is irreversible. The condition causes a distortion in the transfer of weight from the femur to the foot. Tibial torsion will cause more weight on the medial side of the foot, thereby increasing the likelihood of pronated feet. Some sources distinguish between tibial *yarum* (twisting) and tibial *torsion* (bowing). Indeed, this distinction may be helpful when one occurs without the other.

REVIEW AND APPLICATION

Table 3.1 provides a very abbreviated review of the major concepts related to the structure and actions of the ankle, tarsus, and toes.

Femur

The *thigh* (femur) is that portion of the anatomy between the hip joint and the knee joint. The femur is the bone of the thigh. The femur is the longest bone of the body. Knowledge of the bony landmarks on the femur is essential to understanding the placement of muscle attachments (see Figure 3.13). At the lower extremity of the femur are two chunks of bone, the medial and lateral condyles of the femur. Posteriorly, between the condyles, is the *intercondular notch*. Anteriorly, the *patellar surface* is between the condyles. The condyles, as just noted, are labeled *medial* and *lateral,* and on the side of each condyle is a small "pimple" of bone called the *medial* or *lateral epicondyle.* The medial epicondyle is the most medial aspect of the medial condyle of the femur. The lateral epicondyle is the most lateral aspect of the lateral condyle of the femur. On the posterior, superior surface of the medial condyle of the femur is another "pimple" of bone called the *adductor tubercle.* The *shaft of the femur* runs between the condyles and the upper portion of the femur. Running almost the entire length of the posterior of the shaft of the femur is the *linea aspera,* a major muscle attachment. The anterior and posterior views of the upper portion of the femur are very different in appearance. The anterior view shows the lateral chunk of bone called the *greater trochanter.* Medially and inferior to the greater trochanter one can see the *lesser trochanter* protruding from behind. The *neck of the femur* is the narrow portion of the femur between the greater trochanter and the *head of the femur.* (The angle formed by the central axis of the neck of the femur and the central axis of the shaft of the femur is a major factor determining locomotor efficiency that will be discussed at greater length in the discussion of the hip joint.) Another bony landmark visible on the anterior view is the *intertrochanteric line:* a small

TABLE 3.1   Summary of differences among ankle, tarsus, and toes

Joint	Structure of Joint	Possible Actions	Primary Restrictions of Actions	Proper Alignment and Problematic Individual Differences
Ankle	Articulation of tibia fibula talus	Plantar flexion	Muscular tightness of muscles which dorsiflex the ankle	Enlarged os trigonum
		Dorsiflexion	Muscular tightness of muscles which plantar flex the ankle	Exostosis on anterior inferior aspect of the tibia
		No abduction or adduction no rotation	Medial and lateral malleoli of tibia and fibula	Tibial torsion
Tarsus	Articulation of talus calcaneous navicular cuboid 3 cuneiforms	Pronation (combination of abduction and eversion)	Ligamentous and muscular (inelasticity of supinators)	Criteria for assessing pronation and supination based on three bony landmarks: 1. medial head of first metatarsal 2. tuberosity of navicular 3. medial aspect of calcaneous
		Supination (combination of adduction and inversion)	Ligamentous and muscular (inelasticity of pronators)	
		No plantar-flexion or dorsiflexion	*Ligamentous structure	
Toes	Articulation of phalanges metatarsals	Flexion extension hyper-extension	Muscular inelasticity of opposing muscles	Hallux valgus Bunions on head of first metatarsal; tailor's bunion on tuberosity of fifth metatarsal
		Very slight abduction and adduction of toes	Some ligamentous restriction in extremes of range of motion	
		No rotation of toes	Ligamentous structure	

*In some "loosely strung together" individuals, *very slight* plantar flexion and dorsiflexion are possible.

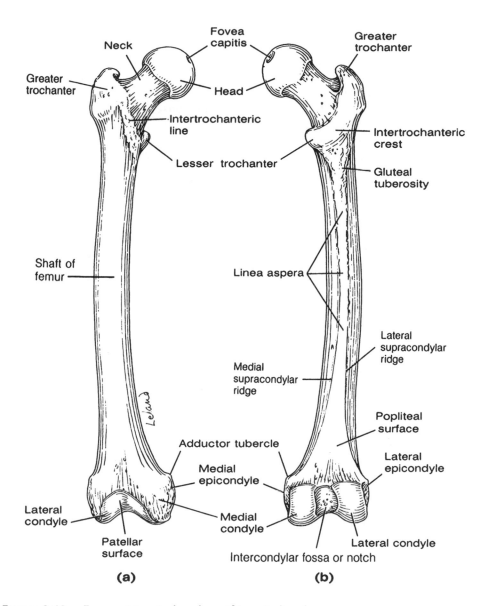

Neck

Fovea capitis

Greater trochanter

Greater trochanter

Head

Intertrochanteric line

Lesser trochanter

Intertrochanteric crest

Gluteal tuberosity

Shaft of femur

Linea aspera

Lateral supracondylar ridge

Medial supracondylar ridge

Popliteal surface

Adductor tubercle

Lateral epicondyle

Medial epicondyle

Lateral condyle

Medial condyle

Patellar surface

Lateral condyle

Intercondylar fossa or notch

(a)

(b)

FIGURE 3.13.   Femur: (*a*) anterior view; (*b*) posterior view

ridge of bone that runs from the greater trochanter to the lesser trochanter on the anterior of the femur. The posterior view of the upper portion of the femur shows the posterior of the greater trochanter and gives a much better view of the lesser trochanter. A sizable crest of bone runs between the greater and lesser trochanters, posteriorly, and is called the *intertrochanteric crest*. The *gluteal tuberosity* is a bony protrusion at the superior end of the linea aspera. The *pectineal line* is a small ridge of bone lateral to the lesser trochanter.

Knee Joint

The knee is formed by the articulation of the femur and tibia and is encased in the joint capsule, which is lined with synovial membrane (see Figure 3.14). The convex condyles of the femur sit in the concave superior articulating surfaces of the tibia. The intercondular eminence partially protrudes up into the intercondular notch, but it leaves considerable space for the internal ligaments of the knee to pass through the notch. The patella, another sesamoid bone, is encased in the tendon of the quadriceps muscles and rides anterior to the knee joint, fitting into the patellar surface of the femur. Technically, the patella is not part of the true knee joint, but rather an anterior bony protection for the tissue within the knee joint. The bony restrictions of motion at the knee joint are minimal. Actually, if the bony restrictions were the only limitation of movement, the knee would have incredible mobility, including unrestricted abduction, adduction, hyperextension, and rotation; but conversely it would have terrible stability. The stability of the knee joint and the primary restrictions of actions are provided by the complex ligamentous structure of the knee. Because the knee is a major site of dance injuries, full analysis of the ligamentous structure of the knee is presented.

Ligaments of the Knee

There are six major ligaments that support the knee joint: two collateral ligaments, two cruciate ligaments, and two popliteal ligaments (see Figure 3.15). The two *collateral ligaments* are located on the medial and lateral sides of the knee, running from the respective epicondyles of the femur

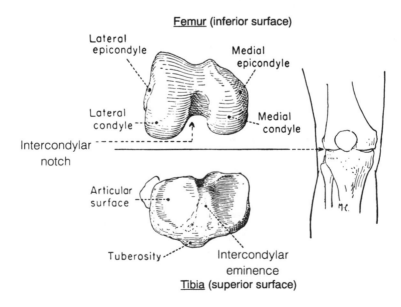

FIGURE 3.14.   Knee joint

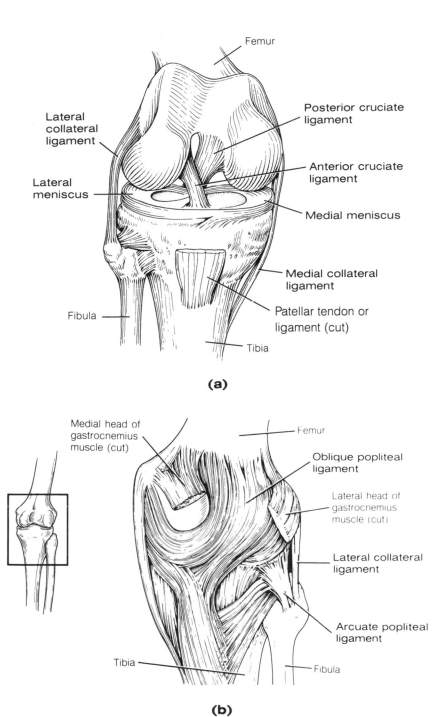

FIGURE 3.15. Ligaments of the flexed right knee: (a) anterior view; (b) posterior view

down to the tibia on the medial side and to the head of the fibula on the lateral side. The collateral ligaments provide lateral stability for the knee joint. They restrict any possible abduction and adduction of the knee joint and totally restrict rotation of the knee in an extended position. The collateral ligaments are taut (tight) when the knee is in the extended position. However, when the knee is flexed, the collateral ligaments are slightly slack. This allows for a slight degree of inward and outward rotation of the knee joint in a flexed position. The *anterior cruciate* ligament runs from the anterior of the tibia to the posterior of the femur, through the intercondular notch. The *posterior cruciate ligament* runs from the posterior of the tibia to the anterior of the femur, also going through the intercondular notch. The two cruciate ligaments are the primary restrictors of anterior/posterior sliding of the knee joint. Without these ligaments, the femur could literally slide off the tibia. In addition to the restriction of anterior/posterior sliding, the cruciate ligaments also contribute to the restriction of rotation at the knee. It is the cruciate ligaments that take over the restriction of rotation where the collateral ligaments leave off, and they serve as the final restriction of rotation of the knee in a flexed position. The *popliteal* ligaments (oblique and arcuate) run from the posterior of the femur to the posterior of the tibia. These ligaments are the primary restrictors of hyperextension of the knee. The popliteal ligaments also contribute to the restriction of anterior/posterior sliding of the knee joint. The ligaments of the knee, therefore, restrict abduction, adduction, lateral/medial sliding, anterior/posterior sliding, hyperextension, and rotation in the extended position.

Additional Stability of the Knee

Further stability of the knee joint is provided by the *medial meniscus* and *lateral meniscus,* otherwise known as the medial and lateral *semilunar cartilages.* These half-moons of cartilage lie on the superior articulating surfaces of the tibia and are attached to the tibia. They serve to deepen the indentation into which the condyles of the femur fit. The menisci are thicker at the outer edges and thinner in the centers, somewhat like a cushion that is pressed down in the center. Indeed, the menisci do serve as shock-absorbing cushions for the knee joint and also increase the stability of the joint. A small ligament called the *transverse* ligament attaches the two menisci to each other. The medial meniscus is firmly attached to the joint capsule, and the lateral meniscus is more loosely attached to the joint capsule. On the lateral side of the knee joint, the distal end of the *fascia lata* (or *iliotibial tract*) provides additional stability for the lateral aspect of the knee joint.

There are two factors which contribute to the higher incidence of injury to the medial side of the knee than to the lateral side. First, the attachment of the medial meniscus to the joint capsule seems to encourage tearing of the medial meniscus. Second, the lateral side of the knee is fortified by the iliotibial tract (fascia lata). Because the medial side of the knee is more susceptible to injury, pronation of the tarsus (which transfers more weight to the medial side of the knee) is more dangerous than supination.

Anterior to the knee joint, the patellar ligament/tendon runs from the inferior border of the patella to the tibial tuberosity. (Anatomists call it a *ligament* because it technically attaches bone to bone. Kinesiologists call it a *tendon* because it serves as the distal attachment for the quadriceps muscles. We will call it a *tendon*.) The patellar tendon adds to the anterior/posterior stability of the knee joint. As mentioned before, the patella (while technically not part of the knee joint) rides anterior to the knee joint and provides protection for the internal structure of the knee, which would otherwise be relatively exposed. Table 3.2 presents a summary of restrictions and possible actions at the knee joint.

TABLE 3.2   Summary of Knee Restrictions and Actions

Potential Actions of the Knee Joint Allowed By Bone Structure	Nature of Restriction (Partial or Total)	Restricting Structure
Abduction and adduction	Total	Collateral ligaments
Lateral sliding	Total	Collateral ligaments assisted by fascia lata on lateral side and meniscus
Anterior/posterior sliding	Total	Cruciate ligaments assisted by popliteal ligament, patellar tendon, and meniscus
Rotation in an extended position	Total	Collateral ligaments
Rotation in a flexed position Slight rotation possible in a flexed position	Partial	Cruciate ligaments
Flexion Flexion of the knee is possible	No restriction until calf contacts back of thigh	
Extension Extension of the knee is possible	No restriction to 180 degrees	
Hyperextension Slight hyperextension is possible for some individuals	Total in some individuals; partial in some individuals, allowing for slight hyperextension	Popliteal ligaments assisted by anterior and posterior cruciate ligaments

Possible Actions of the Knee Joint and Analysis of Joint Actions

When all of the restrictions of actions at the knee are taken into account, two primary actions and one secondary action remain. The possible actions of the knee are *flexion, extension,* and *slight rotation when the knee is in a flexed position.* Some individuals have a longer popliteal ligament, and that condition allows for slight hyperextension of the knee joint, but this action is not possible for all individuals.

In the analysis of joint action at the knee, there is only one position of extension but an infinite number of positions of flexion. Any action toward the position of extension is called *extension.* Any movement away from the position of extension is called *flexion.* Again the *direction of the action* determines the labeling of an action as either flexion or extension. Rotation of the knee is labeled according to the relative facing of the tibia. When the tibial tuberosity points more medially, the knee is inwardly rotated. When the tibial tuberosity points laterally, the knee is outwardly rotated. As a reminder, slight rotation of the knee occurs only in a flexed position.

Individual Differences in Knee Structure

Two variances in the knee structure are commonly called *knock-knees* and *bowlegs.* These variances depend on the relative height (superior/inferior depth) of the medial and lateral condyles of the femur. When the medial condyle is taller than the lateral condyle, the discrepancy results in knock-knees. When the lateral condyle of the femur is taller than the medial condyle, bowlegs occur. There is no possible correction for knock-knees or bowlegs, but in the dance studio, certain adaptations must be made for these conditions. The person with knock-knees finds it impossible to stand with the feet touching in parallel without either overlapping the knees or pressing the knees to a hyperextended position. Knock-kneed dancers should not be forced to stand in parallel with the feet touching, but rather should be allowed to stand with the feet slightly apart to allow space for the knees without making compensations. Knock-kneed dancers should also be particularly careful to avoid pronated feet, as the misalignment of knock-knees adds to the susceptibility to injury on the medial side of the knee.

Bowlegs tend to transfer the weight to the lateral side of the knee, which is more stable. Like supination, bowlegs are not as dangerous as knock-knees, but the aesthetic line may be distorted in parallel.

Another individual difference at the knee is caused by a variation in the placement of the tibial tuberosity relative to the center of the knee joint. The most frequent occurrence of misplaced tibial tuberosity is when it is lateral to the center of the bone. This placement may be related to tibial torsion and/or knock-knees. When this misalignment exists, the patella is pulled laterally and, instead of riding in the patellar surface of the femur, actually rides over the lateral condyle of the femur. This causes friction, erosion, and irritation of the posterior surface of the patella. The irritation may cause buildup of bony scar tissue which results in a consistent grating and crunching of the knee in movement. This condition is called *chondromalacia of the patella.* (Exercises to help this condition are included in Chapter 19 of this book.) Chondromalacia should not be confused with the normal popping of the knee on the first few *pliés* of the day. This normal popping occurs because the first movements of the joint after a period of rest stimulate the synovial membrane, which secretes synovial fluid and lubricates the joints. In the first major movements of the day, the synovial membrane has not yet "done its thing." Thus there is a normal popping of the joints on the first few movements of the joint until the joint is "greased."

Another condition in this area is an inflammation and irritation of the tibial tuberosity called *Osgood-Schlatter disease.* The tibial tuberosity is the distal attachment for the quadricep muscles of the thigh. It is located on the upper epiphyseal line (growth line) of the tibia. An active adolescent may feel soreness at the tibial tuberosity particularly during growth spurts. Fracture of the tibial tuberosity is also identified as Osgood-Schlatter disease by some authorities. A dancer with intense soreness of the tibial tuberosity should see an orthopedic specialist.

Proper Alignment of the Knee

When the knee is flexed, great care should be taken to keep the tibia/fibula directly in alignment (on the same sagittal plane) with the femur. This general rule can do more to prevent knee injuries than any other. This precaution minimizes the rotary action of the knee joint in a flexed position. The rotary action of the knee places great stress on the ligamentous structure of the knee joint, thus increasing the likelihood of injury. Turning the feet out (by pronating the tarsus or outwardly rotating the knee, or both) farther than the knee in *plié* results in a torque of the knee and places great stress on the medial side of the knee (Figure 3.9). Be reminded that in this position the knee is *very* susceptible to injury.

Hyperextension of the knee joint is the other major misalignment of the knee. When one has a tendency to hyperextend the knees, muscular contraction of the flexors of the knee is needed before the knee can unlock. This makes knee flexion a slower process and may result in injury. While some teachers of dance believe that a hyperextended knee is aesthetically pleasing, the relative potential for injury must be considered. If hyperextended knees are demanded in the dance studio, special precautions should be taken to make the dancer aware of the potential injury. Hyperextended knees often initiate a chain reaction of postural misalignments and are particularly dangerous on landings from jumps or leaps.

REVIEW AND APPLICATION

Table 3.3 presents a list of several figures in Chapter 3 and the page number where each can be found. Analyze the joint position or action, and also the action of gravity.

Tables 3.4 through 3.7 show the correct answers for the analyses.

TABLE 3.3   **Practice Analyses**

Figure 3.2 (on page 30)	Analyze the position of ankle, tarsus, and toes.
Figure 3.3 (on page 31)	Analyze the position of ankle, tarsus, and toes.
Figure 3.5 (on page 33)	Analyze the action of ankle and tarsus from a to b.
Figure 3.9a (on page 38)	Analyze the position of the knee.

TABLE 3.4   **Analysis of Figure 3.2 (page 30)**

Identification	Joint Position or Action	Action of Gravity
Ankle (position)	Plantar flexion	Relaxation to neutral which is a direction of dorsiflexion.
Tarsus (position)	Supination	Relaxation to neutral which is a direction of pronation.
Toes (position)	Flexion	Relaxation to neutral which is a direction of extension.

TABLE 3.5   **Analysis of Figure 3.3 (page 31)**

Identification	Joint Position or Action	Action of Gravity
Ankle	Dorsiflexion	Plantar flexion
Tarsus	Pronation	Supination
Toes	Hyperextension	Flexion
(All positions)		

TABLE 3.6   **Analysis of Figure 3.5 (page 33)**

Identification	Joint Position or Action	Action of Gravity
(Analysis of action from a to b, with gravity analyzed at a)		
Ankle	Maintain plantar flexion	Dorsiflexion
Tarsus	Pronation*	Supination

TABLE 3.7   **Analysis of Figure 3.9a (page 38)**

Identification	Joint Position or Action	Action of Gravity
Knee	Flexion	Flexion

CHAPTER 4

Pelvis and Spine

Including hip joints and lumbar, thoracic,
and cervical regions of the spine

The Pelvis and Hip Joint

Structure of the Pelvis

The pelvis is made up of the sacrum and the right and left *os coxae* (hip-bones).[1] The pelvis is a complex three-dimensional structure. It is difficult to comprehend, spatially, from two-dimensional drawings. If possible study the pelvis in three dimensions, actually looking at a skeleton, while referring to the illustrations of the pelvis.

The os coxa is made up of the *ilium, ischium,* and *pubis* (see Figure 4.1). The three bones are adjacent but separate at birth. They ossify into one bone with age. There are a number of bony landmarks on the ilium, ischium, and pubis which serve as muscle attachments.

The ilium is the most superior bone of the os coxa. There are four spines of the ilium: the *anterior superior iliac* spine, the *anterior inferior iliac* spine, the *posterior superior iliac spine,* and the *posterior inferior iliac* spine. The arching ridge of bone on the superior aspect of the ilium is the *iliac crest.* On the outside of the ilium, there is a large indentation called the *gluteal fossa.* Three lines are found on the gluteal fossa: the *posterior gluteal* line, the *anterior gluteal* line, and the *inferior gluteal* line. On the inside of the ilium is another large indentation, the *iliac fossa.* The pubis is the most anterior bone of the os coxa. The *symphysis pubis* is formed where the right and left pubic bones articulate with each other. An "arm" or *ramus* is sent off from the pubis up to the ilium, called the *ascending ramus.* On the superior aspect of the ascending ramus is the *pectineal crest.* A ramus is also sent down from the pubis to the ischium; this is called the *descending ramus.* The two ascending rami are formed in part by the pubis and in part by the ilium. Likewise, the two descending rami are formed in part by the pubis and in part by the ischium. The ischium is the most inferior bone of the os coxa. The *ischial tuberosity* is the section of rough sur-

---

1. The os coxae are also called the *innomenate* bones by some authorities.

53

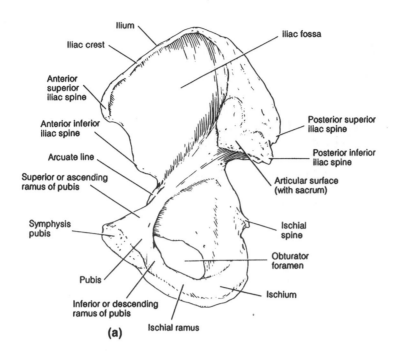

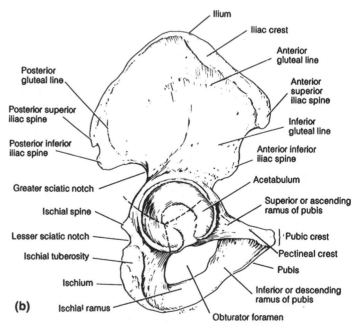

FIGURE 4.1.   Os coxae: (*a*) medial view; (*b*) lateral view

face on the most inferior aspect of the ischium. In dance, the ischial tuberosity is known as the "sit bone." The *acetabulum* (the hip socket) is actually made up of a fusion of the three bones of the os coxa, with the greatest portion of the acetabulum being contributed by the ilium; the ischium and the pubis form smaller sections of the socket. The ilium articulates with the sacrum at the *sacroiliac joint*. This joint is, ideally, a non-movable joint, supported by a network of ligaments. If an individual has had an injury to the ligamentous structure (such as a fall, landing on the "tail"), there may be very slight movement possible at the sacroiliac joint. Movement of this joint frequently causes pain because of the concentration of nerves in this area. A movement of the sacroiliac joint will therefore be likely to pinch a nerve.

The pelvis is actually shaped like a bowl, with the sacrum forming the back of the bowl, the ilium forming the sides, the ischium forming the bottom, and the pubis forming the anterior portion (which is lower than the back and sides). Functionally, the pelvis is a solid unit, with movement of one part of the bowl causing movement of the whole bowl. Three joints allow motion of the pelvis: the articulation of the sacrum with the fifth lumbar vertebra; and the two hip joints, where the femurs articulate with the two sides of the pelvis at the acetabula. The whole pelvis moves as a unit with the fulcrum for movements being the sacro-lumbar joint and the hip joints.

Structure of the Hip Joint

The hip joint is made up of the head of the femur fitting into the acetabulum of the pelvis (see Figure 4.2). In addition to the natural soundness provided by the ball-and-socket structure of the joint, the hip is further secured by a series of ligaments. The major ligaments of the hip joint are the *iliofemoral* ligament, the *pubofemoral* ligament, and the *ischiofemoral* ligament (see Figure 4.3). These ligaments originate from around the acetabulum of the pelvis, wrap obliquely around the neck of the femur, and attach to the femur. The three external ligaments are joined by an internal liga-

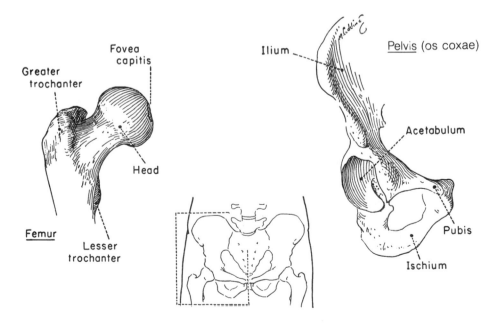

FIGURE 4.2. **Hip joint**

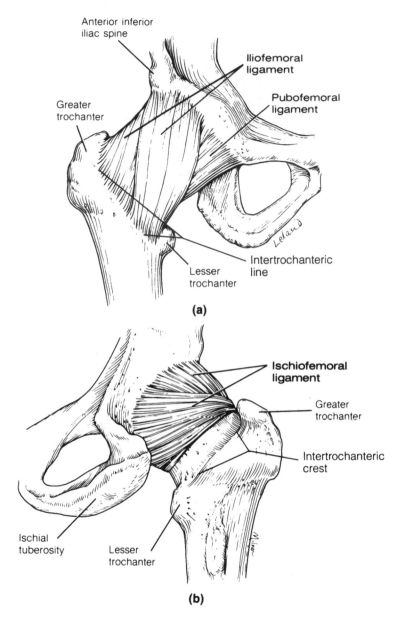

FIGURE 4.3.   Ligaments of the right hip joint: (*a*) anterior; (*b*) posterior

ment, the *teres* ligament, which, like a short yo-yo string from the center of the acetabulum to the center of the head of the femur, holds the head of the femur tight in the acetabulum. The bone structure and the ligamentous structure join to provide the major restrictions of action at the hip.

Actions and Restrictions at the Hip Joint

Action occurs on all three planes of action at the hip joint (see Table 4.1). Because the hip is a primary weight-bearing joint and because the mainte-

TABLE 4.1 Actions and Restrictions at the Hip

Planes of Action	Possible Actions	Restrictions of Actions
Sagittal plane	Flexion	Free to a certain point. With knee flexed, restriction is by contact of thigh with chest. With knee extended, restriction is by hamstring muscles.
	Extension	From a position of flexion, extension is relatively free to approximately 180 degrees. Restriction prior to reaching 180-degree extension is caused by tightness of the hip flexor muscles.
	Hyperextension not possible	Iliofemoral ligament ("Y" ligament) prevents any hyperextension of the hip joint.
Frontal plane	Abduction	When hip joint is not rotated, restriction of abduction is caused by contact of the greater trochanter with the ilium, just above the acetabulum. When hip joint is outward rotated, restriction of abduction comes from the inelasticity of the adductor muscles. (When hip joint is outwardly rotated, the greater trochanter no longer contacts the ilium. Therefore, to achieve abduction of more than approximately 45 degrees, outward rotation must accompany abduction).
	Adduction	Primary restriction of adduction comes from contact with the other leg. When the other leg is out of the way, restriction is caused by inelasticity of the abductor muscles.
Transverse plane	Outward rotation	Primarily restricted by inelasticity of the muscles of inward rotation and the major ligaments of the hip joint. If the acetabulum faces forward there may be restriction of outward rotation due to contact between the neck of the femur and the posterior rim of the acetabulum.*
	Inward rotation	Primarily restricted by inelasticity of the muscles of outward rotation and the major ligaments of the hip. If the acetabulum faces laterally there will be greater range of motion in outward rotation.*
	Circumduction	Term used by anatomists to describe action, but seldom used in actual analysis of joint and muscular action. Because circumduction involves movement on more than one plane at a time, it must be subdivided before muscular analysis can be completed. It is a handy term for gross analysis of joint action, but more cumbersome than it is worth for the specific analysis of joint and muscular action called for in this book. This is the only place in this book where reference is made to circumduction.

*The relative depth of the acetabulum is also thought to have an effect on the range of rotation at the hip joint, with a shallower acetabulum resulting in greater range of rotation and a deeper acetabulum resulting in restricted range in rotation. Some authorities cite the depth of the acetabulum as a male-female difference in pelvic structure, with the male acetabulum being deeper.

nance of a neutral position on any of the planes of action may require muscular effort to counteract the action of gravity, analysis of action at the hip joint should always include analysis of *all three planes of action.* The necessity for this triplane analysis will become apparent in Chapter 9. Reviewing the planes of action, we recall they are the sagittal plane (flexion and extension), the frontal plane (abduction and adduction), and the transverse plane (inward and outward rotation). Actually, all six of these actions are possible at the hip joint, yet each action is limited in some way. Table 4.1 charts the actions of the hip joint and the potential restrictions of those actions. A clarification: the term *hip* refers *only* to the articulation of the head of the femur and the acetabulum (the true hip joint) and is not meant to imply the os coxa (the hipbone) or pelvis.

One question that usually arises following a presentation of the restriction of action at the hip joint is over the complete restriction of hyperextension of the hip joint. The question, "What about arabesque? You cannot deny the fact that the leg goes back in arabesque and that is hyperextension." The response: "Yes, that is hyperextension, but in most cases it is not of the hip joint." Try the following experiment: place one hand on the front of the hip joint (in dance terms sometimes called the "crease"). Place the other hand on the lumbar spine. Swing the leg directly to the front (flexing the hip). Keeping the torso vertical, from a position of flexion of the hip, begin slow extension of the hip joint, letting the leg descend to the floor. Feel the action of hip joint extension with the hand on the front of the hip. Then as the leg moves past 180-degree extension, feel the movement shift to hyperextension of the lumbar spine and hip joint itself remain static at a position of 180-degree extension. For most individuals, and even most dancers, *there is no hyperextension of the hip joint.* In some exceptional cases there may be very slight hyperextension due to laxity of the iliofemoral ligament, but it is only slight. The hyperextension that occurs in arabesque is actually made possible by action in the lumbar spine with an accompanying forward tilt of the pelvis. The iliofemoral ligament prevents hyperextension of the hip joint.

Proper Alignment of the Pelvis

Pelvic alignment can be assessed from two views: from the front and from the side. In the *front view* of pelvic alignment, one checks for bilateral symmetry and whether the two anterior superior spines of the ilium are the same distance from the floor. Actually, an easier way to check these features of alignment is to check the relative length of the legs by having the subject lie supine on the floor with both legs at a right angle to the floor. (Most dancers can achieve this position, but if not—owing to tightness of the hamstring muscles—the examiner must make adjustments to check leg length.) Instruct the subject to make sure that both sides of the sacrum are equally on the floor and the feet are not touching each other. The ankle is dorsiflexed. The examiner can then check the relative length of the right and left leg. If one leg is longer, as is quite common, the subject will have one side of the pelvis higher than the other in the standing position.

The *side view of pelvic alignment* is assessed by recording the relative position of three bony landmarks: the anterior superior spine of the ilium, the posterior superior spine of the ilium, and the symphysis pubis (see Figure 4.4). In *ideal pelvic alignment,* the anterior superior spine of the ilium and the posterior superior spine of the ilium are on the same horizontal (transverse) plane and the anterior superior spine of the ilium is on the same vertical (frontal) plane as the symphysis pubis. Deviations from the ideal position of the pelvis are called *increased pelvic inclination* and *decreased pelvic inclination.* (Increased pelvic inclination makes the rear look larger, or increased.) *Increased* pelvic inclination is indicated when the anterior superior spine of the ilium is lower than the posterior superior spine of the ilium and the anterior spine forward of the symphysis pubis. Increased pelvic inclination is sometimes called "butt-sprung" and almost always occurs simultaneously with swayback. *Decreased* pelvic inclination is indicated when the anterior superior spine of the ilium is higher than the posterior superior spine of the ilium and back from the symphysis pubis. This condition is called "tucked" pelvis in the dance studio. When one is assessing the alignment of pelvis from the lateral view, it is critical to use these bony landmarks as checkpoints because the muscular contour of the buttocks can be deceiving, owing to individual differences in pelvic structure. Ideal alignment of the pelvis is critical for the achievement of efficiency of action both at the hip joint and at the lumbar spine.

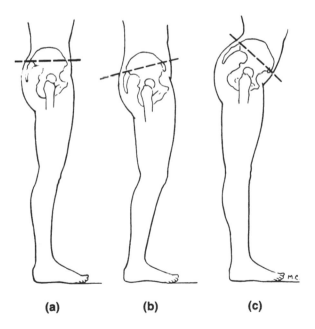

(a)   (b)   (c)

FIGURE 4.4.   Assessment of pelvic alignment: (*a*) ideal alignment; (*b*) decreased pelvic inclination; (*c*) increased pelvic inclination

Individual Differences in Pelvic Structure and Hip Joint Action

Individual differences in pelvic and femoral structure account for some individual differences in efficiency, range of motion, and contour of the pelvic region. Every anatomy book discusses the differences between the male pelvis and the female pelvis. Generally, the male pelvis is narrower than the female pelvis. The difference is primarily caused by a difference in the width of the sacrum, not a major difference in the size of the os coxa. A wider sacrum, inserted between the two iliac bones, spreads the os coxae farther to the sides. This makes the female, with a wider pelvis, less efficient for locomotion. The femur descends to the knee joint at an oblique angle for the female, while the narrower male pelvis allows the femur to be closer to vertical. Of course there are some females with a relatively narrow pelvis, and those females have the potential for greater efficiency in locomotion than females with a wide sacrum. Characteristically, black people have a narrower pelvis than white people. This may be another reason (in addition to the relative length of the calcaneous) why blacks seem to excel at running and jumping. There is, however, an effect on the contour of the pelvic region that may be disadvantageous to any dancers with a narrow pelvic structure. When the pelvis is narrower, there is less posterior space for muscle tissue to spread out to the sides. Consequently, it naturally protrudes to the rear. Looking at the pelvic contour of the narrow-hipped dancer with protruding buttocks may lead to the erroneous assumption that there is increased pelvic inclination. Many dancers with this condition are told to "tuck" the pelvis to a point where they actually decrease the pelvis inclination. For this reason, it is critical to assess the alignment of the pelvis by reference to the bony landmarks, not by appearance of the contour. The contour can be misleading, and reference to the contour can cause overcorrection.

Another difference between the male and female pelvis is the relative amount of lateral flaring of the ischium. As the ischium descends, the female pelvis flares out to the sides and back, while the male ischium is closer to vertical. This characteristic of the female pelvis makes it easier for the fetus to pass through the birth canal. It also makes it easier for the female to "get up onto the sit bones" when sitting with the legs straight. The male pelvis, with the ischii descending an almost vertical line, accentuates to a greater extent the male's relative inflexibility at the hip joint. Females are recognized to have greater mobility of the hip joint than males.

In Table 4.1, two additional individual differences in hip joint structure were noted: relative facing of the acetabulum and relative depth of the acetabulum. The facing of the acetabulum, even though the variance is relatively small, allows for differences in range of motion on the transverse plane. The more anterior the acetabular facing, the greater the range of inward rotation. The more lateral the acetabular facing, the greater the range of outward rotation. This anatomical feature in part explains why some dancers have "natural turnout" while others have to fight for every degree of outward rotation. In fifteen years of assessing the alignment of dancers, I have found that there seems to be a correlation between a narrower pelvic structure and the anterior facing acetabulum. No formal research has been done to validate this observation, but I include it here, hoping to reduce the self-flagellation for limited outward rotation which is frequently practiced by narrow-hipped dancers. Yes, there really is a reason why outward rotation is limited for some. This restriction can be further accentuated by the presence of a deep acetabular structure. The shallower acetabulum allows for greater range of both inward and outward rotation. However, all of these characteristics (narrower pelvis, deeper acetabulum, and restricted range of rotation) make the hip joint more efficient for locomotion. Getting "air" on jumps and leaps is much easier for the narrow-hipped dancer than for the wide-hipped dancer.

The final individual difference in this region is the variance found in the angle between the neck of the femur and the shaft. (See Figure 4.5.) The wider the pelvic structure, the smaller the angle between the neck and shaft of the femur. Therefore, the male has a tendency to a greater *angle of obliquity* (sometimes called the "Q" angle) than the female. This angle variance and the variance in pelvic width form the structural reasons for women's running "funny." The wider the pelvis, the smaller the angle of obliquity, and the "funnier" the run.

Information on each of the individual differences contributes to the dancer's understanding of the reasons for differing movement potential. Forcing a movement at the hip joint beyond the range allowed by the bone structure can result in abnormal erosion of the hip socket. It is my contention that forcing the hip into a position of outward rotation beyond the natural range has been a major factor in causing arthritic hips in aging

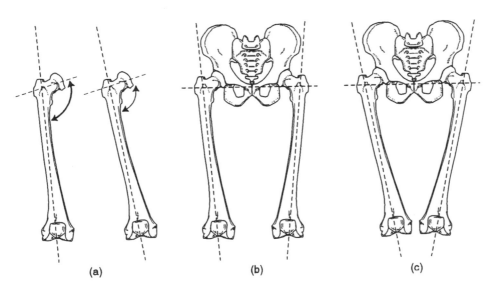

(a) (b) (c)

FIGURE 4.5.   The "Q" angle of the (a) femur and its effect on alignment of the legs for (b) the male and (c) the female.

dancers. So far, no research has been conducted to validate this hypothesis, but the incidence of arthritic hips in aging dancers is quite high.

Over the years, turnout has become a sacred cow: 180-degree turnout puts a dancer in highly esteemed company. In my opinion, the importance of the ability to turn out at the hip joint has been overemphasized. Why do dancers turn out in the first place? Certainly not for aesthetics; the awkward appearance of turned-out feet is far less pleasing than feet that are parallel to each other. Certainly the reason cannot be efficiency, for the foot is clearly designed for movement on the sagittal plane. I believe the answer is to be found in tradition stemming from original ballet technique designed for the proscenium stage. Performance was traditionally done facing the front. This made locomotion to the sides difficult because the feet got in the way when the feet crossed. Therefore the feet were turned out to allow free locomotor movement to the sides of the stage. How much turnout is needed to accomplish this action? Certainly not 180 degrees. Another reason for turnout is to allow greater range of motion in abduction of the hip joint. However, considerably less than 180 degrees is sufficient to prevent contact between the greater trochanter and the ilium above the acetabulum. It is not expected that this observation of turnout will change dance tradition. However, it is hoped that dancers with a limited turnout will at least think about the possible consequences before jamming their hip joints into a 180-degree turnout when their natural bony range of motion is less.

There is also a restriction of rotation at the hip joint that is muscular in nature. Tightness of the inward rotators restricts outward rotation and tightness of the outward rotators restrict inward rotation. That restriction can be changed by stretching the tight muscles, but the restriction provided by the bone structure cannot be changed without doing damage to the structure of the joint. Ideally, there should be a balanced range of inward and outward rotation of the hip joint. When there is a balance of these two actions, the feet will "track" in parallel in normal walking. Many dancers walk turned out (duck-footed) owing to tightness of the outward rotators. This characteristic can contribute to the development of bunions on the head of the first metatarsal and can also contribute to sciatic syndrome (to be discussed in Chapter 13, on muscular imbalances). A "turned-out" walk is not desired.

Analysis of Joint Action at the Hip Joint

Analysis of action at the hip joint, like the other joints of the body, can be the analysis of either static position or actions. There is one position of extension of the hip joint but an infinite number of positions of flexion. The position of extension is the normal standing position. There are an infinite number of positions of inward rotation and outward rotation, but only one position of neutral rotation, which is parallel position. There are an infinite number of positions of abduction and adduction and a single position of neutral ab/adduction. Therefore, a normal standing position (feet hip-width apart and parallel) would be identified as extension, neutral rotation and neutral ab/adduction of the hip joint. A wide second position would be identified as extension, abduction and outward rotation of the hip joint. A "tailor" sitting position on the floor (legs crossed) would be identified as a flexed, abducted and outward rotated position of the hip joint.

As is true of the joints previously presented, analysis of action is dependent upon the *direction of action*. Any movement of either lever (the pelvis or the femur) that lessens the anterior angle between the pelvis and the femur is called an action of *flexion*. The femur can be the moving lever and the pelvis stabilized, the pelvis can be the moving lever with the femur stabilized, or both levers can move. The reverse direction of action is called *extension*.

Any movement of either lever that decreases the lateral angle (whether movement of the femur, the pelvis, or both) is called *abduction*. The action in the opposite direction is called *adduction*. Any movement that rotates hip joint outward (whether the pelvis or the femur is the moving lever, or if both move) is called *outward rotation*. The reverse action is called *inward rotation*. Figures 4.6 and 4.7 illustrate the positions and actions of the hip joint on the three planes of action.

A word of caution: Students are frequently confused when the pelvis (rather than the femur) becomes the moving lever. They tend to look at the contour of the hip region at the skin surface rather than at the angle formed by the femur and the pelvis at the joint itself. In standing on two feet and shifting the pelvis to the right, the action is *adduction of the right hip* and *abduction of the left hip*. Granted, the right ilium is "out to the side" farther, but the right hip joint is adducted. One must look with x-ray vision, and *not* focus on the contour.

The same sort of problem can occur in identifying the direction of rotation when the pelvis is the moving lever (see Figure 4.16 later in the chapter). When one stands with both feet firmly planted on the floor and rotates the pelvis and torso to the right, the *right hip joint is rotating inward* and the *left hip joint is rotating outward*. Again one must focus on the joint, not on the contour.

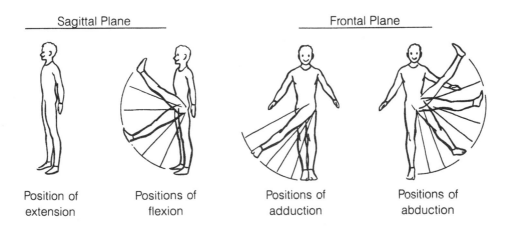

Sagittal Plane		Frontal Plane	
Position of extension	Positions of flexion	Positions of adduction	Positions of abduction

Figure 4.6. **Positions of the hip joint on the sagittal and frontal planes**

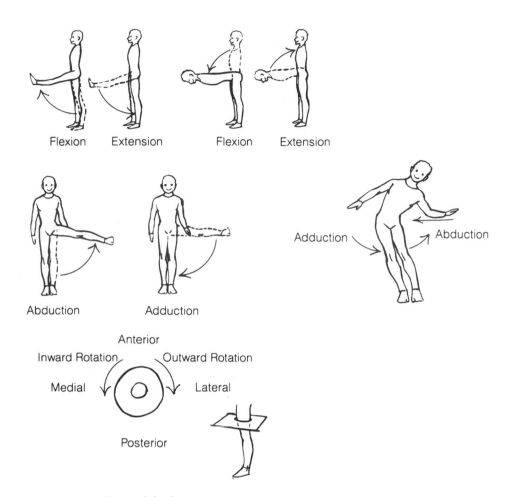

FIGURE 4.7.   Actions of the hip joint

Focusing on the contour can lead to confusion and errors in analysis of hip joint action. Correction of this problem requires changing the perceptual reference to the x-ray perspective and focusing on the relationship between the femur and the pelvis, and on the joint itself.

You are encouraged to experiment with analysis of positions and actions of the hip joint. The action of the hip joint is admittedly complex, but intensive experimentation and analysis at this point can lay the foundation for understanding. To ignore confusion now is to magnify that confusion later, when muscular analysis is added.

The Spine

Structure of the Spine

Humans balance their full weight on a remarkably small support surface. Migrating upward from the sacrum, the spine supports all of the weight of the upper body. A remarkable structure, it provides both relative stability and mobility.

The vertebral column is made up of the *coccyx* (actually a fusion of bones), the sacrum (also a fusion of bones), five *lumbar vertebrae*, twelve *thoracic vertebrae*, and seven *cervical vertebrae* (see Figure 4.8). The spine serves as the support structure for the entire upper body. The sacrum and the vestigial tail, the coccyx, have been included in the discussion of the pelvis, since they form its posterior aspect. Proceeding upward from the sacrum is the movable spine: the lumbar, thoracic, and cervical vertebrae of gradually decreasing size. The two uppermost vertebrae (the atlas and the axis) support the skull at the top of vertebral column and are modified in shape to perform that task. The rib cage (twelve ribs on each side) articulates with the twelve thoracic vertebrae.

The natural curves of the spine are evident in Figure 4.8. Those curves serve the function of allowing the spine to efficiently bear the weight above. The curve of hyperextension in the lumbar region shifts the supporting column anteriorly so that it can efficiently support the weight of the rib cage and thorax above it. The thoracic curve of flexion also serves to assist the centering of weight above the lumbar vertebrae by shifting the center of weight posteriorly. The cervical curve of hyperextension again shifts the support structure anteriorly to effectively support the weight of the head. The thoracic curve (and the sacral curve as well) is called a *primary* curve because the curve of flexion is present in the fetal position. The *secondary* curves of the spine (hyperextension, found in the cervical and lumbar) appear after birth. The cervical curve begins to appear as the infant lifts its head from a prone position; the lumbar curve begins to appear as the infant assumes a seated position. Both these secondary curves must be present before efficient standing or locomotion is possible. These anterior-posterior curves of the spine are essential to efficient weight bearing in an upright position. The relative weight of an individual, or the mass which must be supported by the spine, will often have an effect on the relative depth of the curves of the movable spine. The more weight, the deeper the curves. A heavy individual will usually have deeper spinal curves and a slender person shallower curves. A notable shift in the lumbar curve occurs during pregnancy, when a considerable weight is "hung" on the front of the body. In order to balance that weight, the upper torso must be shifted backward, and the fulcrum for that motion is the lumbar spine. Other distortions of the normal anterior-posterior curves of the spine will be discussed later.

There are a number of bony landmarks on each vertebra. While the shape and size of those landmarks may vary from one spinal region to another, the names remain the same. Figure 4.9 illustrates those bony landmarks. Critical bony landmarks on the vertebrae include: the *body*, the *spine* or *spinous process*, two *transverse processes*, two *superior articulating facets*, and two *inferior articulating facets*. Students in my classes have nicknamed the superior and inferior articulating facets the "ears" and "jowls" of the vertebrae respectively. Those nicknames may help the reader get a sense of where those landmarks are located.

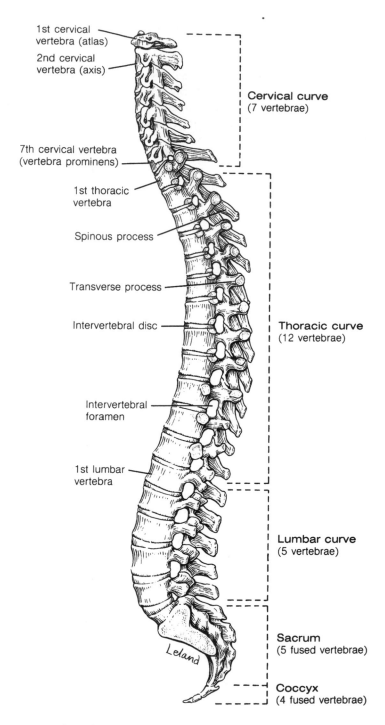

1st cervical
vertebra (atlas)

2nd cervical
vertebra (axis)

Cervical curve
(7 vertebrae)

7th cervical vertebra
(vertebra prominens)

1st thoracic
vertebra

Spinous process

Transverse process

Intervertebral disc

Thoracic curve
(12 vertebrae)

Intervertebral
foramen

1st lumbar
vertebra

Lumbar curve
(5 vertebrae)

Leland

Sacrum
(5 fused vertebrae)

Coccyx
(4 fused vertebrae)

FIGURE 4.8.   **The spine**

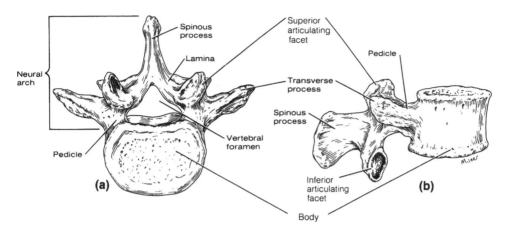

FIGURE 4.9.   A single vertebra

Adjacent vertebrae articulate with each other at the respective superior and inferior surfaces of the bodies of the vertebrae, and at the respective superior and inferior articulating facets. (The "ears" of the vertebra below articulate with the "jowls" of the vertebra above.) The intervertebral discs lie between the bodies of the vertebrae and serve as shock-absorbing cushions between the bodies of the vertebrae.

Actions and Restrictions of the Spine

Actions of the spine, like the actions at other joints, occur on the sagittal, frontal, and transverse planes. Flexion, extension, and hyperextension are movements on the sagittal plane. Right rotation and left rotation are the movements on the transverse plane. Instead of abduction and adduction (which would be confusing terms to use because the center is actually moving) the movements on the frontal plane are called *right lateral flexion* and *left lateral flexion*. The terms *right* and *left* reflect the direction of the action. For example, right rotation is rotation to the right; left lateral flexion is lateral flexion toward the left side. Figure 4.10 illustrates the movements of the spine.

The relative shape and size of the bony landmarks of the vertebrae have an effect upon the possible actions in the three regions of the spine. Beginning at the bottom, the articulation and shape of the lumbar vertebrae allow for a free range of motion on the sagittal plane with flexion, extension, and hyperextension being possible. Lateral flexion is also free in the lumbar region. However, the angle of the articulating facets prevents all but minimal rotation in the lumbar spine (see Figure 4.11). Some experts claim that rotation is possible in the lumbar region, but it is my position that the inferior articulating facets fitting inside the angle of the superior articulating facets of the vertebra below (refer back to Figure 4.9) limit most rotation in the lumbar region. The rotary shifting of the pelvis occurs at the hip joints. In the thoracic spine, the movements of lateral flexion

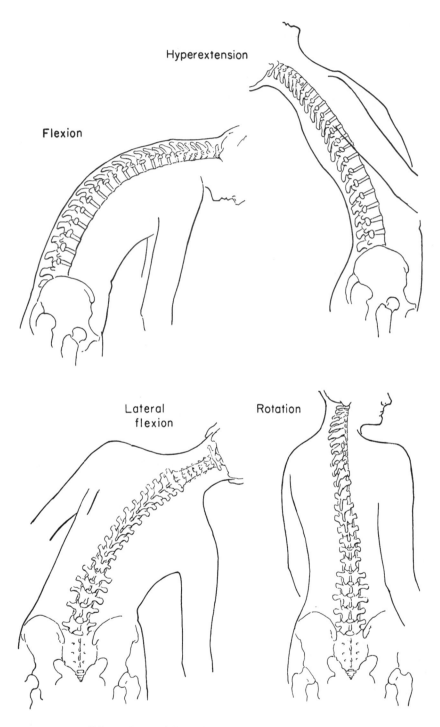

FIGURE 4.10.   Possible actions of the spine

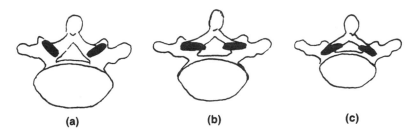

FIGURE 4.11. Angles of the articulating facets in the (*a*) lumbar; (*b*) thoracic; and (*c*) cervical regions of the spine

and rotation are quite free (lateral flexion being restricted only by contact between adjacent ribs). Flexion and extension are possible, but extension is limited to only approximately 180 degrees by the downward-projecting spinous process. Hyperextension (extension beyond 180 degrees) is prohibited in the thoracic spine by the angle of the spinous processes. The side view of an "arched" back appears to be one continuous curve. However, the action in the spine actually takes the shape of a flattened curve, with hyperextension occurring in the lumbar and cervical regions and only extension (180 degrees) occurring in the thoracic region. Because the ribs protrude to the front, the external contour of the curve seems to include the thoracic region; but in fact the hyperextension is occurring only in the cervical and lumbar regions. In the cervical spine, all possible motions are quite free, including flexion, extension, hyperextension, rotation, and lateral flexion. Table 4.2 reviews the actions and restrictions of actions of the three areas of the spine.

Anyone who has ever tried to balance a broom on a fingertip knows the core of the problems of gravity and the spine. The instant that the broom is even slightly off-center, something must be done to counteract the pull of gravity if the broom is going to be kept in a vertical position: either the base of support must be moved to a position under the weight of the broom or the broom must be grabbed. If nothing is done, the broom will fall to the floor in the direction that it was off-center. The spine is more complicated in its response to gravity because it is segmented, but the principles of balance remain the same as the example of the broom. If the weight of the spine is not centered over the base of support—the pelvis and legs—the spine will fall in the direction that it is off-center. For example, if the spine is slightly laterally flexed to the right, gravity will initially continue that direction of action. If the lateral flexion is behind the frontal plane that bisects the vertebrae, hyperextension will be added to the action of gravity, and in the process some rotation may also occur. If the lateral flexion is straight to the side or slightly anterior, flexion of the spine will accompany the right lateral flexion, with some rotation also possible. In normal circumstances, the spine will eventually migrate to a position that is centered on the sagittal plane (toward either hyperextension or flexion), but the actions that occur in the process are not easily reduced to "rules." The action of gravity on the spine is a complex matter and is com-

TABLE 4.2 Actions and Restrictions of the Spine

Spinal Region	Actions Possible	Actions Not Possible	Bony Restrictions
Lumbar	Flexion		A few minor restrictions possible in some people; see individual differences.
	Extension		None.
	Hyperextension		None.
		Rotation	Angle of the articulating facets.
	Lateral flexion		None.
Thoracic	Flexion		Minimal restriction by rib cage.
	Extension		Limited to 180 degrees.
		Hyperextension	Angle of the spinous process pointing downward.
	Rotation		Relatively free.
	Lateral flexion		Restricted only by ribs contacting each other.
Cervical	Flexion Extension Hyperextension Lateral flexion Rotation		No major bony restrictions; primary restrictions provided by musculature.

plicated even more by the fact that individual patterns of strength, weakness, elasticity, and inelasticity interact with the pull of gravity. I wish I could give you some neatly packaged formula for analysis of the actions of gravity at the spine, but there is none. There is no getting around the fact that the action of gravity on the spine is complicated. The best I can do is to suggest that you experiment with off-centered positions while maintaining a solid base of support to let your body teach you about gravity and the spine.

Individual Differences in the Spine

Individual differences in the spine can be categorized as those which involve (1) variation in the curves of the spine and (2) variations in movement potential based on variations in the number or shape of the vertebrae. While there is a standard number of vertebrae in each of the sections of the spine, there are occasions when an individual will have one fewer lumbar vertebra than normal, one more lumbar vertebra than normal, or other similar variations in the other two regions of the spine. There is also variation in the level of the spine at which the shift from one vertebral shape to another occurs. These individual variations encompass such a wide range of possibilities that to discuss all of them is beyond the scope of this book. Nevertheless, variation in the shape and structure of the individual vertebrae can have a direct effect on the movement potential of the spine. For example, the uppermost aspect of the superior articulating facets in the lumbar region is called the *mamillary process*. The process serves as a muscle attachment and can develop a ridge of bone that hooks over the top of the inferior articulating process of the vertebra above. When this happens, there can be a restriction of flexion in the lumbar spine that somewhat limits the normal range of motion in the lumbar region.

Variations in the number of vertebrae in a given region of the spine also have a direct effect on the curves of the spine. For example, if an individual has only four lumbar vertebrae, the lumbar curve will be sharper than when an individual has all five vertebrae and the curve is spread over a longer distance. Having an extra vertebra in the thoracic region can extend the thoracic curve of flexion down into the lumbar region. In some instances the shape of the twelfth thoracic vertebra resembles more the shape of a lumbar vertebra, and the lumbar curve of hyperextension then extends up into the lower thoracic region. As mentioned, the relative depth of the curves can vary from one individual to another. When the curves are very shallow, the condition has been labeled "flat back." This condition may be related to function, reflecting the response to weight-bearing, or it might be congenital (present at birth), genetically determined.

Each of the individual differences discussed here has an effect on the movement potential of the spine, and also has implications for the conditioning of the muscles of the spine. Careful assessment of the alignment of the spine is essential to discovering these individual differences and subsequently dealing with them effectively.

Assessment of Spinal Alignment

Each of the normal sagittal curves of the spine can be accentuated and result in a misalignment such as kyphosis in the thoracic region or lordosis in the lumbar region. Misalignment of the spine can also reflect an abnormality that occurs on two planes of movement, as is the case with scoliosis. Table 4.3 lists potential misalignments of the spine, identifying the region where misalignment occurs and the nature of the misalignment.

Causes of abnormalities in spinal alignment are usually traceable either to habitual postural patterns or to variations in bone structure, such as leg length. Consistently carrying a purse or dance bag (noted for weighing a ton) on one shoulder can cause scoliosis. Carrying a backpack can cause round shoulders. Being left-handed can cause a scoliosis because of the postural adjustment needed to write efficiently. Forward head may be caused by poor eyesight. Wry neck may be caused by hearing problems. These examples serve to illustrate that any habitual postural pattern may

TABLE 4.3   **Misalignments of the Spine**

Plane of Action	Nature of Curve	Spinal Region	Name of Misalignment
Sagittal (side view) (see Figure 4.12a)	Flexion (excessive)	Thoracic	Kyphosis (round shoulders)
	Hyperextension (excessive)	Lumbar	Lumbar lordosis (swayback)
		Cervical	Cervical lordosis (often accompanied by forward head)
Frontal and transverse combined	Lateral flexion and rotation combined	Can be located in any of the three regions of the spine	Scoliosis
Frontal	Lateral flexion	Cervical	Wry neck (this may be a scoliosis)

result in a deviation from the ideal alignment of the spine. In the early phases of habit formation, the postural deviation is functional or temporary. If the habit continues over a long period of time, the individual vertebrae adapt to the stress and actually change shape. For example, the body of the vertebra is normally cylindrical with the height equal at all points on the circumference of the cylinder. Consistent misalignment can compress the vertebra on one side, resulting in a "wedge-shaped" vertebra. Once the bone structure has adapted to the stresses caused by the misalignment, the abnormality is unchangeable (structural rather than functional). When an abnormal curve of the spine is structural, corrective exercise will not reverse the condition but may prevent further deterioration. It seems quite clear that the earlier a spinal misalignment is observed, the greater the possibility for correction. Periodic assessment of alignment by the teacher of young dancers can do much to prevent structural misalignments.

Assessment of the deviations viewable from the side is relatively simple, since they are accentuations of the normal curves and can be observed and identified. Assessment of scoliosis is more complicated because this condition combines misalignment on two planes: the transverse and the frontal. Scoliosis is a combination of lateral flexion and rotation. Usually the lateral flexion and rotation are in the same direction (right lateral flexion accompanied by right rotation and left lateral flexion accompanied by left rotation), but scoliosis is a complex phenomenon and other combinations are also possible.

There are two approaches I have found helpful in assessing scoliosis. One is very simple and can be easily used in the studio but gives less spe-

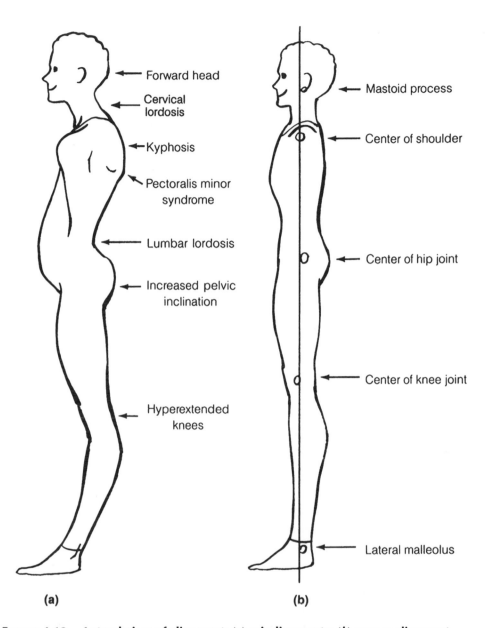

FIGURE 4.12. Lateral view of alignment: (*a*) misalignments; (*b*) proper alignment

cific information than the other. Figure 4.13 illustrates the simple test for scoliosis. The subject bends over as if to touch the floor, flexing at the hip and in all areas of the spine. The evaluator sits behind the subject and looks for "humps" on either side of the spine as the subject slowly curls up to a standing position. A "hump" on one side indicates a lateral curvature of the spine. Usually the hump is on the concave side of the curve. Using this simple assessment technique, the evaluator can chart the presence and general nature of the curve by referring to the numbering of the verte-

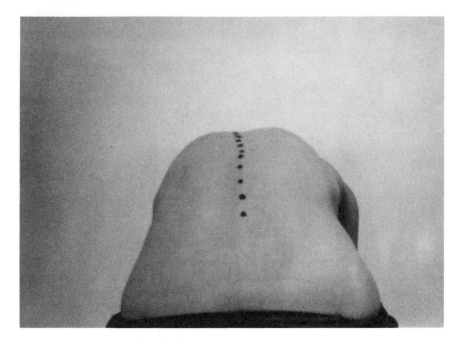

FIGURE 4.13.   Simple test for scoliosis

brae. For example: a subject might have a long C-curve, concave to the right, extending from the fifth lumbar to the eighth thoracic vertebrae. (This long C-curve seems quite common for individuals with a variance in leg length. In this case the right leg would probably be longer.) Another common occurrence is an S-shaped curve, reflecting the compensation required to remain erect. The simple test for scoliosis can also be done with less specificity in the technique class if the teacher will just take the time to visually scan the backs of the students when they are performing a hamstring stretch. This very quick scan can identify major abnormalities. The second test for scoliosis is more complicated but yields more specific information (see Figure 4.14). In this test, the examiner marks the spinous processes of the subject's spine with a grease pencil, taking care to mark the exact center of the spinous processes, not the sides. The subject then stands facing away from the examiner, and any deviations are noted. I tend to prefer the simpler test for scoliosis because it does not *require* disrobing and can be done easily in the dance studio.

Any abnormal structural curve of the spine results in unequal pressure on the cartilagenous disk between the bodies of the vertebrae. This can result in a herniated disk (slipped disk) if the pressure squeezes the disk out to one side. When the displaced disk puts pressure on surrounding nerve tissue, extreme pain is the result. This condition requires the attention of a doctor, preferably an orthopedic specialist.

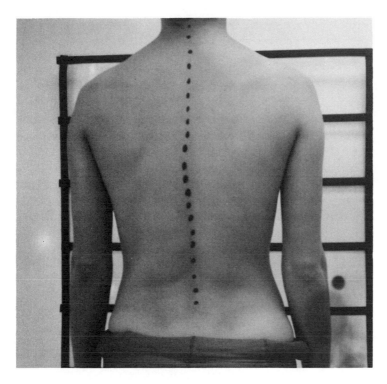

FIGURE 4.14. Spine "marking test" for scoliosis

Misalignments of the spine and its base of support, the pelvis, come in many forms and have serious negative consequences. Two of the most common misalignments of this region are increased pelvic inclination and unequal leg length. Each of these problems initiates a chain reaction of compensations in the spine. The extreme mobility of the spine makes sprains, strains, and spasms common consequences of overmovement and overuse.

No discussion of the spine would be complete without at least a mention of muscular back pain. Common sites for back pain include the low back, the neck, and the region between the shoulder blades (scapulae). Frequently, pains in these areas are the result of strain on the musculature caused by misalignment of the skeletal structure. Understanding of these aches and pains depends on knowledge of the muscular system. For this reason, specific discussion of back pain is postponed until you have knowledge of the muscular structure. Chapter 13 discusses muscular imbalances of the spine and Chapter 19 presents corrective exercises.

PRACTICE DEMONSTRATIONS

Figures 4.15, 4.16, and 4.17 will give you an opportunity to practice analysis of joint position and action. Tables 4.4 to 4.6 will allow you to check the accuracy of your analysis. The figures and tables are on pages 76–78.

FIGURE 4.15.   Analyze the position of the right and left hips.

TABLE 4.4   Analysis of Figure 4.15

Identification	Joint Position or Action	Action of Gravity
Right hip	Flexed	Extend
	Abducted	Adduct
	Outward rotated	Inward rotate
Left hip	Extended	Flexion
	Outward rotated	Inward rotation
	Neutral Ab/adduction*	Adduction

*Actually the position of the left hip is *slightly* adducted because the weight is on one leg and the center of gravity must be shifted to the left.

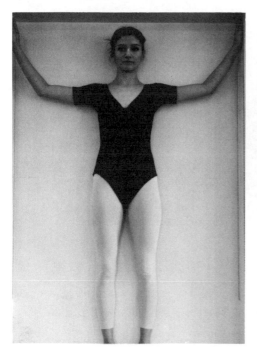 

(a)   **(b)**

FIGURE 4.16.   Analyze the action of the right and left hips from (*a*) to (*b*), with gravity at (*b*).

TABLE 4.5   Analysis of Figure 4.16 (Action of right and left hips from *a* to *b*)

Identification	Joint Position or Action	Action of Gravity
Left hip	Abduction Slight outward rotation Maintenance of extension	*Return to starting position (Adduction, slight inward rotation, and flexion)
Right hip	Adduction Slight inward rotation Maintenance of extension	*Return to starting position (Abduction, outward rotation, and flexion)

*Analysis of gravity is admittedly somewhat confusing in this analysis. The primary reason for including this specific demonstration is to check for x ray vision in analyzing the hip joint action on the frontal plane (abduction/adduction).

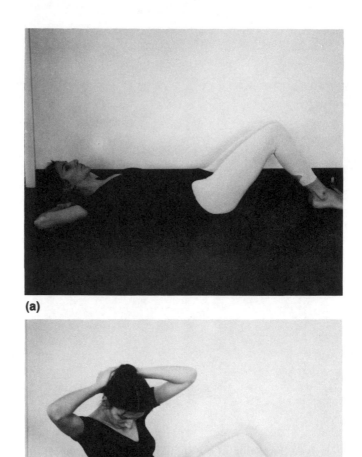

(a)

(b)

FIGURE 4.17.   Analyze the action of the torso (lumbar and thoracic regions) and neck (cervical region) from (a) to (b), with gravity at (b).

TABLE 4.6   Analysis of Figure 4.17 (Action of the torso and neck from a to b)

Identification	Joint Position or Action	Action of Gravity
Torso	Flexion Rotation to the right Perhaps slight right lateral flexion	Extension Rotation to the left Slight lateral flexion to the left
Neck	Flexion Perhaps slight rotation to the right	In first phases gravity will extend and in the last phases gravity will maintain flexion

CHAPTER 5

Scapula and Humerus

The Scapula

The shoulder girdle is made up of the *clavicle* and the *scapula*. It is a freely moving structure, sitting over the rib cage like a set of shoulder pads. The unique feature of the shoulder girdle is the freedom of motion allowed by the minimal bony restrictions. The only bony articulation with the supporting structure occurs at the articulation between the clavicle and the sternum (see Figure 5.4, later in this chapter). Other than that single bony articulation, the shoulder girdle is freely mobile. The shoulder girdle is separate from the shoulder joint in kinesiological analysis. For that reason, calling the actions of the shoulder girdle actions of the *scapula* helps to prevent confusion. From this point on, actions of the shoulder girdle will be called *actions of the scapula* to prevent inappropriate transfer of information and confusion with the shoulder joint.

Bone Structure

The *scapula* is a triangular-shaped bone which has three borders, three angles, three protrusions, and four fossae (see Figure 5.1). The names of the borders and angles of the scapula follow anatomical logic. The borders are *vertebral*, *axillary* (or *lateral*), and *superior*. The angles are *inferior*, *superior*, and *lateral*. The first two protrusions are seen from the posterior view of the scapula where a major bony ridge runs horizontally across the scapula. The ridge is called the *spine of the scapula*. The most lateral aspect of the spine of the scapula is called the *acromion process*. The third protrusion is a hook of bone that protrudes anteriorly and is called the *coracoid process*. The *glenoid fossa* is the socket for the shoulder joint and actually cuts off the "point" of the lateral angle of the scapula. Posteriorly, there is a fossa above the spine of the scapula and one below it. They are named *supraspinous fossa* and *infraspinous fossa*, respectively. Anteriorly, the entire surface of the scapula is concave. That large anterior fossa is called the *subscapular fossa*. The subscapular fossa forms the posterior definition for the area, which I call the "sandwich" area, where the muscles are sandwiched between the scapula and the rib cage.

The scapula articulates with the clavicle at the acromio-clavicular joint, which is a relatively nonmovable joint. Since the acromio-clavicular joint

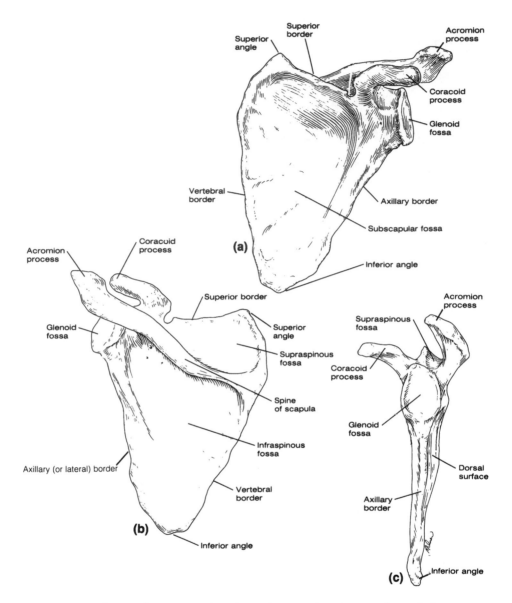

FIGURE 5.1.   Left scapula: (*a*) anterior view; (*b*) posterior view; (*c*) lateral view

moves in conjunction with the scapula, this text focuses on the movements of the scapula. (A "shoulder separation" injury tears the ligaments that hold the joint together. When this happens, slight movement may be possible at the acromio-clavicular joint.) The clavicle, viewed from above, is an S-shaped bone with the medial curve convex to the front and the lateral curve concave to the front. The clavicle articulates with the sternum at the sterno-clavicular joint. It is at this joint that all of the movements of the scapula occur, because the acromio-clavicular joint is a nonmovable joint. The only individual difference worthy of note at the scapula and clavicle is the relative depth of the curves of the clavicle. The deeper the curves of the clavicle, the greater the likelihood of round shoulders or pectoralis minor syndrome (a muscular imbalance discussed in Chapter 13). If, in adolescence, the shoulders are held forward, the constant pressure can cause an increased bowing of the clavicle prior to ossification. This condition is quite common in female adolescence if the young girl is tall or if she is embarrassed by the recently developed breasts. It is also quite common for competitive swimmers because of the frequent occurrence of pectoralis minor syndrome in that group.

Possible Movements of the Scapula

All of the actions of the scapula conform somewhat to the shape of the rib cage, since the scapula slides over the rib cage in different directions for all of its actions.

There are seven and a half actions possible at the scapula. They are listed in Table 5.1, and illustrated in Figure 5.2.

TABLE 5.1 Actions of the Scapula

Action	Description
Elevation	From a normal position of the shoulders, elevation is the raising of the scapula (and clavicle) straight up toward the ears.
Depression	Depression of the scapula is pressing the scapula down onto the rib cage. Return from elevation is also called depression.
Abduction	Abduction of the scapula is lateral movement of the scapula away from the spinal column. Return from adduction is also called abduction.
Adduction	Adduction of the scapula is medial movement of the scapula toward the spinal column. Return from abduction is also called adduction.
Upward rotation	Upward rotation of the scapula is rotation about the center point of the scapula in a direction defined by the glenoid fossa pointing upward and the inferior angle moving laterally and upward. Return from downward rotation is also called upward rotation.
Downward rotation	Downward rotation of the scapula is rotation of the scapula around its centerpoint in a direction defined by the glenoid fossa pointing downward and the inferior angle moving medially. Return from upward rotation is also called downward rotation.
Forward tilt	Forward tilt of the scapula occurs when the scapula slides upward and over the top of the rib cage, moving more to the front. (Some authorities call this action upward tilt, but I believe the use of forward tilt prevents possible confusion with upward rotation.)
Return from forward tilt	This is the half-action. In this action the scapula returns from forward tilt. However, since the rib cage is directly beneath the scapula, true backward tilt is not possible.

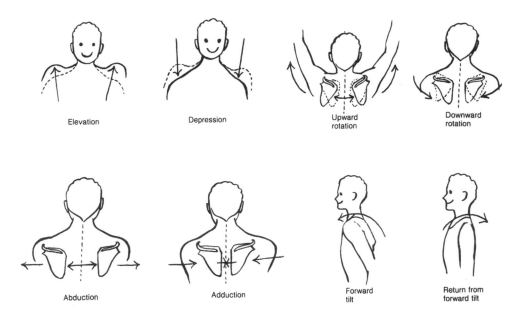

Elevation   Depression   Upward   Downward
                                       rotation   rotation

Abduction   Adduction   Forward   Return from
                                      tilt   forward tilt

FIGURE 5.2.   **Actions of the scapula**

It has been my experience that the actions of the scapula most difficult to understand are upward and downward rotation. Imagine a thumbtack stuck through the scapula at its centerpoint (just under the spine of the scapula and an equal distance from the vertebral border and the glenoid fossa) and holding the scapula fixed there. Let your imagination go one step further and take hold of the inferior angle of the scapula and move the inferior angle laterally; that is *upward rotation*. The reverse action is *downward rotation.*

The great freedom of movement of the scapula is restricted primarily by the muscular structure and secondarily (somewhat) by the relative convex shape of the rib cage and concave shape of the scapula (subscapular fossa). The fact that the scapula is considerably more mobile than the pelvis is one reason for the greater range of motion possible at the shoulder than at the hip. The movements of the scapula facilitate movements of the shoulder joint. The exact nature of that facilitation is presented after the nature and function of the shoulder joint are discussed.

The Humerus

Bone Structure

The *humerus* is the long bone of the upper arm. Like the femur, it has a *head, neck,* protrusions near the head, a shaft, and a *medial* and *lateral epicondyle* (see Figure 5.3). But there are some additional bony landmarks that must be noted. The *head* of the humerus is at the proximal end of the bone. Just distal to the head is the *anatomical neck* (a relatively small in-

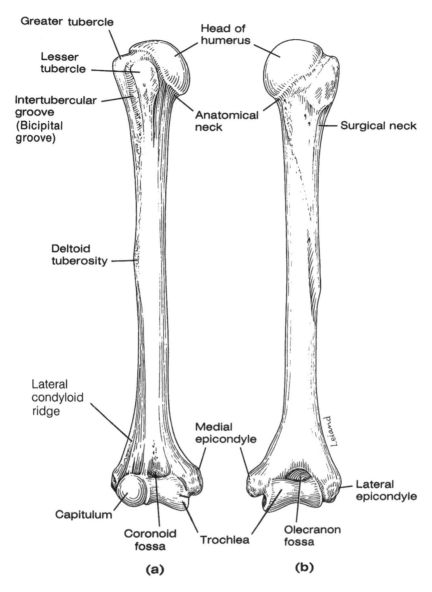

FIGURE 5.3. **Right humerus: (*a*) anterior view; (*b*) posterior view**

dentation). Laterally, there is a chunk of bone called the *greater tuberosity* (greater tubercle), and medially on the anterior of the humerus is the *lesser tuberosity* (lesser tubercle). Between the greater and lesser tuberosities is the *bicipital groove* (intertubercular groove) through which the tendon of the biceps brachii muscle passes. Just below the greater and lesser tuberosities is the *surgical neck* of the humerus. About halfway down the shaft of the humerus on the lateral side is the *deltoid tuberosity,* the attachment of the three deltoid muscles. Distally on the humerus are the *medial* and *lateral epicondyles.* Anteriorly, on the distal end of the humerus, are the *coronoid fossa,* the *trochlea,* and the *capitulum.* On the posterior of the distal end of the humerus is the *olecranon fossa,* and the trochlea is also visible from the rear. Proximal to the lateral epicondyle is the *lateral condyloid ridge,* running up the lateral side of the humerus.

The Shoulder Joint

The shoulder joint is the articulation between the head of the humerus and the glenoid fossa of the scapula. While the shoulder joint is a ball-and-socket joint like the hip, the socket of the shoulder joint is nowhere near as deep as the acetabulum (see Figure 5.4). In fact, it is really only an indentation. This is one reason for the extreme mobility of the shoulder compared with the hip joint. Another reason for the greater mobility of the humerus is the structure of the scapula and its free-floating system as compared with the solid structure of the pelvis. The movement at the shoulder joint is so free that the bipolar terms do not apply. Terms like *abduction* and *adduction* presume that the action will go just so far and then will have to return. That is not true at the shoulder joint. For example, start with the arm hanging at your side and start abducting at the shoulder joint, moving the arm away from the midline. Keep going, and the humerus will begin to move back *toward* the midline once your arm is above horizontal. Then we hit another area of befuddlement when we continue the same action past vertical, crossing the midline of the body. This is why the range of motion at the shoulder joint makes the existing labeling structure obsolete. Many kinesiology textbooks simply pretend that the problem does not exist by not dealing with actions above horizontal. Instead, I have developed a modified use of the labeling system to account for action above the head.

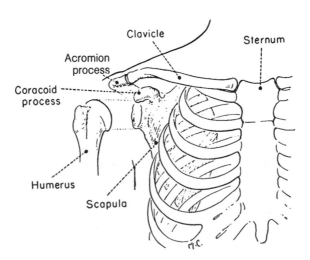

FIGURE 5.4.   **Right shoulder joint**

Positions and Actions of the Shoulder Joint

The actions at the shoulder joint include abduction, adduction, hyperabduction, hyperadduction, flexion, extension, hyperflexion, hyperextension, horizontal flexion, horizontal extension, inward rotation, and outward rotation. On the sagittal plane, there is one position of extension, one position of complete flexion (or extension above the head), and an infinite number of positions of flexion. On the frontal plane, there is one neutral position and an infinite number of positions of both abduction and adduction. On the transverse plane, there is one neutral position of rotation and an infinite number of positions of both inward and outward rotation. Figures 5.5 and 5.6 illustrate the positions and actions of the shoulder joint.

Starting from a "position of extension," any movement toward flexion and continuing in that direction is labeled either flexion or hyperflexion. The opposite direction is called *extension* or *hyperextension*. (Be careful

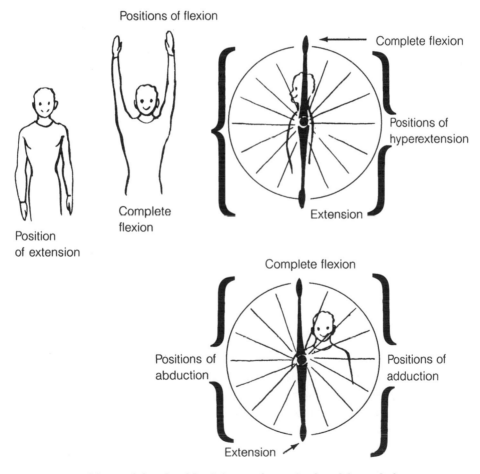

FIGURE 5.5.   **Positions of the shoulder joint on the sagittal and frontal planes**

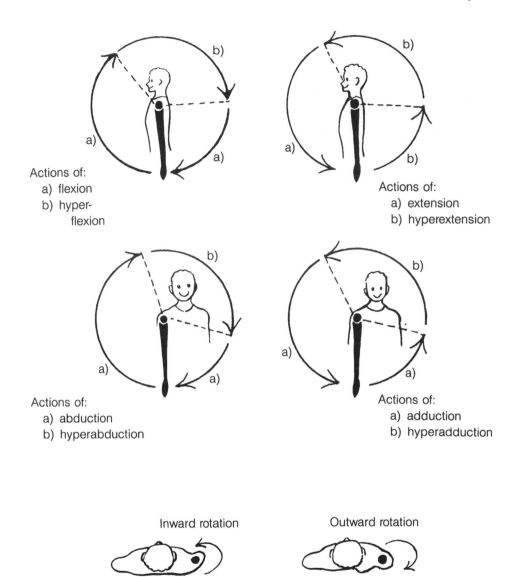

Actions of:
a) flexion
b) hyper-
   flexion

Actions of:
a) extension
b) hyperextension

Actions of:
a) abduction
b) hyperabduction

Actions of:
a) adduction
b) hyperadduction

Inward rotation

Outward rotation

FIGURE 5.6.   Actions of the shoulder joint

not to confuse a *position* of hyperextension with an *action* of hyperextension.) On the frontal plane, starting again from a position of extension,
movement out to the side and continuing in that direction is called *abduction* or *hyperabduction*. The opposite action (moving across the midline) is
called *adduction* or *hyperadduction*. However, it must be noted that adduction from a position of extension must be accompanied by either slight
flexion or extension, or else the humerus makes contact with the body. Actually, most of the "hyper" actions require some kind of compensatory action on another plane.
     Luckily, inward and outward rotation are more limited than flexion and
extension or abduction and adduction, and labeling of actions and posi-

tions is consequently simpler. Horizontal flexion and horizontal extension are actually combinations of actions on the frontal and sagittal planes. *Horizontal flexion* describes the *action* (not position) of flexion and adduction with humerus perpendicular to the side of the body. *Horizontal extension* combines abduction and extension with the humerus perpendicular to the side of the body. Each of these actions of the shoulder joint is facilitated by specific actions of the scapula.

Combined Action of Shoulder and Scapula

In the initial stages of analysis of joint action, you are encouraged to analyze the actions of the shoulder joint and the scapula separately. It is very easy to confuse adduction/abduction of the scapula with adduction/abduction of the shoulder joint, yet they are *not* the same action. It is also easy to confuse upward and downward rotation of the scapula with inward and outward rotation of the shoulder joint, simply because the word *rotation* is used in both sets of terms. Separation of the shoulder and scapula in the initial stages of analysis is purely academic, and is encouraged to help to clearly distinguish between the actions of the two joints. In actual movement of the shoulder joint and scapula, the two joints act synergistically to allow great range of motion at the shoulder. This synergism is neurologically controlled, and there are four rules of association which govern the combined actions of the shoulder/scapula.

1. When the humerus is more than 2 to 3 degrees away from a position of extension, the scapula is upwardly rotated. (Exception: When the shoulder joint is hyperextended and adducted, sort of tucked behind the back, the scapula is downwardly rotated.)
2. When the humerus is anterior to the frontal plane bisecting the shoulder joint, the scapula is abducted.
3. When the humerus is posterior to the frontal plane bisecting the shoulder joint, the scapula is adducted.
4. When the shoulder joint is hyperextended, with inward rotation, the scapula is forward tilted.

These rules of association are very helpful in identifying the positions and actions of the scapula. Since the scapula is covered with muscle tissue, it is difficult to directly observe the actions of the scapula. The rules of association will make analysis much easier.

PRACTICE DEMONSTRATION

For Figure 5.7, analyze the action of the shoulder and scapula first from (a) to (b) with gravity at (a), and second from (b) to (c) with gravity at (c). Table 5.2 (p. 89) shows the correct analysis.

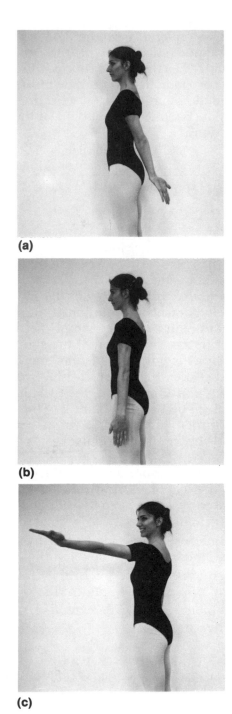

(a)

(b)

(c)

FIGURE 5.7.   Analyze the action of the shoulder joint and scapula from (a) to (b), with gravity at (a) (slightly adducted behind the back), and from (b) to (c), with gravity at (c).

TABLE 5.2 Analysis of Figure 5.7

Identification	Joint Position or Action	Action of Gravity
Shoulder (a) to (b)	Flexion Slight abduction Outward rotation	Flexion Abduction* Outward rotation
Scapula (a) to (b)	Abduction Slight upward rotation Return from forward tilt	Abduction Slight upward rotation Return from forward tilt
Shoulder (b) to (c)	Flexion Abduction Outward rotation	Extension Adduction Inward rotation
Scapula (b) to (c)	Abduction Upward rotation Slight elevation	Adduction Downward rotation Depression

*From the angle of the photograph, it is difficult to see the initial adduction of the shoulder joint, but it is there.

CHAPTER 6

Radius, Ulna, and Hand

Including elbow joint, radio-ulnar joints, wrist, and fingers

The Forearm

Radius and Ulna

The radius and ulna are the bones of the forearm (see Figure 6.1). The *ulna* is a long bone with the head at the distal end and a "hook" of bone at the proximal end. The hook is made up of three sections: posteriorly, there is a protrusion called the *olecranon process;* anteriorly, there is a protrusion called the *coronoid process* (not to be confused with the coracoid process of the scapula); between the two processes is the *semilunar notch* (or trochlear notch). Distal and lateral to the coronoid process (distal to "the hook") is the *radial notch,* which articulates with the head of the radius. At the distal end of the *shaft* of the ulna are the *head* of the ulna and the *styloid process* (the "wrist bone" on the little finger side).

The *radius* is a long bone with the head at the proximal end. The superior surface of the head is concave rather than convex, as if the top of the head had been cut off. On the antero-medial surface of the radius, just below the head, is the *radial tuberosity.* The *shaft* of the radius extends distally, and the *styloid process* is the most distal point on the bone (the "wrist bone" on the thumb side). On the medial side of the distal end of the radius is the *ulnar notch,* which articulates with the head of the ulna. On the radius and ulna, the terms *medial* and *lateral* refer to the anatomical position (the arms at the sides with the thumb out to the side). Assuming anatomical position when locating bony landmarks can reduce the possibility of confusion.

Elbow Joint

The elbow joint is made up of the articulation of the humerus with the ulna and the radius (see Figure 6.2). The primary articulation is between the humerus and the ulna. The semilunar notch of the ulna fits into the trochlea of the humerus, with the olecranon process of the ulna fitting into the olecranon fossa of the humerus and the coronoid process of the

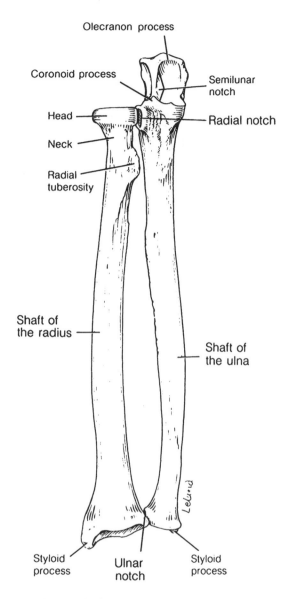

FIGURE 6.1. Radius and ulna (right front view)

ulna fitting into the coronoid fossa of the humerus. The secondary articulation of the elbow joint is between the radius and the humerus. The capitulum of the humerus fits into the concave superior surface of the radius (where the head is "cut off"). The structure of the trochlea and the semilunar notch prevents any action at the elbow joint other than flexion and extension. In some individuals, extension beyond 180 degrees (hyperextension) is possible because of a shorter olecranon process or a deeper olecranon fossa, or both. Neither rotation nor ab/adduction is possible at the elbow joint. If the radius and ulna are not the same length, as is true for some individuals, the lower arm and the humerus do not form a

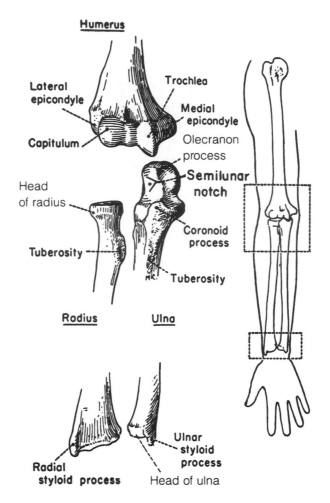

FIGURE 6.2.   Elbow and radio-ulnar joints (right)

straight line; the lower arm actually appears to be in an abducted position. This occurs when the ulna is longer than the radius and is functionally similar to knock-knees. Some authorities think this condition is a primary cause of stress-related conditions at the elbow joint, such as tennis elbow, little league elbow, and bursitis.

The analysis of action at the elbow joint is quite simple. There is one position of extension and an infinite number of positions of flexion. The action of flexion takes the forearm closer to the humerus, and the action of extension takes the forearm away from the humerus.

Radio-Ulnar Joints

There are two articulations between the radius and the ulna: one proximal, involving the head of the radius and the radial notch of the ulna; and one distal, involving the head of the ulna and the ulnar notch of the radius (refer back to Figure 6.2). The head of the radius rotates in the radial notch, while the ulnar notch of the radius rotates around the head of the ulna, allowing the actions of pronation and supination. Rotating the palm forward in the anatomical position is supination. Rotating the palm backward in the anatomical position is pronation. (Memory aid: supination "holds soup.") When the radio-ulnar joints are supinated, the radius and ulna are parallel to each other. In pronation, the radius and ulna are crossed. It is important to point out that the radius rotates around the stationary ulna in pronation and supination. This information will be used in identifying actions of muscles at the elbow and radio-ulnar joints.

The Wrist and Hand

Most kinesiology books spend a great deal of time discussing the wrist and hand. This is understandable when one considers the involvement of the hand in so many sports skills. However, in dance the hand is used minimally; consequently, the presentation of information on the wrist and hand is relatively rudimentary in this text.

Like the foot, the hand is divided into three regions: carpal bones, metacarpal bones, and phalanges (see Figure 6.3). There are eight bones in the *carpal region.* The carpal bones are arranged in two curved rows (one proximal and one distal). The proximal row articulates with the radius and ulna to form the wrist joint. The distal row articulates with the *five metacarpal* bones (numbered one through five for identification purposes). Distal to the metacarpal bones are the *phalanges:* two on the thumb and three on each of the fingers.

Wrist

The wrist joint is the articulation between the first row of the carpal bones and the radius and ulna (see Figure 6.4). Possible actions at the wrist include flexion, extension, hyperextension, abduction, and adduction. All of these actions are identified with reference to the anatomical position. Confusion can occur in the labeling of abduction and adduction, because analysis of action is difficult when one is not in the anatomical position. For this reason, I use the terms *radial deviation* and *ulnar deviation* as replacements for *abduction* and *adduction*. It is easy to remember that the thumb is on the radial side, and therefore it is no longer necessary to return to anatomical position to identify an action as abduction or adduction. Abduction is radial deviation and adduction is ulnar deviation. Movement at the wrist toward the little finger is ulnar deviation. Movement at the wrist toward the thumb is radial deviation.

Thumb

The actions of the thumb are quite complicated and are difficult to describe. Figure 6.5 illustrates the movements of the thumb. The illustration

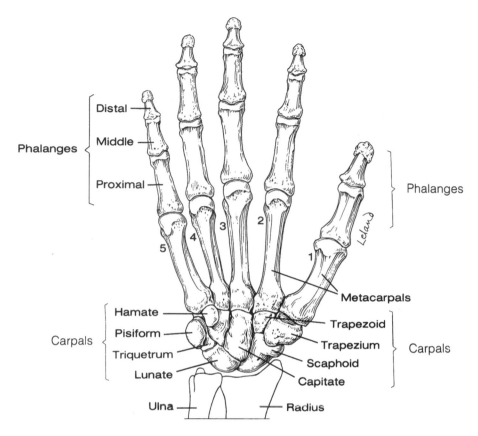

FIGURE 6.3.   **Bones of the hand**

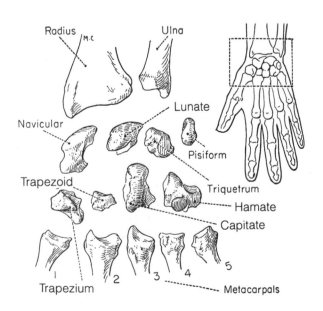

FIGURE 6.4.   **Wrist and carpal bones (right)**

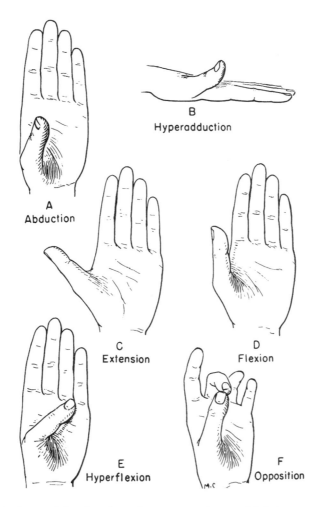

FIGURE 6.5. **Actions of the thumb at the carpometacarpal joint**

is included only for background information. This book will not focus on the actions of the thumb.

Fingers

The actions of the fingers include flexion, extension, abduction, and adduction. Making a fist is primarily flexion of the fingers, and opening the hand is extension. Abduction is spreading the fingers wide, and adduction is bringing the fingers back together.

This description of the actions of the wrist and hand is extraordinarily simple compared with the complex function of the hand. Once again, the rationale for this simplification lies in the simple use of the hand in dance. Furthermore, one could easily spend a whole textbook on the actions and individual differences in actions of the hand.

Understanding of the information to be presented in Section III is contingent upon thorough comprehension of the skeletal structure. The following will assist in the review process.

1. List the possible actions and restrictions of actions for the following joints:

   toes
   tarsus
   ankle
   knee
   hip
   lumbar spine
   thoracic spine
   cervical spine
   scapula
   shoulder joint
   elbow joint
   radio-ulnar joints
   wrist

2. Point out the following bony landmarks of the foot:

   head of the first metatarsal
   navicular
   cuboid
   first cuneiform
   second cuneiform
   third cuneiform
   talus
   calcaneous
   tuberosity of the navicular
   tuberosity of the fifth metatarsal

3. Point out the following bony landmarks of the leg:

   Tibia
       medial malleolus
       anterior border
       medial border
       interosseous border
       medial surface
       lateral surface
       posterior surface
       tibial tuberosity
       medial condyle
       lateral condyle
       intercondular emminence
   Fibula
       lateral malleolus

shaft
head
Femur
  medial condyle
  lateral condyle
  medial epicondyle
  lateral epicondyle
  intercondular notch
  adductor tubercle
  shaft
  linea aspera
  greater trochanter
  lesser trochanter
  intertrochanteric crest
  intertrochanteric line
  neck
  head

4. Point out the following bony landmarks of the pelvis:
   Ox coxa
     Ilium
       anterior superior spine
       anterior inferior spine
       posterior superior spine
       posterior inferior spine
       iliac fossa
       gluteal fossa
       crest of the ilium
     Ischium
       ischial tuberosity
     Pubis
       symphysis pubis
       ascending ramus
       descending ramus
   Sacrum
   Coccyx

5. Point out the following bony landmarks of the spine:
   Vertebra
     spinous process
     transverse processes
     body
     supcrior articulating facets
     inferior articulating facets
   Lumbar vertebra distinctions
   Thoracic vertebra distinctions
   Cervical vertebra distinctions

6. Point out the following bony landmarks of the scapula:
    inferior angle
    superior angle
    lateral angle (glenoid fossa)
    medial border (vertebral)
    lateral border (axillary)
    superior border
    spine of the scapula
    supraspinous fossa
    infraspinous fossa
    subscapular fossa
    acromion process
    coracoid process

7. Point out the following bony landmarks on the arm:
    Humerus
        head
        surgical neck
        anatomical neck
        greater tuberosity
        lesser tuberosity
        bicipital groove
        deltoid tuberosity
        medial epicondyle
        lateral epicondyle
        olecranon fossa
        coronoid fossa
    Radius
        radial tuberosity
        head
        shaft
        ulnar notch
        styloid process
    Ulna
        olecranon process
        coronoid process
        semilunar notch
        radial notch
        head
        styloid process
        shaft

8. Describe the following misalignments of the skeletal structure:
    pronated or supinated feet
    increased and decreased pelvic inclination
    lumbar lordosis
    kyphosis
    cervical lordosis
    forward head
    pectoralis minor syndrome

The Muscular System

CHAPTER *7*

Overview of the Muscular System

The muscular system provides the power for both movement through space and maintenance of a given position in space. All controlled movement is a constant "tug-of-war" with gravity. Stabilization of a position in space is as vital to human movement as production of movement through an arc in space. Stabilization may be against the pull of gravity or against the pull of another muscle, but regardless of the source of the opposing action, stabilization is critical to effective human movement. Kinesiological analysis to identify the muscles essential to a given action must include those contractions which stabilize the joints against unwanted actions.

The primary focus of kinesiological analysis of muscular action is to determine which muscles perform a given action and which muscles stabilize the body to allow only that action. In this chapter your major responsibility will be to perform that analysis. There is, however, a lot of background information that adds to understanding of the process. Such information includes the roles muscles play, the general classification of muscles, the microscopic structure of muscle tissue, the nature of the motor unit, the mechanism of contraction (including the neurological, chemical, and mechanical cycles), the muscle spindles, the nature of the stretch reflex and the sensory organs involved, and the classification of voluntary muscles. There is no need to memorize; read for basic understanding of the processes.

Basic Understanding of the Processes

Roles of Muscles

The nature of muscles is that they can produce force in only one direction. *Muscles can only pull, they cannot push.* Yet the possible joint actions are generally two-directional: flexion-extension, inward and outward rotation, and so on. Because muscles are limited to pulling, there are opposing sets of muscles called *agonists* and *antagonists* for each joint action. The *agonist* is the muscle which contracts to produce a given action; the *antagonist* is the muscle which contracts to produce the opposite action. *Agonist* and *antagonist* are relative terms; that is, they can be assigned only if one

101

knows the joint action. Indeed, the roles of agonist and antagonist reverse if the action reverses.

The muscle most effective in the production of a given action is the *prime mover.* In some cases the prime mover may not be strong enough for the task, and other muscles must be recruited to help it. Muscles that contribute to a given action are called *assistors.* In other cases, two or more muscles perform the identical action at a joint; these muscles are called *synergists.* The prime movers, the assistors, and the synergists are considered agonists, for they all play a role in the production of a given action. In addition, *stabilizers* and *neutralizers* also play a major role in the production of a given action, but they may or may not be considered agonists, depending on their action at the joint. The meaning and application of each of these terms will become clear with actual muscular analysis.

General Types of Muscles

There are three general types of muscle tissue in the human body: *cardiac* muscle, *smooth* muscle, and *striated* muscle. Each of these performs a spe-

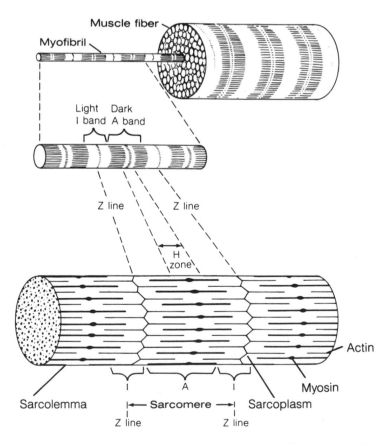

FIGURE 7.1.   Microscopic structure of striated muscle, including muscle fiber, myofibril, and sarcomere

cific role in human functioning. Cardiac muscle tissue is particularly adapted to the demands on the muscles of the heart. Smooth muscle is particularly adapted to the demands on the viscera. Striated muscle is adapted to the demands for voluntary movement. Kinesiology focuses only on the striated muscles, since they provide the force for voluntary movement and stabilization.

Microscopic Structure of Striated Muscle

All striated muscles are made up of many fibers (see Figure 7.1). Each of those muscle fibers is made up of many myofibrils. Both the fibers and the myofibrils run the full length of the belly of the muscle. The myofibrils are encased in a plasma membrane called the *sarcolemma*. The sarcolemma and connective tissue are a bit like a sausage skin, encasing the contractile mechanism of the fiber at the belly of the muscle, continuing to the muscle attachment as part of the tendon (as if the sausage had been squeezed out). Consequently, the tendon—sometimes erroneously thought of as distinct from the muscle—is actually the merging of all of the connective tissue from all the myofibrils and is an integral part of the muscle.

Each myofibril is longitudinally segmented into sections called *sarcomeres* (see Figure 7.2). Each sarcomere contains a viscous, gelatinous fluid called *sarcoplasm* (refer back to Figure 7.1). Suspended in the sarcoplasm are two types of protein filaments called *actin* and *myosin*. The myosin is not attached to the ends of the sarcomere, but rather "floats" in the center of the tubelike structure of the sarcomere. The actin filaments are attached to the two ends of the sarcomere. Neural stimulation at the junction between nerve and muscle causes activation of the entire sar-

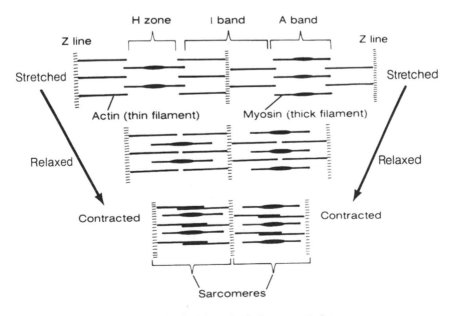

FIGURE 7.2. Sarcomere in stretched, relaxed, and contracted states

colemma, which in turn causes bridges or ratchetlike protrusions to reach from the myosin to the actin. The actin is then pulled toward the center of the sarcomere from both ends of the sarcomere. The summative effects of contraction of all of the sarcomeres in a myofibril, all of the myofibrils in a fiber, and all of the fibers in a muscle produce a maximal contraction of that muscle. In its contracted state the sarcomere is shortest. In a relaxed state the sarcomere is longer. (The actin is no longer being pulled to the center of the sarcomere.) When an external force is applied by gravity, contraction of the antagonistic muscle, or some other external force, the sarcomere can be stretched to a length that is longer than the relaxed length. It must be noted that *a muscle cannot stretch itself.* There must be an external force to produce the stretch.

The Motor Unit

Graded contraction of muscle is possible because there are many motor units in each muscle (see Figure 7.3). The *motor unit* is a functional unit

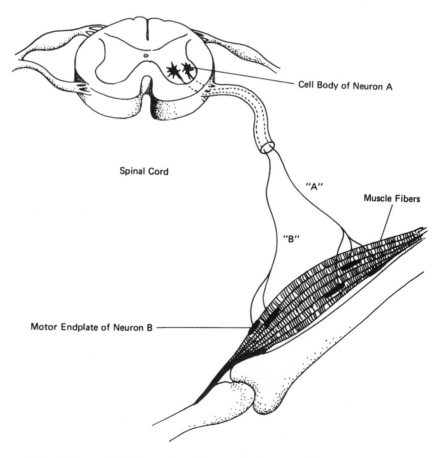

FIGURE 7.3.   Schematic illustration of motor unit. Note that neurons A and B have a different number of motor end plates and activate a different number of fibers.

that includes the motor neuron, and its parts, the axon, motor end plate, as well as muscle fibers activated by a nerve.

When a nerve is activated, all of the fibers connected to the nerve contract. This principle is called the *"all or none" law.* Yet not all the motor units need contract at the same time. Different demands require either fewer or more motor units. Rarely does the dancer need the simultaneous contraction of all of the motor units of a given muscle (maximal contraction). In most instances, the motor units work in a rotation system: working for a while and resting for a while. If motor units are stronger, fewer are needed to perform the same task, and this allows longer rest periods for the motor units between bouts of work. This delays the onset of fatigue. Graded contraction of a muscle is further facilitated or discouraged by the fact that the motor units of different muscles include different numbers of myofibrils. The muscles of the eye and hand have a relatively small number of fibers activated by each motor unit. These muscles therefore have a potential for fine degrees of gradation of contraction. Other muscles like the gluteus maximus have far more fibers activated by a single motor unit. Fine gradations of contraction are difficult to perform with these muscles. It is thought that selective activation of specific motor units may be the primary factor that allows the remarkably fine isolations of movement often called for in dance.

The Mechanism of Muscle Contraction

There are three components to the mechanism of muscular contraction: *neurological, chemical,* and *mechanical.* Approaching the process with extreme simplicity, when the neuron of a motor unit is activated or stimulated, there is a depolarization of the sarcolemma followed by a chemical reaction within the sarcomeres. The chemical reaction involves the breakdown of adenosine triphosphate, which releases the energy used in the mechanical shortening of the myofibrils. Once the adenosine triphosphate is broken down, a resynthesis of adenosin triphosphate begins utilizing creatin phosphate, adenosin diphosphate, and glycogen. Resynthesis of adenosin triphosphate eventually produces a by-product called *lactic acid,* which in turn is resynthesized by oxygen. When more lactic acid is produced than can be managed by the existing oxygen at the muscle site, additional oxygen from the bloodstream is needed. (*Anaerobic* activities are those which do not require that extra oxygen. *Aerobic* activities continue over time; therefore, more lactic acid is built up, and the resynthesis process depends upon the respiratory and cardiovascular systems to supply the additional oxygen.) The presence of lactic acid is the most immediate cause of muscle fatigue.

The exact mechanism of transfer from chemical energy from the breakdown of adenosin triphosphate into the mechanical energy produced by the sliding of the actin filaments over the myosin is quite complicated. Let's just say it happens. Luckily, even without our understanding it, the transfer does take place and the muscle shortens. Muscle fibers can shorten up to approximately one half of their resting length. When the muscle fiber shortens, it pulls on both ends of the fiber simultaneously. (This information will have implications for stabilization with the specific analysis of muscular action.)

The Muscle Spindles

Imbedded between the muscle fibers are muscle *spindles* (or "mini-muscles"). Figure 7.4 illustrates the general location of the muscle spindles. The regular muscle fibers are called *extrafusal* muscle fibers. The muscle fibers within the spindle itself are called *intrafusal* muscle fibers. The muscle spindle is an "in-house" monitor of muscular activity. It is a sensory receptor that is sensitive to stretch, contraction, and possibly velocity of contraction of the muscle tissue in which it is imbedded. These muscle spindles report the status of the muscle to the central nervous system. The *alpha* neurological system is the primary system which causes contraction of the extrafusal fibers. The alpha and gamma systems of neurological activation and monitoring work together to produce contraction and modify that contraction according to the information provided.

The Stretch Reflex

The muscle spindles play an essential role in the stretch reflex. The stretch reflex is a fundamental function of the neuromuscular system. When a muscle is stretched, there is a reflexive contraction of that muscle following the stretch. The stretch reflex can be utilized to advantage in movement skills, such as the windup or backswing in many motor skills. A

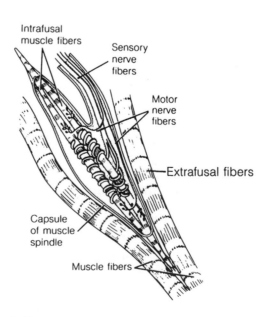

FIGURE 7.4.   Muscle spindle

backswing or windup creates a stretch of the muscles that produce the swing or throw. The *plié* is the dancer's "windup" for a jump. The first activation of these muscles is, then, reflexive and is provided by the stretch reflex. The stretch reflex is both the friend and the enemy of athletes and dancers. It is a protective mechanism that can prevent overmovement of a joint. But it is also a major block to achieving flexibility.

Once again, the stretch reflex is a contraction response to the stretching of the same muscle. Figure 7.5 is a schematic diagram of the mechanism of the stretch reflex.

When a muscle is stretched, the extrafusal and the intrafusal fibers are stretched. When the intrafusal fibers are stretched, they activate the annulospiral receptor at the center of the spindle. This activation stimulates the afferent neuron which eventually synapses (connects) with the alpha motor neuron at the spinal level, which in turn, causes a contraction of the same extrafusal fibers that were originally stretched. This is called an alpha reflex loop. Backtracking to the synapse, information is sent to the brain (neuromuscular feedback), thus keeping the brain informed of the

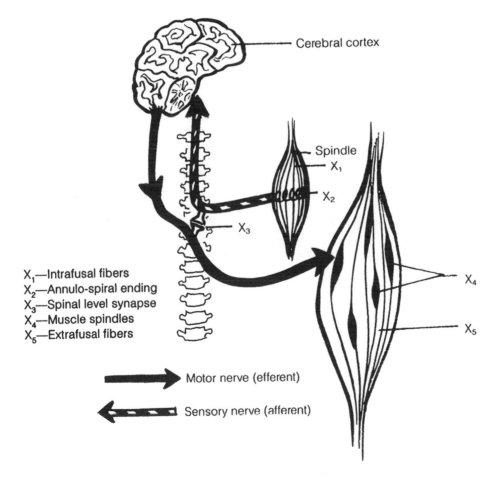

Cerebral cortex

Spindle
X_1

X_2

X_3

X_4

X_5

X_1—Intrafusal fibers
X_2—Annulo-spiral ending
X_3—Spinal level synapse
X_4—Muscle spindles
X_5—Extrafusal fibers

Motor nerve (efferent)

Sensory nerve (afferent)

FIGURE 7.5. Schematic diagram of the stretch reflex

immediate activity of the system. It is possible to *block the stretch reflex* through conscious control from the higher centers of the brain. This is how we perform a "long-sustained stretch," which will be discussed in Chapter 19. Another block of the stretch reflex is called reciprocal inhibition or reciprocal relaxation, and occurs at the spinal level synapse. The block of the stretch reflex by reciprocal inhibition is chemical in nature, temporary, and partial. Reciprocal inhibition will be discussed more completely in Chapter 19. A third means of blocking the stretch reflex is by activation of the Golgi tendon organ.

The Golgi Response

Golgi tendon organs are sensory organs in the muscle (see Figure 7.6). They are located in the area of the muscle between the belly of the muscle and the tendon. These organs are sensitive to pressure caused by "pull" on the tendon. Thus the Golgi receptors provide information to the central nervous system regarding muscle tension. Activation may be caused either by contraction or by stretch of the muscle. When the Golgi receptors are maximally activated, they completely block the stretch reflex for a short time. But a word of caution to the dancer who might say, "That's what I'll use to get more stretch." The Golgi tendon organs are slow to activate maximally and then respond only when the tendon is about to pull off the bone. The severity of the pull required to activate maximally and stimulate the reflex makes this a potentially dangerous way to try to achieve greater mobility. However, some dancers may have experienced the Golgi response during an intense stretching session. The sensation is one of total release of the muscle being stretched, usually accompanied by a sensation of warmth, and the range of motion is increased considerably. The muscle feels as if it has turned to Jell-O—which, in a way, it has. The blocking of the stretch reflex totally deactivates the neural stimulation of the "bridges" between the actin and myosin. Without the pull from those bridges, the sarcoplasm takes whatever length is allowed by the connective tissue. When the actin and myosin filaments are not connected, the sarcomere is actually like a jelly-filled tube, with the filaments floating in the tube.

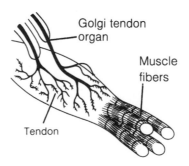

Golgi tendon organ

Muscle fibers

Tendon

FIGURE 7.6.   **Golgi tendon organ**

Types of Striated Muscle

Striated, or *voluntary,* muscles can be classified by color, shape, and function. Everyone who has sat down to a family Thanksgiving dinner knows that there is light meat and dark meat. Humans also have light meat and dark meat. The "dark meat" is composed of muscles more reddish in color because of their higher myoglobin count. These muscles have a great potential to continue contraction over time. They have been nicknamed the "holder" muscles. These red holder muscles are usually deeper and slower to activate and deactivate than their counterparts, the white muscles, because red muscles have a greater proportion of slow twitch fibers. The white muscles have a lower hemoglobin content and have been nicknamed the "mover" muscles. The white muscles activate and deactivate quickly because of a greater proportion of fast twitch fibers.

Another classification of muscles is by shape. There are five basic shapes of muscle: fusiform, pennate, bipennate, multipennate, and radiate (see Figure 7.7). The *fusiform,* or spindle-shaped, muscle is a long muscle, usually with a tendonous attachment at both ends. It has a relatively small cross section of contractile tissue. The *pennate, bipennate,* and *multipennate* muscles are all characterized by one tendonous attachment (usually distal) and one attachment where the belly of the muscle butts right up to the periostium of the bone (bone covering) with no tendon (usually the proximal attachment).

Muscular force is related to the total cross section of muscle tissue. Therefore radiate and multipennate are the most powerful of the muscle shapes and the fusiform is the least forceful. Speed of lever action is related to the length of the muscle and the relative amount of shortening that is possible. Remember that a muscle can shorten up to one half of its resting length. Since the fusiform muscles are the longest muscles, they have the greatest potential for shortening, which indirectly can produce lever speed. Interestingly enough, the fusiform muscles are also usually white muscles, so lever speed is also facilitated by the speed of neural activation.

Still another classification of muscle tissue is based on engineering and focuses attention on the mechanical efficiency of given muscles for a specific task. *Spurt* and *shunt* are categories of muscles based on the distance from the moving joint to each of the attachments. When the proximal attachment is closer to the moving joint than the distal attachment, the muscle is called a *shunt* muscle. When the proximal attachment is farther away from the moving joint than the distal attachment, the muscle is called a *spurt* muscle. Analysis of mechanical efficiency shows that spurt muscles are most effective for moving tasks and shunt muscles are most efficient for stabilizing tasks. These two labels are of interest in biomechanics. Definitions are included for information only.

Integration of Background Information

Pulling together some of the isolated facts from the foregoing presentation explains some of the mysteries of muscle phenomena. For example, why

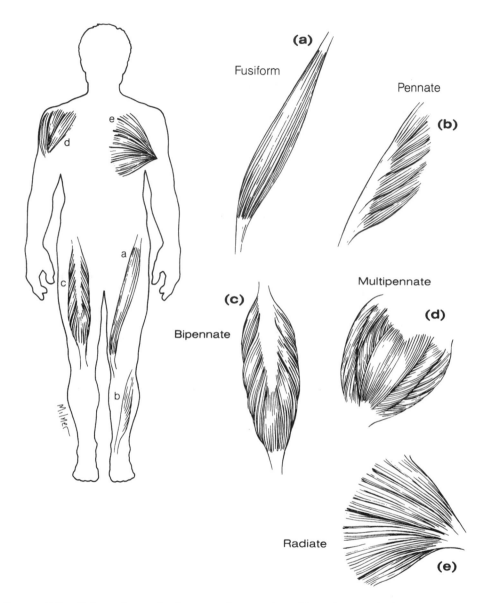

Figure 7.7.   Selected muscle shapes and examples of locations in the body

do some muscles tear more frequently than others? For one thing, most of the extensor muscles have more muscle spindles than the flexors; therefore the stretch reflex is more powerful in the extensor muscles. This facilitates maintenance of an upright position. (As a rule, gravity flexes in the lower extremity and spine, and the stretch reflex responds with contraction of the extensors.) The extensor muscles also tend to be deep, red, holding muscles. This means that they will activate and deactivate more slowly than the flexors. This is a valuable characteristic in the antigravity process, but when a flexor muscle contracts quickly, there are times when the extensors do not have time to deactivate and therefore can be torn. There are some flexor muscles that are deep holding muscles, and it is predictable that these muscles (notably the deep muscles of the groin) are often torn. Although there are exceptions, this concept may explain why some muscles are more susceptible to tearing. Another factor that contributes to susceptibility to tearing is the number of joints a muscle crosses. Two-joint muscles (hamstrings, rectus femoris, gastrocnemius, gracilis, and others) are more likely to be torn than single-joint muscles, perhaps because of contradictory demands for movement and/or stabilization of the two joints.

Additional integration of information will occur throughout the text, topic by topic. While not all of this background information is essential to the actual analysis of muscular action, such knowledge encourages more understanding of the remarkable processes of production, control, and refinement of human motion.

Kinesiological Analysis

Principles of Analysis

Analysis of human motion for the purpose of identifying the muscles that produce action is guided by a number of principles. These principles take into account the potential of a muscle for contraction, the effect of gravity on all motion, and the antagonistic roles of gravity and the musculature. Each principle will be stated and discussed. Please pay close attention to these principles, for confusion over any principle could totally distort the analysis process. Because of the importance of these principles to accurate kinesiological analysis, they are repeated in Table 7.1.

1. *Muscles only pull; they do not push.* This has been stated often enough to make it clear that this point is critical to understanding the action of the musculature. Yet in the process of muscular analysis, students often seem to need a reminder.

2. *Muscles contract in the center and pull equally on both ends.* When the bridges are sent down from the myosin to the actin and the actin is pulled to the center of the sarcomere, it is impossible to give directional signals.

TABLE 7.1 **Principles of Kinesiology**

1. Muscles only pull; they do not push.
2. Muscles contract in the center and pull equally on both ends.
3. The action of a muscle on a joint will be determined by the attachments and the path of the muscle.
4. Muscles must oppose gravity to produce a movement or maintain a position.
5. Three types of contraction are possible in opposing gravity:
   a. Shortening contraction: force greater than the resistance;
   b. Static contraction: force equal to the resistance;
   c. Lengthening contraction: force less than the resistance.

That is, it is impossible to apply the force of muscular contraction to only one of the muscle attachments. It is a given that when a muscle contracts, both levers (attachments on the levers) move, unless one of the levers is stabilized by another muscle, by gravity, or by some other outside force. Without some form of stabilization, contraction will produce movement of *both* levers. It should be noted that when one lever *is* stabilized, all of the contractile power is focused on the moving lever and fewer motor units are needed to perform the action. The movement is easier. All movements of the limbs require some stabilization of the proximal attachment (stabilization of the center). Anyone who has had abdominal surgery knows that even in simple walking, the abdominal muscles are crucial: they stabilize the pelvis to allow more efficient action by the flexors and extensors of the hip joint. Stabilization of the center of the body demands strength in the muscles of the torso and scapula; these needs will be considered in Chapter 19.

3. *The action of a muscle on a joint will be determined by the joint structure, the attachments, and path of the muscle.* Muscles pull in a straight line and pull both attachments closer to the point where the muscle crosses the joint. A muscle must cross a joint to produce an action at that joint. A muscle that crosses straight across a joint will have only one action (action on only one plane). A muscle that crosses a joint obliquely (wraps around the bones) will have more than one action (or actions on more than one plane). For example, suppose you want to lift a board and you reach under the board and grab the opposite side and pull. The board will lift, twist, and perhaps pull slightly toward the right if you are pulling with your right hand. Likewise, muscles that cross a joint with an oblique path will have more than one action at the joint.

4. *Muscles must oppose gravity to produce a movement or maintain a position.* Gravity is a constant force. In Section II, you were shown the process of identifying the action of gravity on a given joint in a given position. In order to identify which muscle or muscles will be effective in producing a movement or maintaining a position, it is also necessary to be aware of the action of gravity. For example, if gravity is a flexor of a joint, the extensor muscles must be used to oppose gravity.[1] Any action of a joint that occurs with control must use the muscle group that produces the action opposite to the action of gravity. The line of gravity descends vertically through the center of the joint to be analyzed. Gravity pulls the moving lever down, toward that line. In the analysis of the action of gravity on a joint it is necessary, in most cases, to *hold all other joints constant* in order to accurately identify gravity's action on the joint in question.

The key in the initial stages of muscular analysis is, "If gravity does it, the muscles won't." It helps to think of gravity and muscular force as two opponents in a tug-of-war to move the body. Gravity is pulling in one direction, and the muscles are pulling in the opposite direction. Sometimes

---

1. Unless the desired action is the same as that produced by gravity and the action is faster than gravity would produce.

one opponent gains ground, sometimes the other gains ground, and sometimes the forces are equal and there is no movement.

5. *Three types of contraction are possible in opposing gravity: shortening, static, and lengthening.* The tug-of-war mentioned above involves two forces and one mass. One force is the force of gravity, called *resistance* (or weight). The other force is the force of muscular contraction. The mass is the human body or a segment of the body. The three types of muscular contraction are distinguished by different relationships between resistance and force.

If the force is greater than the resistance, force wins the tug-of-war and the mass moves opposite to the pull of gravity. This is called *shortening contraction.*

If the force is equal to the resistance, neither opponent wins the tug-of-war; there is no movement. This is called *static contraction.*

If the resistance is greater than the force, gravity wins the tug-of-war and the mass moves with the pull of gravity. This is called *lengthening contraction* and is discussed below.

The Paradox of the Lengthening Contraction

In a tug-of-war, the opponents don't stop pulling during the contest, yet it is possible to lose ground because the opposing team is stronger. In a lengthening contraction the muscles are still pulling, but there is a *gradual decrease in the number of active motor units* and gravity is winning the tug-of-war. For example: Let your right arm hang down in a position of extension from where you are sitting. Put your left hand over the biceps of the right arm. Flex the elbow and, with your left hand, feel the biceps contracting. Next hold a flexed position. The biceps are still contracting. Gradually lower the arm back to a position of extension. The biceps continue to contract until you get to the position of extension, and there they relax. In the first action, power is greater than resistance and action of the elbow is caused by a shortening contraction of the flexors of the elbow joint (gravity is an extensor). In the maintenance of the flexed position, power and resistance are equal and the result is a static contraction of the flexors (the biceps). Lowering the forearm back down to a position of extension *with control* requires gradually decreasing the number of active motor units in the biceps and thereby allows gravity to win: a lengthening contraction.

Using this same example, two exceptions can be noted. The first is when the forearm is simply dropped down to a position of extension. In this situation, there is no contraction of the biceps. The muscle simply relaxes to allow gravity to do its thing. The second exception is when the mass moves faster than gravity would move it. From a position of flexion of the elbow joint, *snap* the arm down to a position of extension of the elbow. Going faster than gravity requires some assistance from the extensors (the triceps). Did you feel it? While these exceptions must be noted, they do tend to confuse the definitions previously given. A review of the descriptions of the three types of contractions may reduce confusion.

One additional note is required regarding the shortening and lengthening contractions. In other references they may be referred to as *concentric* (shortening) contraction and *eccentric* (lengthening) contraction. These names were probably given to reduce the confusion caused by the paradox of the lengthening contraction. Yet the paradox still exists, and you must deal with it. I use the terms *lengthening* and *shortening* contractions because they are considered easier to remember.

Assumptions of This Approach to Kinesiological Analysis

A number of assumptions underlie my approach to kinesiological analysis of human motion. *The first assumption* is that the movement will be performed with the smallest possible number of muscles contracting and those muscles will be prime movers or exactly matched in function to the demands of the task. That is, efficiency and economy of muscular contraction are the guidelines for identifying active muscle groups. In any action it is possible to use what I call muscular "overkill." It is always possible to use far more muscles than necessary for a given action. This may be caused by weakness of the prime mover, requiring assistance from other muscles. It may be caused by a need to "control" every tiny motion that requires co-contraction of agonist and antagonist for precise control. It may be due to inelasticity of the antagonistic muscles, causing a need to overcome not only gravity but the opposing muscles as well. Finally it may be due to misalignment of the skeletal system, making contraction of more muscles necessary in order to accomplish a movement task. Beginning dancers frequently experience overkill. Gaining movement skill in dance, like athletics, is a process of gradually paring the contractions down to use just the prime movers. When a dancer or athlete has reduced the number of active muscles to the bare minimum, the movement has a clear, simple, easeful sense of efficiency: "It looks so easy." It is my contention that a sense of ease can do much to prolong the life of the dancer by reducing the stress of overkill on muscles and joints. Admittedly, there will be times when, for a given effect, a choreographer will specifically call for high levels of tension and simultaneous use of agonist and antagonist. The dancer should be able to produce that quality of motion when it is called for, but should also be able to reduce the action to contraction of only the muscles which efficiently produce the desired movement.

The second assumption of my approach to kinesiological analysis is that one must take the action of gravity into account. Movement does not occur in a vacuum. Gravity does have a lot of pull. Before one can identify the muscles producing a given action, one must identify the action of gravity at the joint involved.

The third assumption is that all of this information is valuable only when it is carried in the dancer's head. Dancers do not carry kinesiology books into the studio with them. Yet it is in the studio that the benefits of this information are felt. Doing an "open book" muscular analysis is, in my opinion, an exercise in academic futility. Particularly in modern dance, where the combinations often change every day, either one analyzes the action in the studio or the opportunity is lost. Admittedly, a lot of preliminary memorization must take place before the dancer can use kinesiological analysis effectively in the studio. But the "payback" is worth it because injuries can be prevented; conditioning for a specific performance role can be approached efficiently and effectively; specific weaknesses can be acknowledged and dealt with wisely; and particular strengths can be used effectively.

Specific Muscle Actions

There is no easy way to learn the muscle actions. You must learn the attachments, learn the path, and thereby learn the actions. One thing that has helped many of my students is a "hands-on" approach. I have had students go so far as to draw the muscles on their own bodies and then recite the muscle names. There are many different approaches to learning the actions of muscles, but the more you use your own body as your textbook, the easier it will be for you to take it with you wherever you go. Many students use flash cards in the initial phases of learning the attachments and action of muscles, and they have worked well in many cases. But whatever gimmicks you use, the task remains: you must memorize the information before you can use it. Figures 7.8 and 7.9 illustrate most of the major muscles of the body. Tables 7.2, 7.3, and 7.4 list all of the major muscles of the body (excluding the intrinsic muscles of the foot and hand—those muscles which do not also cross the ankle or wrist joint) and identify which joint is affected by contraction. These figures and tables were developed to give you an overview of the muscular system, not to give you a heart attack. *Don't panic* at the number of muscles. As you begin to work systematically at learning the musculature from the bottom up, you will find patterns that will help you remember names, locations, and actions. It will be helpful to return to these figures and tables once the memorization process has begun. They can serve as guides for self-testing.

The information in following chapters on muscle attachments is done in chart form to facilitate studying. Preceding each chart is a paragraph or two giving an overview of structure and function, a review of possible joint actions, and "helpful hints to homeowners" for studying. The charts themselves include the muscle names, the attachments, the joints crossed, the path of the muscle as it crosses the joint, and the actions of the muscles.[2] When two or more muscles have exactly the same actions, they are noted as synergistic on the charts. Normally, a kinesiology book does not include the path of the muscle, but for some muscles this information is crucial to accurate identification of action. Following each chart is a discussion of specific muscles intended to clear up points which often seem to muddle students. At least one demonstration analysis is presented for each of the muscle sections. Finally, specific implications for dancers are discussed.

---

2. Specific placement of muscle attachments may vary up to approximately one-fourth inch, or even more, from individual to individual. This variation can make a muscle either more or less efficient at performing a given joint action.

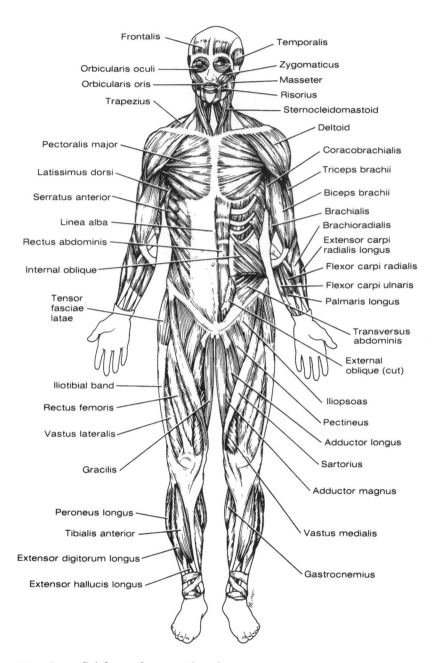

Frontalis
Temporalis
Orbicularis oculi
Zygomaticus
Orbicularis oris
Masseter
Trapezius
Risorius
Sternocleidomastoid
Pectoralis major
Deltoid
Latissimus dorsi
Coracobrachialis
Serratus anterior
Triceps brachii
Linea alba
Biceps brachii
Rectus abdominis
Brachialis
Internal oblique
Brachioradialis
Tensor fasciae latae
Extensor carpi radialis longus
Flexor carpi radialis
Flexor carpi ulnaris
Palmaris longus
Transversus abdominis
External oblique (cut)
Iliotibial band
Iliopsoas
Rectus femoris
Pectineus
Vastus lateralis
Adductor longus
Gracilis
Sartorius
Adductor magnus
Peroneus longus
Tibialis anterior
Vastus medialis
Extensor digitorum longus
Extensor hallucis longus
Gastrocnemius

FIGURE 7.8.   **Superficial muscles: anterior view**

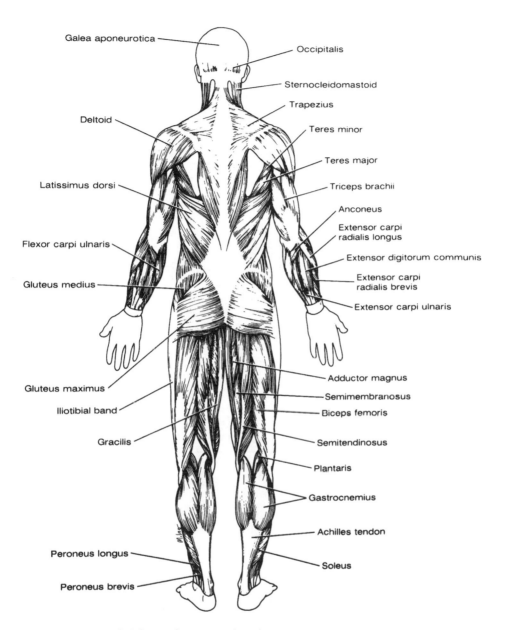

Galea aponeurotica
Occipitalis
Sternocleidomastoid
Trapezius
Deltoid
Teres minor
Teres major
Latissimus dorsi
Triceps brachii
Anconeus
Extensor carpi radialis longus
Flexor carpi ulnaris
Extensor digitorum communis
Gluteus medius
Extensor carpi radialis brevis
Extensor carpi ulnaris
Adductor magnus
Semimembranosus
Gluteus maximus
Biceps femoris
Iliotibial band
Semitendinosus
Gracilis
Plantaris
Gastrocnemius
Achilles tendon
Peroneus longus
Soleus
Peroneus brevis

FIGURE 7.9. **Superficial muscles: posterior view**

TABLE 7.2 Major Muscles of Toes, Tarsus, Ankle, Knee, Hip

Toes	Tarsus	Ankle	Knee	Hip
Intrinsic muscles of the foot				
Flexor digitorum longus				
Flexor hallux longus				
Extensor digitorum longus				
Extensor hallus longus				
	Tibialis anterior			
	Tibialis posterior			
	Peroneus longus			
	Peroneus brevis			
	Peroneus tertius			
		Soleus gastrocnemius		
		Plantaris		
			Popliteus	
			Medial vasti	} Quadriceps
			Intermediate vasti	
			Lateral vasti	
			Rectus femoris	
			Gracilis	
			Sartorius	
			Semitendinosus	} Hamstrings
			Semimembranosus	
			Biceps femoris	
				Adductor brevis
				Adductor longus
				Adductor magnus
				Pectineus
				Iliacus
				Psoas (major)*
				Gluteus maximus
				Gluteus medius
				Gluteus minimus
				Tensor fascia lata
				Six deep rotators

*The psoas major also crosses the lumbar spine joints and therefore have an effect on that set of joints.

118

TABLE 7.3   Major Muscles of Torso, Neck, Scapula, Shoulder

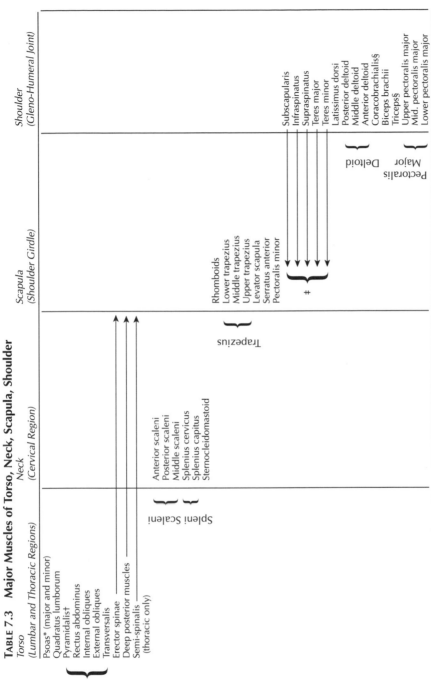

Torso (Lumbar and Thoracic Regions)	Neck (Cervical Region)	Scapula (Shoulder Girdle)	Shoulder (Gleno-Humeral Joint)
Psoas* (major and minor)			
Quadratus lumborum			
Pyramidalis†			
Rectus abdominus			
Internal obliques			
External obliques			
Transversalis			
Erector spinae			
Deep posterior muscles			
Semi-spinalis (thoracic only)			
	Anterior scaleni		Subscapularis
	Posterior scaleni		Infraspinatus
	Middle scaleni		Supraspinatus
	Splenius cervicus	Rhomboids	Teres major
	Splenius capitus	Lower trapezius	Teres minor
	Sternocleidomastoid	Middle trapezius	Latissimus dorsi
		Upper trapezius	Posterior deltoid
		Levator scapula	Middle deltoid
		Serratus anterior	Anterior deltoid
		Pectoralis minor	Coracobrachialis§
			Biceps brachii
			Triceps§
			Upper pectoralis major
			Mid. pectoralis major
			Lower pectoralis major

ABDOMINALS

Splenii   Scaleni

Trapezius

‡‡

Pectoralis Major   Deltoid

* Psoas major also acts on hip joint.
† Low lumbar only.
‡ These five muscles act primarily on the shoulder joint, but since they all attach to the scapula, they may have a secondary action on the scapula.
§ Also acts on elbow joint.

TABLE 7.4 Major Muscles of Elbow, Radio-Ulnar Joints, Wrist, Hand

Muscle	Elbow	Radio-Ulnar Joints	Wrist	Hand (Fingers and Thumb)
Biceps brachii	✓	✓		
Triceps	✓			
Brachioradialis	✓	✓		
Brachialis	✓			
Anconeus	✓			
Pronator teres	✓	✓		
Flexor carpi radialis	✓		✓	
Flexor carpi ulnaris		XXXXXXXXXXXXXXXXXX	✓	
Extensor carpi ulnaris		XXXXXXXXXXXXXXXXXX	✓	
Extensor carpi radialis longus			✓	
Extensor carpi radialis brevis			✓	
Palmaris longus			✓	
Flexor digitorum superficialis		XXXXXXXXXXXXXXXXXX	✓	✓
Extensor digitorum		XXXXXXXXXXXXXXXXXX	✓	✓
Supinator		✓		
Pronator quadratus		✓		
Extensor pollicis longus				✓
Abductor pollicis longus				✓
Flexor digitorum profundus				✓
Flexor pollicis brevis				✓
Extensor indicis				✓
Extensor digiti minimi				✓
Intrinsic muscles of the hand				✓

XXXXXXX: No action at the radio-ulnar joint. Muscles must attach to the radius to have an action of pronation or supination, since the ulna does not move on these actions.

- - - - - -: Minimal action on joint.

CHAPTER 8

Muscles of the Toes, the Tarsus, and the Ankle

Muscles and Paths

The muscles of the ankle, the tarsus, and the toes run from the tibia and fibula on the proximal end down to the bones of the foot, distally. Obviously a muscle must cross a joint to cause action at that joint. Those muscles that do not attach to the phalanges do not cause action of the toes.

The possible actions of the toes include flexion, extension, and hyperextension. The possible actions of the tarsus are pronation and supination. The possible actions of the ankle joint are plantar flexion and dorsiflexion.

The path for the muscles of the toes may be plantar or dorsal. *Plantar* refers to the sole of the foot and *dorsal* to the top of the foot. Muscles having a plantar path will cause flexion of the toes on contraction. Muscles following a dorsal path will extend the toes. The path of the muscles crossing the tarsus joint may be either medial or lateral to the midpoint of the tarsus. The lateral muscles cause pronation; the medial muscles cause supination. The path for the ankle joint is either anterior or posterior to the center of the ankle joint. The anterior muscles will dorsiflex the ankle and the posterior muscles will plantar-flex the ankle. The term *hallux* refers to the great toe. The term *digitorum* refers to the four lesser toes.

Table 8.1 lists the muscles of the ankle, tarsus, and toes. Specifically noted are attachments, joints crossed, path, and action. Figures 8.1–8.4 illustrate the muscles listed in Table 8.1. Figure 8.5 illustrates the intrinsic muscles of the foot—for information only.

Muscle Actions

Understanding the action of the toes is relatively simple: if the muscle is on the plantar surface, it is a flexor; if it is on the dorsal surface, it is an extensor. It is when one starts adding analysis of the ankle and tarsus that confusion arises. An action of the foot seldom happens at only the ankle or tarsus. Because two joint regions are combined in the analysis of foot action (three when you add the toes), students sometimes become confused about which specific muscles are performing an action. In order to deter-

121

TABLE 8.1 Muscles of Ankle, Tarsus, Toes

Muscle Name	Proximal Attachment	Distal Attachment	Joint(s) Crossed	Path	Actions
Flexor digitorum longus	Posterior surface of tibia	Distal phalanx of toes 2 through 5 (plantar)	Toes (2 through 5) Tarsus Ankle	Plantar Medial Posterior	Flexion Supination Plantar flexion
Flexor hallux longus	Lower two-thirds of posterior fibula	Distal phalanx of the great toe (plantar)	Toe (1) Tarsus Ankle	Plantar At midpoint Posterior	Flexion Slight supination Plantar flexion
Extensor hallux longus	Midanterior of fibula and interosseous membrane	Dorsal surface of the distal phalanx of the great toe	Toe (1) Tarsus Ankle	Dorsal At midpoint Anterior	Extension Slight supination Dorsiflexion
Extensor digitorum longus	Anterior surface of upper three-fourths of fibula and interosseous membrane	Dorsal surface of phalanges of toes 2 through 5	Toes Tarsus Ankle	Dorsal Lateral Anterior	Extension Pronation Dorsiflexion
Tibialis anterior	Lateral condyle and upper two-thirds of the lateral surface of the tibia	Medial surface of first cuneiform and first metatarsal	Tarsus Ankle	Medial Anterior	Supination Dorsiflexion
Tibialis posterior	Posterior surface of the tibia, fibula, and interosseous membrane	Tendons to cuboid, navicular, and all three cuneiforms on plantar surface	Tarsus Ankle	Medial Posterior	Supination Plantar flexion

122

Muscle	Origin	Insertion	Joint	Location	Action
Peroneus longus	Lateral upper two-thirds of fibula (synergistic with peroneus brevis)	Tendons to plantar surface of first cuneiform and base of first metatarsal	Tarsus Ankle	Lateral Posterior	Pronation Plantar flexion
Peroneus brevis	Lower two-thirds of fibula (synergistic with peroneus longus)	Tuberosity of the fifth metatarsal	Tarsus Ankle	Lateral Posterior	Pronation Plantar flexion
Peroneus tertius	Lower one-third of anterior fibula and interosseous membrane	Dorsal surface of fifth metatarsal	Tarsus Ankle	Lateral Anterior	Pronation Dorsiflexion
Gastrocnemius	Posterior aspect of medial and lateral condyles of the femur	Tuberosity of the calcaneous (via the Achilles tendon)	Ankle Knee	Posterior Posterior	Plantar flexion Flexion
Soleus	Posterior surface of upper third of fibula and middle third of tibia	Tuberosity of the calcaneous via the Achilles tendon	Ankle	Posterior	Plantar flexion
Plantaris*	Posterior surface of femur above the lateral condyle	Tuberosity of the calcaneous via the Achilles tendon	Ankle Knee	Posterior Posterior	Plantar flexion Flexion

*Not a primary muscle of either the ankle or the knee joints. It is mentioned only because of injuries to it, which will be discussed later. This muscle tears when one changes direction quickly.

123

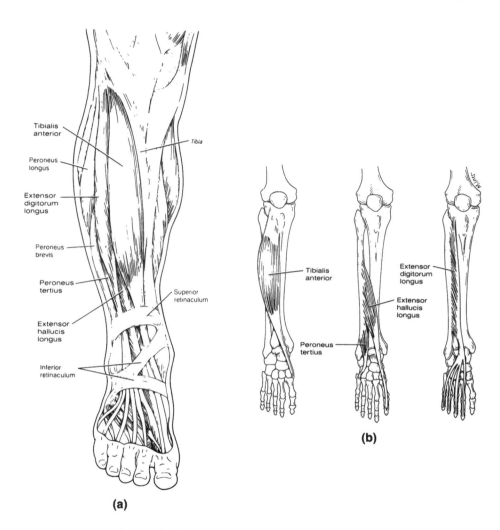

(a)

(b)

FIGURE 8.1.   **Muscles of the lower leg, anterior view: (*a*) superficial layer; (*b*) deep layer**

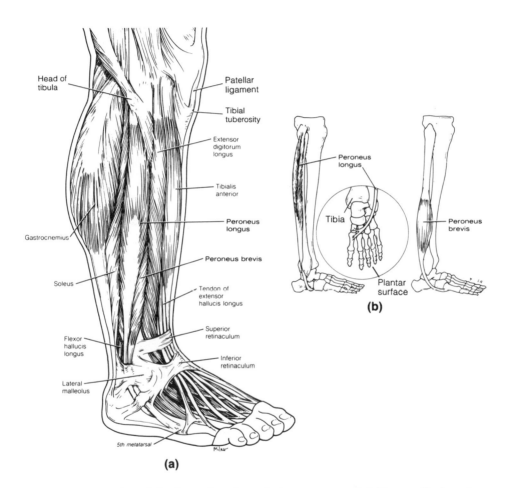

FIGURE 8.2. **Muscles of the lower leg, lateral view: (*a*) superficial layer; (*b*) deep layer**

126

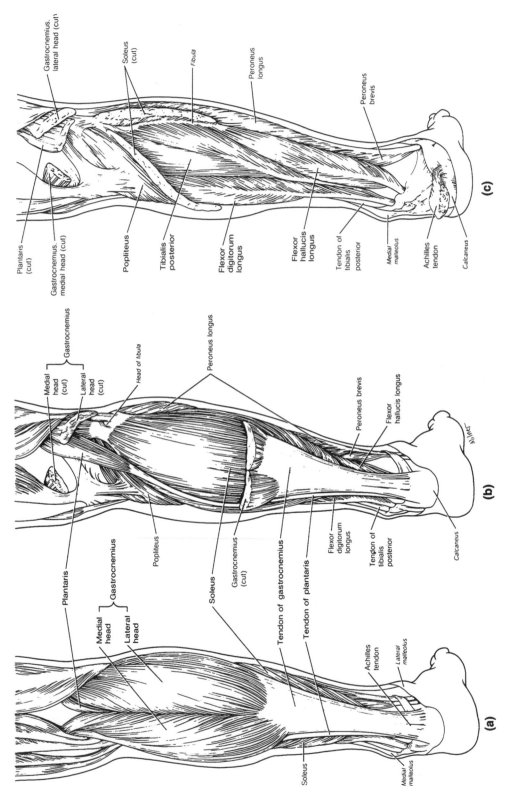

FIGURE 8.3. Muscles of the lower leg, posterior view: (a) superficial layer; (b) middle layer; (c) deep layer

Gastrocnemius, lateral head (cut)

Soleus (cut)

Fibula

Peroneus longus

Peroneus brevis

Plantaris (cut)

Gastrocnemius, medial head (cut)

Popliteus

Tibialis posterior

Flexor digitorum longus

Flexor hallucis longus

Tendon of tibialis posterior

Medial malleolus

Achilles tendon

Calcaneus

(c)

Gastrocnemius

Medial head (cut)

Lateral head (cut)

Head of fibula

Peroneus longus

Plantaris

Medial head

Lateral head

Gastrocnemius

Popliteus

Soleus

Gastrocnemius (cut)

Tendon of gastrocnemius

Tendon of plantaris

Peroneus brevis

Flexor hallucis longus

Flexor digitorum longus

Tendon of tibialis posterior

Calcaneus

(b)

Achilles tendon

Lateral malleolus

Soleus

Medial malleolus

(a)

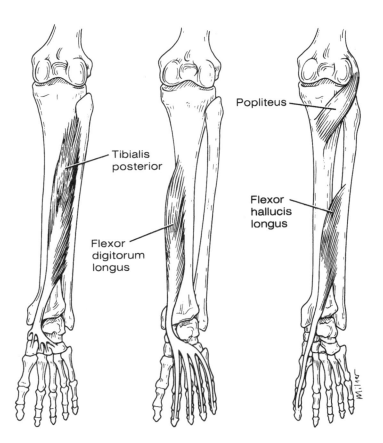

FIGURE 8.4. Muscles of the lower leg, posterior view, deepest layer (with calcaneus removed)

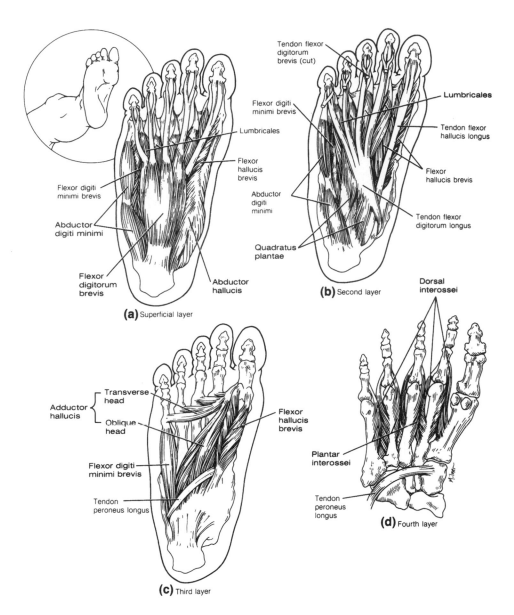

Figure 8.5. **Intrinsic muscles of the foot: (*a*) superficial; (*b*) second layer; (*c*) third layer; (*d*) deepest layer**

mine exactly which muscles are most efficient at performing a given action, one must take all joints into consideration. It's a bit like a cross-reference: the kinesiologist needs to know what is happening at all joints to identify the efficient muscles. Table 8.2 identifies the four quadrants of possible movements at the ankle/tarsus combination and lists the actions in those quadrants and which muscles perform the actions.

TABLE 8.2   Muscles of ankle and tarsus by quadrant of action

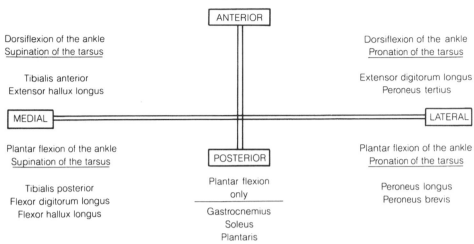

PRACTICE DEMONSTRATION

The next step is analysis, taking the demonstration form partially presented in Section II through to completion by adding the analysis of muscle group, type of contraction, and specific muscles. A sample of the completion of the demonstration form would probably be helpful at this point. Figure 8.6 illustrates an action of the ankle, tarsus, and toes. Table 8.3 shows a completed demonstration form, analyzing the action presented in Figure 8.6. The action takes place between (*a*) and (*b*).

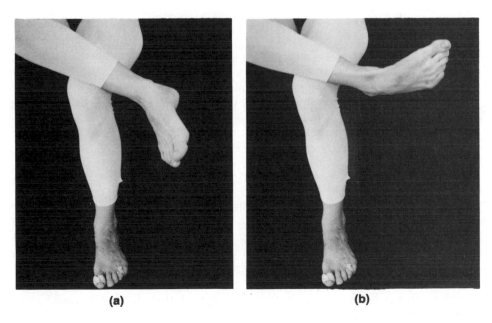

(a)   (b)

FIGURE 8.6.   **Analyze the action of the ankle, tarsus, and toes from (*a*) to (*b*), with gravity at (*b*).**

TABLE 8.3   **Analysis of Figure 8.6**

Joint	Joint Position or Action	Action of Gravity at (b)	Muscle Group and Type of Contraction	Specific Muscles
Toes	Flexion	Relaxation actually allows extension (gravity at toes is difficult to determine)	Shortening Contraction of flexors	Flexor dig. long. Flexor hall. long.
Tarsus	Supination	Pronation*	Shortening Contraction of supinators	Tibialis posterior† Flexor digitorum longus
Ankle	Plantar	Dorsi-flexion‡	Shortening Contraction Plantar flexors	Tibialis posterior Flexor digitorum longus Gastrocnemius§ Soleus

*Remember, action is identified by direction.
†Why not tibialis anterior? Because it is a dorsiflexor.
‡The *direction of action* is dorsiflexion.
§Did you forget the "gastrox" and soleus in the effort of getting the tarsus muscles? It's easy to do—*be careful*. While they may not be "prime movers" (that do *all* the actions), they certainly can contribute to the plantar flexion component.

Figure 8.7 (p. 131) is another demonstration for analysis. Analysis of the joint action and the action of gravity is found in Chapter 7. This analysis completes the process. Table 8.4 is a blank form for analysis. Table 8.5 is the correct analysis of the demonstration presented in Figure 8.7. It should be clear that one or two sample demonstrations do not give sufficient practice at the analysis task. It is suggested that you go back to other illustrations in Section II for further practice.

IMPLICATIONS FOR DANCERS

The muscles of the ankle, the tarsus, and the toes are of critical importance to the dancer. Balance of strength in agonist and antagonist is important, particularly in the tarsus region. Imbalance in strength of the pronators and supinators of the tarsus can lead to a tendency to pronate or supinate in a non-weight-bearing position (for example, in air). Landing with a misaligned tarsus increases the likelihood of ankle sprains.

All dancers will have far greater strength in the plantar flexors of the ankle than in the dorsiflexors (after all, dancers lift all of their body weight with the plantar flexors, so it is predictable that the plantar flexors will be stronger). It is also natural to grip with the toes when one is in *relevé* because one of the major muscles counteracting the pull of gravity at the ankle (plantar flexor) and at the tarsus (supinator) is also a flexor of the toes

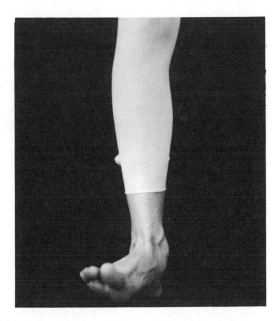

FIGURE 8.7.   Analyze the position of the ankle, tarsus, and toes.

(flexor digitorum longus). In order to achieve proper performance (no toe gripping) it is necessary to compensate muscularly by activating the extensors of the toes to reduce gripping. It is possible, but it certainly is not natural. Many of the errors in performance common among beginning dancers are muscularly caused and explained by this kind of kinesiological analysis.

TABLE 8.4   Practice Analysis of Figure 8.7

Joint	Joint Position or Action	Action of Gravity	Muscle Group and Type of Contraction	Specific Muscles
Ankle				
Tarsus				
Toes				

TABLE 8.5   Analysis of Figure 8.7

Joint	Joint Position or Action	Action of Gravity	Muscle Group and Type of Contraction	Specific Muscles
Toes	Hyper-extended	Flexion	Static contraction of extensors	Extensor digitorum longus Extensor hallux longus
Tarsus	Pronated	Supination	Static contraction of pronators	Peroneus tertius (and extensor digitorum longus)
Ankle	Dorsiflexed	Plantar flexion	Static contraction of dorsiflexors	Extensor digitorum longus, peroneus tertius, and extensor hallux longus

Note: It is not absolutely essential to list the muscles repeatedly for the different joints. It is done so here for clarity.

The flexor hallux longus is an important muscle to dancers because it is a plantar flexor and assists in supination (both antigravity actions). A common ailment of dancers (particularly in ballet) is a condition called *long flexor tendonitis.* This condition occurs when more is asked of the muscle than it is prepared to give. Constant contraction can lead to this form of tendonitis. More will be said about tendonitis in Chapter 18, but for now it is important to point out that long flexor tendonitis is quite common in dancers.

Another form of tendonitis quite common in dancers is Achilles tendonitis. The symptoms of this condition are tenderness of the Achilles tendon, consistent grating or crunching on movement, and pain on forcible plantar flexion of the ankle joint. This condition is aggravated by the amount of time many dancers spend in a plantar flexed position. If the dancer is careful about stretching out the gastrocnemius and soleus after class, rehearsal, and performance, the likelihood of Achilles tendonitis is reduced. But, realizing now that the Achilles tendon is actually the attachment of the gastrocnemius, soleus, and plantaris, you must also realize that to totally stretch the Achilles, you must dorsiflex the ankle with the knee *both flexed and extended.* The gastrocnemius is a superficial, white, fast, "mover" muscle. Therefore it will be the more efficient muscle in performing the *action* of plantar flexion for locomotion (runs, jumps, etc). After a class full of locomotor activity the dancer should stretch with the ankle dorsiflexed and *knee straight* to stretch the gastrocnemius most effectively. The soleus is a deep, red, "holding" muscle. It is therefore more adapted to *maintaining a position* of plantar flexion (as in *relevé* or *pointe* work). If a class is predominantly *adagio* work, with many long, extended balances, the soleus should be the prime target for the stretch, with the ankle dorsiflexed and *knee eased into a flexed position*. This second stretch for the soleus will also be effective for the other plantar flexors, *if the stretch is done in parallel*. If the stretch is done in an outwardly or inwardly rotated position, there will be an unequal stretch of the medial and lateral muscles.[1]

Shin splints are another stress-related condition in the lower leg where the muscles of the ankle and tarsus attach. The description and explanation of shin splints will be presented in Chapter 18. However, every dancer has at least some idea of what shin splints are. At this time we will say that shin splints are pain resulting from overuse of specific muscles. One of the most common sites of shin splints is the tibialis anterior, but shin splints can also occur in the tibialis posterior, flexor digitorum longus, flexor hallux longus, peroneus longus, peroneus brevis, and peroneus tertius. Classic causes of shin splints in dancers fall into three categories: those caused by improper landing (not coming through the ankle to full dorsiflexion—heel down—on jumps and leaps); those caused by dancing on hard surfaces, like cement (or cement disguised by tile flooring); those caused by consistently carrying the weight too far forward on the balls of the feet or too far back on the heels (certainly related to the first cause, but not exactly the same), requiring a constant contraction of the dorsiflexors of the ankle.

Spasm (cramp) in the peroneal muscles (longus, brevis, and tertius) and the extensor digitorum longus may be a symptom of sciatica (tight outward rotators of the hip pinching the sciatic nerve). Sciatica will be discussed at length in Chapter 13. Spasm of the peroneals can also occur when a dancer is first trying to correct a sickled (supinated) *relevé* position.[2]

Wobbling feet on *relevé* or *pointe* may indicate weakness of the pronators and supinators of the tarsus. All dancers should do additional conditioning for these muscles because they provide the lateral and medial stability for the foot. Such conditioning should be an integral part of rehabilitation after an ankle sprain. Actually, most injuries labeled *ankle sprains* are caused by overmovement of the tarsus (supination), causing the common injury of tearing the anterior talofibular ligament.

1. If rotation (pronation or supination) of the tarsus is included in this stretch, care should be taken to minimize stress on the knee.
2. Gradual preconditioning of these muscles often reduces the occurrence of overuse symptoms (soreness or spasms). See Figure 19.15.

CHAPTER 9

Muscles of the Knee and the Hip

Muscles of the Knee

The primary restrictions of actions at the knee joint are provided by the complex ligamentous structure of the knee. You are encouraged to review the restrictions of action. Possible actions at the knee joint are flexion and extension, plus the possibility of slight rotation when the knee is flexed. Because the actions of the knee are limited, analysis of the possible actions of muscles on the knee is relatively straightforward. If a muscle passes anterior to the joint, it will be an extensor of the knee. A posterior path means that the muscle will flex the knee. To analyze the rotary action of the muscles of the knee requires one to focus on the line of pull between the two attachments. Unfortunately, there is no simple formula for determination of the actions of inward and outward rotation such as there is for flexion and extension. One must look at the line of pull of each muscle to determine the direction of rotation, if there is any.

Muscle Actions

There are two major sets of muscles at the knee joint: the *quadriceps* and the *hamstrings*. Each set includes a number of muscles, and these individual muscles should be learned separately because they do not have exactly the same actions. For example, the two medial hamstrings (semitendonosus and semimembranosus) have an action of inward rotation of the knee, but the lateral hamstring (biceps femoris) has an action of outward rotation at the knee. Furthermore, when you get to the actions of the two joint muscles at the hip, it will be necessary for you to think of the individual muscles of the quadriceps and the hamstrings separately.

Table 9.1 shows the attachments and actions of the muscles of the knee. You will note that the attachments of the gastrocnemius and plantaris are not repeated in this table. As a review exercise, you can fill in these two muscles from memory. Figures 9.1, 9.2, and 9.3 illustrate the muscles listed in Table 9.1.

134

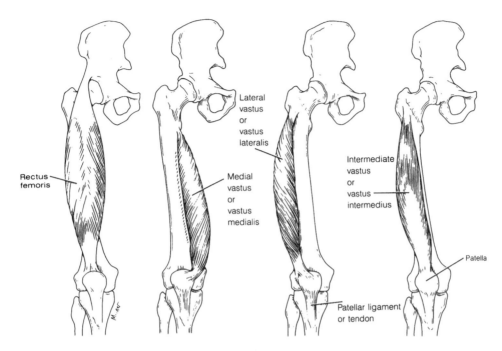

FIGURE 9.1.   The four muscles of the quadriceps

Most anatomy and kinesiology books do not note the rotary effect of the medial and lateral vasti. Indeed, it is quite difficult to distinguish between their actions on the transverse planes. However, if you extend the knee while seated, pressing the heel forward medially (trying to maintain outward rotation of the knee joint), I think you can feel more contraction from the lateral vasti. Conversely, if you extend the knee with the heel pressing laterally (inward rotation), you can feel more contraction from the medial vasti. While this hypothesis regarding the rotary potential of the vasti has not been proven electromyographically in the laboratory, it may be of assistance in conditioning for chondromalacia of the patella (covered in Chapter 19). I share this information with you in the hope that someone might find the question of rotary action of the vasti fascinating enough for a research project using electromyography to see if knee extensions with medial and lateral heel presses might somewhat selectively activate the medial and lateral vasti.

Many authorities have noted that the vasti reach full contraction in the last 10 to 15 degrees of extension of the knee. The rectus femoris is the prime mover up to that point. To check this selection of muscle contingent upon the angle of pull, sit with your right and left hands over the lateral and medial vasti. Then extend the knee slowly. You will be able to feel the full activation of the vasti in the last degrees of the extension action. This full extension of the knee is called "setting the quads," it is frequently used in conditioning for the quadriceps, and the exercises are called "quad-sets."

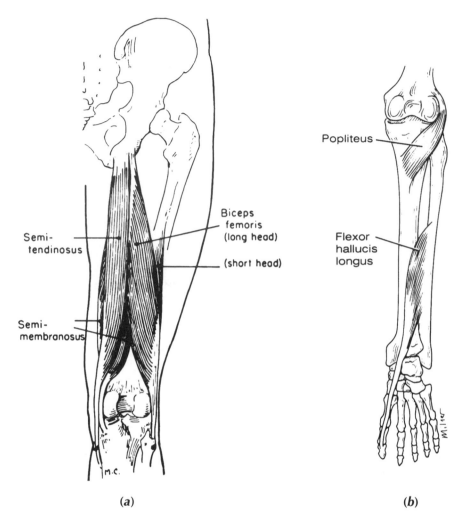

(*a*)   (*b*)

FIGURE 9.2.   **The three hamstring muscles: semitendinosus, semimembranosus, and biceps femoris (*a*); and the popliteus (*b*).**

Types of Contraction

Since the muscles of the knee are relatively simple to learn, this is an excellent place to practice applying the concepts of lengthening, static, and shortening contractions. For example, going down in a *plié* is giving in to gravity with control.[1] Therefore gravity is winning the tug-of-war, and the muscles fighting gravity are extensor muscles. When going down in a *plié*, the action of gravity is flexion. The active muscle group is the extensor group, and the type of contraction is a lengthening contraction. The specific muscles are the rectus femoris, the medial vastus, the lateral vastus, and the intermediate vastus. When the dancer is rising from a *plié*, gravity

---

1. A *plié* is an action that involves the hip and ankle joints just as much as the knee joint. However, this analysis focuses on the knee only.

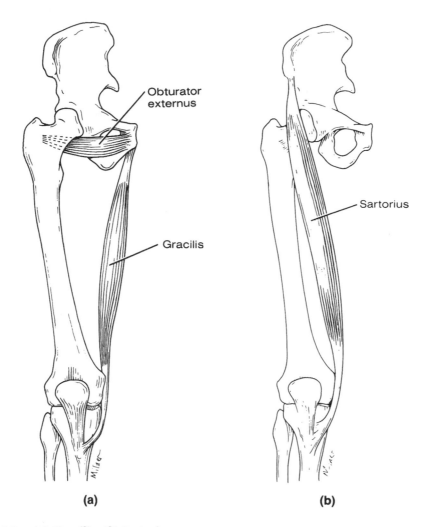

Figure 9.3. (*a*) **Gracilis;** (*b*) **Sartorius**

is still a flexor, and the muscles opposing gravity in the tug-of-war are therefore still extensors. The type of contraction would change, because now the muscles are winning the tug-of-war, and rising from a *plié* requires a shortening contraction of the extensors of the knee. Again the specific muscles are the rectus femoris, medial vastus, lateral vastus, and intermediate vastus. Holding a *demi-plié* position requires contraction of the same muscles (gravity still has the same action—flexion), but now the type of contraction is a static contraction. A helpful general rule to remember is, *the muscles that get you there are the muscles that hold you there and let you down (up) from there.*

PRACTICE DEMONSTRATION

Analysis of Figure 9.4 (p. 140) will give you a chance to practice. Table 9.2 (p. 141) is blank for your answers. Table 9.3 (p. 141) gives the correct

TABLE 9.1 Muscles of the Knee

Muscle Name	Proximal Attachment	Distal Attachment	Joint Crossed	Path	Action
Medial vasti	Medial lip of linea aspera	Tibial tuberosity via the patellar tendon	Knee	Anterior Medial	Extension Inward rotation
Intermediate vasti	Anterior surface of shaft of femur	Tibial tuberosity via the patellar tendon	Knee	Anterior	Extension
Lateral vasti	Greater trochanter and lateral lip of linea aspera	Tibia tuberosity via the patellar tendon	Knee	Anterior Lateral	Extension Outward rotation
Rectus femoris	Anterior inferior iliac spine	Tibial tuberosity via the patellar tendon	Knee Hip	Anterior Anterior	Extension Flexion
Semitendinosus	Medial aspect of ischial tuberosity (synergistic with semimembranosus)	Proximal, medial surface of tibia, just below the distal attachments of the gracilis and sartorius	Knee	From posterior, wrapping to anterior	Flexion Inward rotation
			Hip	Posterior and medial	Extension, adduction, and inward rotation
Semimembranosus	Medial aspect of ischial tuberosity (synergistic with semitendinosus)	Just posterior to semitendinosis attachment on the proximal medial surface of tibia	Knee	Same as semi-tendinosus	Flexion Inward rotation
			Hip	Posterior and medial	Extension, adduction, and inward rotation

Muscle	Origin	Insertion	Joint	Line of pull	Action
Biceps femoris	Long head: Lateral aspect of ischial tuberosity Short head: Lateral lip of linea aspera	Posterior lateral condyle of tibia and lateral head of fibula (both heads have a common distal attachment)	Knee (both heads)	Posterior Lateral	Flexion Outward rotation
			Hip (long head)	Posterior and lateral	Extension (assist abduction) Outward rotation
Gracilis	Anterior, inferior aspect of symphasis pubis	Medial, proximal surface of tibia	Knee	Posterior and medial	Flexion Inward rotation
			Hip	Medial, inferior, and slightly anterior	Adduction Inward rotation Assist in flexion
Sartorius	Anterior superior iliac spine	Just anterior to Gracilis attachment on medial condyle of tibia	Knee	Posterior and medial	Flexion Inward rotation
			Hip	Obliquely wrapping from superior to medial inferior	Flexion Outward rotation Assist in abduction
Popliteus	Lateral condyle of the femur	Medial posterior surface of tibia	Knee	Posterior and diagonal from high lateral to low medial	Flexion Inward rotation

Gastrocnemius (review from Table 8.2)
Plantaris (review from Table 8.2)

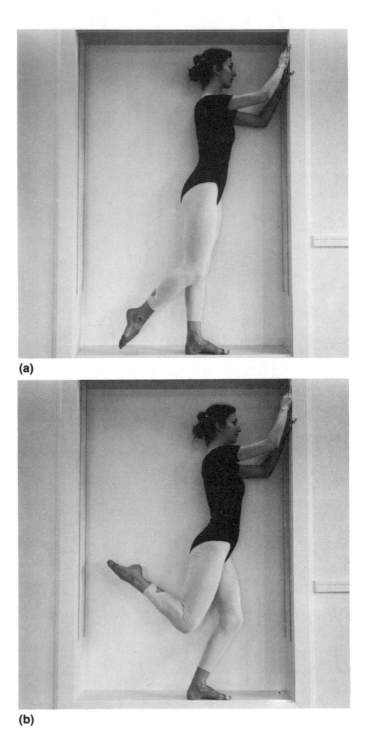

(a)

(b)

FIGURE 9.4.   Analyze the action of the right and left knees from (a) to (b), with gravity at (b).

TABLE 9.2 **Analysis of Figure 9.4**

Joint	Joint Action or Position	Action of Gravity	Muscle Group and Type of Contraction	Specific Muscles
Right knee				
Left knee				

TABLE 9.3 **Analysis of Figure 9.4**

Joint	Joint Action or Position	Action of Gravity	Muscle Group and Type of Contraction	Specific Muscles
Right knee	Flexion	Extension	Shortening Contraction of flexors	Gastrocnemius Semitendinosus Semimembranosus Gracilis Biceps femoris Sartorius*
Left knee	Flexion	Flexion	Lengthening Contraction of extensors	Rectus femoris Lateral vastus Intermediate vastus Medial vastus

*Possible assistance from popliteus and plantaris.

analysis. Try to do the analysis without reference to the key; then check your answers.

Students often experience some confusion when first doing muscular analysis. If you had problems, review the appropriate material. That is, if you got confused about "type of contraction," reread the section earlier in this chapter. If the specific muscles boggled you, study Table 9.1. If you had the action of gravity wrong, remember that gravity pulls in an absolutely vertical line through the center of the joint. If you had the action of gravity right but had the wrong muscle group, remember that *if gravity does it, the muscles won't*. The muscle group must be opposite to the action of gravity. If you did not get the joint action right, go back to Chapter 3 and review the analysis of joint action. Each step in the process is critical, and accuracy at each step is essential. *Don't try to "fake" your way through if you don't understand*. The confusion will only snowball as you go along. Clear up any misconceptions and problems now.

IMPLICATIONS FOR DANCERS

The healthy performance of the knee joints is certainly crucial to dancers. No dancer can hear the words, "Oh, my knee!" without turning white with fear. The knee is, indeed, an incredible mechanism that supports most of the weight of the body in all kinds of distorted positions. One of the positions most stressful to the knee is the deep squat position—the *grand plié*. The internal pressure on the knee joint itself rises incredibly as the flexion of the weight-bearing knee increases. While some *grand pliés* may be necessary to maintain the strength in the deepest ranges of flexion of the knee, extensive work in *grand plié* is bound to take its toll. I therefore advise that the number of *grand pliés* be limited and that other means be used to strengthen the quadriceps (see Chapter 19).

The strength of the muscles of the knee can certainly add stability to the knee joint. A balance of strength in the flexors and extensors of the knee joint is called for by most authorities, and many cite an imbalance of strength in these two muscle groups as a primary cause of injuries to the knee. Of course, I would add misalignment of the tarsus to the primary causes of knee injuries in dancers (not having the knees over the toes—or pronating the tarsus), resulting in unwanted rotation of the knee. Hamstring tears are the most predominant injury to the muscles of the knee for the general population, but for dancers there are some other tears that also occur with frequency.

The plantaris muscle is a flexor of the knee and assists in plantar flexion of the ankle. The belly of the muscle is located directly behind the knee, and the remainder of the muscle is tendonous in nature. When a dancer is performing a combination requiring sudden stops and direction changes, the plantaris is particularly susceptible to tears. This danger is heightened if the dancer is wearing shoes (such as tennis shoes) that increase friction between the foot and the floor. When the plantaris tears, there is a sensation of popping in the calf, and sometimes the sensation is actually accompanied by a popping sound that is quite loud.[2] When this happens, the dancer should get off the leg immediately and seek medical help.

The popliteus is also located directly behind the knee joint. It is effective in the initial stages of flexing a "locked" knee. If a dancer has a tendency to hyperextend the knees, he or she may "slam" into the hyperextended position and tear the popliteus. "Losing it" on a landing from a jump or leap could press the knee into hyperextension on the landing, markedly increasing the likelihood of tearing the popliteus.

---

2. Some authorities attribute this sound to a tearing of the gastrocnemius or soleus.

The relative frequency of hamstring tears is thought to be, in part, related to the fact that the hamstrings have a larger number of muscle spindles and therefore have a stronger stretch reflex. The fact that the hamstrings activate and deactivate more slowly than the quadriceps may also contribute to the frequency of hamstring tears. Adequate warm-up for the hamstring muscles is critical.

The importance of strength and mobility conditioning for all of the muscles surrounding the knee cannot be overstressed.

Muscles of the Hip Joint

There is no getting around the fact that the hip joint is complex. Actions occur on all three planes of action, including flexion, extension, (no hyperextension), abduction, adduction, inward rotation, and outward rotation. Because the hip is a major weight-bearing joint, it is necessary to analyze any action of the hip on *all three planes of action*. Maintenance of a position requires muscular contraction against gravity and is as important as "moving actions" in the analysis of hip action. In the first stages of muscular analysis of the hip joint, you must consciously remind yourself to focus on all three planes of action. It is easy to forget.

The complexity of the hip joint is amplified by the fact that almost all muscles have multiple actions. Only one muscle, the rectus femoris, has a singular action at the hip joint. All other muscles have actions on all three planes. Yet analysis is not an impossible task; there are some keys that will help.

Keys to Analysis at the Hip Joint

Muscles that pass anterior to the center of the hip joint will flex the hip. Posterior muscles will extend the hip. Inferior muscles will adduct, and superior muscles will abduct. Unfortunately, there is no neat little package of rules for determining the rotary effect of a muscle. (I have tried to develop such a rule and the rule—intended to simplify the process—turned out to be more complex than just looking at the path of the muscles to determine rotary action.) Remembering that a muscle will pull both attachments toward the center of the muscle makes identification of rotary action quite clear. Table 9.4 lists the paths for the sagittal and frontal planes, but lists no paths for the transverse plane. By putting one hand on one attachment and the other hand on the other attachment and bringing the two points closer together, you can determine all of the actions of a given muscle. Again, this hands-on approach is most helpful for dancers who seem to be more attuned to kinesthetic learning than to verbal learning.

A Trip Around the Hip

One way to help clear up the confusion so predominant in the initial stages of learning the muscles of the hip is to take a "trip" around the hip,

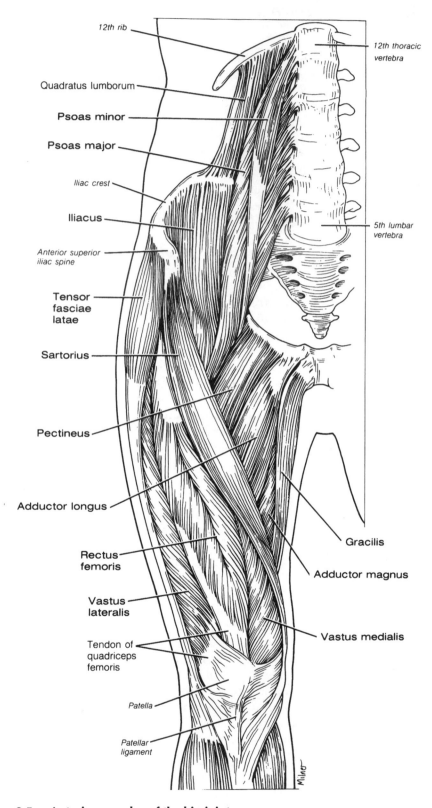

FIGURE 9.5.   Anterior muscles of the hip joint

144

noting the overlap of muscular action as one goes from anterior to medial, from medial to posterior, from posterior to lateral, and from lateral to anterior. A visual guide to the trip is provided in Figures 9.5–9.9.

Starting at the sagittal plane bisecting the hip joint, we begin on the front of the hip (Figure 9.5). Here we find the one muscle that has a singular action: the rectus femoris that flexes the hip (and also extends the knee). As soon as we move medially (still anterior), we have muscles that adduct and flex. In this section we find six muscles: iliopsoas, pectineus, adductor brevis, adductor longus, the anterior fibers of the adductor magnus, and gracilis (Figures 9.6–9.7). Five of those six muscles are also outward rotators. The gracilis is the only inward rotator that also flexes and adducts.

Moving along, we cross over to the posterior muscles, which are also medial (Figure 9.8). These muscles will extend and adduct. There are three muscles in this section: semitendinosus, semimembranosus, and posterior fibers of the adductor magnus. All three of these muscles also rotate inward.

From here we move laterally (still posterior) to identify those muscles which extend and abduct: long head of the biceps femoris, upper fibers of

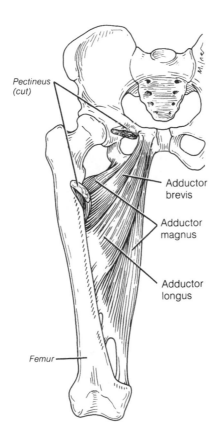

FIGURE 9.6. **Adductor group of the hip joint**

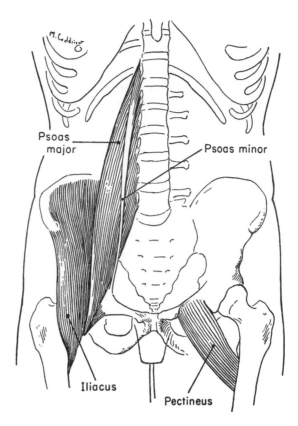

FIGURE 9.7.   Iliopsoas (illiacus, psoas major, and psoas minor) and pectineus

the gluteus maximus, posterior fibers of the gluteus medius, and the upper three of the six deep rotators (Figure 9.9). While in this location, we find four muscles which run beneath the center of the joint (resulting in an adduction action): the inferior fibers of the gluteus maximus, and the lower three of the six deep rotators. Analyzing the rotation action in this area (posterior and lateral) is simple; all the muscles rotate outward, including the long head of the biceps femoris, the entire gluteus maximus, all six deep rotators, and the posterior fibers of the gluteus medius.

Passing the anterior-posterior midpoint again, we move into the anterior-lateral quadrant where we find muscles which flex and abduct. There are four muscles here: anterior fibers of the gluteus medius, gluteus minimus, tensor fascia lata, and the sartorius. (Some books split the gluteus minimus into two sections: anterior and posterior. It has been my experience that the proximal attachment of the gluteus minimus usually does not flare back behind the center of the joint. I therefore list it as one muscle with actions of flexion, abduction, and inward rotation. If it did flare back, as some authorities say, the posterior fibers would extend, abduct, and rotate outward.) The sartorius is an outward rotator of the hip, and all three other muscles are inward rotators.

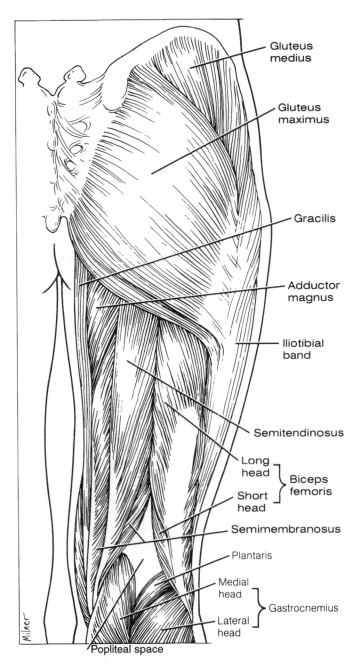

FIGURE 9.8. **Posterior muscles of the hip joint**

Here we are, back at the front again with the rectus femoris. It is hoped that journeying around the hip and locating the muscles of the hip in their respective quadrants of action has given you an overview of the musculature of the hip joint. Now you are more prepared to study Table 9.4.

Another helpful study guide is to list all of the muscles according to specific actions. Table 9.5 shows the possible combinations of actions on the

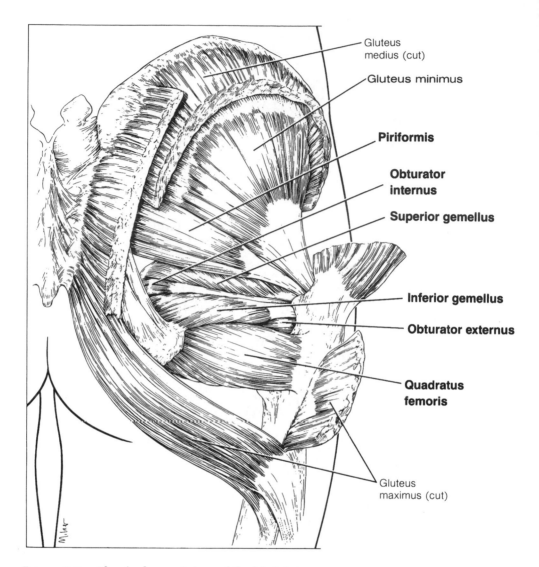

FIGURE 9.9.   The six deep rotators of the hip joint

three planes of actions and lists all of the muscles which perform those actions. Table 9.6 identifies the six actions of the hip and then lists all the muscles which perform those actions. Both tables are intended to serve as study guides, but you are encouraged to develop additional guides.

Clusters of Muscles Commonly Used in Dance

There are a number of clusters of actions that frequently occur at the hip joint. The first of these clusters is the *antigravity group*. Remember, gravity is a flexor, adductor, and inward rotator of the hip joint in a normal standing position. Therefore, the antigravity group will include the abductors, extensors, and outward rotators. Text continues on p. 153, after Table 9.4.

TABLE 9.4 Muscles of the Hip

Muscle Name	Proximal Attachment	Distal Attachment	Joint Crossed	Path	Action
Rectus femoris (review)					
Sartorius (review)					
Iliopsoas		Via a common tendon to the lesser trochanter of femur	Hip (whole iliopsoas)	Anterior Medial* Inferior	Flexion Adduction Outward rotation
Iliacus	Iliac fossa				
Psoas major	Transverse processes, bodies and intervertebral disks of the lumbar vertebrae	Psoas minor attaches distally to iliopect-ineal eminence on the ascending ramus†	Lumbar spine (psoas only)	Anterior	Flexion Lateral flexion to same side Hyperextension‡
Psoas minor			Note: The psoas minor does not cross the hip joint.		
(Iliacus is synergistic with pectineus, adductor brevis, longus, and anterior magnus)					
Pectineus	Ascending ramus of pubis on the pectineal crest	Pectineal line of femur (posterior and inferior to the lesser trochanter)	Hip	Anterior Medial Inferior	Flexion Adduction Outward rotation
(Synergistic with iliacus, adductor brevis, longus, and anterior magnus)					
Adductor group					
Adductor brevis	Descending ramus of pubis	Upper part of linea aspera	Hip	Anterior Medial Inferior	Flexion Adduction Outward rotation

TABLE 9.4 (*continued*)

Muscle Name	Proximal Attachment	Distal Attachment	Joint Crossed	Path	Action
(Synergistic with adductor longus)					
Adductor longus	Ascending ramus of pubis	Middle third of linea aspera	Hip	Anterior Medial Inferior	Flexion Adduction Outward rotation
(Synergistic with adductor brevis)					
Adductor magnus§ (anterior and posterior fibers) (Anterior fibers synergistic with adductor longus and brevis)	Descending ramus	Whole length of linea aspera, ending at the adductor tubercle	Hip (anterior, superior fibers) (posterior, inferior fibers)	Anterior Medial Inferior Posterior Medial Inferior	Flexion Adduction Outward rotation Extension Adduction Inward rotation
Gracilis (review)					
Semitendinosus (review)					
Semimembranosus (review)					
Biceps femoris (review)					
Six deep rotators					
Piriformis Obturator internus Superior gemellus	Sacrum and ilium (upper three)‖	Posterior aspect of greater trochanter	Hip	Posterior Lateral Superior	* { Outward rotation Abduction Extension
Obturator externus	Ischium (lower three)‖	Posterior aspect of greater trochanter and below it	Hip	Posterior Medial Inferior	Outward rotation Adduction Extension * {
Inferior gemellus Quadratus femoris					*All actions apply to all three muscles.

Abductor group	Origin	Insertion	Joint		Action
Gluteus minimus	Gluteal fossa, between the anterior and inferior gluteal lines	Anterior surface of the greater trochanter	Hip	Anterior Lateral Superior	Flexion# Abduction Inward rotation#
(Synergistic with tensor fascia lata)					
Gluteus medius	Gluteal, fossa, between the posterior and anterior gluteal lines	Superior and lateral surface of the greater trochanter	Hip (anterior fibers)	Anterior Lateral Superior	Flexion Lateral Abduction Inward rotation
			Hip (posterior fibers)	Posterior Lateral	Extension Abduction
				Superior	Outward rotation
			Hip (all fibers contracting simultaneously)		ABDUCTION (other actions cancel out)
(Anterior fibers synergistic with gluteus minimus, posterior fibers synergistic with anterior gluteus maximus)					
Gluteus maximus	Posterior surface of sacrum and coccyx and gluteal fossa, on the posterior gluteal line	Gluteal tuberosity of the femur and the iliotibial band of the fascia lata (posteriorly)	Hip (superior, anterior fibers)	Posterior Lateral Superior	Extension Abduction Outward rotation
			Hip## (inferior, posterior fibers)	Posterior Medial Inferior	Adduction Extension Outward rotation

(continued)

TABLE 9.4 (*continued*)

Tensor fascia lata	Just lateral to the anterior superior spine of the ilium	Anterior of the iliotibial band of the fascia lata	Hip	Flexion Abduction Inward rotation
(Synergistic with gluteus minimus)				Anterior Lateral Superior

* The iliopsoas "scoops" under the viscera and crosses over the front rim of the pelvis (the ascending rami) and descends laterally to the lesser trochanter, with the psoas minor stopping to attach to the ascending ramus.

† This is a change from the first edition, where the distal attachment of the psoas minor was erroneously listed as the lesser trochanter.

‡ The action of hyperextension is possible only when the extensor muscles of the upper spine are contracting to stabilize the torso. This action of the iliopsoas is sometimes called the "paradox of the iliopsoas."

§ Like other multipennate muscles, the adductor magnus has more than one action at the hip joint, according to the placement of the different fibers. Functionally it divides into two muscles.

‖ The sciatic nerve passes under the piriformis and above the other (lower) five of the six deep rotators.

Posterior fibers may extend and rotate outward.

These fibers are the most efficient for returning to standing from a turn-out *pliá*. They are some times called the "air muscles" (for they get you up into the air), or nicknamed the "goosers."

152

TABLE 9.5 Combined Actions of the Hip Joint and Muscles That Perform Those Actions

Flexion *Adduction* *Outward Rotation*	*Flexion* *Adduction* *Inward Rotation*	*Flexion* *Abduction* *Outward Rotation*	*Flexion* *Abduction* *Inward Rotation*

Iliopsoas
Pectineus
Adductor brevis
 	
Adductor longus
Anterior fibers
  Adductor magnus
Rectus femoris
  (flexion only)
	Gracilis
	
	Rectus femoris
	  (flexion only)
		Sartorius
		
		Rectus femoris
		  (flexion only)
			Tensor fascia lata
			Gluteus minimus
			Anterior gluteus
			  medius
			
			Rectus femoris
			  (flexion only)

Extension *Adduction* *Outward Rotation*	*Extension* *Adduction* *Inward Rotation*	*Extension* *Abduction* *Outward Rotation*	*Extension* *Abduction* *Inward Rotation*

Lower gluteus
  maximus
Lower 3 of the
  6 deep
  rotators
	Semitendinosis
	Semimembranosis
	Posterior fibers
	  Adductor
	  magnus
		Posterior
		  Gluteus
		  medius
		Upper (anterior)
		  gluteus
		  maximus
		Long head of
		  biceps femoris
		Upper 3 of the
		  6 deep rotators
			None

Other clusters of muscles are related to the nature of dance. Flexion, outward rotation, and neutral ab/adduction are common, as in a *grand battement*. Unfortunately, this action has been commonly labeled "extension" by dancers, presumably reflecting the position of the knee joint. Regardless of what dancers call it, the joint *action* is flexion at the hip with outward rotation. The sartorius is critical in this action and may be assisted by other flexor/outward rotators, including a balance of abductors and adductors to maintain the neutral ab/adduction.

Another cluster common in dance is the group used for the arabesque, including extensors and outward rotators. A common problem in performance of arabesque occurs because the gluteus maximus, long head of the biceps, posterior gluteus medius, and upper three of the six deep rotators (all of which are extensors and outward rotators) *also abduct*. A common error in performance is abduction of the moving leg.[3] In order to perform

---

3. The term *working leg* is not used in this text. Frequently the standing leg is working as hard as, or harder than, the so-called "working leg." The terms *moving leg* and *standing leg* will be used.

TABLE 9.6   Isolated Actions and Muscles*

Flexion	Extension	Abduction
Anterior gluteus medius	Posterior adductor magnus	Upper gluteus maximus
Gluteus minimus	Semitendinosus	Gluteus medius
Tensor fascia lata	Semimembranosus	Gluteus minimus
Sartorius	Long head: biceps femoris	Tensor fascia lata
Rectus femoris	Gluteus maximus	Upper 3 of 6 deep rotators
Iliopsoas	6 deep rotators	Sartorius (assist)
Pectineus	Posterior gluteus medius	
Adductor brevis		
Adductor longus		
Anterior adductor magnus		
Gracilis (assist)		

Adduction	Inward rotation	Outward rotation
Iliopsoas	Tensor fascia lata	6 deep rotators
Pectineus	Gluteus minimus	Gluteus maximus
Adductor brevis	Anterior gluteus medius	Posterior gluteus medius
Adductor longus	Gracilis	Long head: biceps femoris
Adductor magnus	Posterior adductor magnus	Sartorius
Semitendinosus	Semitendinosus	Iliopsoas
Semimembranosus	Semimembranosus	Pectineus
Lower fibers: gluteus maximus		Adductor brevis
Lower 3 of 6 deep rotators		Adductor longus
Gracilis		Anterior adductor magnus

*While this table may be of some help, it should not be a primary focus of study. Actions seldom, if ever, occur in isolation. For this reason, Table 9.5 is better for memorization, since it includes the three planes of action.

the arabesque properly, without either abduction or adduction, it is necessary to activate the lower gluteus maximus and lower six deep rotators. If the semitendinosus and semimembranosus are used to correct the abduction, the outward rotators have to work even harder to maintain outward rotation because the "semis" rotate inward. Small wonder that proper performance of the arabesque is difficult.

Still another cluster of muscles commonly used in dance includes the muscles that *stabilize the pelvis and keep it level when the weight is on one leg.* Like a teeter-totter, the pelvis balances on one femur when the weight is on one leg. Since the support structure is so far to one side of the pelvis (one femur) there is a *natural tendency for the supporting hip to adduct.* That is, the weight of the pelvis will drop down on the unsupported side (see Figure 9.10). Two muscle groups contract to stabilize the pelvis in a

(a)

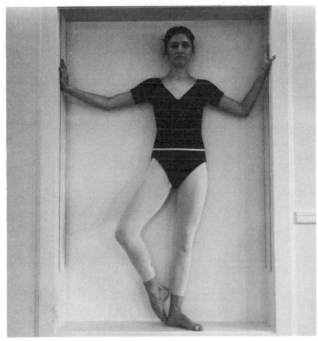

(b)

FIGURE 9.10.   Pelvic alignment with weight on one foot (a) *Wrong:* weight "dumped" into the standing hip with adduction of left hip and left lateral flexion of torso in lumbar region; (b) *Correct:* correction produced by contraction of abductors of left hip and right lateral flexors of torso.

level position when the weight is on one leg: the abductors of the hip on the weight-bearing side and the lateral flexors of the torso on the non-weight-bearing side. Since the lateral flexors of the torso have not yet been presented, this discussion will focus on the muscles of the hip which stabilize (abduct) the standing hip. The gluteus medius is one of the primary abductors of the hip. It is the prime mover in stabilizing the pelvis. Still another factor must be considered: the weight of the moving leg. As the moving leg changes its position, the prime movers of stabilization will adjust to counterbalance the weight. For example, if one is standing with the weight on the left leg and the right leg as the moving leg, the left hip abductors will be the primary stabilizers. When the right hip is flexed (as in a dance "extension"), the weight of the right leg is anterior and the counter-balancing muscle(s) must be posterior. Consequently, in this position, gravity would adduct, flex, and still inwardly rotate the left hip. Counter-acting the action of gravity would require contraction of the abductors, extensors, and outward rotators.[4]

If the right leg is moved to the side (abducted) as in the first section of a *grande ronde jambe,* the primary action of gravity on the left hip will be adduction and the abductors will counteract gravity. As the leg continues in the *grand ronde jambe* and is taken posteriorly, the action of gravity will be to extend the left hip (remember the teeter-totter action) and still adduct. The muscles to counteract that action will be the flexors and abductors of the left hip. In all balances on one leg when the torso is vertical or close to vertical, the abductors of the standing hip must be activated to keep the pelvis level. They are assisted by the lateral flexors of the torso on the un-supported side of the pelvis.

There are many other clusters of muscles commonly used in dance; perhaps these few examples will stimulate you to identify others.

Efficiency of Specific Muscles

Another aspect of analysis of muscular activity at the hip joint is relative efficiency of certain muscles based on their fiber arrangement and whether they are spurt or shunt muscles. For example, in extension of the hip, the hamstrings are most efficient in the "ballpark" of 120 degrees to 180 degrees.[5] The gluteus maximus, however, is more efficient when the femur is closer to a right angle to the pelvis. This makes the hamstrings the prime movers in locomotion on a level surface, but the gluteus max-imus takes over in climbing stairs or a steep hill, or in a deep lunge posi-tion. Of course, if one performs a maximal contraction of the extensors, the "whole team" comes off the bench, but in less-than-maximal contractions there is selection based on mechanical principles of efficiency.

4. Remember that there is also an action of the torso, but this analysis focuses on the hip joints.
5. With 180 degrees being extension of the hip.

PRACTICE DEMONSTRATIONS

Figure 9.11 shows an action of the right hip and a position of the left hip. Analyze the demonstrated action and position in Table 9.7. Check your answers with the key in Table 9.8.

IMPLICATIONS FOR DANCERS

Dance focuses much attention on the hip joint. The implications for dancers have been categorized as (A) muscular imbalances common in dance; and (B) synergistic action of the hip joint and the torso.

(A) FOUR MUSCULAR IMBALANCES OF THE HIP JOINT

Four muscular imbalances are quite common among dancers: (1) tightness and weakness of the abductor muscles; (2) imbalance in strength and mobility between the inward rotators and the outward rotators; (3) tightness of the hip flexors; and (4) imbalance in mobility between the medial and lateral hamstrings. Each of these muscular imbalances can cause performance problems and/or pain for the dancer. Because they are so common in dance, each of these muscular imbalances of the hip will be discussed.

1. *Tight and weak abductor muscles.* The role of the abductor muscles in the stabilization of the pelvis when the weight is on one leg was discussed previously in this chapter. Because in dance the abductor muscles are often called on to counterbalance the pull of gravity at the hip joint, these muscles are the focus for one muscular imbalance at the hip. One would think that, because these muscles are used so frequently by dancers, they would be quite strong, but that is not the case. Actually, most dancers show considerable weakness of the abductors of the hip. To check strength of the abductors, have a dancer lie on his or her side and abduct the top hip (side leg lift) against resistance. The tester presses down with the hand on the side of the dancer's leg as the dancer tries to lift the leg straight up to the side (abduction). Check the relative strength when the hip is rotated outward and parallel. For most dancers there will be a marked imbalance in strength. It is thought that the low-grade contraction required for stabilization of the pelvis in standing on one leg is not sufficient to build strength in the parallel abductors. The almost constant low-grade contraction of the abductors of the hip facilitates inelasticity but does not build strength. Therefore, dancers' abductors are often weak and inelastic. This is thought to be one of the primary causes of "lateral snapping hip." Lateral snapping hip is characterized by the greater trochanter "popping" out to the side when the hip is adducted. Actually, the tightness of the abductor muscles is the primary cause of this phenomenon. Remember that the gluteus medius and gluteus minimus attach to the greater trochanter. When those muscles are tight and the hip is adducted, eventually the greater trochanter slips out from under the gluteals posteriorly and protrudes to the side. Some dancers erroneously call this phenomenon "throwing the hip out of joint." Actually the hip joint remains intact, but the greater trochanter sliding out from under the gluteals makes the lat-

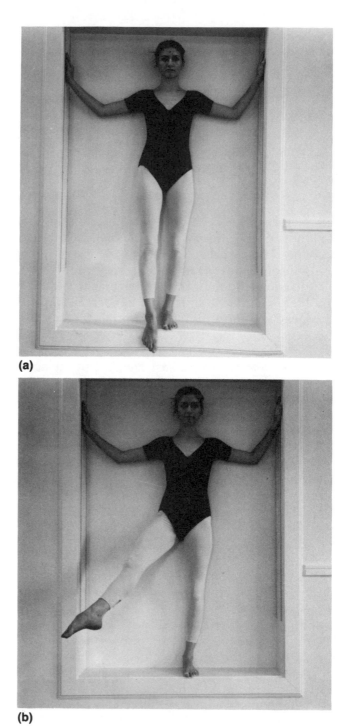

(a)

(b)

FIGURE 9.11. Analyze the action of the right hip from (a) to (b), with gravity at (b).

TABLE 9.7 Demonstration Analysis

Identification	Joint Action	Action of Gravity	Muscle Group and Type of Contraction	Specific Muscles
Right hip				
Left hip				

TABLE 9.8 Analysis of Figure 9.11

Identification	Joint Position or Action	Action of Gravity	Muscle Group and Type of Contraction	Specific Muscles
Right hip	Flexion Abduction Outward rotation	Extension Adduction Inward rotation	Shortening Contraction Flexors Abductors Outward rotators	*Sartorius Iliopsoas Pectineus (also possible: adductor brevis, longus and anterior magnus) Gluteus medius (also possible: tensor fascia lata and gluteus minimus)
Left hip	Maintain Extension Neutral rotation Slight adduction	Flexion Inward rotation Adduction	Static contraction Extensors Abductors Outward rotators	Posterior gluteus medius Anterior (upper) gluteus maximus Upper 3 of the 6 deep rotators Long head of biceps femoris

*No single muscle effectively does all three actions (sartorius only assists in abduction); there are many possible combinations, with only one listed.

160

eral contour appear distorted. Conditioning for this problem should include strengthening and stretching the abductors of the hip. If the muscles are strengthened, fewer motor units will be required to perform the stabilization task. Stretching the muscles will allow the gluteals to stretch when the hip joint is adducted, and while the greater trochanter will still protrude, it won't be forced to pop out from under the muscles. The "snapping" caused when the abductors are inelastic creates an eroding shock to the internal structure of the hip joint which may contribute to the high incidence of arthritic hips among aging dancers. Both stretching and strengthening of the abductors of the hip joint are covered in Chapter 19.

  2. Imbalance between inward and outward rotators. The second muscular imbalance common to dance is the imbalance between the mobility of the inward and outward rotators of the hip joint. Because so much of dance activity is performed with the hip outwardly rotated, the outward rotators get very tight and the inward rotators get very elastic. It is this imbalance of muscular elasticity that causes many dancers to walk "duck-footed." With tight outward rotators, it becomes difficult for the dancer to even approach a neutral position on the transverse plane of the hip joint. Parallel position actually feels inwardly rotated for many dancers. Some dancers may even think that this imbalance is "cute"—at least until they start to experience sciatic syndrome, which is characterized by pain deep in the buttocks and pain radiating down the leg, following the path of the biceps femoris and the peroneal muscles on the lateral side of the leg. It is thought that one of the major causes of sciatic syndrome, and its high incidence among dancers, is the tightness of the outward rotators of the hip joint. The six deep rotators are prime movers in outward rotation of the hip. The sciatic nerve weaves through the six deep rotators, in most cases passing under the upper three and over the lower three. If the six deep rotators are very tight, they can pinch the sciatic nerve and cause intense pain in all of the muscles activated by that nerve. Experiencing the pain of sciatic syndrome once is all it takes to convince a dancer to stretch the outward rotators. Dancers with a natural turnout are more susceptible to sciatic syndrome than dancers who naturally have greater inward rotation, because holding a position of outward rotation allows the six deep rotators to shorten. A common question asked by dancers who have this condition is, "If I stretch my outward rotators and increase my potential to turn in, won't I lose some of my ability to turn out?" The answer is "no," not if you also continue to stretch the inward rotators to maintain the range of motion.[6] Dancers should remember that the hip joint flexes and extends most efficiently in a parallel position. While work in the studio requires almost consistent outward rotation, the dancer should try to utilize the parallel position outside of the studio to more effectively maintain a balance of elasticity between the inward and outward rotators.

6. A study of conditioning for dancers showed that it was possible to increase the range of inward rotation possible at the hip joint without decreasing the potential for outward rotation (Fitt, *Dance Research Journal,* 14/1 and 2, 1981-82).

3. *Tightness of hip flexors, low back pain, bubble buns and thunder thighs, anterior snapping hip.* The third muscular imbalance common among dancers is tight hip flexors. This condition is not so much a function of the demands of dance as it is a function of the consistent use of the seated position in this culture. Tight hip flexors are common in any culture that sits as much as we do. To repeat: muscles will shorten to the joint position which is consistently held. Because we spend so much time sitting, the flexors of the hip joint have ample opportunity to shorten. Then when we stand up, those tight hip flexors (all of which either attach to or cross over the front rim of the pelvis) pull down on the front rim of the pelvis, causing increased pelvic inclination and lumbar lordosis. In an attempt to straighten up, we "grip" with the gluteus maximus to force extension of the hip joint. The tight hip flexors then pull on the femur, forcing the knee to flex slightly. Then we grip with the quadriceps to maintain an extended knee. The gripping with the gluteus maximus and the quadriceps causes hypertrophy (development of muscle bulk) of those muscles. Then the individual not only has tight hip flexors, increased pelvic inclination, and lumbar lordosis, but also has "bubble buns" and "thunder thighs." To add insult to injury, these individuals often experience "low back pain" because of their consistent misalignment of the lumbar spine. It really sounds depressing, doesn't it? Yet the solution to these problems is really quite simple in theory. *Stretch the hip flexors.* I have had remarkable and immediate results with dancers who come into my office with these problems, simply by stretching the hip flexors. Increasing the elasticity of the hip flexors reduces the pull of the front rim of the pelvis and on the femur. The pelvis assumes a position closer to an ideal pelvic alignment, and the stress on the lower back is reduced. One dancer who embarked on a conscientious program of stretching the hip flexors lost one and a half inches from the circumference of her thighs in approximately six weeks. I am not saying that this kind of remarkable result is guaranteed, but reduction of tension in the hip flexors can certainly make the maintenance of an upright position more efficient. Of course not all low back pain can be explained by tight hip flexors. Before starting a stretching program for the hip flexors, a dancer with severe low back pain ought to see an orthopedic surgeon to make sure that there is no problem with the bony structure of the spine.

In some dancers, another problem accompanies the tight hip flexor. Anterior snapping hip is a result of tendons sliding over the ascending ramus with force. The muscles commonly involved in anterior snapping hip may be the iliopsoas, the sartorius, and the rectus femoris. Tightness of any of these muscles can cause anterior snapping when the tight muscle and tendon slide over the uneven superior surface of the ascending ramus. Again, stretching the hip flexors may reduce the occurrence of anterior snapping hip.

4. *Imbalance between medial and lateral hamstrings.* The fourth muscular imbalance common in dance is an imbalance of elasticity between the medial and lateral hamstrings. Most dancers exhibit remarkable elasticity of the semitendinosus and semimembranosus. This mobility comes from

all of the intensive stretching done in stride position and in seated second position, with the hip abducted during the stretch. Because of the common positions used for stretching the hamstrings, which incorporate an abducted position of the hip joint, the biceps femoris is stretched less often than the semitendinosus and semimembranosus. Stretches for the hamstrings should be performed in three different positions of the hip. Flexion in parallel position of the hip joint (no rotation, no ab/adduction) will moderately stretch all of the hamstrings. Stretching with the hip flexed, abducted, and rotated outward will focus the stretch on the semitendinosus and semimembranosus because their actions are extension, adduction, and inward rotation. Stretching in a position of flexion, adduction, and inward rotation will focus the stretch on the biceps femoris, since its actions are extension, abduction, and outward rotation. Once again, each of these positions should be utilized in stretching the hamstrings. Remember, the knee must be extended in all hamstring stretches.

These four muscular imbalances (tightness and weakness of the abductors of the hip; imbalance between the elasticity of the inward and outward rotators; tightness of the hip flexors; and imbalance of mobility between medial and lateral hamstrings) are all quite common in dance, and are also covered in Chapter 13 (muscular imbalances) and in Chapter 19 (conditioning).

(B) SYNERGISTIC ACTION BETWEEN HIP JOINT AND TORSO

There is a functional interface between the actions of the hip and the actions of the torso. In order to facilitate movement of the leg, the muscles of the torso contract to stabilize the pelvis. Remembering that muscles contract in the center and pull on both attachments equally, unless there is stabilization of one of the levers, gives us the reason for the functional interface between the torso and the hip joint. For example, efficient flexion of the hip joint (as in a dance "extension") requires contraction of the anterior torso muscles to stabilize the front rim of the pelvis. A common error in performance of a dance "extension" occurs because the hip flexors pull the pelvis forward into an increased inclination, hyperextending the lumbar spine at the same time as they pull the femur into a flexed position. Let's get one thing straight right now. *The hamstrings do not flex the hip in a dance "extension."* Muscles only pull; they do not push. There is simply no way that the hamstrings can contract to cause a dance "extension." Yet many teachers of dance have said that the hamstrings do the work of a dance "extension." When I first encountered this obvious error, I thought, "How stupid; the hamstrings just can't do it." I puzzled over this blatant error because I know that teachers of dance *are not stupid folk.* As I took the analysis a step further, I realized that, in the studio, the dance teacher experiments with techniques to obtain proper performance. In the process of correcting the common misperformance in dance "extensions," the teachers must have sensed a "down in back" sensation and equated it with contraction of the hamstrings. Actually, that sensation was caused by an "up in front" contraction of the abdominals to stabilize the pelvis. When the abdominals are contracted, the front rim of the pelvis is held stable as the hip flexors contract to lift the leg (hip flexion). Because one lever is stabilized, the contractile force provided by the hip flexors is all applied to the moving lever, the femur; and the action seems remarkably easier than when the abdominals are not contracted. Because the pelvis is a solid unit, pulling up on the front with the abdominals causes the posterior of the pelvis to drop down, like a rocking bowl, and that downward sensation may have originally been interpreted as contraction of the hamstrings. I have included this puzzle for a specific reason. Teachers of dance, in the past, have not had the benefit of kinesiological training. They have found practical solutions to practical problems in the dance studio. Then, using limited anatomical knowledge, they have explained the phenomenon incorrectly. That does not mean that the solution is wrong—only that the explanation is in error. My experience with the puzzle of the hamstrings causing hip flexion made me realize that it is frequently necessary not to make hasty judgments, but rather to take the analysis a step further to get beyond an erroneous explanation and get to an accurate, practical solution. This is thought to be an important perspective for all kinesiologists dealing with dancers, and it is equally important for students of dance who are simultaneously studying kinesiology. When there is a marked discrepancy between the information presented in the studio and the information presented in kinesiology class, the student is encouraged to take the analysis a step further to try to find the principle underlying the apparent error.

The functional interface between the torso and the hip joint is also found in the arabesque. From the material on the skeletal system, we know that the hip joint cannot hyperextend. An arabesque combines action of the hip joint and the lumbar spine to get the leg back behind the body in a position of "hyperextension." Actually, the hip joint is extended to its full range (usually about 170 to 180 degrees). The remainder of the action is performed in the lumbar spine with hyperextension of that area. Strength of the muscles of the lower back is critical for accurate performance of the arabesque. Short-waisted individuals may have difficulty with the arabesque because the ribs may actually come into contact with the crest of the ilium, as the lumbar spine hyperextends. Another obvious restriction of the arabesque may be tight hip flexors, discussed above. The torso and the hip joint work together to allow proper performance of the arabesque.

Another functional interface between the torso and the hip joint has an effect on the relative mobility of the two regions. I call this the *mobility gradient,* since there seems to be an inverse relationship between the mobility of the hip joint and the mobility of the torso for many dancers. Excessive mobility in the spine (particularly in flexion, but also in other actions) reduces the stretch required at the hip joint in most stretching exercises. For example, the standard seated hamstring stretch may show only mobility of the spine, with very little actual flexion of the hip occurring if the spine is very mobile. Conversely, if the hip joint is very mobile, the demands on the extensors of the spine are reduced. Any stretch should focus separately on both the hip joint and spine, and dancers should become aware of the specific limitations that might exist in their overall mobility and adjust the stretch to those needs. Stretching with a "flat back" can focus the stretch on the hamstrings. To effectively stretch the torso's posterior muscles usually requires other stretches for dancers. These are included in Chapter 19.

CHAPTER 10

Muscles of the Torso and the Neck

Functionally, the spine can be divided into two sections for the purpose of muscular analysis: the torso and the neck. The torso includes the lumbar and thoracic sections of the spine; the neck is, obviously, the cervical region. Some muscles, like the erector spinae and the deep posterior muscles, run the entire length of the spine and have the same actions throughout. But the abdominal muscles run up only as far as the rib cage and therefore have no effect on the cervical spine. With one exception, the muscles of the neck also have no direct effect on either the thoracic spine or the lumbar spine. For these reasons, and for easier muscular analysis, I have divided the spine into the two sections called *torso* and *neck*. There are also muscles which act directly on the rib cage in the thoracic region. Those muscles will be covered in Chapter 14. Following the pattern established throughout the text, the lower section (the torso) will be presented first, followed by the neck.

Muscles of the Torso

Table 10.1 presents the attachments and actions of the muscles of the torso. Figures 10.1–10.5 illustrate these muscles.

Reviewing the actions possible at the torso, we remember that, on the sagittal plane, flexion, extension, and hyperextension are possible when the lumbar and thoracic regions are combined. Lateral flexion to the right and to the left are the possible actions on the frontal plane. Rotation to the right and to the left are the movements possible on the transverse plane (occurring primarily in the thoracic region).

The muscles of the torso, with one exception, are classified as anterior or posterior muscles (see Figures 10.1–10.5). Anterior on the torso are all of the flexor muscles, the abdominals (Figure 10.1), including the transversalis, the internal obliques, the external obliques, and the rectus abdominis. The pyramidalis muscle (Figure 10.2) is also on the anterior of the torso (below the umbilicus—the belly button). It is a very small muscle (and actually absent in some individuals) and is seldom mentioned in kinesiology textbooks because of its limited action. Yet it is an important

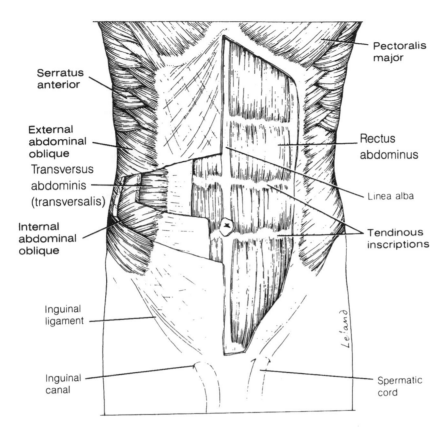

Serratus anterior

External abdominal oblique

Transversus abdominis (transversalis)

Internal abdominal oblique

Inguinal ligament

Inguinal canal

Pectoralis major

Rectus abdominus

Linea alba

Tendinous inscriptions

Spermatic cord

FIGURE 10.1.   **Abdominals including rectus abdominus, internal obliques, external obliques, and transversalis**

muscle for dance and is often quite developed in skilled dancers. The psoas, presented with the muscles of the hip (see Figure 9.7), is anterior to the spine but can serve as either a flexor or a hyperextensor of the lumbar spine (iliopsoas paradox, discussed later in this chapter).

Posterior on the torso are the extensor muscles, including the erector spinae, the semispinalis (thoracic region of the torso only), and the deep posterior muscles. This listing of the extensor muscles of the spine is deceptively simple, noting only three muscle groups. But the key word is *groups*. The erector spinae includes three sections: the iliocostalis, the longissimus, and the spinalis (see Figure 10.3). The deep posterior muscles include the multifidus, the rotatores, the interspinalis, and the intertransversarius (see Figure 10.4). The semispinalis muscle, which extends into the neck region, has three sections: the capitis, the cervicis, and the thoracis (see Figure 10.8—included with muscles of the neck). The clustering of the muscles into three major groups reduces the amount of memorization required and simplifies the process of analysis. While some specificity is lost by clustering, the benefits of simplicity outweigh this loss.

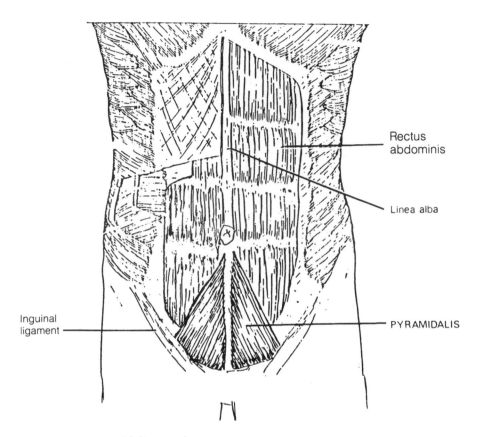

FIGURE 10.2.   Pyramidalis muscle

The one exception to the anterior-posterior grouping of the muscles of the torso, referred to earlier, is the quadratus lumborum (Figure 10.5). It is a lateral muscle and, because of its attachments and action, can be classified as neither a flexor nor an extensor, although it stabilizes the lumbar spine in both positions.

There are duplicate sets of each of the muscles of the torso and the neck on the right and the left sides of the body. That seems rather obvious to some of you, but to others it will clear up some confusion. You might be surprised at how many times I have been asked whether these muscles are present on both the right and the left. The muscles on the right side will contract to produce lateral flexion to the right, and the muscles on the left will contract to produce lateral flexion to the left. Anteriorly, the right and the left sides are separated by a connective tissue junction called the *linea alba* (a little like a "connective tissue seam" down the front of the abdominal wall from sternum to pubis). The division of labor is not nearly so clear for the rotation. Many of the muscles of the torso cross diagonally to assist in rotation. Whether they rotate to the same side (i.e., right internal obliques rotating the torso to the right) or the opposite side (i.e., right external obliques rotating the torso to the left) depends on the relationship of the attachments. In some cases, the lower attachment is more lateral

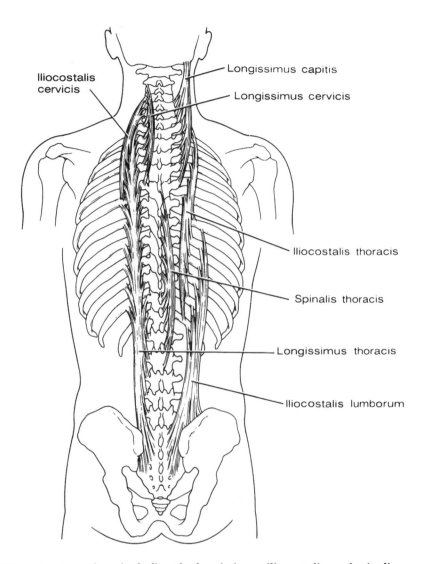

FIGURE 10.3.   Erector spinae including the longissimus, iliocostalis, and spinalis
THESE MUSCLES OVERLAP AND LAYER TO FORM THE LONGITUDINAL MUSCLE BULK ON EITHER
SIDE OF THE SPINE.

and the upper attachment is more medial. In other cases, the relationship
of the attachments is reversed. It is this diagonal path of the muscles of
the torso that produces rotation to either the same side or the opposite
side.

The clustering of the muscles of the torso makes identification of the
use of specific muscles relatively easy—except when we get to rotation
provided by extensor muscles. Some fibers on the right of the torso rotate
to the right, while others on the right rotate to the left. Rather than memo-
rizing all of the infinitely small fibers of the extensor muscles, I have
found that it is adequate, for the purposes of dance kinesiology, to say sim-

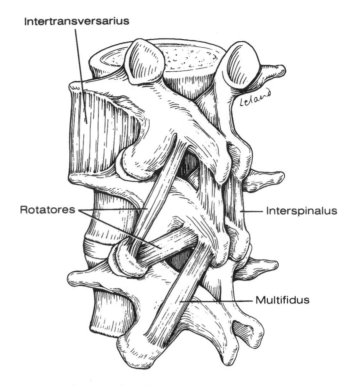

FIGURE 10.4.   Deep posterior muscles of the spine

ply "right rotation fibers of the erector spinae" (or of the deep posterior muscles). For example: turning the shoulders to face the left is a joint action involving a maintenance of extension and active rotation to the left. (Remember that gravity is a flexor of the spine in an upright position.) This would require a static contraction of the extensor muscles (extension

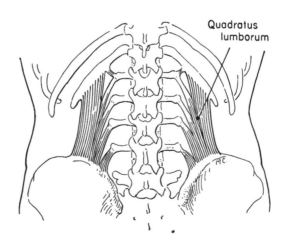

FIGURE 10.5.   Quadratus lumborum

TABLE 10.1 Muscles of the Torso

NOTE: Reference to "same side" or "opposite side" implies "the side muscle is on."

Muscle	Proximal Attachment	Distal Attachment	Joint Crossed	Path	Action
Erector spinae					
The erector spinae is a complex system of muscles arising from the lower portion of the back; as it rises, it splits into three sections: iliocostalis, longissimus, and spinalis. The specific attachments are more complicated than they are worth, since the erector spinae have the same action through the torso and the neck.					
Iliocostalis					
Longissimus					
Spinalis			Torso	Posterior Lateral	Extension Lateral flexion (one side only) Rotation*
			Neck	Posterior Lateral	Extension Lateral flexion (one side only) Rotation*
Deep posterior muscles					
The deep posterior muscles include the complex network of the small muscles running from vertebra to vertebra, specifically, multifidus, rotatores, interspinalis, and intertransversarius. As with the erector spinae, the actions remain constant throughout the torso and neck regions.					
Multifidus					
Rotatores					
Interspinalis					
Intertransversarius			Torso and neck	Posterior Lateral	Extension Lateral flexion (one side only) Rotation (to either side depending on fibers)

(continued)

TABLE 10.1 (*continued*)

Muscle	Proximal Attachment	Distal Attachment	Joint Crossed	Path	Action
Semispinalis	Transverse processes thoracic and seventh cervical vertebra	Spinous processes of the second cervical through the fourth thoracic vertebrae and the occipital bone	Upper torso (thoracic)	Posterior from low lateral to high medial	Extension Lateral flexion (one side) Rotation to the opposite side
			Neck (cervical)	Posterior from low lateral to high medial	Extension Lateral flexion (one side) Rotation to the opposite side
Abdominals <u>Transversalis†</u>	Lumbodorsal fascia, last six ribs (post), inguinal ligament, and iliac crest	Linea alba and anterior half of iliac crest	Torso	Wraps from posterior to anterior like a "waist cincher"	Pulls the abdominal wall back into visceral cavity the (cinches the waist)
Internal obliques	Inguinal ligament, iliac crest, and lumbodorsal fascia	Linea alba and lower 4 ribs	Torso	Go from low lateral to high medial, anteriorly	Flexion Lateral flexion (one side) Rotation to the same side

Muscle					Action
External obliques	External surface of the lower 8 ribs	Linea alba and anterior half of iliac crest	Torso	Go from low medial to high lateral, anteriorly	Flexion Lateral flexion (one side) Rotation to the opposite side
Rectus abdominus	Pubic crest	Xiphoid process of sternum and costal cartilages of ribs 5 through 7	Torso	Runs straight up the front, on either side of the linea alba	Flexion Lateral flexion (one side)
Pyramidalis	Pubic crest	Linea alba below the umbilicus	Lumbar region of torso	Anterior, like a reverse pubic hair triangle	Flexion (lift and stabilize the front rim of the pelvis)
Quadratus lumborum	Iliac crest and iliolumbar ligament	Inferior border of twelfth rib and transverse processes of the upper lumbar	Torso (lumbar region)	Like "guy wires" for the lumbar spine Lateral	Lateral flexion (one side) Stabilize lumbar spine through flexion, extension and hyperextension (both sides)

Psoas major and minor (review)

*The rotation action of the erector spinae can either be to the same side as the muscle is on or to the opposite side, depending on the fibers which are activated.
†Also called *transversus abdominus* by some authorities.

173

fibers of erector spinae, deep posterior muscles and semispinalis) and a shortening contraction of the left rotators (left rotation fibers of the erector spinae and the deep posterior muscles, and the right side of the semispinalis).

When rotation of the torso is accompanied by flexion of the torso, as in the first half of a left-twisting sit-up, we can identify the specific rotation muscles. Lying on the back (supine) means that gravity will be an extensor. Therefore, the joint action of flexion and rotation to the left is produced by a shortening contraction of the flexors and left rotators (the rectus abdominus, the left internal oblique, and the right external oblique).

The identification of specific muscles producing lateral flexion to the right or left and the identification of specific muscles producing flexion, extension, and hyperextension are not nearly so complicated as the identification of muscles for rotation.

The analysis of the action of gravity is actually the trickiest part of muscular analysis of the torso. Consequently, in identifying the proper muscle group—which depends on accurate identification of the action of gravity—mistakes can easily be made. Let us take the example of slow lateral flexion to the left (straight to the left) from a vertical position. Once the torso is off center, gravity will cause the lateral flexion to the left and the muscle group and type of contraction will be a lengthening contraction of the *right lateral flexors*. Also, the maintenance of extension (going straight to the side) requires a static contraction of the erector spinae, deep posterior muscles, and semispinalis.

PRACTICE DEMONSTRATIONS

Two practice demonstrations are included in this section. The first is a simple analysis of the torso (see Figure 10.6). Table 10.2 is blank for you to fill in to check your comprehension of the information. Table 10.3 shows accurate analysis of Figure 10.6. Figure 10.7 is a demonstration that focuses on both the hip joint and the torso. It is included to illustrate the interface between the hip and torso. Tables 10.4 and 10.5 are for analysis of Figure 10.7.

In addition to these demonstrations and the previous discussions of the action of the torso muscles, four specific muscles deserve special attention, not because they are more important than the other muscles in producing action of the torso, but because their exact placements and actions may still be unclear. Those four muscles are the transversalis, the pyramidalis, the quadratus lumborum, and the psoas.

The *transversalis* attaches to the posterior connective tissue, wraps around the viscera like a waist cincher, and attaches to the linea alba with fingers of connective tissue that attach to the rectus abdominus. It is thought that the transversalis functions to pull the abdominal muscles farther into the abdominal cavity in an action like a "Graham contraction."[1] Unfortunately, the transversalis muscle is not automatically activated

1. Martha Graham developed a technique (*Graham technique*) for training modern dancers. One component of that technique is the Graham contraction.

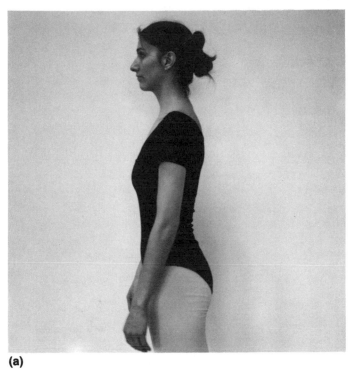

(a)

(b)

FIGURE 10.6. Analyze the action of the torso from (*a*) to (*b*), with gravity at (*b*).

TABLE 10.2   Analysis of Figure 10.6

Identification	Joint Action	Action of Gravity	Muscle Group and Type of Contraction	Specific Muscles
Torso				

TABLE 10.3 Analysis of Figure 10.6

Identification	Joint Position or Action	Action of Gravity	Muscle Group and Type of Contraction	Specific Muscles
Torso (from a to b)	Flexion	Flexion	Lengthening Contraction of extensors	R and L erector spinae R and L deep posterior muscles R and L semispinalis

(a)

(b)

FIGURE 10.7. Analyze the action of torso and hips from (*a*) to (*b*), with gravity at (*a*).

TABLE 10.4 Analysis of Figure 10.7

Identification	Joint Action	Action of Gravity	Muscle Group and Type of Contraction	Specific Muscles
Torso (from a to b)				
Hip (from a to b)				

TABLE 10.5 Analysis of Figure 10.7

Identification	Joint Position or Action	Action of Gravity	Muscle Group and Type of Contraction	Specific Muscles
Torso	Extension	Flexion	Shortening contraction of extensors	Erector spinae Deep posterior muscles Semispinalis
Hips	Flexion Maintain neutral ab/ad and neutral rotation	Extension (dump back into coccyx)	Shortening contraction of flexors	Iliopsoas* Rectus femoris Possible assistance from pectineus, adductor group, tensor fascia lata, and gluteus minimus if iliopsoas and rectus are too weak.

*Can also contribute to hyperextension of lumbar region because of attachment on anterior of lumbar vertebrae.

180

when the other abdominal muscles contract. Conscious activation is necessary to strengthen and tone the transversalis. The abdominal "hollowing" action of the transversalis was first described to me by Dr. John Wilson of the University of Arizona.

The *pyramidalis* muscle[2] also must be consciously activated. When this muscle is discussed (which is seldom), the action is usually recorded as "tightening the linea alba." However, if it can pull down on the linea alba, it can also pull up on the front rim of the pelvis. When strength and muscle tone are built in this muscle it is thought that it can assist in the stabilization of the front rim of the pelvis without activating so much of the abdominal wall. This allows for greater freedom of movement (less "lockjaw") while still stabilizing the front of the pelvis to make hip flexor contraction more efficient.

The *quadratus lumborum*, because of the fingerlike attachments (interdigitations) to the transverse processes of the lower vertebrae, serves as a set of "guy wires" for the lower torso. With the guy wires on the sides of the spine, the muscle allows free movement from front to back, making flexion, extension, and hyperextension possible but providing lateral stabilization of the lower torso in all of those actions. In addition to its lateral stabilization role, the quadratus lumborum also serves as a prime mover for lateral flexion of the torso, and contributes to stabilization of the pelvis when the weight is on one leg.

The *psoas* (including the psoas major and psoas minor) is the portion of the iliopsoas that attaches to the lumbar spine on the anterior of the bodies of the vertebrae, the transverse processes, and the disks between the vertebrae. Because it is anterior, it theoretically has the potential for contributing to flexion of the lumbar spine, but that is possible only when the erector spinae and deep posterior muscles are not activated to maintain a vertical position. With stabilization of the upper spine by the erector spinae and deep posterior muscles, the psoas pulls the lumbar spine forward while the upper spine remains stable, resulting in hyperextension of the lower torso. For the psoas to act exclusively on the hip joint, stabilization of the pelvis by contraction of the abdominals and pyramidalis is necessary. This is particularly true of a seated position, which makes the psoas a critical muscle for assisting the seated dancer who is trying to "get up on the sit bones" (see Figure 10.7). Essentially, the hyperextension of the lower torso is actually caused by a flexion of the hip, with the pelvis serving as the moving lever, and the femur and the upper spine being stabilized. Tightness of the hamstrings can also restrict the action, because hip flexion is a central aspect of the action.

The iliacus was discussed in Chapter 9, and we have just completed a brief discussion of the psoas. I think this is the place for my "iliopsoas disclaimer." The iliopsoas is, admittedly an important and complex muscle whose contraction has an effect on both the hip joint and the lumbar

2. At the University of Utah, the pyramidalis has been nicknamed "Carol's Muscle." It was questioning by Carol Warner that forced me to search the anatomy books until I found it, and subsequently theorized about its function based on Carol's kinesthetic awareness.

spine. It is particularly important to dancers because its contraction produces both flexion and outward rotation of the hip joint. Moreover, its contraction can kinesthetically heighten the awareness of "center." But the iliopsoas is not the answer to every question asked about the function of the hip joint and the lumbar spine. It is, after all, a combination of three muscles. If it could do all that it is purported to do in some dance studios, it would have at least forty-five attachments. Listening to some teachers of dance, one would think that the iliopsoas could perform a triple pirouette all by itself. While it is an important muscle for dancers, it is not the answer to every dance problem. Nevertheless, with the correction of the distal attachment of the psoas minor in this second edition of *Dance Kinesiology* (see Table 9.4), I must admit having made an error regarding the potential action of the iliopsoas. In the first edition, the distal attachment of the psoas minor was listed as the lesser trochanter of the femur. I was wrong. The psoas minor actually attaches to the iliopectineal eminence of the ascending ramus of the pubis. This may seem like an inconsequential change, but it is not. Before the change, there was no way that the psoas could contribute to the upward stabilization of the front rim of the pelvis. The correct attachment on the front rim of the pelvis adds the potential action of lifting the front rim of the pelvis. For years, Bill Evans and I have disputed the potential action of the psoas. Now I must say, "I was wrong, Bill. The psoas minor can stabilize the front rim of the pelvis." But the psoas major cannot.

IMPLICATIONS FOR DANCERS

Strength and mobility of the torso are critical for dancers. The concept of motion starting "from the center" is more than an aesthetic ideal; it is an anatomical necessity. Specifically, the torso region must be stabilized for efficient use of the muscles of the hip joint. In some cases the muscles of the torso are directly involved in the performance of dance skills, such as the arabesque. In other cases, the musculature of the torso contracts to stabilize the pelvis, as in the case of a dance "extension." Whether the torso is directly or indirectly involved in the performance of a movement combination, the fact remains: *movement does start at the center.* If the muscles of the torso are weak, a galaxy of compensations must be made—such as recruiting other muscles to aid in the task. The torso conditioning sequence (included in Chapter 19) is designed to provide dancers with the torso strength required to meet the demands of dance. Many conditioning programs focus on building the strength of the abdominals, but few focus on the strength of both anterior and posterior rotators, and even fewer focus on building strength in the lateral flexors. The conditioning program in Chapter 19 is designed to give equal attention to all of these muscle groups.

While most dance conditioning programs include building strength and muscular endurance in the abdominal region, the programs do not always approach that conditioning from a kinesiologically sound basis. Sit-ups are frequently used to build strength. Yet two-thirds of sit-ups are performed by the hip flexors. Frequently sit-ups are done rapidly, and then the "bouncing off the floor" provides momentum so that the abdominals (active in the first third of a sit-up) are only minimally contracted. It is also thought that "crunches," as practiced in spas across the country, are not as valuable as slow abdominal curls for isolating the abdominals through the full range of contraction. I have seen no research on the respective effects of the two types of abdominal strengthening exercises. Until I do, I tend to stick with recommending the curls, performed at varying tempos. In abdominal curls, the hip flexors become considerably less efficient, and consequently more is demanded of the abdominals, if the knees are bent and the feet placed on the floor closer to the buttocks. It is my contention that five abdominal curls, done slowly through the difficult range of motion with knees bent, will build more strength in the abdominals than 25 sit-ups. However, this hypothesis has not been documented through research at this point.

Another exercise that was often done in the past to build strength in the abdominals was the double leg lift. This exercise is actually dangerous and is only indirectly effective for building strength of the abdominals. One of the prime movers for the double leg lift is the iliopsoas (hip flexor). The abdominals are activated only to stabilize the pelvis to make the iliopsoas more efficient. A much more direct route to strengthening the abdominals is the use of abdominal curls, where the demand is directly on the abdominals. Moreover, the specific attachment of the psoas muscles on the front of the lumbar vertebrae *and the disks between,* makes the double leg lift potentially dangerous because the powerful contraction of the psoas can pull the disks forward. Thus, double leg lifts can actually *cause* a herniated disk in the lumbar region. This is particularly true if the abdominals are weak and cannot adequately stabilize the pelvis during the exercise. As a rule, I would recommend against the use of double leg lifts. The potential benefits are simply not worth the risk of a low back injury.

Dancers are often advised, in any exercise designed to strengthen the abdominals, not to "bunch the muscles." We know from the discussion of the sarcomere, actin, and myosin in Chapter 7 that *contraction of a muscle always requires "bunching."* Every muscle "bunches" when the actin is pulled in to the center of the sarcomere. It is impossible to contract the abdominals without bunching the muscles. The question is, or should be, Where do you put your bunch? Simultaneous contraction of the transversalis, accompanying abdominal contractions, will pull the abdominals back toward the spine, thus giving the "scooped-out" look which is desirable in dance. Dancers should be encouraged to actively contract the transversalis during abdominal curls, since it will not automatically be activated. However, exhalation during contraction can facilitate activation of the transversalis during an abdominal curl. Another muscle that must be consciously activated during abdominal curls is the pyramidalis.

To build strength in the pyramidalis, the dancer must first kinesthetically find where it is. One of the ways that I have found to locate the pyramidalis is effective, if not very refined. The dancers lie on the floor in the hook position (on their backs, knees bent, and feet on the floor in alignment with the centers of the hip joints); they are directed to contract the abdominals to press the lower back down to the floor; they are then instructed to imagine that they are stopping a stream of urine. The isolated compression in the lower abdominal region, below the belly button, is the contraction of the pyramidalis. Once the dancer has "found" the pyramidalis, he or she must consciously contract it during curls to build strength. The next step is using the pyramidalis to assist in the stabilization of the front rim of the pelvis in a standing position.

The final implication for dancers related to the torso muscles is to deal with the stabilization of the pelvis when the weight is on one leg. This discussion was begun in Chapter 9 with the identification of hip muscles involved in stabilization. You will remember that the muscles of the hip that contribute to maintenance of a level pelvis when the weight is on one leg are the abductors of the standing hip. On the unsupported side, stabilization is provided by the lateral torso muscles. Specifically, the internal obliques and the quadratus lumborum are involved in lateral stabilization of the pelvis. These two muscles are effective in the task of laterally stabilizing the pelvis because of their respective attachments to the ilium. They serve as the "skyhooks" which pull the unsupported side of the pelvis up, from above. Students often find it fascinating to feel these muscles at work. Place your hands on your iliac crests, with your thumbs toward the spine. Walk with the hands in this position, and you will feel the lateral torso muscles contracting, alternating right and left as you walk. In practice, the combined efforts of the abductors of the standing (supported side) hip joint and the lateral flexors of the torso on the unsupported side of the pelvis result in the maintenance of a level pelvis when the weight is on one leg. Grading the amount of contraction to exactly what is needed to keep the pelvis horizontal is sometimes difficult for beginners. In beginning stages of dance training, it is common to find the students either "dumped into the standing hip" (no stabilization contraction initiated), or standing with the unsupported hip too high (too much activation of the stabilizing muscles). It takes some time, and periodic feedback from the instructor or from mirrors, to register exactly how much contraction is needed to keep the pelvis level.

Muscles of the Neck

Table 10.6 lists the muscles of the neck. Some muscles of the neck have been excluded from this list, but the major muscles are included. Figures 10.8–10.11 illustrate the muscles of the neck.

The skeletal structure of the neck allows great freedom of movement, and possible actions include flexion, extension, hyperextension, lateral flexion, and rotation. It is the musculature of the neck that stabilizes the head atop the cervical spine. Following the pattern established for the torso, the anterior muscles will flex the neck, the posterior muscles will extend/hyperextend, and the lateral muscles will laterally flex the neck. Specific rotary action again depends on the placement of the two attachments of the individual muscles. Three muscles of the torso extend up into the neck region: the erector spinae, the deep posterior muscles, and the

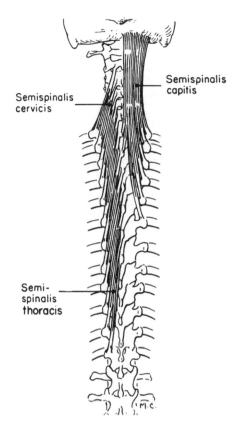

Semispinalis capitis

Semispinalis cervicis

Semi-spinalis thoracis

FIGURE 10.8.   Semispinalis

semispinalis (Figure 10.8). Added to those muscles are the three scaleni (Figure 10.9), the sternocleidomastoid (Figure 10.10), and the two spleni (Figure 10.11).

Analysis of actions of the neck is similar in procedure to analysis of actions of the torso, and the same problems present themselves. The head performs a tricky balancing act on the spine, and gravity (in a normal upright position) will flex the neck. However, as soon as the head is moved off center, gravity will cause or facilitate that action.

PRACTICE DEMONSTRATION

Figure 10.12 shows two actions of the neck from a neutral position. Table 10.7 is for practice analysis, and Table 10.8 is the key.

IMPLICATIONS FOR DANCERS

Many dancers seem to carry excessive tension in the muscles of the neck. This may be due to the frequent balancing of the weight of the head in an off-center position. It may also be due to simultaneous contraction of antagonistic muscles of the scapula, which is demanded in dance. Attention is given to this problem in Chapter 19.

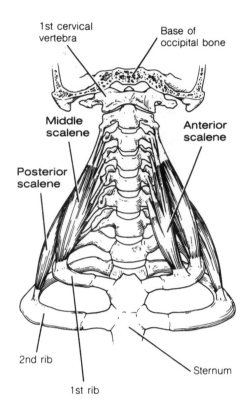

1st cervical vertebra

Base of occipital bone

Middle scalene

Anterior scalene

Posterior scalene

2nd rib

1st rib

Sternum

FIGURE 10.9. The three scaleni muscles

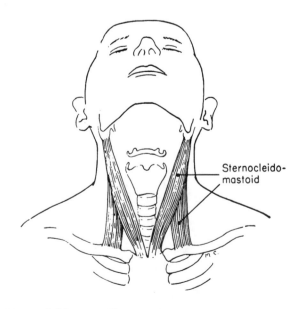

Sternocleido-mastoid

FIGURE 10.10. Sternocleidomastoid

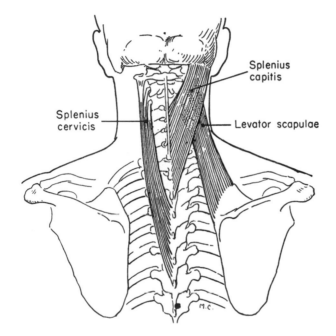

FIGURE 10.11.   Spleni muscles (splenius cervicis and splenius capitis) and levator scapulae. (Although the levator scapulae is a muscle that acts primarily on the scapula, this illustration shows it with posterior neck muscles.)

TABLE 10.6 Muscles of the Neck

Muscle	Proximal Attachment	Distal Attachment	Joint Crossed	Path	Action
Erector spinae (review)					
Deep posterior muscles (review)					
Sternocleidomastoid	By two heads to medial clavicle and the sternum	Mastoid process of temporal bone	Neck	Wrapping from high posterior to low anterior	Flexion Lateral flexion (one side) Rotation to opposite side*
Three scaleni	Transverse processes of cervical vertebrae	Upper two ribs	Neck	Anterior Section	Flexion Lateral flexion (one side) Rotation to opposite side*
				Middle Section	Lateral flexion (one side)
	When all three scaleni contract simultaneously, the resultant action is lateral flexion			Posterior Section	Lateral flexion (one side) Extension Rotation to same side
Two spleni Splenius cervicus Splenius capitus	Spinous processes of the seventh cervical and upper thoracic vertebrae and the ligamentum nuchae	Occipital bone, mastoid process of the temporal bone, and transverse processes of the upper three cervical vertebrae	Neck	From low medial to high lateral	Extension Lateral flexion (one side) Rotation to same side
Semispinalis (review)					

*Reminder: *opposite side* means opposite to the side the muscle is on.

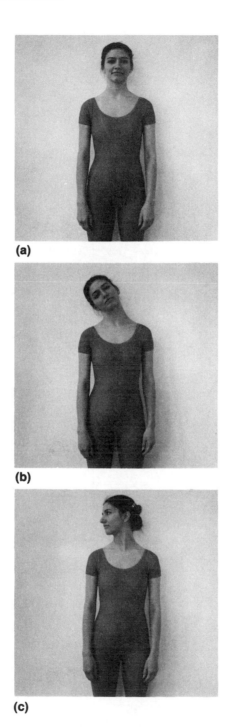

(a)

(b)

(c)

FIGURE 10.12. Analyze the action of the neck from (a) to (b) with gravity at (b); and from (a) to (c) with gravity at (c).

TABLE 10.7 Practice Analysis of Figure 10.12

Identification	Joint Action	Action of Gravity	Muscle Group and Type of Contraction	Specific Muscles
Neck from (a) to (b)				
from (a) to (c)				

TABLE 10.8 Analysis of Figure 10.12

Identification	Joint Position or Action	Action of Gravity	Muscle Group and Type of Contraction	Specific Muscles
Neck or from (a) to (b)	Lateral flexion to right Maintain extension	Lateral flexion to right flexion (possibly slight rotation to right)	Following a brief contraction by right lateral flexors to initiate the action, lengthening contraction of left lateral flexors Static contraction of extensors (and possibly left rotators)	Right scaleni (all 3 just middle) Left scaleni (posterior rotates to left) Left erector spinae Left deep posterior Left erector muscles Left spleni (also rotate to left) Not left sternocleidomastoid, because it flexes
Neck from (a) to (c)*	Rotation to right Maintain extension Perhaps slight right lateral flexion	Rotation to left Flexion Slight right lateral flexion	Shortening contraction of right rotators Static contraction of extensors Initial shortening contraction of right lateral flexors, followed by static contraction of left lateral flexors	Right spleni Right posterior scaleni Erector spinae* Deep posterior muscles* Left semispinalis Right rotation fibers*

*If there is lateral flexion, right lateral flexion would require recruitment of the right side of the erector spinae and deep posterior muscles, and less activity from the left semispinalis. A static contraction of the left lateral flexors would recruit the left side of the erector spinae and deep posterior muscles and recruit less from the right spleni and right posterior scaleni.

CHAPTER 11

Muscles of the Scapula and the Shoulder

Muscles of the Scapula

Technically, all of the muscles attached to the scapula have the potential for creating an action of the scapula. However, only those also attached to the supporting structure (the spine) are included in this chapter. Muscles that cross the shoulder joint and attach to the humerus are included as muscles of the shoulder, since their primary action is there.

As a review, the scapula has seven and a half possible actions: elevation, depression, adduction, abduction, upward rotation, downward rotation, forward tilt, and (half action) return from forward tilt.

Starting from the deepest of the muscles of the scapula and moving toward the surface, we find the *rhomboids* and *levator scapulae* on the posterior of the spine. The *pectoralis minor* and the *subclavius* are deep muscles on the anterior of the rib cage. The *serratus anterior* is a deep lateral muscle. Superficially, on the posterior aspect, the *trapezius* is a large flaring muscle which is divided into three major sections: upper, middle, and lower. Table 11.1 lists the attachments of the muscles of the scapula. Figures 11.1 and 11.2 illustrate the muscles of the scapula.

In Section II, "The Skeletal System," Chapter 5 presents four "rules of association" that govern the synergistic action between the scapula and the shoulder joint. A review of those rules is appropriate at this time to remind you of the close association between the two joints.

1. When the humerus is more than 2 to 3 degrees away from a position of extension, the scapula is upwardly rotated. (Exception: When the shoulder joint is hyperextended and adducted, sort of "tucked behind the back," the scapula is downwardly rotated.)
2. When the humerus is anterior to the frontal plane bisecting the shoulder joint, the scapula is abducted.
3. When the humerus is posterior to the frontal plane bisecting the shoulder joint, the scapula is adducted.
4. When the shoulder joint is hyperextended with inward rotation, the scapula is tilted forward.

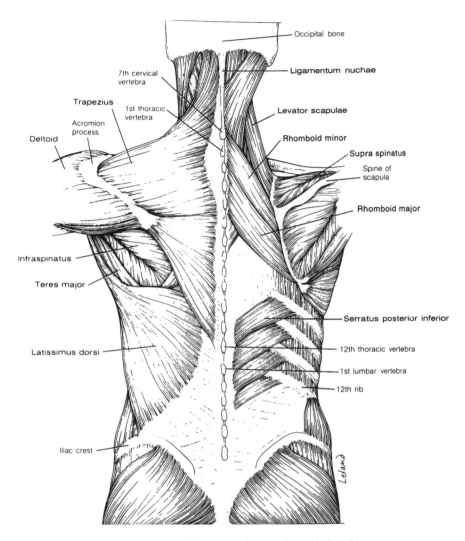

FIGURE 11.1. **Posterior muscles of the scapula, trunk, and shoulder**

Without the associated action of the scapula, the shoulder joint would be far more limited in its actions. The scapula moves to allow a much greater range of motion for the shoulder joint. For example, the action of abduction of the shoulder joint would be restricted by the humerus contacting the acromion process if the scapula did not simultaneously rotate upward. The upward rotation of the scapula to facilitate the actions of the shoulder joint (when taking the humerus away from position of extension), allows the full range of motion human beings have at the shoulder joint. However, this synergistic action between the scapula and the shoulder joint has some negative effects for dancers.

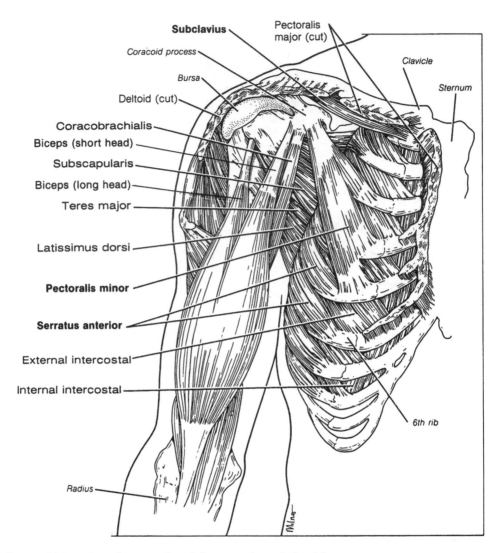

FIGURE 11.2. **Anterior muscles of the scapula and shoulder**

IMPLICATIONS FOR DANCERS

Upper back tension. When dancers raise their arms above their heads, they are told to "keep the shoulders down." This is not an automatic response; it is, instead, a learned coordination. Nondancers will exhibit a natural elevation of the scapula when they raise the arms above the head. This is an automatic action because the muscles which rotate the scapula upward also elevate the scapula. The upper trapezius is the prime mover in this action of the scapula, producing the actions of both upward rotation and elevation. It is essential that the scapula be rotated upward to allow the position of complete flexion (or extension above the head) of the shoulder joint. We see that, in order to get the necessary upward rotation, we also must accept the action of elevation. Then the dance teacher says, "Get your shoulders *down.*" In order to depress the scapula, one must activate the lower trapezius, the pectoralis minor, and the subclavius. In effect, we then have the elevators and depressors contracting simultaneously. Whenever there is a constant activation (co-contraction) of antagonistic muscles, tension will build. It is no wonder that many dancers have excessive tension in the upper back and neck. The very nature of the aesthetics of dance brings tension into that region. While we cannot expect the aesthetics of dance to change and allow the shoulder to rise with arm movements that go above the head, we can do exercises to stretch out the tense muscles. Such exercises are included in Chapter 19.

Pectoralis minor syndrome. Another implication for dancers is a common tendency toward pectoralis minor syndrome. This problem is due to a tight, inelastic pectoralis minor. Consistent contraction of the muscles (as is needed to keep the shoulders down) increases base-level tension in the muscle, and thus the scapula is consistently pulled into a forward-tilted position. This action causes the posterior "winging" of the scapula, where the inferior angle of the scapula protrudes to the rear. Because of the slight abduction action of the pectoralis minor, the rhomboids and the levator scapulae are put into a state of constant stretch. The stretch reflex is constantly being activated for those muscles, and the rhomboids and the levator scapulae subsequently get constant impulses to contract. Sooner or later, the posterior muscles give up and actually go into spasm (cramp), causing intense pain in the upper back. When pectoralis minor syndrome reaches this point, it is frequently very painful to rotate the cervical spine. Another symptom of pectoralis minor syndrome is numbness in the fingers on the ulnar side of the hand that may be accompanied by pain in the ulnar side of the arm. The brachial plexus passes directly under the pectoralis minor. When the muscle is very tight, it can press on the brachial plexus, causing numbness and pain in the area activated by those nerves. (We also see this pattern of muscle tightness, pressure on nerve, and resultant pain at the hip joint with sciatic syndrome.) The primary pain of pectoralis minor syndrome occurs in the posterior muscles, yet the source of the problem lies anterior with the pectoralis minor. Deep-pressure massage on the pectoralis minor can frequently relieve the painful condition, although relief often follows the massage by about two to three hours. It seems that it takes some time for the posterior muscles to get the message that they can relax. This syndrome is common among dancers because of the demand to keep the shoulders down, but it is also common among nondancers. Swimmers are highly susceptible to pectoralis minor syndrome, as are keyboarders, pianists, flutists, and string players. Students who spend a lot of time hunched over books are also susceptible to pectoralis minor syndrome. Stretches for the pectorals are included in Chapter 19.

TABLE 11.1 Muscles of the scapula

Muscle	Proximal Attachment	Distal Attachment	Joint Crossed	Path	Action
Rhomboids (major and minor)	Spinous processes of seventh cervical and upper five thoracic vertebrae	Vertebral border of the scapula from spine of scapula to inferior angle	Scapula	Low lateral to high medial	Adduction Elevation Downward rotation
Levator scapulae	Transverse processes of the upper four cervical vertebrae	Vertebral border of scapula, above the spine of the scapula	Scapula*	Low lateral to high medial	Elevation Assist in adduction Assist in downward rotation
Pectoralis minor	Anterior surface of the third, fourth, and fifth ribs	Coracoid process of scapula	Scapula	Anterior	Forward tilt Assist in depression Assist in abduction
Serratus anterior	Outer (lateral) surfaces of the upper nine ribs	Entire length of the anterior surface of the vertebral border of the scapula	Scapula	"Sandwich" muscle between scapula and rib cage with fibers reaching out to sides of the rib cage	Abduction (all fibers) Upward rotation (lower fibers only)

TABLE 11.1 (*continued*)

Muscle	Proximal Attachment	Distal Attachment	Joint Crossed	Path	Action
Subclavius	Outer surface of the first rib	Inferior surface of the lateral portion of the clavicle	Scapula	From the lateral clavicle, down and medially	Depression May assist in forward tilt and abduction (slightly)
Trapezius	Occipital bone, ligamentum nuchae, and the spinous processes of the seventh cervical and all thoracic vertebrae	Lateral third of the clavicle, acromion process, and the spine of the scapula	Scapula	Upper†	Elevate Upward rotate Adduct
				Middle†	Adduct
				Lower†	Adduct Upward rotate Depress

*Neck: can assist in lateral flexion of the neck when the scapula is stabilized.
†When all fibers contract simultaneously, the resultant action is adduction and upward rotation.

Muscles of the Shoulder

At the shoulder joint we find three large, superficial, multipennate muscles and eight deeper muscles. The multipennate muscles are the *latissimus dorsi*, the *deltoid*, and the *pectoralis major*. The pectoralis major and the deltoid muscles each have three sections, which have separate actions. Luckily, the latissimus dorsi has only one set of actions. The eight deeper muscles include the *coracobrachialis*, the *biceps brachii*, and the *subscapularis* on the anterior of the shoulder joint. Posterior to the center of the shoulder joint are the *infraspinatus*, the *teres minor*, the *teres major*, and the *triceps brachii*. Superior to the center of the shoulder joint is the *supraspinatus*.

Reviewing the actions of the shoulder joint, there are twelve possible actions: flexion, extension, hyperflexion, hyperextension, abduction, adduction, hyperadduction, hyperabduction, inward rotation, outward rotation, horizontal flexion, and horizontal extension. Complete analysis of possible actions of the shoulder joint must include all of these actions. However, in the initial stages of muscular analysis it is necessary to keep the demonstrations relatively simple. As soon as the humerus is above horizontal, many of the actions of specific muscles shift slightly. That shifting of actions causes great confusion to beginning dance kinesiologists, and to the experienced as well. For this reason, most of the discussion of the actions of the muscles deals exclusively with the actions of the shoulder joint below horizontal, or in the actions on the horizontal plane of horizontal flexion and horizontal extension. Table 11.3 lists the attachments of the muscles of the shoulder joint, and Figure 11.3 illustrates the shoulder muscles.[1]

Some pairs of muscles at the shoulder joint have similar paths and attachments. Consequently, they are "partners" or synergistic to each other. It is hoped that listing the synergists of the shoulder joint will simplify, somewhat, the learning of the information about the shoulder muscles. Table 11.2 lists the muscles that operate synergistically at the shoulder joint.

A question frequently asked regarding the action of the lower third of the pectoralis major is, "How can this section of the muscle, being anterior, extend the joint?" Indeed, it cannot perform the action of hyperextension, but it can extend the shoulder joint from a position of flexion, particularly when there is resistance to the action and the individual is actually pressing the arm down against resistance in front of the body. Without external resistance, and assuming a normal upright position, the lowering of the arm from a position of flexion of the shoulder joint would be performed by a lengthening contraction of the flexors. (Did you follow that little jump over into resistance and type of contraction? If you did, you are beginning to integrate the information.)

A helpful demonstration of the three actions of the pectoralis major is done with students sitting at a desk or table. First, put the right hand,

1. See Figure 11.1 for the posterior superficial muscles of the shoulder.

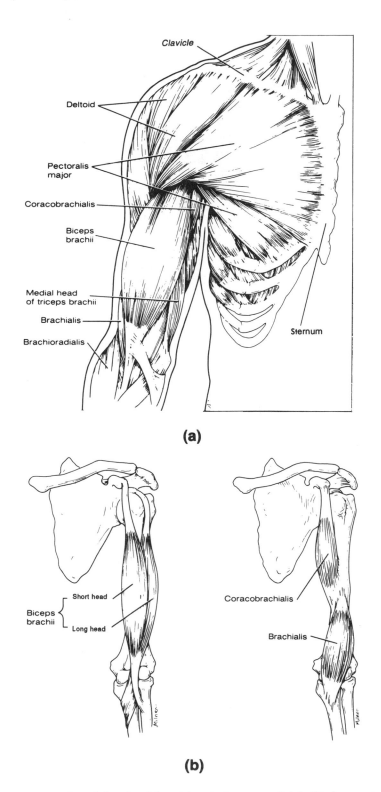

(a)

(b)

FIGURE 11.3.   Muscles of the shoulder: (*a*) anterior, superficial; (*b*) deep anterior

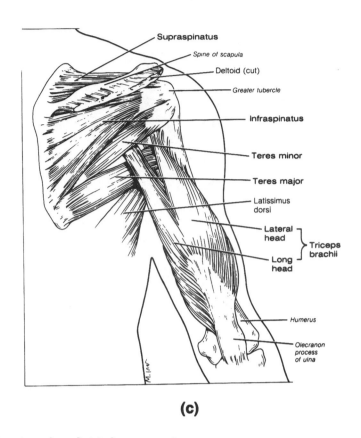

(c)

FIGURE 11.3. (*continued*) (*c*) deep posterior

TABLE 11.2   Shoulder Joint Synergists

Muscle Pairs	Common Actions
Latissimus dorsi Teres major	Even though the latissimus dorsi goes down to the iliac crest, and the teres major goes only to the inferior angle of the scapula, the two muscles cross the shoulder joint in the same path and therefore have the same actions: extension, adduction, and inward rotation.
Teres minor Infraspinatus	With almost exactly the same paths and attachments, it is easy to see that these two muscles are synergists. Their actions are extension, outward rotation, and horizontal extension.
Supraspinatus Middle deltoid	Following the same path across the shoulder joint, these muscles abduct the shoulder joint.

Coracobrachialis
  Short head of the
  biceps brachii
	Both of these muscles attach to the coracoid process of the scapula and cross the shoulder joint anteriorly. Their actions are flexion and adduction, and they can assist in horizontal flexion.

Subscapularis Middle pectoralis major	Both adduct and inwardly rotate the shoulder, and both are involved in horizontal flexion.

TABLE 11.3 Muscles of the Shoulder Joint

Muscle Name	Proximal Attachment	Distal Attachment	Joint Crossed	Path	Action
Pectoralis major upper middle lower	Medial clavicle, the sternum, the cartilages of the upper six ribs and the aponeurosis of the external obliques	Lateral lip of bicipital groove	Shoulder	Radiate muscle running from the front of the chest to the anterior humerus with distal fibers twisting so the lower proximal fibers attach uppermost on the humerus	*Upper fibers:* Flexion Adduction* Inward rotation *Middle fibers:* Adduction Inward rotation Horizontal flexion *Lower fibers:* Extension Adduction* Inward rotation
Latissimus dorsi Synergistic with teres major	Spinous processes of the lower six thoracic vertebrae, sacrum, posterior iliac crest, lower three ribs, all via the lumbodorsal fascia	Medial lip of bicipital groove	Shoulder†	Tendon of the latissimus passes under the armpit, twisting as it attaches to the anterior of the humerus	Extension Adduction Inward rotation Horizontal extension only with inward rotation

(*continued*)

TABLE 11.3 (*continued*)

Muscle Name	Proximal Attachment	Distal Attachment	Joint Crossed	Path	Action
Deltoids anterior middle posterior	Lateral third of the clavicle, acromion process, and spine of the scapula	Deltoid tuberosity of humerus	Shoulder	Deltoids combine to form a cap sleeve of muscle over the top of the shoulder joint. Lower fibers of anterior and posterior go below joint.	*Anterior deltoid:* Flexion Adduction‡§ Inward rotation Horizontal flexion *Middle deltoid:* Abduction *Posterior deltoid:* Extension Outward rotation Adduction§ Horizontal extension
Teres major Synergistic with latissimus dorsi	Posterior surface of the inferior angle of the scapula	Medial lip of bicipital groove of humerus, just medial to attachment of latissimus	Shoulder	Like the latissimus, the teres major runs under the armpit and attaches to the anterior of the humerus	Extension Adduction Inward rotation Assist in horizontal extension when the shoulder is inwardly rotated
Teres minor Synergistic with infraspinatus	Axillary border of scapula	Posterior aspect of greater tubercle of humerus (posterior to infraspinatus)	Shoulder	Posterior	Extension Adduction Outward rotation Horizontal extension when shoulder is outwardly rotated

Muscle	Origin	Insertion	Joint	Location	Action
Infraspinatus Synergistic with the teres minor	Infraspinous fossa of the scapula	Posterior aspect of the greater tubercle of the humerus, anterior to the teres minor	Shoulder	Posterior	Extension Adduction Outward rotation Horizontal extension when shoulder is outwardly rotated
Coracobrachialis	Coracoid process of the scapula	Medial surface of humerus, opposite deltoid tuberosity	Shoulder	Anterior Under joint	Flexion Adduction Horizontal flexion
Supraspinatus Synergistic with the middle deltoid	Supraspinous fossa of scapula	Lateral portion of top of the greater tubercle of the humerus	Shoulder	Over top of joint	Abduction
Subscapularis	Subscapular fossa of scapula	Lesser tuberosity or tubercle of the humerus	Shoulder	"Sandwich muscle" between scapula and rib cage, which runs under armpit to anterior humerus	Inward rotation Assists in horizontal flexion and adduction

(continued)

Table 11.3 (*continued*)

Muscle Name	Proximal Attachment	Distal Attachment	Joint Crossed	Path	Action
Biceps brachii	Long head: above glenoid fossa of scapula	Radial tuberosity on radius	Shoulder	Anterior, running through the bicipital groove above the joint	Flexion Assists in abduction
	Short head: coracoid process of scapula	Radial tuberosity on radius	Shoulder	At the shoulder it follows a path similar to the coraco-brachialis	Flexion Assists in adduction and horizontal flexion
			Elbow (both heads)	Anterior	Flexion
			Radio-ulnar joints	(both heads)	Supination
Triceps brachii	Long head: under glenoid fossa of scapula	Olecranon process of ulna	Shoulder	Posterior Under the joint	Extension Adduction
	Medial head: posterior surface of upper humerus	Olecranon process of ulna	Elbow	Posterior	Extension
	Lateral head: posterior surface of lower humerus	Olecranon process of ulna	Elbow	Posterior	Extension

*When all fibers contract simultaneously, the resultant action is horizontal flexion (adduction) and inward rotation.
†If both the shoulder and the pelvis are stabilized, the latissimus can assist in lateral flexion of the torso.
‡When all fibers of the deltoid contract simultaneously, the resultant action is abduction.
§Adduction action of anterior and posterior deltoids occurs only when each contracts alone.

palm down, on top of the table and the left hand on the right pectoralis major. Pressing down on the table or desk, the student will feel (with the left hand) the contraction of the lower pectoralis major. Second, put the right hand, palm up, under the desk or table and press up against the table or desk. With the left hand, you can then feel the contraction shift to the upper fibers of the pectoralis major. Third, reach out to the right, to the corner of the table or desk, and attempt to pull it to the left. Now the left hand will feel the middle fibers of the pectoralis major. (In this third action, if there is a maximal contraction, you may feel all of the fibers of the pectoralis major contracting together in horizontal flexion.)

Another question frequently asked deals with the ab/adduction actions of the anterior and posterior fibers of the deltoid muscle: How can a muscle both abduct and adduct? Contraction of all of the fibers of the deltoid muscle, simultaneously, causes abduction. However, when the anterior or posterior fibers contract separately, each of these sections of the deltoid can assist in adduction: the anterior deltoid assisting in adduction combined with flexion, and the posterior deltoid assisting in adduction combined with extension.

PRACTICE DEMONSTRATION

Figure 11.4 illustrates an action of the shoulder and scapula for analysis. Table 11.4 is for practice analysis. The correct answers to this demonstration are in Table 11.5

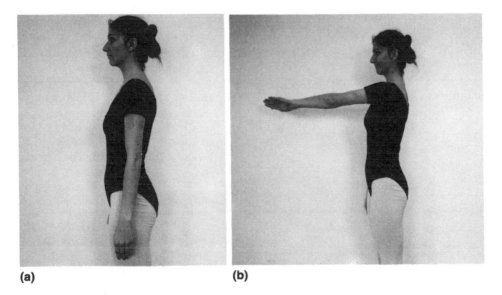

(a)　　　　　　　　　　　**(b)**

FIGURE 11.4. **Analyze the action of the shoulder joint and the scapula from (a) to (b), with gravity at (b).**

TABLE 11.4   Analysis Chart for Figure 11.4

Identification	Joint Action	Action of Gravity	Muscle Group and Type of Contraction	Specific Muscles
Shoulder joint*				
Scapula				

*Because the rules of association depend on the action of the shoulder joint, it is advisable to analyze the shoulder joint first.

TABLE 11.5   Analysis of Figure 11.4

Identification	Joint Position or Action	Action of Gravity	Muscle Group and Type of Contraction	Specific Muscles
Shoulder	Flexion Adduction Inward rotation	Extension Abduction Outward rotation	Shortening contraction Flexors Adductors Inward rotators	Upper pectoralis major Middle pectoralis major Biceps brachii Coraco brachialis Subscapularis Anterior deltoid
Scapula	Abduction Upward rotation Forward tilt	Adduction Downward rotation Return from forward tilt	Shortening contraction Abductors Upward rotators Forward tilters	Serratus anterior Pectoralis minor

IMPLICATIONS FOR DANCERS

Conditioning. The implications related to the shoulder joint for dancers are the same as for athletes. Because of the extreme mobility of the shoulder joint, special conditioning is necessary before the arms can effectively and safely support weight (one's own weight or the weight of another dancer). If a particular dance work or technique requires a lot of weight support on the arms, extra conditioning is recommended. Special exercises for the shoulder are given in Chapter 19.

Shoulder problems. The structure of the shoulder joint makes it particularly susceptible to dislocations when it is three-quarter flexed (the front high diagonal). The only structure to support the shoulder joint in that low, posterior quadrant is muscle tissue. Therefore, strength of the latissimus dorsi and teres major is essential to protect the shoulder joint in this position.

Other common problems of the shoulder joint include bicipital tendonitis (which involves an inflammation of the tendon of the long head of the biceps as it passes through the bicipital groove) and inflammation of the bursa (bursitis) immediately beneath the belly of the anterior deltoid. Preconditioning can be a major factor in the prevention of these two painful conditions.

Lifting. The demands for shoulder strength have traditionally been more extreme for the male dancer than the female. However, contemporary choreography now has the female doing many lifts. Thus, consideration of the special nature of lifting is appropriate for all dancers. While the intention here is not to do an intensive biomechanical analysis of lifting, it is necessary to note certain principles of efficient lifting. Six basic principles are:

1. Start with and maintain good alignment.
2. Lower your own center of gravity before lifting.
3. Apply as much force as possible with your legs.
4. Apply the force at the lifted dancer's center of gravity.
5. Apply the force in a vertical direction.
6. Keep the lifted dancer's center of gravity over your own base of support.

Different lifters will find certain foot positions more effective than others (first position, wide second position, or parallel first position). It is thought that this individual difference is due to variances in the relative strength of the specialized hip extensors activated in the different positions. Often a lifter will automatically assume the position in which he or she has the greatest strength.

Muscular analysis of lifting will certainly identify different muscles for different lifts, but some muscle groups are active in most lifts. Key muscle groups which should be strengthened prior to lifting are:

1. Flexors and abductors of the shoulder joint
2. Upward rotators of the scapula

3. All muscles of the torso (for stabilization)
4. Extensors of the knee and hip

General preconditioning for lifting should include building strength in all of these muscle groups. Conditioning for a specific lift, with special requirements, should be done at the specific joint angle to be used in the lift and should build to lifting *more* weight than will be lifted in performance.

You now have the necessary information to analyze the specific muscular requirements of lifts. Identifying the specific muscles which work in a lift is the first step in systematically building the strength essential to ease and safety. Information included in Chapter 19 will allow you to design an efficient conditioning program for lifting tasks.

PRACTICE DEMONSTRATION

Analyze Figure 11.4 from a to b, using the blank form (Table 11.4). Answer key is given in Table 11.5.

CHAPTER 12

Muscles of the Elbow, Radio-Ulnar Joints, Wrist, and Hand

Muscles of the Elbow

The muscles of the elbow are divided into the flexors on the anterior of the arm and the extensors on the posterior. In the flexor group are the *biceps brachii,* the *brachioradialis,* the *brachialis,* the *pronator teres,* and the *flexor carpi radialis.* There are other muscles that cross the elbow joint anteriorly, but their actions are minimal at the elbow joint. The extensor group includes the triceps and the *anconeus,* with some minor assistance from the *supinator.*

Muscles of the Radio-Ulnar Joints

The lack of a neat pattern for identifying rotation remains consistent as we view the muscles that act upon the radio-ulnar joint. A reminder: only those muscles that attach to the radius can have an effect on the radio-ulnar joint, because the radius is the moving bone in the actions of pronation and supination of the forearm. Those muscles that have a primary action at the radio-ulnar joint must be learned. The "hitchhikers" (the extensor carpi radialis longus and brevis) also supinate. The *palmaris longus* pronates, and the *flexor carpi radialis* assists in pronation. The one remaining muscle having an action on the radio-ulnar joints is the *brachioradialis.* Its action is another of those paradoxes: it can both pronate and supinate, depending on the starting position of the joint action. From extreme supination the brachioradialis will pronate to a neutral position. From a position of extreme pronation, the brachioradialis will supinate to a neutral position.

Muscles of the Wrist

The muscles of the wrist are also relatively easy to divide into flexors, extensors, radial deviators, and ulnar deviators. Once again, a trip around the joint can give us a sense of the overlapping actions of the muscles of the wrist. Starting at center front, we find the *palmaris longus*, the *flexor digitorum profundus*, the *flexor digitorum superficialis*, and the *flexor pollicis longus*. Each of these four muscles flexes the wrist. Moving laterally (in anatomical position) to the radial side we find the flexors that also radially deviate (abduct). This group includes the *flexor carpi radialis* and the *abductor pollicis longus*. Laterally, there are two muscles that have the sole action at the wrist of radial deviation: the *extensor pollicis longus* and the *extensor pollicis brevis*. Crossing over to the posterior side, we find two "hitchhiking muscles," the *extensor carpi radialis longus* and the *extensor carpi radialis brevis*, which extend and radially deviate the wrist. The muscles directly posterior extend the wrist. They include the *extensor digitorum*, the *extensor indicis*, and the *extensor digiti minimi*. On the posterior, ulnar side we find the muscle that extends and ulnar-deviates (adducts): the *extensor carpi ulnaris*. Crossing again from posterior to anterior, we find the muscle that flexes and ulnar-deviates the wrist: the *flexor carpi ulnaris*. Again, the actions of a muscle on the wrist are determined by the path: anterior path flexes; posterior path extends; radial path radially deviates; and ulnar path ulnar deviates. The names of the muscles provide wonderful keys to their actions.

Table 12.1 lists the attachments and actions of the muscles of the elbow, the radio-ulnar joints, the wrist and the hand. Figures 12.1 and 12.2 illustrate the location of the muscles.

PRACTICE DEMONSTRATIONS

Figures 12.3–12.5 are the practice demonstrations for the elbow, radio-ulnar joints, and wrist. For each demonstration, a blank table and key (Tables 12.2–12.7) are included.

IMPLICATIONS FOR DANCERS

There are not many special implications for dancers related to the forearm. However, there is one problem many dancers have in the beginning of training which can be explained by the movement possibilities of the shoulder, elbow, and radio-ulnar joints. Many dancers have difficulty finding the desired position of the arms for the second position. Figure 12.6 illustrates the usual error (a) and the correction to proper placement (b). The correction requires inward rotation of the shoulder joint to get the elbows pointing toward the back and then requires supination of the forearm to get the palm to face forward. Functionally, the arm is rotating inward at the shoulder end and outward at the hand end (supination). This is obviously difficult and feels very awkward to the beginning dancer. It is doubtful that dance aesthetics will change to accommodate dance kinesiology, but knowing that a skill is not supposed to be easy sometimes makes dealing with the difficulties of learning it a bit easier.

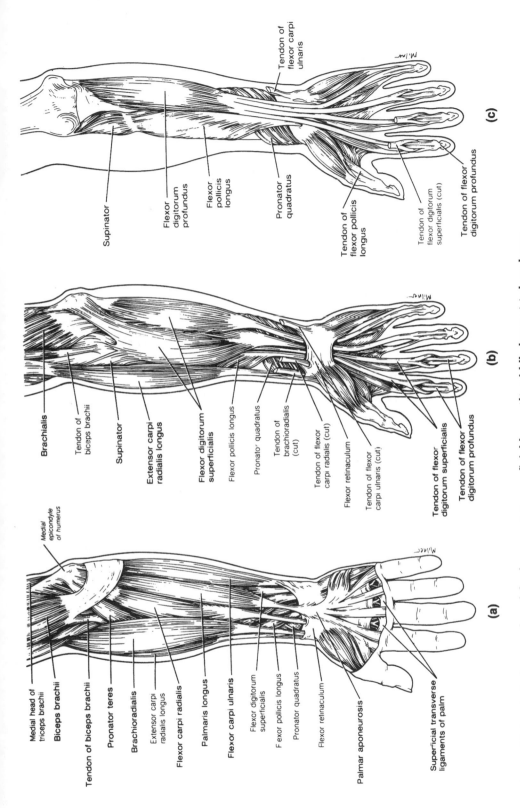

Medial head of triceps brachii

Biceps brachii

Tendon of biceps brachii

Pronator teres

Brachioradialis

Extensor carpi radialis longus

Flexor carpi radialis

Palmaris longus

Flexor carpi ulnaris

Flexor digitorum superficialis

Flexor pollicis longus

Pronator quadratus

Flexor retinaculum

Palmar aponeurosis

Superficial transverse ligaments of palm

Medial epicondyle of humerus

(a)

Brachialis

Tendon of biceps brachii

Supinator

Extensor carpi radialis longus

Flexor digitorum superficialis

Flexor pollicis longus

Pronator quadratus

Tendon of brachioradialis (cut)

Tendon of flexor carpi radialis (cut)

Flexor retinaculum

Tendon of flexor carpi ulnaris (cut)

Tendon of flexor digitorum superficialis

Tendon of flexor digitorum profundus

(b)

Supinator

Flexor digitorum profundus

Flexor pollicis longus

Pronator quadratus

Tendon of flexor carpi ulnaris

Tendon of flexor pollicis longus

Tendon of flexor digitorum superficialis (cut)

Tendon of flexor digitorum profundus

(c)

FIGURE 12.1.   Anterior muscles of the forearm: (*a*) superficial layer; (*b*) middle layer; (*c*) deep layer

211

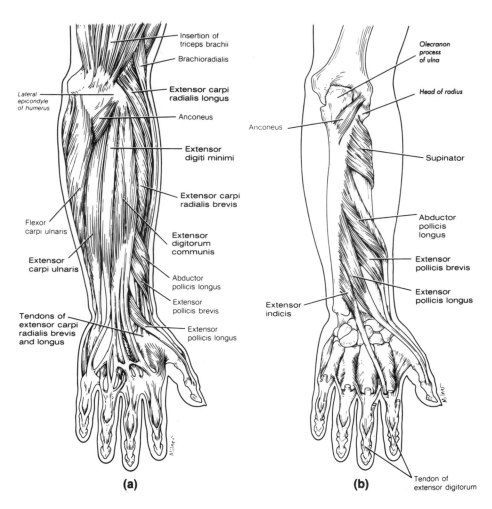

Figure 12.2. Posterior muscles of the forearm: (*a*) superficial layer; (*b*) deepest layer

TABLE 12.1   Muscles of the Elbow, Radio-Ulnar Joints, Wrist, Hand

Muscle	Proximal Attachment	Distal Attachment	Joint Crossed	Path	Action
Biceps brachii (review)			Elbow Radio-ulnar		
Triceps brachii (review)			Elbow		
Brachialis	Anterior surface of the distal half of the humerus	Coronoid process of ulna	Elbow	Anterior	Flexion
Brachio radialis	Lateral condyloid ridge of humerus	Styloid process of radius	Elbow	Anterior	Flexion
			Radio-ulnar	Straight path on radial side of forearm	Pronation from extreme supination to neutral Supination from extreme pronation to neutral
Anconeus	Lateral epicondyle of the humerus	Lateral surface of olecranon process of ulna	Elbow	Posterior	Extension
Pronator teres	Medial epicondyle of humerus and coranoid process of ulna	Middle of lateral surface of shaft of radius	Elbow	Anterior	Flexion
			Radio-ulnar	Proximal medial to distal lateral	Pronation

(continued)

TABLE 12.1 (*continued*)

Muscle	Proximal Attachment	Distal Attachment	Joint Crossed	Path	Action
Flexor carpi radialis	Medial epicondyle of the humerus	Palmar surface of second and third metacarpals	Elbow	Anterior	Flexion
			Radio-ulnar		Assists pronation
			Wrist	Anterior Radial side	Flexion Radial deviation (abduction)
Flexor carpi ulnaris	Medial epicondyle of humerus, olecranon process, and proximal two-thirds of posterior surface of ulna	Lateral carpal bones and fifth metacarpal (palmar surface) (may assist in elbow flexion)	Wrist	Anterior Ulnar side	Flexion Ulnar deviation (adduction)
Extensor carpi ulnaris (may assist in elbow extension)	Lateral epicondyle of humerus	Base of fifth metacarpal (posterior)	Wrist	Posterior Ulnar side	Extension Ulnar deviation (adduction)
Extensor carpi radialis longus (synergistic to extensor carpi radialis brevis) (may assist in elbow extension)	Lateral condyloid ridge of humerus	Posterior surface of base of second metacarpal	Radio-ulnar		Supination
			Wrist	Posterior Radial side	Extension Radial deviation (abduction)

Muscle	Origin	Insertion	Joint	Location	Action
Extensor carpi radialis brevis (synergistic to extensor carpi radialis longus)	Lateral epicondyle of humerus	Posterior surface of base of third metacarpal	Wrist	Posterior Radial side	Extension, Radial deviation (abduction)
(may assist in elbow extension)					
Palmaris longus (may assist in elbow flexion)	Medial epicondyle of humerus	Palmar aponeurosis	Radio-ulnar		Pronation
			Wrist	Anterior	Flexion
Flexor digitorum superficialis	Medial epicondyle of humerus, coronoid process of ulna, and anterior surface of radius	Palmar surface of middle phalanges of fingers 2 through 5, by four tendons	Wrist	Anterior	Flexion
(may assist in elbow flexion)			Fingers	Palmar	Flexion
Extensor digitorum	Lateral epicondyle of humerus	Posterior surface of phalanges of fingers 2 through 5, by four tendons	Wrist	Posterior	Extension
(may assist in elbow extension)			Fingers	Posterior	Extension
Supinator	Lateral epicondyle of humerus	Proximal end of lateral surface of radius	Radio-ulnar		Supination
Pronator quadratus	Distal, anterior surface of ulna	Distal, anterior surface of radius	Radio-ulnar		Pronation
Extensor pollicis longus	Posterior surface of middle of ulna and interosseus membrane	Base of distal phalanx of thumb	Wrist	Radial Side	Radial Deviation (abduction)
(may assist in radio-ulnar supination)			Thumb		Extension Abduction

(continued)

215

TABLE 12.1 (*continued*)

Muscle	Proximal Attachment	Distal Attachment	Joint Crossed	Path	Action
Abductor pollicis longus	Posterior surface of middle of radius, ulna, and interosseus membrane	Palmar base of first metacarpal	Wrist	Anterior Radial side	Flexion Radial deviation (abduction)
(may assist in radio-ulnar supination)			Thumb		Abduction Extension
Flexor digitorum profundus	Anterior surface of upper two-thirds of ulna	Palmar surface of middle phalanges of fingers 2 through 5, by four tendons	Wrist Fingers	Anterior Palmar	Flexion Flexion
Flexor pollicis longus	Anterior surface of radius and interosseus membrane	Palmar surface of distal phalanx of thumb	Wrist	Anterior	Flexion
			Thumb		Flexion Abduction
Extensor pollicis brevis	Posterior surface of middle of radius	Posterior surface of base of first phalanx of thumb	Wrist	Radial side	Radial deviation (abduction)
			Thumb		Extension Abduction
Extensor indicis	Posterior surface of distal end of ulna and interosseous membrane	Tendon of extensor digitorum to index finger	Wrist	Posterior	Extension
			Index finger	Posterior	Extension
Extensor digiti minimi	Proximal tendon of extensor digitorum*	Distal tendon of extensor digitorum*	Wrist	Posterior	Extension
(may assist in elbow extension)			Fifth finger	Posterior	Extension

*This is a slender muscle running parallel to the extensor digitorum and having common proximal and distal attachments with the extensor digitorum.

216

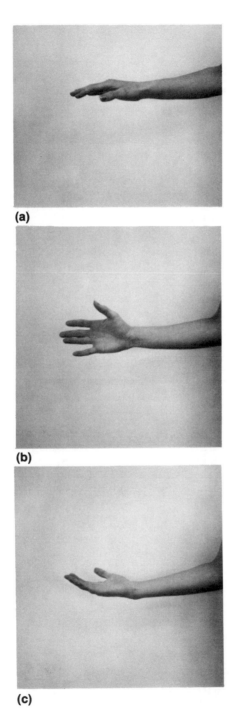

(a)

(b)

(c)

FIGURE 12.3. Analyze the action of radio-ulnar joints from (*a*) to (*b*), with gravity at (*a*); and from (*b*) to (*c*), with gravity at (*c*).

TABLE 12.2 Analysis of Figure 12.3

Identification	Joint Action	Action of Gravity	Muscle Group and Type of Contraction	Specific Muscles
Radio-ulnar joints From (a) to (b)				
From (b) to (c)				

TABLE 12.3 Analysis of Figure 12.3

Identification	Joint Position or Action	Action of Gravity	Muscle Group and Type of Contraction	Specific Muscles
Radio-ulnar joints (a) to (b)	Supination	Pronation	Shortening contraction of supinators	Supinator Biceps brachii Brachioradialis

From (b) to (c)	Supination	This will vary with different muscular balances: (1) if pronators are very tight, *relaxation* will cause return to pronation; (2) if pronators are elastic, gravity will supinate	1. Continued shortening contraction of supinators
			
			2. Lengthening contraction of pronators
				1. Supinator
				   Biceps brachii
				
				2. Pronator teres
				   Pronator quadratus
				   Brachioradialis

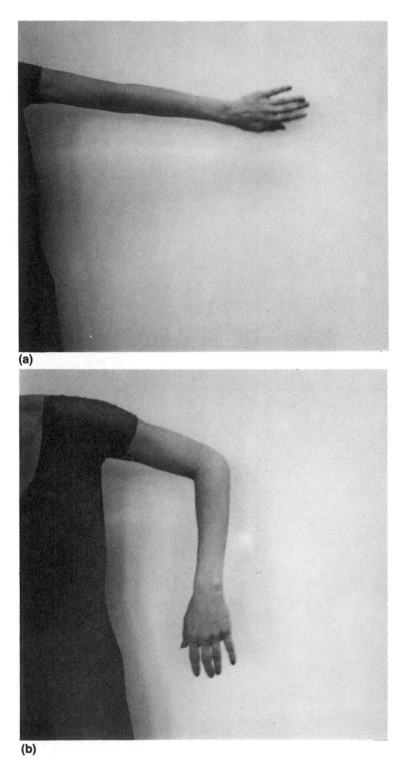

(a)

(b)

FIGURE 12.4. Analyze the action (with control, not dropped) of the elbow joint from
  (a) to (b) with gravity at (a).

TABLE 12.4 Analysis of Figure 12.4

Identification	Joint Action	Action of Gravity	Muscle Group and Type of Contraction	Specific Muscles
Elbow From (a) to (b)				

TABLE 12.5 Analysis of Figure 12.4

Identification	Joint Position or Action	Action of Gravity	Muscle Group and Type of Contraction	Specific Muscles
Elbow	Flexion	Flexion	Lengthening contraction extensors	Triceps Anconeus

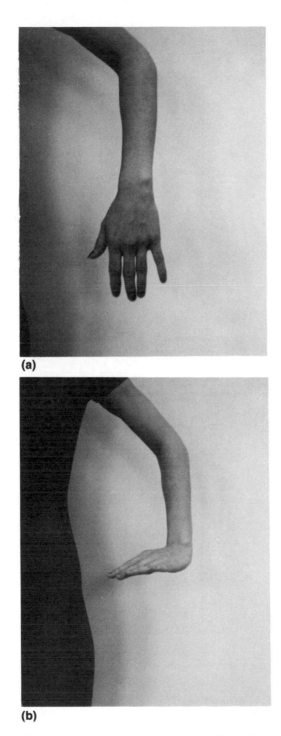

(a)

(b)

FIGURE 12.5. Analyze the action of the wrist from (*a*) to (*b*), with gravity at (*b*).

TABLE 12.6   Analysis of Figure 12.5

Identification	Joint Action	Action of Gravity	Muscle Group and Type of Contraction	Specific Muscles
Wrist From (a) to (b)				

TABLE 12.7 Analysis of Figure 12.5

Identification	Joint Position or Action	Action of Gravity	Muscle Group and Type of Contraction	Specific Muscles
Wrist From (a) to (b)	Hyperextension Radial deviation	Flexion Ulnar deviation	Shortening contraction: Extensors Radial deviators	Extensor carpi radialis longus and brevis Extensor pollicis longus and brevis Extensor digitorum (possible assistance from extensor indicis and extensor digiti minimi)

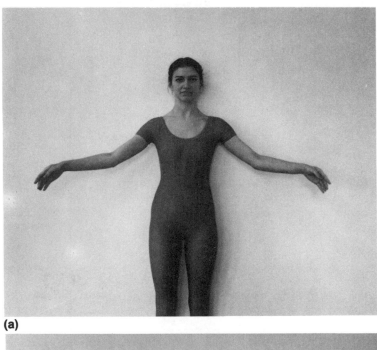

(a)

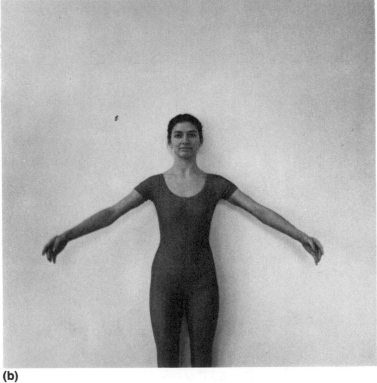

(b)

FIGURE 12.6.   Second position arms. (*a*) *Wrong:* shoulder joint in neutral rotation, radio-ulnar joints in neutral position, and wrists flexed and ulnar-deviated. (*b*) *Correct:* shoulder joint inward rotated (to get the elbow up to the back), radio-ulnar joints supinated (to have the palms face forward), and wrist in a position of extension.

Misalignments and Muscular Imbalances Common in Dance

and suggestions for corrective approaches

The Process of Assessment

Sources of Problems: Two Critical Questions

Two questions are paramount in the assessment and identification of misalignments and muscular imbalances. First, "Have I accurately identified the source of the problem?" Second, "Is the source of the problem changeable?"

PAIN AS AN INDICATOR

In dealing with the first question, pain is one indicator, but we have seen that the location of pain may or may not be near the source of the problem.

For example, pain in the lumbar spine is the effect most frequently felt accompanying tight hip flexors. The standard approach to this problem has often been to treat the location of the pain and stretch the extensors of the lumbar spine with supine pelvic tilts and curls which draw the knees to the chest. If tight hip flexors are the cause of this particular lumbar pain, the normally prescribed stretches for the extensors of the spine will only postpone the return of the pain. Effective treatment of low back pain resulting from tight hip flexors can be found only by dealing with the cause of the problem, the tight hip flexors. (A warning is necessary: to be on the safe side, all low back pain should be screened by an orthopedic surgeon to rule out the possibility of structural problems, before one embarks on an exercise program to stretch the hip flexors.)

Treating a pain by focusing exclusively on the location of the pain will solve the problem if the cause and the pain are in the same location. However, if the pain is caused by a resultant contraction in response to tight-

227

ness of the muscles on the opposite side of the body, as described above, working on the pain site offers only temporary relief. The more complex the chain reaction causing the problem, the more difficult it is to track down the primary cause of the pain. However, if we are diligent, we can often find the source of the problem. In the search, it is necessary to combine knowledge of the muscular system (presuming this is a muscular pain) with listening to the body with our internal receptors. Dancers often "know" when stretching a given muscle is the key to relief. The response is often, "Wow! That's it!" or "Ooooo, that hurts so good!" I have learned, over the years, to listen carefully to these comments by "body-wise" dancers as they search for a culprit muscle that is causing them pain. If a dancer responds to the question, "Is that any better?" with a statement like, "Well, sort of, I guess," it tells me that we have *not* found the culprit. We then continue the search, trying other possibilities, until we get the "Wow!"

KEYS TO MANAGEMENT OF A
NONCHANGEABLE PROBLEM

The second paramount question is, "Is the problem changeable?" When a muscular imbalance results from a structural, nonchangeable cause, correction is not possible and we must move into the domain of pain management. A good example here is the characteristic scoliosis that results from one leg being longer than the other. Since surgical removal of a section of the long leg is a bit extreme, the best approach to this situation is *management* of the pain caused by the scoliosis and corrective exercises to prevent an increase in the depth of the scoliotic curve. I know this problem well, for my left leg is almost three-quarters of an inch longer than my right. My body has compensated for this variance with a sharp curve in the lower lumbar region, concave to the left. This means that my left quadratus lumborum is very susceptible to tightening up—to the point of spasm if I neglect it. When I get that old familiar nagging in the left side of my low back, I do a set of exercises that I have found effective for me.

What are the keys to management represented in this example? First is *awareness of the nonchangeable problem.* Second is *analysis and identification of compensatory corrections* that are probable accompaniments to the problem. Third is *sensory awareness* of the problem area, with heightened sensitivity to the "nipping" or "gnawing" that often signals the onset of a chronic condition. Fourth is *development of an effective exercise sequence* that keeps the condition from progressing to the painful stage.

When a problem is structural in nature—such as leg-length variance, Morton short toe, knock-knees, bowed legs, narrow or wide pelvis, or structural scoliosis—my advice to young dancers is "Learn to fake it with class, and try to equalize muscular strength and elasticity around the problem." Trying to change a permanent structural misalignment is an exercise in futility and only leads to frustration and self-chastisement. Acceptance of the problem and effective management of the muscle tissue surrounding the problem are a much more productive investment of time and energy.

Attitude toward the Assessment Process

A dancer's negative attitude toward the process of assessment of alignment and/or muscular imbalances can derail the best of efforts. Students in my kinesiology classes are required to do an intensive analysis of their own bodies, including bone structure anomalies, muscular strengths and weaknesses, alignment habits that are balanced and unbalanced, and patterns of muscular elasticity and tightness. I often hear the comment, "This is so depressing, to list all my problems." This is a normal first response to the process of analysis and assessment; but if one gets stuck in that attitude, the negativity can be demoralizing and can serve to block effective use of the information. The key word here is *information*. A systematic analysis of alignment and assessment of strengths and weaknesses will allow the wise dancer to approach improvement and/or management from a knowledgeable position. Denial and disgust do not lend themselves to a positive approach to growth and development.

Realistic self-acceptance is essential in dealing with nonchangeable problems. Likewise, a bulldog-like determination is essential to bring about a change in habit or conditioning that can correct an identified misalignment or muscular imbalance.

Assessment of Alignment

Alignment is assessed with the subject in a standing position, weight evenly balanced on both feet, feet directly under the centers of the hip joints, and arms hanging relaxed at the sides. Because different components of alignment are more visible from certain viewpoints, three views of the subject are necessary: front, back, and side. Posture grids can help the assessor by providing a visual background of absolute vertical and absolute horizontal. Another aid is a plumb bob suspended from above, indicating the vertical coordinate. Photos of the subject from the three views can be a permanent record, as can checklists filled out by an evaluator. A helpful aid, when photos are used, is the use of "stick-on dots" (in a color contrasting with the leotard worn) which are applied at critical bony landmarks and then used as reference points in assessment.

Figures 13.1 and 13.2 illustrate the use of the posture grid and stick-on dots. In Figure 13.1, stick-on dots have been used to indicate the most anterior point on the acromion process of the scapula; the anterior and superior spines of the ilium; and the center of the superior border of the patella. The dots can assist the evaluator in identifying shoulder height, hip height, and patellar facing. In Figure 13.2, the dots are placed on the mastoid process, the center of the shoulder joint, the most superior portion of the greater trochanter, the lateral aspect of the posterior superior spine of the ilium (or on the side of the gluteus maximus at the level of the posterior superior spine of the ilium, so it can be seen from the side), the lateral aspect of the anterior superior spine of the ilium, the midpoint of the knee joint, and the lateral malleolus. These points should be familiar to you. All of them have been discussed in Section II in relation to the assessment of total alignment and the assessment of pelvic alignment.

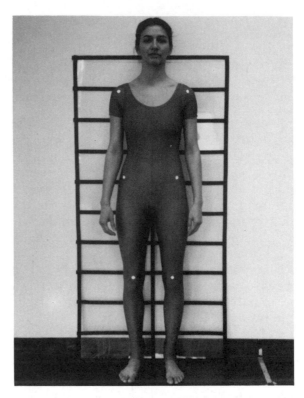

**FIGURE 13.1.   Assessment of alignment from the front view using a posture grid and
dots on acromion processes, anterior superior spines of the ilium, and center top of
the patella.**

Tables 13.1 and 13.2 are two different approaches to the same task: doc-
umentation of the assessment of alignment.

Assessment of Muscular Balance (Strength and Elasticity)

Muscular balance is indicated by a balance in strength and elasticity of agonists and antagonists which perform opposing possible actions at the
various joints of the body. Accurate testing of both strength and elasticity
of musculature is frequently quite complicated, testing strength with
strain gauges and testing elasticity or range of motion with *goniometers*
(tools used to identifying degrees of motion produced at a given joint).
(You will notice that I not use the word *flexibility,* since I believe it can
lead to inappropriate transfer by being confused with *flexion.* I prefer the
word *elasticity* because it more accurately represents the condition that is
being measured.)

In a laboratory setting, these kinds of specific measures are necessary to
obtain accurate measurements. But although these techniques yield specific information, it is thought that the hassle of using them might dis-

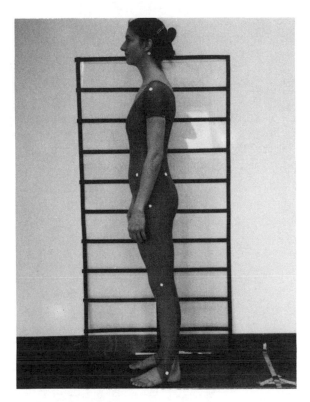

FIGURE 13.2. **Assessment of alignment from the side view using a posture grid and dots on the mastoid process, midpoint of the shoulder, anterior superior spine of the ilium, posterior superior spine of the ilium, greater trochanter, midpoint of knee joint, and lateral malleolus.**

courage dancers and teachers of dance. For this reason, in the following system assessment of strength is based on manual testing and range of motion is based on visual estimation. Such measurement techniques should not be used in a research project, but for general assessment they are thought to be adequate.

MANUAL STRENGTH TESTING

Manually testing for strength requires the evaluator to have knowledge of the muscle groups of the body. The evaluator places a hand on the body part, resists a given joint action, and estimates the relative strength of the muscle group as strong, average, or weak. The position of the hand is then shifted to the other side of the body part, and the antagonistic muscles are tested. Since the evaluator depends on kinesthetic perception of the force of the contraction, it is important to test both agonist and antagonist of the right and left sides in sequence, so the kinesthetic reference is immediate. A brief rest period of five to ten seconds between testing of agonist and antagonist is recommended to give the muscle groups an opportunity to deactivate before the opposite muscle is tested. Contracting against re-

TABLE 13.1 Posture Screening

Side View Check Points	Front View Check Points	Deviations
*Mastoid process	Eyes level—facing front	*Side view:*
*Midpoint of shoulder	Shoulders level	—Forward head
	Spine straight	—Round shoulders
		—Swayback
		—Increased pelvic inclination
		(anterior lower)
Arms hang directly at sides		—Decreased pelvic inclination
Pelvis level	Hips level	(posterior lower)
		—Hyperflexed knees
*Slightly anterior to	Leg length equal	—Hyperextended knees
midpoint of hip joint		—Forward lean
	Knees facing front (neither	—Backward lean
	knock-knees nor bowlegs)	
	Feet neither pronated nor supinated	*Front view:*
*Slightly posterior to		—Wry neck (head off to one side)
center of knee joint	*Quick check for scoliosis:*	—Shoulder height unequal
	Have the person face away	—Scoliosis
	from you and bend over to the	—Unequal leg length
	front, letting the arms, head,	—Knock-knees
*Slight anterior to ankle bone	and torso hang toward the	—Bowlegs
	floor. If one side of the back is	—Cross-eyed knees
	higher, scoliosis is possible	—Supination of tarsus
	and more specific tests are	—Pronation of tarsus
	called for.	

*On same vertical line.

TABLE 13.2 Posture assessment sheet

NAME _____

DATE _____

Area	Possible Deviations	No Deviation (OK)	Slight Deviation	Moderate Deviation	Marked Deviation	Comments
Side View	Total: ____Forward ____ Backward					
	Knees: ____Hyperextended ____ Hyperflex					
	Plevis: ____ Increased ____Decreased					
	Lumbar spine: swayback					
	Hip flexors: (tight)					
	Thoracic spine: Round Shoulders					
	Pectoralis minor syndrome					
	Cervical spine: Forward head					
	Arm position: ____hang forward ____back					
Front or Back View	Tarsus: ____ pronated ____supinated					
	Tibial torsion					
	Patella alignment ____lateral ____ med.					
	Knees: Knock-knees					
	Bowlegs					
	Cross-eyed					
	Leg length ____ R. longer____ L. longer					
	Hip height					
	Scoliosis Lumbar					
	(also see Thoracic					
	below) Cervical					
	Shoulder tension					
	Shoulder height ____R. high____ L. high					
	Head off to one side ____R. ____ L.					

Other Comments

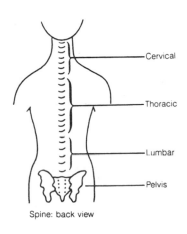

Spine: back view

Indicate on diagram the direction and location of existing scoliosis.

TABLE 13.3 Testing for Balance of Strength and Mobility

Joint Actions	Strength		Mobility		Check below for major muscular imbalances
	Right	Left	Right	Left	
Tarsus					
Supination					
Pronation					
Ankle					
Dorsiflexion					
Plantar flexion					
Knee					
Flexion					
Extension					
Hip					
Flexion					
Extension					
Inward rotation					
Outward rotation					
Abduction					
Adduction					
Torso					
Flexion					
Extension					
Hyperextension					

Lateral flexion (right and left)

Rotation (right and left)

Neck

Flexion

Extension

Hyperextension

Lateral flexion (right and left)

Rotation (right and left)

Shoulder

Abduction

Adduction

Flexion

Extension

Inward rotation

Outward rotation

Horizontal flexion

Horizontal extension

Strength scoring: 3 = Strong; 2 = Average; 1 = Weak
Mobility scoring: 3 = Extreme; 2 = Average; 1 = Restricted
Alternative scoring for greater refinement
Strength: 5 = Very strong; 4 = Strong; 3 = Average; 2 = Somewhat weak; 1 = Very weak
Mobility: 5 = Extreme; 4 = Above average; 3 = Average; 2 = Somewhat restricted; 1 = Very restricted

sistance does create a certain amount of neuromuscular tension, and for this reason it is suggested that all of the strength testing be done at once, and a longer period of relaxation be allowed before testing for elasticity and range of motion. Of course, the order could also be reversed, with range of motion tested first.

RANGE-OF-MOTION TESTING

Dancers, as a group, are much more sophisticated at assessing range of motion than other groups. Dancers spend a lot of time in the studio working for increased range of motion. Therefore, they seem to be able to identify extreme mobility, average mobility, and limited mobility easily, quickly, and accurately. Admittedly, what is classified as extreme mobility for a dancer would be considered "out of sight" for the normal population.

USE OF THE MUSCULAR IMBALANCE CHART

Table 13.3 presents one approach to recording muscular strength and mobility throughout the body. Each set of joint actions is presented, but cross-references to actions of adjacent joints are not listed. For example, a complete testing of strength and mobility of the tarsus really should be performed in both a plantar and a dorsiflexed position of the ankle. Also, testing of inward and outward rotation of the hip joint should include base positions of both flexion and extension of the hip. This cross-referenced testing of strength and elasticity is advisable, but it would make Table 13.3 prohibitively long. The basic testing in Table 13.3 can be used as an indication of muscular imbalances. If additional information is needed, evaluators can design cross-referenced testing of both strength and elasticity. If Table 13.3 is to be used "as is," testing of strength and elasticity on one plane of action should be performed in a neutral range of the other planes. For example, testing of abduction and adduction of the hip joint would be tested in parallel position, neither fully flexed nor fully extended. It is helpful to indicate the relative position of the joint on the other planes if subsequent testing is planned, so that the test can be replicated with some degree of consistency.

Chain Reactions of Conditions

We have to this point viewed the human body in segments, with only an occasional discussion of interfaces between segments. Yet the body operates not as isolated segments of action but rather as a unified whole. Misalignment in one area almost always causes a need for compensation in adjacent areas, and these compensations, in turn, cause still another set of compensations farther up (or down) the line. Radiating out from one primary misalignment may be a whole series of secondary misalignments (or accommodations)—a chain reaction. Three examples of chain reactions are given below: side effects of pronation of the tarsus, side effects of variance in leg length, and side effects of tight hip flexors. These three examples were chosen because of their frequency in the dance community.

Pronation of the Tarsus and Chain Reactions

Pronation of the tarsus has effects in both directions: distally it affects the weight-bearing patterns of the foot; proximally it affects the alignment of the knee and hip, and possibly even the spine.

A characteristic pattern of pronation of the tarsus will cause a shift of weight to the medial side of the foot. Accompanying this shift, there is a tendency to use the medial side of the head of the first metatarsal as the pushoff in locomotion. (This pattern is even more pronounced in dancers, who have a tendency to walk "duck-footed," or in a consistently turned-out position of the hip joint.) The stress on the medial aspect of the head of the first metatarsal is extreme. The body responds by building up bone tissue, resulting in the formation of *bunions*.

Gravity is a pronator of the tarsus in a normal standing position. If the ligamentous structure of the foot allows for pronation of the tarsus, the supinator muscles must be stronger to counteract the pull of gravity. With the supinator muscles stronger than the pronator muscles, when the foot is not weightbearing, the tarsus will be pulled into a position of supination, because of the greater strength of the supinator muscles. If the tarsus is supinated in a non-weight-bearing position, the likelihood of *ankle sprains* is greatly increased. (Actually, these are tarsus sprains caused by landing on a supinated tarsus and rolling over the outside of the foot.)

The chain reaction of effects of a pronated tarsus in the opposite direction (toward the knee) has equally dangerous consequences. The shift of weight to the medial side of the foot causes a tendency to outwardly rotate the knee joint, with the foot splaying out to the side. In this case the foot shows a greater degree of "turnout" than is shown by the facing of the knee. In extreme cases, the knees actually look cross-eyed, with the patellas seeming to look at each other. With the foot turning out farther than the hip joint, the stress localizes at the knee joint, placing an inordinate torquing and twisting pressure on the knee and increasing the likelihood of *knee injuries*. Dancers who force turnout can be seen doing a demiplié, turning the feet out farther, and then returning to a standing position. *This technique for increasing false turnout (that which occurs at the knee and the tarsus instead of the hip) puts great stress on the knee joint and consequently should be forbidden.* In extreme cases of pronation of the tarsus, there may also be a tendency to *hyperextension of the knees* to counteract the torque at the knee joint.

Moving up to the hip joint, the chain reaction continues. With pronation there is a tendency for the hip joint to inwardly rotate, and this means that there is greater demand for contraction of the outward rotators of the hip to maintain proper alignment of the knee over the foot. This can lead to *increased tension* or *spasm of the deep rotators of the hip joint* and a subsequent flareup of *sciatic syndrome*.

This chain reaction of compensations can continue up into the spine, though the consequences of pronated feet listed above are the most common.

Variance in Leg Length and Chain Reactions

When one leg is longer than the other, the pelvis will tip to one side and the torso will shift (laterally flex) toward the side of the long leg in order to maintain a vertical, upright posture, which is facilitated by the neurological righting reflexes. Thus a person with one leg longer than the other will often have compensatory *scoliosis*. The most common pattern of the scoliosis is a long C-curve extending up the spine that is concave toward the side of the long leg, but other patterns of scoliosis are possible. (My own left leg is three-quarters of an inch longer than my right leg. As mentioned before, my particular scoliosis is a sharp curve to the left side at the level of the fourth and fifth lumbar vertebrae, with an x-ray showing major compression of the left sides of the bodies of those two vertebrae. This scoliotic pattern results in a tightening—or shortening—of my left quadratus lumborum that can go into spasm if I don't take care of it by stretching the left quadratus.) The patterns of scoliotic compensation for variance in leg length are specific to the individual, and careful examination is necessary to correctly identify a specific pattern.

While scoliosis is a common consequence of variance in leg length, another possible accommodation is to maintain slight flexion of the hip on the side of the long leg. Maintaining slightly greater hip flexion on one side than the other results in a twisting of the pelvis on the support structure. This twisting can result in an *imbalance of strength and elasticity of the right and left hip flexors and extensors.*

Still another pattern that can accompany variance in leg length occurs in moving and dancing. The dancer tends to prefer balancing on the longer leg. (After all, if he or she stands on the shorter leg, the long leg tends to hit the floor on leg swings and the unsupported side of the pelvis must be lifted to prevent this "toe-stubbing.") This preference often results in *less elasticity and greater stability with the long leg* and *greater mobility and less stability with the short leg.* If the long leg is preferred for balancing actions, the antigravity muscles will be stronger for the long leg than for the short leg. Once again we see a chain reaction of effects radiating out both proximally and distally from the source of the problem.

Tight Hip Flexors and Chain Reactions

The extended amount of time we spend sitting in this culture allows the hip flexors to tighten up. Even though dancers spend a lot of time on their feet, they too are subject to tight—or short—hip flexors resulting from excessive sitting. When an individual with tight hip flexors stands up, the hip remains in a semiflexed position. The front rim of the pelvis is pulled down in front, causing *increased pelvic inclination* which in turn causes *swayback.* The hyperextension of the lumbar spine caused by increased pelvic inclination allows the extensors of the lumbar spine to tighten. As those muscles get shorter and shorter, two things happen: the *muscles of the low back tend to go into spasm,* and the thoracic spine must compensate for the backward movement of the spine by *increasing the flexion curve in the thoracic region.*

This chain reaction can continue upward into the cervical spine as well, but let's go back to the hip region and look at the chain reaction of tight hip flexors going downward. A dancer with tight hip flexors battles the pelvic misalignment by contracting the extensors of the hip and particularly by gripping the gluteus maximus to achieve the "look" of an aligned pelvis. This does not change the fact that the hip flexors are tight; the hip stays in a semiflexed position, and that causes the knees to flex. To counteract the flexion of the knees, the extensors of the knees are gripped (the quadriceps). The constant gripping action in the gluteus maximus and the quadriceps results in the classic *"bubble buns"* and *"thunder thighs."* This continues the chain reaction and results in a tendency to *hyperextended knees*. All of this results from tight hip flexors!

The point of this rather lengthy discussion of chain reactions resulting from misalignments or muscular imbalances is, I hope, by now clear. *No misalignment happens in isolation. There are always accommodations and compensations.* Careful, systematic analysis of alignment and muscular balance can make ideal alignment more immediately achievable by the dancer. For this reason, specific conditions and imbalances that can cause chain reactions of compensations are presented in the next section of this chapter.

Specific Conditions and Imbalances

The following discussion of specific conditions and imbalances does not cover every possible problem. Additionally, there will be some individuals whose condition does not fit into the usual pattern of misalignment and/or muscular imbalance. The aim is, rather, to focus the reader's attention on some of the most common problems in dance, and the most usual consequences of those problems. If your situation does not fit the description given, analyze and experiment with possible solutions that seem appropriate. In addition to the exercises listed in the discussions below, the reader is also referred to the chapter on conditioning (Chapter 19), and specifically to the mini-programs toward the end of that chapter, which are designed for specific problems.

Just as we started at the foundation and moved up through the body in the chapters on the skeletal system and the muscular system, this discussion will also start at the foundation.

Foot and Lower Leg

Hallux valgus is a condition in which the phalanges of the great toe angle off toward the lateral side of the foot. This condition may be congenital, or it may be caused by wearing shoes that are too narrow in childhood, when the foot is still taking its final ossified shape. In early stages, this condition may be changeable if it is due to a muscular imbalance. If, however, ossification has occurred and the joint structure itself is the cause of the misalignment, change is impossible, or at best very unlikely. The foot with a hallux valgus will be less efficient in locomotion when the feet are in parallel position, since the big toe is not in straight alignment with the metatarsal to provide extra "push-off" forces. This foot may be susceptible to tendonitis of the muscles of the great toe (hallux), and attention to the strength and elasticity of the flexor hallux longus and the extensor hallux longus may be indicated.

For dancers, the most common location of *bunions* is on the medial aspect of the head of the first metatarsal. It is thought that the consistent maintenance of outward rotation of the hip joint, resulting in a duck-footed walk, may contribute to the development of bunions at this location. Walking in a turned-out position puts continual stress on the medial aspect of the first metatarsal, since it is, in outward rotation, the last part of the foot to leave the ground. The continual stress causes buildup of bony scar tissue at the site of the irritation, resulting in bunions. To reduce the stress, walking in parallel position, with the feet tracking straight ahead, is strongly encouraged. This will not remove old scar tissue, but by reducing stress it may prevent buildup of new scar tissue. Severe cases of bunions must be treated surgically.

Flat feet may be an indication of laxity of the plantar ligaments of the foot, or weakness of the musculature that supports the medial side of the foot (the supinators that also plantar-flex). There is no way to tighten up loose ligaments, but it is possible to supplement lack of ligamentous support with additional strength of the musculature of the foot and tarsus. One approach to increasing strength to supplement lax ligaments is to strengthen the intrinsic muscles on the plantar surface of the foot. These are the intrinsic flexors of the toes. Although these muscles were not individually identified in Chapter 8, they can be approached in a general sense. The toe gripper exercise in Chapter 19 (Figure 19.12) is an effective way to strengthen the intrinsic muscles of the foot. Strengthening the supinator/plantar flexors (tibialis posterior, flexor digitorum longus, and flexor hallux longus) that cross the ankle and tarsus may also assist in supporting the arch of the foot. The ankle/tarsus series (Figure 19.15) can develop strength in these muscles. Always remember to stretch out after strengthening exercises.

In *Morton short toe*, as discussed in Chapter 3, the first metatarsal is shorter than the second metatarsal. There are two primary consequences of this condition: buildup of a callus beneath the head of the second metatarsal, and instability when the dancer is on relevé or half toe. There is a natural tendency to supinate the foot in this position. In studio language, this is a *sickled foot*. A sickled foot is dangerous because it increases the likelihood of ankle/tarsus sprains. Moving a sickled foot to an ideally aligned position requires contraction of the plantar flexors/pronators of the ankle tarsus (peroneus longus and peroneus brevis). The ankle/tarsus series noted above (Figure 19.15) is excellent for beginning the conditioning of these muscles. In addition, contracting these muscles against the resistance of a theraband or another elastic device will develop strength in these muscles rapidly, but remember to stretch out after exercise by supinating and dorsiflexing the ankle/tarsus region.

Pronation and *supination of the tarsus* are both misalignments. (Assessment of alignment of the tarsus is discussed in Chapter 3.) Pronation is the more serious of the two, as was illustrated in the discussion of chain reactions resulting from habitual pronation. The consequences of pronated feet may be reflected in a relatively minor nagging pain in the knee joint or may appear as a serious traumatic injury to the knee due to inordinate stress when landing from a jump or leap. A dancer with pronated feet in a normal standing position will have a marked muscular imbalance between the muscles that pronate and supinate the tarsus, particularly those that also plantar-flex. (Pronation in a plantar-flexed ankle position will be almost nonexistent.) A tendency to pronate in a normal standing position translates into a tendency to supinate in a non-weight-bearing position of the tarsus (such as being midair in a jump or leap). For this reason both the pronator/plantar flexors and the supinator/plantar flexors need to be strengthened with more repetitions for the pronators to facilitate the balancing of strength. The ankle tarsus series (Figure 19.15) is specifically designed to meet this need. Once again, theraband exercises are also recommended.

Tibial torsion is a bowing and simultaneous twisting of the tibia as reflected in the line of the anterior border of the tibia. The bowing is most usually convex out to the lateral side of the lower leg, with the uppermost and lowermost portions of the tibia being more medial. The bowing and twisting of the tibia may also contribute to cross-eyed knees and/or condromalacia of the patella. This condition is structural and therefore cannot be corrected. The dancer with tibial torsion may be more susceptible to shin splints than dancers with no tibial torsion. Furthermore, tibial torsion tends to accentuate any tendency toward pronation of the tarsus, since the weight is transferred to the foot on the medial side. Exercises to strengthen and stretch the musculature of the ankle/tarsus are suggested to prevent overuse syndromes such as shin splints and tendonitis.

Knee and Thigh

Knock-knees and *bowlegs* are structural conditions resulting from variation in the relative height of the medial and lateral condyles of the femur. No correction is possible.

Cross-eyed knees is a condition where the patellas of the two knees seem to be looking at each other. This condition may be structural and therefore uncorrectable, or it may be a result of misalignment above or below the knee joint. Misalignment from below comes from a tendency to pronate the tarsus in a normal standing position, as discussed with regard to the chain reaction to pronation. This causes an outward rotation of the knee joint (with the tibia rotated laterally), which gives an appearance of facing medially. The other cause may be lack of outward rotation in the hip joints that is equal to the outward rotation of the feet. Clearly, both causes have the same result: oppositional rotation at the knee joint, with the thigh rotating one way and the tibia rotating the other way. Correction of this condition can be approached either from above (increasing the outward rotation of the hip joints) or from below (supinating the tarsus to a neutral position). I tend to encourage dancers to correct the alignment of the tarsus, since that is the foundation. Once again, the ankle-tarsus series (Figure 19.15) is recommended to strengthen the supinators that also plantar-flex the ankle. In this instance, a theraband or some other elastic resistance device is particularly helpful, since the specific muscular actions can be targeted.

Placement of the tibial tuberosity is ideally at the center-front of the tibia. However, the *tibial tuberosity may be congenitally displaced* to either the medial or the lateral aspect of the tibia. The most common displacement of the tibial tuberosity is to the lateral side. Remembering that the tibial tuberosity is the muscular attachment for the quadriceps muscles, whose tendons encase the patella, it is easy to see why a laterally placed tibial tuberosity will pull the patella laterally. When this happens, the patella rides over the convex surface of the lateral condyle of the femur rather than over the concave surface of the intercondular notch. As the knee flexes and extends, the posterior surface of the patella rubs against the lateral condyle of the femur, causing bony irritation, followed by buildup of scar tissue, and finally is accompanied by consistent grating and crunching of the knee joint on flexion and extension of the knee. This condition is called *chondromalacia of the patella.* It is thought that strengthening the medial vasti can serve to pull the laterally displaced patella over toward the middle of the joint, thus reducing the bony erosion of the posterior of the patella. The question becomes, How do we selectively strengthen the medial vasti? First of all, remember that the vasti are most efficient in extension of the knee in the last 10 to 15 degrees of extension. Consequently, full extension of the knee, with an emphasis on the last 10 to 15 degrees, is necessary to fully activate the vasti. To selectively activate the medial vasti, also supinate the tarsus while extending the knee. This tarsus action seems to focus the contraction more on the medial vasti. Heel presses (Figure 19.11) with a supinated tarsus are thought to selectively strengthen the medial vasti.

Tightening of the fascia lata (ilio-tibial band, also known as the *I-T band)* is a new one to me. In the years since the publication of the first edition, there has been a marked increase among dance students of running to maintain cardiorespiratory fitness. It seems that running has a tendency to stress the I-T band, resulting in the tightening of that fascial plane (which is what the I-T band is). What I have observed is that the tightening of the I-T band puts pressure on the knee joint from the lateral side. This seems to be a cause of knee pain, but not on the lateral side of the knee. The pain occurs on the medial, inferior aspect of the patella or slightly under the patella in that location. The pain has been described as a "nagging twinge," irritating but not excruxiating. Deep massage of the I-T band just above the knee joint can sometimes manually stretch the I-T band. Poke the fingers under the band from the side and from behind, just anterior to the tendon of the biceps femoris, and then place the thumbs on the front side of the band. Then, roll the I-T band between the thumbs and fingers with moderate to deep pressure. This massage technique has given immediate relief to many dancers who were complaining of nagging, twinging pain on the medial, inferior aspect of the patella. Obviously, if this pain is associated with a traumatic injury, consult a physician. However, if the pain sort of "oozes in on you" for no obvious reason, and you are increasing the amount of locomotion in your daily routine, you might try the massage technique described above. If the pain persists, see a physician.

Variance in leg length is a structural problem and simply must be accepted. You are not going to change the length of the leg. However, the consequences of the variance can be managed so that they do not worsen over time. A common consequence of having one leg longer than the other is compensatory scoliosis that is concave to the side of the long leg. The curve can vary considerably in length, but the depth of the curve will reflect the degree of difference in length of the legs. Another common consequence of variance in leg length is a slight rotation of the entire pelvis to the side of the long leg. Each of these misalignments that may result from differences in leg length needs attention so that the musculature does not become excessively imbalanced. Generally speaking, if the left leg is longer, the muscles on the left side of the spine will be tighter than those on the right, the inward rotators of the left hip will be tighter than those on the right, and the outward rotators of the right hip will be tighter than those on the left. Of course there may be individual variations on this theme. Whatever the muscular imbalances, they are likely to get more severe if they are ignored. A regular program of specific stretching is recommended. The latissimus stretch (Figure 19.10e) and the long-C stretch (Figure 19.10a) are effective for the tightness in the torso. The yoga sit stretch (Figure 19.10d), the seated frog press (Figure 19.46), the lying frog press (Figure 19.48), the lying knee press (Figure 19.47), and the hip greaser (Figure 19.50) are effective for the rotators of the hip joint.

Pelvis and Hip Joint

Pelvic width is determined by the relative width of the sacrum and is an individual difference that cannot be changed. Individuals with a narrow pelvis are likely to excel at running and jumping because the "Q angle" (the angle between the neck and the shaft of the femur) is smaller and the levers of the leg track more directly beneath the hip joints, with the femur closer to vertical. An individual with a wide pelvis will be far less efficient in locomotion because of the smaller "Q angle" and because the leg descends at an angle instead of vertically. I have observed that individuals with a narrow pelvis tend to have greater range of motion in inward rotation and those with a wider pelvis tend to have greater range of motion in outward rotation. Perhaps there is a positive correlation between pelvic width and forward- or sideward-facing acetabulae.

The structure of the acetabulae can vary in two ways. First, the sockets may face either to the front or to the side. Clearly, dancers with forward-facing sockets will have greater inward rotation and those with the sockets facing toward the side will have greater outward rotation. Second, the sockets can vary in depth. A deeper socket will be more stable but will have less range of motion. A shallower socket will have greater mobility and less stability. Ignoring these natural limitations and trying to force rotation of the hip joint in either direction can damage the internal structure of the joint and may be a precursor of degenerative arthritis of the hip joint.

Tight hip flexors can play a central role in a number of problems, including *increased pelvic inclination, swayback, low back pain,* and *anterior snapping hip.* If a joint position is habitual, the muscles will shorten to that length. As discussed in the section on chain reactions, in our culture the amount of time spent seated is excessive. Therefore, the hip flexors tighten. When they do, they pull down on the front rim of the pelvis, causing increased pelvic inclination and swayback. In this case the muscles of the low back are the ones that frequently go into spasm as a result of the tight hip flexors. In another scenario resulting from tight hip flexors, the tendons of the sartorius, the rectus femoris, and/or the iliopsoas are pulled tight across the front rim of the pelvis. As the joint position is changed, those muscles which are pulled tight against the ascending remus "twang" as they move over the bone, much like a plucked guitar string. In fact, the iliopsoas has been nicknamed the "twanger" by some dancers. This "twanging" is the condition called *anterior snapping hip.* Any one of the three muscles (sartorius, rectus femoris, or iliopsoas) may be doing the snapping. Stretching the hip flexors in a series of positions of abduction and adduction of the hip joint may help the dancer identify which position needs the stretch most. The remedy for tight hip flexors, whether manifested in swayback, low back pain, or anterior snapping hip, is to stretch the hip flexors. The lying hip flexor stretch (Figure 19.44), the stork stretch (Figure 19.24), and the TV stretch (Figure 19.14) are all equally effective. The hip flexor lift, (Figure 19.59) is also effective for releasing the tension of the hip flexors.

Weak and tight abductors, as noted in Chapter 9, are quite common among dancers because standing on one leg requires constant low-grade contraction by the abductors. The common tightness and weakness of the abductors of the hip joint makes dancers prime candidates for *lateral snapping hip.* The distal attachments of the gluteus minimus and the gluteus medius attach on the greater trochanter. If those muscles are very tight, as is common with dancers, they do not slide fluidly over the greater trochanter. Instead, in certain positions or actions of the hip joint, the tendon "catches" for a moment until the force exceeds the resistance and the tendon suddenly snaps over the bone. To stretch the abductors of the hip joint, the long C-stretch and the lunge stretch (Figures 19.10a and b) are effective. To increase strength in the abductors, side leg lifts in parallel position (Figure 19.9) are recommended.

Sciatic syndrome, or *"sciatica,"* is caused by pressure on the sciatic nerve. The pressure may come from bones, muscles, or other tissue pressing on the nerve. The condition that is most usual for dancers is pressure on the sciatic nerve by the six deep rotators. Remember that the sciatic nerve "basket weaves" through the deep rotators, passing under the upper muscles and coming out over the lower muscles. When a dancer has been working hard to increase outward rotation in technique class or rehearsal, the six deep rotators frequently tighten up, often to the point of spasm. When that happens the six deep rotators pinch the sciatic nerve. The pain begins deep in the indentation of the buttocks; travels down the lateral and posterior aspect of the thigh, following the path of the biceps femoris; continues down to the lower leg, causing pain and/or spasm of the peroneals; and finally travels to the lateral side of the foot, causing spasm and/or pain in the extensor digitorum longus and the peroneus tertius. Any or all of these areas may be painful, depending on the severity of the pressure on the nerve. Stretching the six deep rotators is the first line of defense against sciatica that results from muscular tightness. The yoga sit stretch (Figure 19.49) is most effective. The leg-over stretch (Figure 19.10c) is also quite effective, as is the lift for the outward rotators (Figure 19.65).

Torso and Neck

Lumbar lordosis is commonly known as *swayback*. It is an accentuation of the normal curve of hyperextension in the lumbar region. Symptoms, in addition to the increased curve itself, often include low back pain (sometimes generalized and sometimes sharp and pinpointed). The medical profession has most frequently treated this pain with muscle relaxants, bed rest, and general stretches of the extensors of the spine. However, it is thought that this may be a little like treating a blister on the foot without changing the shoes that caused the blister. In this case, the "blister" is pain in the low back, but a frequent cause of this pain is thought to be tightness of the hip flexors. As has been mentioned earlier, long periods of time spent in a sitting position allow the hip flexors to tighten. Then, when one stands up, the tight hip flexors are not elastic enough to allow full extension of the hip. They pull down on the front rim of the pelvis, causing an increase in the hyperextension curve of the lumbar spine. Stretching and releasing the tension in the hip flexors will often bring immediate relief of low back pain. Six of the exercises described in Chapter 19 can be used to accomplish this: lying hip flexor stretch (Figure 19.44), TV stretch (Figure 19.14), stork stretch (Figure 19.24), hip flop (Figure 19.51), latissimus stretch (Figure 19.10e), pelvic clock (Figure 19.59), and hip flexor "lift" (Figure 19.55).

Thoracic kyphosis is an accentuation of the normal thoracic curve of flexion in the upper back. It is most often caused by weakness of the extensors of the thoracic region of the spine. It should be noted that this condition is quite unusual among dancers, because of the demands for strength that dance places on the extensors of the spine. However, in rare instances a dancer may experience thoracic kyphosis. The reader is warned to clearly distinguish between thoracic kyphosis (an actual increase in the thoracic curve) and pectoralis minor syndrome (which is a consistently held forward tilt of the scapula and is far more common among dancers). The common term "round shoulders" may include one or both of these conditions. Distinguishing between these two conditions allows one to select the precise exercises that will correct the problem, or at least prevent it from getting worse. Corrective exercises for thoracic kyphosis include arches (Figure 19.3), flagman presses (Figure 19.35), lying frog press (Figure 19.48), thoracic clock (Figure 19.57), and mad cat (Figure 19.32). Pectoralis minor syndrome is discussed on p. 247.

Cervical lordosis is an accentuation of the normal hyperextension curve of the cervical region. This condition is often associated with a condition known as *forward head*. When the cervical region is hyperextended, the face will tip upward, making it "difficult" to see in front of the body. The chin juts forward to allow vision to focus forward instead of upward. It is thought that the muscular cause of this condition is tightness of the flexors of the neck, particularly the sternocleidomastoid and the anterior scaleni. Stretching the neck flexors often allows repositioning of the head directly above the center of the spine. Neck stretches and neck circles (Figure 19.38) are effective for this condition.

Scoliosis is a condition which may occur in any region of the spine. It is a more complex condition than lordosis or kyphosis because it involves two planes of action, the frontal and the transverse. Scoliosis involves both lateral flexion and rotation, or a sideward bending combined with a twisting of the spine. The lateral flexion may be concave (indented) on the right or left side, and the rotation may be toward either the right or the left side. This makes "neatly packaged" exercises difficult, if not theoretically impossible, to prescribe. However, if one simply listens to the body, corrective exercises can be found. As a person with scoliosis does exercises for the torso region, it is common to find one side more difficult than the other. If in doing strength exercises such as abdominal curls (Figure 19.2) or arches (Figure 19.3), one side is stronger than the other, do more repetitions on the weak side. If in doing torso stretches, such as those in Figure 19.10, one side is tighter than the other, spend more time stretching the tight side. While this may be a simplistic approach to a complicated condition, it will at least begin to initiate the necessary balancing of strength and mobility in a scoliotic spine. The thoracic clock (Figure 19.57) may serve to identify additional tight or weak zones.

Upper back and neck tension is common among dancers because of the simultaneous contraction of antagonistic muscles (particularly the upper and lower trapezius) called for by proper dance technique. Stretching is an effective way to reduce tension in this area. Some exercises that are thought to be effective for this are neck stretches (Figure 19.38), the arm-over stretch (Figure 19.36), the latissimus stretch (Figure 19.10e), the reciprocal stretch for pectoralis major (Figure 19.39), the doorjamb hang (Figure 19.40), the water ski stretch (Figure 19.58), the shoulder flop (Figure 19.37), the thoracic clock (Figure 19.57), and the shoulder clock (Figure 19.56). Experimentation with these stretches and releasing exercises will point to the exercises that are most effective for an individual. When weakness of the shoulder region is contributing to the tension, the shoulder sequence (Figure 19.29), seated arm circles (Figure 19.28), and flagman presses (Figure 19.35) are also recommended, but remember to stretch out after doing the strength exercises.

Shoulder and Scapula

Pectoralis minor syndrome occurs when the pectoralis minor is tight and constantly pulls the scapula into a forward tilt. The syndrome includes shoulders that angle forward from the chest so that the tip of the acromion process is well in front of the frontal plane that bisects the rest of the body; and a cupping of the shoulders when viewed from the front so that there is a hollowed-out look just beneath the clavicle. The sensory experience of pectoralis minor syndrome includes any combination of the following: severe pain and/or spasm in the area of the upper trapezius, levator scapulae, and/or the rhomboids (this sometimes progresses to the muscles of the neck, so that turning the head is extremely painful, if it is possible at all); and pain radiating down the medial (ulnar) side of the arm, sometimes all the way down to the fourth and fifth fingers. Unfortunately, the pectoralis minor is difficult to stretch: no "backward tilt" is possible, because the scapula makes contact with the rib cage at an inferior angle. For this reason, the most direct route to relief is through deep massage of the pectoralis minor (Figure 19.41). Some stretches provide relief if the condition has not progressed too far. They are the arm-over stretch (Figure 19.36), doorjamb stretch (Figure 19.40), reciprocal stretch for the pectoralis major (Figure 19.39), shoulder flop (Figure 19.37), and shoulder clock (Figure 19.56).

Triceps-biceps interface is a muscular imbalance I discovered at a time when I was playing a lot of golf. The tendon of the biceps brachii, where it runs through the bicipital groove, became very tender, making me think of bursitis or tendonitis. One day, after twenty-seven holes of golf, I was poking around the shoulder, letting my "fingers do the walking" in search of the source of pain. Without thinking about it, my hands started to massage the short head of the triceps, on the posterior of the upper arm. As my fingers probed, I yowled "Ouch!" I long ago learned that any point *that* tender is a potential source of other problems, and I did some painful, deep massage on the tender spot. The next day the pain in the tendon of the biceps was gone—and it stayed gone as long as I stretched out the triceps periodically and continued to do the deep massage on the short head of the triceps. I share this information now, even though I have not yet figured out the exact reason for the interfacing pain, except that the two muscles are antagonistic.

Elbow joint pain is another golf-related pain, presumably related to the amount of pronation and supination of the radio-ulnar joint required in the golf swing. When the elbow starts to throb, stretching the elbow, wrist, and finger flexors seems to reduce the pain. To do the stretch, reach the painful arm straight out in front of you with palm facing up and elbow straight. With the opposite hand, reach underneath, take hold of the fingers, and pull them down toward the floor while keeping the stretching elbow straight. Hold the stretch for at least thirty seconds, and up to two minutes. (Note: One of my friends was taking ibuprofen for pain so that she could play golf. Once she started doing this exercise, she found herself pain-free and no longer needed medication.)

Serratus anterior tightness is a condition that I discovered while working on this very book. Hours and hours at the keyboard (with the arms slightly in front of the body and the scapula slightly abducted) required a continuous low-grade contraction of the serratus anterior. The pain was somewhat similar to pectoralis minor syndrome, focused in the upper back but a little lower (perhaps the middle trapezius?), and radiating around the rib cage (following the path of the serratus anterior). Like the pectoralis minor, the serratus anterior is difficult to stretch, so I just reached up just under the armpit with the opposite hand and did deep, circular massage on the attachments of the serratus on the lateral side of the rib cage. After the massage, the scapula settled back into a nonabducted position and the pain disappeared.

Weakness of the adductors of the scapula and *weakness of the outward rotators of the shoulder joint* are two conditions that are quite common to dancers and nondancers alike. This muscular weakness may be one reason why *rotator cuff injuries* are on the rise. For most of us, the inward rotators of the shoulder joint are quite strong because we use them in everyday activities like driving an automobile. The outward rotators, on the other hand, are often very weak because they are seldom used against resistance. Strengthening the outward rotators of the shoulder joint, coupled with strengthening the adductors of the scapula, may be a wise preventive measure. Rowing exercises are excellent, and flagman presses (Figure 19.35) will also strengthen these muscle groups.

Whole Body—Side View

Forward or backward lean most often results from an imbalance in weight distribution on the front and back of the foot. The site of the shift and the resultant stress is usually the ankle joint. In forward lean, carrying too much weight on the ball of the foot means that the heels seldom make solid contact with the ground. A state of semi-plantar flexion is maintained almost continuously. Achilles tendonitis (the gastrocnemius and soleus) might result from this imbalance of weight distribution. The backward lean, on the other hand, places more weight on the heels, and the dorsiflexors of the ankle must contract to prevent falling on the tush. It is likely that shin splints (particularly of the tibialis anterior and the extensor digitorum longus) will result from carry too much weight on the heels. For anterior shin splints, do the shin splint stretch (Figure 19.17); for Achilles tendonitis and/or posterior shin splints, do the gastrocnemius and soleus stretch (Figure 19.22). Also, for both of these conditions, Rest, Icing, Compression, and Elevation (RICE) are indicated. In addition, some measures should be taken to change standing habits to rebalance the distribution of weight between the front and the back of the foot.

Hyperextended or hyperflexed knees must be analyzed separately because the two conditions result from different causes.

The most common cause of *hyperflexed knees* is tightness of the hamstrings, although tightness of the gastrocnemius may also be a factor. This condition is most common in, but not exclusive to, men who enter dance after intense participation in athletics. Men and women with tight hamstrings and hyperflexed knees have taken my conditioning class, and in the first two or three weeks of the class, many of them have insisted that their hamstrings simply will not stretch. My ever-so-subtle reply is, "Horsepuckey! You just haven't been determined enough about stretching. Give it six weeks of every-other-day stretching, and you will see a remarkable change." (I must add here that I have never been disappointed, but I must also note that I was there to nag, nag, nag.) Stretching exercises for the hamstrings include the second half of the plow (Figure 19.6), the seated reciprocal hamstring stretch (Figure 19.26), and the supine hamstring stretch (Figure 19.45).

Hyperextended knees are a postural habit. The habit is often a side effect of tight hip flexors and/or lumbar lordosis. Changing the primary misalignment often reduces the degree of hyperextension. Still, the habit sometimes persists. For students with a stubborn habit of hyperextension of the knees, I recommend taping an "X" behind the knee joint when it is ever so slightly flexed. Then, when the knee is hyperextended, the tape pulls on the skin, giving immediate sensory feedback regarding the misalignment. Of course, if the tendency to hyperextension is extreme, the tape pulls off altogether. When that happens, I encourage the student to try to keep the tape on for gradually longer and longer periods in class. Quite a few students have corrected their tendency to hyperextended knees using this taping technique. There is still a problem, however. Some dance techniques actually encourage a hyperextended knee for such skills as arabesque because of the aesthetically pleasing line of the leg when the knee is hyperextended. A dancer must decide for himself or herself which is more important, safety or aesthetic line. It is indeed a choice.

Whole Body—Front or Back View

This final check is to assess the relative *equality of the right and left sides of the body.* While much of this information is gleaned from the analysis of muscular strength and elasticity (see Table 13.3), there are some features that need special attention.

Feet: Are there differences in degree of pronation and/or supination? If so, you will want to adjust the number of repetitions of exercises done on each side, to bring the feet closer to balance.

Knees: Are the knees facing in the same direction (with center of patella directly over the space between the first and second toe)? See cross-eyed knees and chondromalacia of the patella, discussed above.

Hips: Are the hips of equal height? (This is related to variance in leg length.) Clearly, there is nothing to be done to make the legs of equal length, but the musculature can be checked for equal strength and elasticity, and programs can be designed to come closer to balance.

Shoulders: Are the shoulders of equal height? Variance here would be related to torso scoliosis.

Head to one side or the other, or *wry neck,* is related to cervical scoliosis. The neck stretches (Figure 19.38) can be done in all directions to identify the direction that is most limited. Once identified, that segment of the stretch should be done regularly. This condition may also be related to hearing loss in one ear.

Applying the Information

All of the information gained from the assessment of alignment and the relative balance or imbalance of strength and mobility is simply worthless unless it is put to use. Going through the whole assessment process does not ensure change. Each dancer must ask, "What am I going to do with this information?" Uses of the information can be classified into two categories: (1) understanding and self-acceptance and (2) taking control of one's own growth and development.

Self-Acceptance and Understanding

In the past, I have been puzzled and dismayed by the demoralizing self-chastisement and self-degradation of dancers who discovered imperfections in their instrument. It seemed that one flaw in an otherwise perfect body became the obsessive focus of all perceptions. Dancers do tend to personalize any limitation they may have and generalize it to everything. ("If I have limited outward rotation of the hip"—or some other limitation—"I am a bad person.") That kind of response to information about capacities and limitations is certainly not the intention of the assessment process. Dancers must realize that there is no such thing as the perfect body for dance. *The demands of dance are too all-encompassing for one body to meet all them.* If a dancer is extremely flexible, it is likely that he or she will have problems with stability, and vice versa. A dancer with a narrow pelvis is likely to have limited range of motion in outward rotation of the hip joints, but is also likely to have a more efficient "machine" for locomotion and will be capable of higher and longer jumps and leaps. A condition which from one perspective seems to be a limitation may be considered a capacity when it is viewed from a different perspective. Kinesiological analysis allows for viewing body function from many different perspectives.

The purposes of assessment of capacities and limitations are (1) to realistically appraise capacities and limitations; (2) to identify those limitations which can be transformed into capacities through exercise and training; (3) to accept those limitations which cannot be changed and learn to work with them, not against them; and last, but certainly not least, (4) to take responsibility for modifying limitations which can be changed. This brings us to the second category of uses of the information: taking control of one's own growth and change.

Taking Control

Dancers often seek the "perfect" technique teacher, in the hope that this teacher will solve all their problems and transform them into perfect dancers. I call this the "do me" or "dance me" phenomenon. The emotionally mature dancer comes to the realization that improvement is to be found only through self-direction and self-discipline. No single teacher is a magic key to dancing—the key is to be found within each dancer, through honest self-appraisal, determined self-discipline, and educated self-direction.

Dance kinesiology plays an important role in self-direction. Through careful assessment of alignment and muscular imbalances, the dancer can identify limitations and strengths. He or she can reduce chronic pain caused by correctable misalignments or muscular imbalances, and can initiate the transformation of some limitations into strengths.

The first time one actually *uses* kinesiological analysis to identify the source of a recurring pain, correct the problem, and stop the pain, there is an incredible sense of appreciation of the information gained through dance kinesiology. One steps out of the role of a helpless victim and into the role of a knowledgeable practitioner who can make changes to reduce the likelihood of recurrance of pain. There is a very real sense of power in this moment: the power of self-knowledge, self-correction, and self-control. Likewise, there is a deep sense of pride when one transforms a limitation into a capacity through self-discipline. Every truly successful dancer has a personal list of physical victories over bad habits. In the "old days" dancers were left on their own to find solutions to their problems. Perhaps now, with a solid kinesiological background, dancers will be able to make the transformation more rapidly and effectively. This is not meant to imply that change becomes easy. No matter how you slice it, changing habits is difficult. But it does help considerably to be working on the right thing.

Kinesiological information, however, should never be used as a cop-out. It is sometimes tempting for a dancer to say, "I have Morton short toe. I'll never be able to balance, so why should I try?" Admittedly, the length of the toe cannot be changed. But the strength of the musculature which stabilizes the ankle/tarsus region can be increased to facilitate better balance. Kinesiological information allows the dancer to identify the problem and create an alternative, workable solution to a seemingly unchangeable problem.

Honest self-appraisal, realistic goals, and determined self-discipline are all critical elements in the making of a dancer. Dance kinesiology can assist in the first two; the dancer must provide the self-discipline.

Physiological Considerations for Dancers

CHAPTER 14

Physiological Support Systems

Certain elements of physiology are fundamental to understanding the functioning of the human body. Dance curricula seldom include separate courses on the physiological bases of exercise. Therefore, the fundamentals of exercise physiology are included here (even though they, technically, are not part of the kinesiological body of knowledge). Three major areas of physiological functioning will be briefly discussed: the cardiovascular system, the respiratory system, and the neurological (nervous) system. Most of the information presented is quite rudimentary, but it does roughly outline the basic physiological functioning of the systems and their responses to conditioning.

The Cardiovascular System

Structure and Function

The cardiovascular system includes the heart and the blood vessels (arteries, capillaries, and veins) which transport blood to the various regions of the body. The heart is the center of the cardiovascular system (see Figure 14.1). It has four chambers: two *atria* and two *ventricles*. The right and left atria receive blood returning from the body and from the lungs, respectively. From the atria, the blood passes into the right and left ventricles and is pumped out of the heart to the lungs and to the body by contraction of the heart. At each junction in the heart (between chambers, between veins and the atria, and between the ventricles and the arteries) there are *valves* which regulate the flow of blood by preventing reversal of the flow. The sounds one hears listening to the heart are actually the closing of the heart valves.

The circulation of blood can be followed by starting at any point in the cardiovascular system and returning to the point of origin. Starting at the right atrium of the heart, the blood passes to the right ventricle and from there, via the pulmonary artery, to the lungs for oxygenation. Returning from the lungs via the pulmonary vein, the oxygenated blood passes through the left atrium and left ventricle to the aorta. It is worthy of note

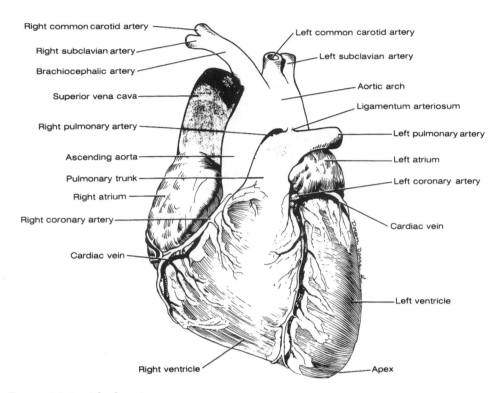

Right common carotid artery

Right subclavian artery

Brachiocephalic artery

Superior vena cava

Right pulmonary artery

Ascending aorta

Pulmonary trunk

Right atrium

Right coronary artery

Cardiac vein

Right ventricle

Left common carotid artery

Left subclavian artery

Aortic arch

Ligamentum arteriosum

Left pulmonary artery

Left atrium

Left coronary artery

Cardiac vein

Left ventricle

Apex

FIGURE 14.1.   The heart

that the pulmonary artery and pulmonary vein are the two exceptions to the rule that arteries carry oxygenated blood and veins carry blood with carbon dioxide. From the aorta, the blood flows through the branching arteries and arterioles to the capillaries (diverging blood bed), where the oxygen is exchanged for carbon dioxide for expulsion. The blood then moves through the converging blood bed (capillaries, venules, veins) and eventually reaches the vena cava, which transports the blood to the right atrium.

The arteries and veins, illustrated in Figures 14.2 and 14.3, differ from each other physically. Artery walls are lined with smooth muscle tissue, and as the blood flows into the artery, the walls of the artery are stretched, causing an elastic recoil that serves as a pumping action and assists circulation through the arteries. With advancing age, the walls of the arteries may lose some of their elasticity, and there may be a buildup of plaque on the inside of the arteries (athersclerosis), which can block the flow of blood through the arteries.

Veins, illustrated in Figure 14.3, have no such pumping action, but instead have valves which prevent the backup of blood. (The contraction of surrounding skeletal muscle does put pressure on the veins and provides a modified pumping action.) The valves are evenly spaced in the veins, with chambers between valves. Once the blood reaches a given chamber, it cannot back up unless a valve is malfunctioning, in which case the blood re-

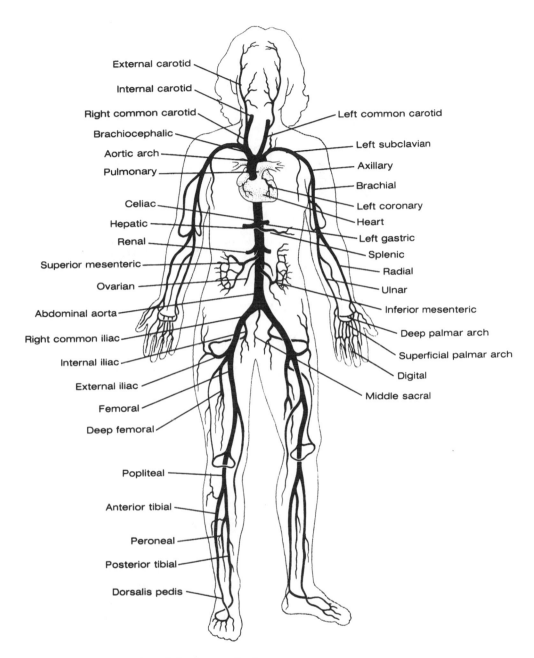

FIGURE 14.2. **Arteries of the human body**

cedes to the preceding chamber, "pooling" there until the following blood pressure forces it onward. Varicose veins are the result of malfunctioning valves and subsequent pooling of blood in the chambers of the veins. The previously mentioned contraction of the musculature in the vicinity of the veins puts pressure on the blood bed and forces the blood in the only direction it can go (because of the valves), which is back toward the heart.

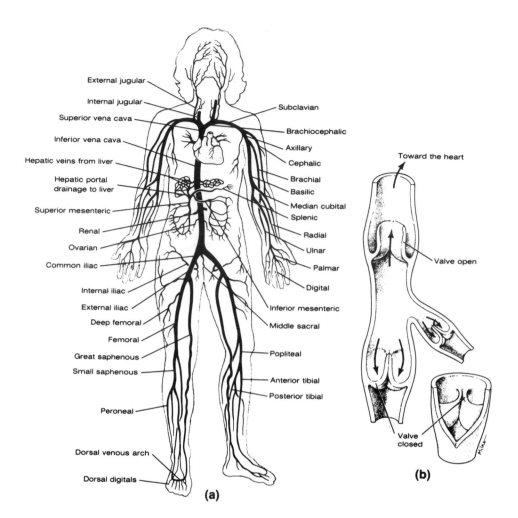

Figure 14.3. (*a*) Veins of the human body; (*b*) valves in the veins

The blood returning to the heart is called *venous return*. Venous return is increased both by the muscular contraction around the veins and by a pumping action of the diaphragm as it ascends and descends between the thoracic and abdominal cavities, putting pressure on the vena cava, which passes through the diaphragm.

Vasoconstriction and Vasodilation

The *capillary bed* is the site where oxygen is exchanged for carbon dioxide. The diameter of vessels in the blood bed can *constrict* (get smaller) or *dilate* (get larger). Vasoconstriction and vasodilation of the arterioles leading into the capillaries aid the system in directing the flow of blood to the active regions of the body and away from the low-use areas. The blood volume in a normal adult does not vary dramatically except for minor fluxuations that accompany increased or decreased activity or dehydration.

Consequently, the blood flow must be regulated and directed to active areas by vasoconstriction and vasodilation. Muscular contraction and exercise will cause vasodilation of the blood vessels supplying the active musculature, and the inactive areas will vasoconstrict. Ingestion of food will cause vasodilation in the visceral area; this is the primary reason for not eating a big meal before a performance. If the visceral blood vessels are vasodilated, there is simply not enough blood to adequately supply the active muscles.

Changes in postural position require changes in vasoconstriction and vasodilation patterns to maintain needed blood flow to all areas of the body. Gravity has just as powerful an effect on the blood as it does on other liquids: in the veins, the blood will run "downhill" and pool at the lowest point unless there is constriction or contraction of surrounding skeletal muscle. Standing for long periods of time often causes pooling of the blood in the legs. Swollen, aching legs can be the result. The responsiveness of the blood bed to changes in posture and activity levels varies from individual to individual. Some people have a system that will adapt quickly, and some have a system that adapts more slowly. Dizziness after standing up quickly is caused by ineffective adaptation to a new posture. When one is seated or lying down, the demands on the circulatory system are less intense than when one is standing. As one stands, the blood flows "downhill" and there is insufficient blood flow to the brain, causing dizziness until the blood vessels in the lower extremities are constricted. These factors contribute to the need for warm-up and cool-down. Gradual adjustment to exercise is necessary at the beginning of exercise (warm-up). Gradual cessation of exercise (cool-down) prevents pooling of blood in the previously active regions of the body.

Blood Pressure

Vasoconstriction and vasodilation are critical in the maintenance of blood flow to the various parts of the body and have an effect on blood pressure. Blood pressure is actually measured in the arteries. For consistency of measurement, the blood pressure cuff is always placed on the right arm at heart level, with the subject seated. This placement measures the blood pressure in the brachial artery. As the heart pumps the blood into the aorta and then into all the branching arteries, there is an initial pressure in the arteries as the blood is forced into the blood vessel, distending the walls of the artery. This pressure is reflected in the higher of the two figures in the standard blood pressure measurement, *systolic* blood pressure. The lower pressure figure is an indication of the pressure exerted by the elastic recoil of the muscular walls of the artery. This second pressure forces the blood along in the artery; it is called *diastolic* blood pressure.

Control of Heart Rate and Blood Pressure

In activity and rest, blood pressure and heart rate increase and decrease to maintain a circulatory balance (*homeostasis*) within normal limits. A number of factors control heart rate and blood pressure.

NEURAL CONTROLS

The pacemaker (or sinoatrial node) stimulates the heart at a steady rate. A speedup of the heart rate is caused by the accelerator branch, which is constantly active. If the accelerator branch were allowed to function without controls, the heart would just keep speeding up, continually. Luckily, the vagus nerve provides deceleration. The vagus nerve is stimulated by heightened blood pressure in the carotid sinus of the carotid artery. When the heart rate accelerates, there is a rise in the blood pressure in all of the arteries, including the carotid artery in the neck. The rise in blood pressure causes a stimulation of the vagus nerve and a subsequent slowing of the heart rate, followed by a lowering of the blood pressure. The sensitivity of the vagus nerve seems to be affected by activity. The higher the activity level and the better the person's physical condition, the more sensitive is the vagus nerve. This variable is called *vagal tone*, and is thought to be a primary reason why trained athletes have a lower resting heart rate than untrained individuals. Another reason is that the stroke volume per beat is greater, thus allowing a slower pulse. While these three neural controls (pacemaker, accelerator branch, and vagus nerve) have a direct effect on the heart rate, there are other phenomena that also affect it.

STROKE VOLUME

The volume of blood pumped by the heart in one cycle is called *stroke volume*. This measure of cardiac function is directly affected by the amount of blood returned from the veins (venous return), with a higher venous return resulting in a higher stroke volume. As the stroke volume rises, the systolic blood pressure also rises, causing stimulation of the vagus nerve and a resultant lowering of the heart rate. In exercise, the sympathetic nervous system overrides the control, and blood pressure rises. If venous return is poor, stroke volume will decrease, causing a lower blood pressure and no stimulation of the vagus nerve, and thus allowing the accelerator branch, which is constantly active, to speed up the heart.

CHEMICAL REGULATION

Another major control of heart rate and blood pressure is chemical. The presence of high levels of carbon dioxide in the system will increase the acidity (a low pH level) in the bloodstream, resulting in a rise in heart rate and blood pressure. Another chemical response is the presence of *epinephrine*, also known as *adrenaline*, in the system accompanying any emotional or stressful situation. Adrenaline will cause a rise in the heart rate and respiratory rate.

AMBIENT FACTORS

Ambient factors such as altitude and temperature also have an effect on heart rate. For example, if the temperature is high, the blood vessels vasodilate and the heart must speed up to maintain homeostasis. A low temperature will cause vasoconstriction and a subsequent slowing of the heart rate to a point. Altitude variations affect respiration because of lower partial pressure of oxygen at high altitudes. The respiratory rate increases at high altitudes, to get sufficient oxygen.

Exercise and the Cardiovascular System

As cardiorespiratory condition is improved with a systematic exercise program, there will be a number of changes in the functioning of the cardiovascular system. The heart size will increase, and the resting heart rate will slow down. (It is not unusual for endurance-trained athletes to have a resting heart rate below fifty beats per minute.) Venous return will be improved by better muscle tone in the musculature, and the stroke volume will thus be increased. There will be a slight increase in blood volume as well as an increased red blood cell count.

TARGET HEART RATE

In order for these changes to occur, stress must be placed on the cardiorespiratory systems. Most dance classes do not focus on cardiorespiratory conditioning. In order to stress the system, a medium to high "target" heart rate must be maintained continuously for fifteen to twenty minutes. In dance class, it is common to cross the floor once and then rest as the other students cross the floor. There is really very little conditioning of the cardiorespiratory systems in these circumstances. In order to build one's cardiorespiratory level, one must identify a target heart rate and then participate in a repetitive activity which maintains that heart rate for fifteen to twenty minutes. One formula that can be used to calculate the target heart rate is in Table 14.1. Another version of the formula is in Chapter 19.

CARDIORESPIRATORY FITNESS FOR DANCERS

Cardiorespiratory fitness is just as important to dancers as it is to athletes, but dance training seldom has paid as much attention to it. While some choreographers are noted for the vigorous demands they place on dancers, it is rare to find sufficient preconditioning for those demands in dance classes. It is usually up to the dancer to prepare for demanding roles. Yet the need for cardiorespiratory fitness goes beyond the preparation for a specific role. High levels of cardiorespiratory fitness delay the

TABLE 14.1   Calculating Target Heart Rate*

A = 220
B = Age in years
C = Resting heart rate (taken after five minutes rest)
D = 60% (0.60)
E = Maximum heart rate (A − B =——)
F = Range or maximum heart rate reserve (E − C =——)
G = Additive factor (F × D =——)
H = TARGET HEART RATE (C + G =——)

*Adapted from *Journal of Health, Physical Education and Recreation*, March/April, 1977.

onset of fatigue and accelerate the recovery rate from vigorous exercise. These factors, coupled with the well-known general health benefits, make cardiorespiratory fitness essential for dancers.

Realistically, one cannot expect the tradition of dance training to change overnight. Moreover, the time required for effective cardiorespiratory conditioning is prohibitive when most dance classes last only one and a half hours. Dance teachers and students are justifiably protective of that time. If there is reluctance to use class time to build necessary levels of cardiorespiratory fitness, the individual dancer must design a program for himself or herself. Suggestions for this type of conditioning are given in Chapter 19.

The Respiratory System

Structure and Function

The respiratory system includes the *trachea* (windpipe), *bronchial tubes, bronchioles, lungs,* and *alveoli* (air sacs) of the lungs (see Figure 14.4a–b). The rib cage houses the lungs. Attached to the rib cage are the primary muscles of respiration, including the intercostals, the serratus posterior superior, the serratus posterior inferior, and the diaphragm (see Figure 14.4c–e). Respiration is controlled autonomically by the medulla, but conscious control from the cerebral cortex can override autonomic control.[1] That is why thinking about breathing makes the process seem unnatural.

The respiratory phenomena—including pulmonary ventilation in the lungs, gaseous transport, and gaseous exchange at the tissue level—provide the body with the oxygen needed to continue activity.

The Flow of Gases in Breathing

All gases in the ambient atmosphere flow into the lungs when the pressure in the lungs is lower than the ambient pressure. Conversely, gases flow out of the lungs when the pressure in the lungs is greater than the ambient pressure. Beyond that, each gas has its own pressure gradient, which varies according to the relative concentration of that gas at a given site. Gases flow passively to the areas of lower concentration.

Gaseous Exchange

The two gases critical to the respiratory process are oxygen and carbon dioxide. When a gas enters the system, it is taken into the blood and transported as a liquid. The relative concentration of oxygen and carbon dioxide governs the process of *gaseous exchange*. Gaseous exchange occurs at the alveoli and again in the capillary bed.

---

1. The autonomic nervous system innervates both smooth and cardiac muscle and controls glandular secretions.

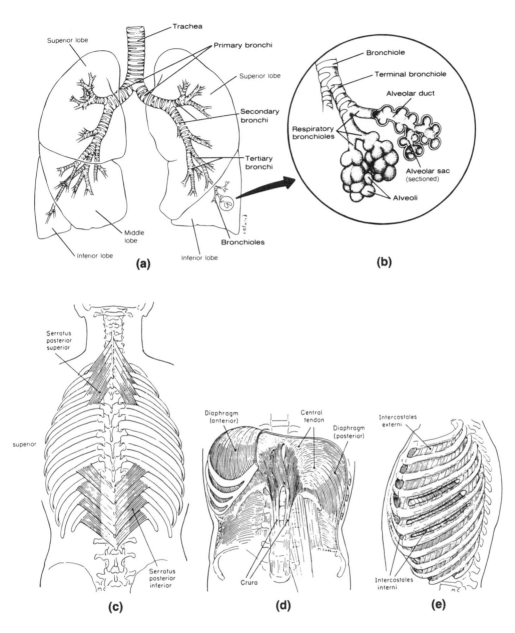

FIGURE 14.4. Respiratory system: (*a*) lungs; (*b*) bronchiole and alveoli; (*c*) serratus posterior superior and inferior; (*d*) diaphragm; (*e*) intercostal muscles

When an individual begins to exercise, carbon dioxide is produced at the site of the active musculature by the metabolism of glycogen and fats and the resynthesis of adenosine triphosphate (ATP) from adenosine diphosphate (ADP). There is an immediate vasodilation at the site of activity in response to higher acidity levels, and that vasodilation facilitates the process of gaseous exchange. In the muscle tissue, following the onset of exercise, there is a higher concentration of carbon dioxide than there is in the capillaries supplying that region. Likewise, the capillaries contain a higher concentration of oxygen than is present in the muscle tissue. The discrepancy in the pressure gradients of oxygen and carbon dioxide causes the exchange of gases, with the carbon dioxide leaving the surrounding tissue by diffusion and entering the blood. The oxygen leaves the hemoglobin and diffuses to the area of lower concentration in the muscle tissue. From this point, the carbon dioxide is carried in the bloodstream back to the heart, where it is pumped to the lungs via the pulmonary artery. Carbon dioxide in the blood is combined with water to form carbonic acid. High levels of acidity in the bloodstream, as already noted, increase heart rate and respiratory rate. Thus, the increase in the levels of carbon dioxide in the blood after exercise is one reason for an increase in heart and respiratory rates.

The presence of potassium and sodium can serve to neutralize or "buffer" the acidity in the bloodstream, thus lowering the immediate acidity levels and thereby maintaining lower heart and respiratory rates.

When the blood, high in acidity owing to carbon dioxide levels, reaches the alveoli, there again is a discrepancy in the pressure gradient for both oxygen and carbon dioxide. There is a higher concentration of carbon dioxide in the alveoli than in the air coming into the lungs. Conversely, the air coming into the lungs has a higher concentration of oxygen than the air in the alveoli. Because gases flow passively to the lower pressure, oxygen flows into the alveoli and carbon dioxide is expelled. High levels of acidity in the alveoli cause an impulse to exhale, thus expelling the carbon dioxide. This is the primary reason for the forced exhalation which occurs with high levels of exercise.

Mechanics of Breathing

The mechanical function of breathing is caused by changing the relative size and volume of the rib cage. When the rib cage is rotated upward and elevated, and the diaphragm is lowered, a vacuum is created in the lungs and the ambient atmosphere rushes into the lungs. When the rib cage is depressed and rotated downward, and the diaphragm has risen, the pressure is increased in the lungs and the air rushes out. The action of the rib cage is controlled by the muscles of respiration, primarily the diaphragm, serratus posterior superior and inferior, and intercostal muscles (refer back to Figure 14.4c, d, e).

The serratus posterior superior elevates and upwardly rotates the rib cage. This action stretches the intercostal muscles, and they respond with a contraction activated by an action similar to the stretch reflex, which further upwardly rotates the rib cage. This action combined with the descent of the diaphragm produces active inhalation.

Active exhalation is initiated by the serratus posterior inferior, which depresses and downwardly rotates the rib cage. Simultaneously, the diaphragm ascends, serving to increase the pressure within the rib cage. In exhalation, like inhalation, the intercostals are stretched and respond with a contraction, thereby increasing the pressure in the rib cage and facilitating exhalation.

The autonomic control of breathing is centered in the medulla but can be overridden by the cerebral cortex. There is a constant impulse to inspire (similar to the constant impulse to speed the heart rate) in the neural control of breathing. The impulse to inspire is broken by high pressure in the alveoli or by feedback from the muscles of respiration. In normal resting breathing, inhalation is active and exhalation is passive. However, in heavy exercise exhalation becomes the more active phase. If a person is unaccustomed to exercise, the muscles of respiration can fatigue and even can go into spasm. This may contribute to a respiratory phenomenon called *side ache* or a "stitch in the side." However, some authorities consider a stitch in the side to be more complex than a simple muscle spasm.

Other Respiratory Phenomena

Other respiratory phenomena include second wind, hyperventilation, elevated postexercise oxygen consumption, and acclimatization to high altitude.

Second wind occurs when, in extreme exertion, the breathing shifts from labored to easy breathing. It is doubtful that this phenomenon is exclusively respiratory, but the major observable effects of second wind are respiratory. It is somewhat as if the body has just shifted into "overdrive": the more efficient fuel consumption makes activity seem easier.

Hyperventilation occurs when unnecessarily high levels of oxygen are present in the system and more carbon dioxide is exhaled than necessary. The result may be forced breathing, dizziness, loss of consciousness, cyanosis (fingernails and lips turning blue), and involuntary flexing of the fingers and toes. Hyperventilation seems to be related to performance in highly emotional states or under extreme stress. Immediate care for hyperventilation involves increasing alveolar levels of carbon dioxide. This can be done by breathing into a paper bag or cupping the hands over the mouth and nose so that the hyperventilator is, in effect, breathing the same air he or she has expelled, which is higher in carbon dioxide than the ambient atmosphere. Following an attack of hyperventilation, an individual should always consult a physician.

Another phenomenon is *elevated postexercise oxygen consumption*. The term *oxygen debt* is sometimes used to describe the energy deficit occurring when the body uses more oxygen than is immediately available. The concept is presently in disrepute with exercise physiologists, but is included here because some authorities still refer to it.

Acclimatization to high altitude is necessary because in higher altitudes the partial pressure of oxygen in the ambient atmosphere is less than at lower altitudes. Consequently, the entire respiratory system must work harder to inhale the same amount of oxygen.

Measurement of Respiratory Capacities

A number of measurements of capacity are used by exercise physiologists to evaluate the functioning of the cardiovascular and respiratory systems. The most common measure of respiratory efficiency is *maximum oxygen uptake* (VO_2 max), which represents the maximal difference between oxygen inspired and oxygen expired. Another, less common measure is *lactate levels* in the bloodstream. Blood samples are drawn and blood lactate levels are measured at different activity levels. At the same activity level, trained athletes will often have a lower lactate level than untrained individuals. Moreover, toleration of higher lactate levels (acidity in the system) is thought to be one indication of superior conditioning. Other measurements include various measures of lung capacity.

Effects of Conditioning

An intensive conditioning program has some definite effects on the respiratory and breathing processes. The hemoglobin count in the bloodstream increases, making the transport of oxygen more efficient. The levels of buffers in the bloodstream increase, making prolonged intense activity more possible. Respiratory rate during submaximal exercise decreases and the recovery time following exercise decreases. These changes make the body better able to withstand the stress of continued exercise for longer periods of time.

The Nervous System

The nervous system is the regulator and director of human interaction with the internal and external environments. It comprises the *central nervous system* (brain, brain stem, and spinal cord) and the *peripheral nervous system* (nerves which radiate to all parts of the body). Figure 14.5 illustrates the central nervous system and the proximal portions of the peripheral nervous system. The *autonomic nervous system* (sympathetic and parasympathetic) regulates the involuntary visceral, respiratory, hormonal, and cardiac functions of the body. The *somatic system* regulates movement and perception of movement and is therefore of primary concern to dancers. To say that the nervous system is complex is a gross understatement. The presentation of the nervous system in this text is an extreme simplification of how the system functions to stimulate, regulate, and adapt human motion to fluctuating demands. Included here are discussions of the neuron, the synapse, the higher centers of motor control, reflexive control of movement, the kinesthetic sense, and both traditional and recent concepts of hemispheric dominance. As with the discussions of the cardiovascular system and the respiratory system, however, an immense amount of information has been excluded. An effort has been made to screen the information and include only that which is directly applicable to dance and dance education.

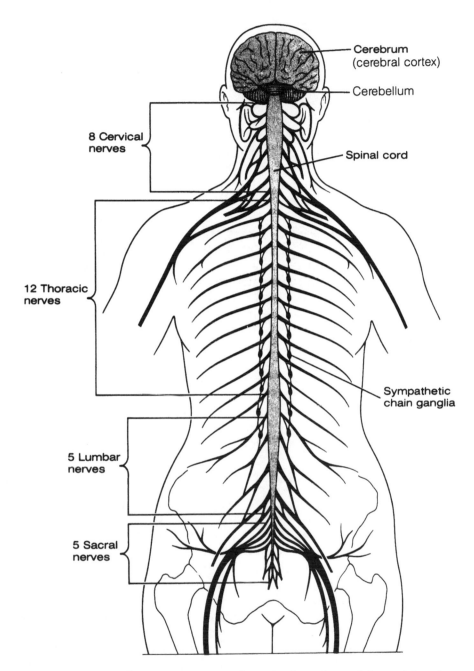

FIGURE 14.5. **Central nervous system and proximal portions of the peripheral nervous system**

Sensory and Motor Neurons

The *neuron* is the most fundamental unit of the nervous system. It consists of a cell body, an axon, and a number of dendrites. Simply speaking, the dendrites receive the stimulation, which then passes through the cell body to the axon, which transmits the impulse to the dendrites of adjacent neurons. The diameter of the neuron varies and has a direct effect upon the speed of the transmission of the impulse. The larger the nerve, the faster the impulse. The *motor unit* is the functional unit which includes the neuron, the motor end plate, and the muscle fibers activated by that nerve.

There are many types of neurons, but the primary classification is *sensory (afferent)* and *motor (efferent)*. Basically, the sensory neurons carry information (input) to the central nervous system (spinal cord and brain), where the information is used to direct or redirect activity. The motor nerves transmit the impulses (output), which stimulate the contraction of muscles. The sensory system is in turn divided into the *exteroceptive system*, which transfers information related to pain, temperature, and touch; and the *proprioceptive* system, which transfers information about muscle contraction, tension, stretch, and joint position. The proprioceptive system is an integral component of the kinesthetic sense, discussed later in this chapter.

The system for classifying the neurons is further subdivided into alpha and gamma systems. The *alpha system* is primarily involved with voluntary, conscious activation of movement. The *gamma system* is primarily concerned with grading of action and making postural adjustments. For comprehensive presentations of the function of these systems, the reader is directed to books on exercise physiology and neurophysiology.[2]

The Synapse

The *synapse* is the junction between the axon of one neuron and the dendrite of another neuron. Between the two neurons is a space called the *synaptic gap*. The impulse from the presynaptic neuron is transmitted to the postsynaptic neuron only when conditions allow transmission over that gap. This unique property of the synapse is the primary controller of the path of neural impulses, and thus of which muscles are activated. A given impulse may be *transmitted* or *blocked*, depending on the chemical balance at the site of the synapse. Furthermore, through patterned usage, the transmission of an impulse can be directed to the neurons that have been activated in the past. This phenomenon is called *synaptic facilitation* and is a primary contributor to motor learning. It is also the feature that makes changing an established motor pattern difficult. Previous movement experiences will, therefore, have a definite effect on neural pathways. Once a neural pathway has been established, it is difficult to change that pattern of transmission because the neural transmission automatically flows (because of synaptic facilitation) in the established pathway.

2. Ragnar Granit, *The Basis of Motor Control*. Academic Press, London, 1970.

Therefore, the synapse is crucial to motor learning and relearning. The problem is, of course, that we do not have direct control over the synapse itself. Changing a motor pattern usually requires changing the image of movement and giving the central nervous system new information about the desired movement. In turn, the central nervous system changes the pattern of activation. The nervous system tries a new pathway, but it may not—on first try—be the desired pathway, so another is tried. This is why making changes in movement patterns takes so much time. The information we give to the central nervous system is not always accurate or complete. The more accurate the information given to the central nervous system, the faster the desired movement combination can be performed.

Neurological Centers Involved in Motor Performance

The central nervous system comprises the brain, the brain stem, and the spinal cord. In different systems of classification there is some overlapping of terms and disagreement regarding exact locations. The brain stem, for example, may be considered part of the brain. When one divides the brain into its geographical areas, the classification is forebrain, midbrain, and hindbrain. This classification includes components which other sources call the brain stem.

Whatever the classification system, there is a set of two cerebral hemispheres (in the forebrain) which include the cerebral cortex, basal ganglia, corona radiata, thalamus, hypothalamus, and corpus callosum (the connection between the two hemispheres). In between and below the cerebrum (hemispheres) is the midbrain, which includes a number of nuclei (concentrations of cell bodies that transmit impulses to and from different regions of the brain), and the anterior portion of the reticular activating system. The posterior portion of the reticular activating system extends back into the hindbrain, which also includes the pons, medulla oblongata, and cerebellum. The spinal cord descends from the hindbrain.

Even this grossly abbreviated list of parts of the brain becomes complicated. Instead of dealing with all of the areas of the brain, we will focus our attention on those which have a direct role in the production and control of movement: the cerebral cortex, the midbrain, the cerebellum and thalamus, and the spinal cord. These are schematically illustrated in Figure 14.6.

CEREBRAL CORTEX

The cerebral cortex is the mastermind, the central decision maker and initiator of motion. The primary impulses for motion are transmitted in the main neural pathways from the cerebral cortex (the pyramidal system). Accompanying this primary stimulus is a secondary, regulatory system that facilitates and blocks certain neural pathways on the basis of desired movement. The secondary system is called the *extrapyramidal* system because of the path of neural tracts radiating from it. These two systems work synergistically to produce movement. The activation or cessation of

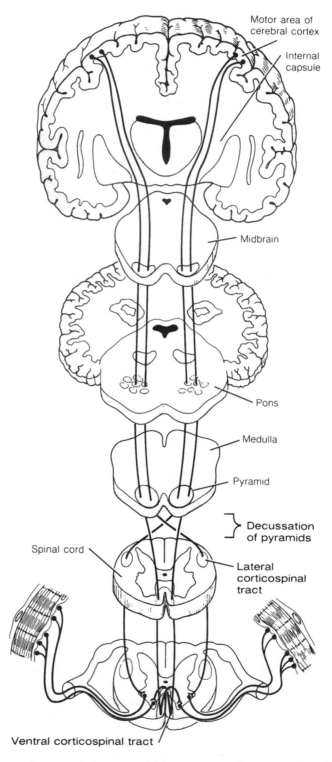

FIGURE 14.6.   Pathways of the pyramidal tracts carrying motor impulses to skeletal muscles

motion is controlled by the cerebral cortex. All complex motor tasks are initiated by the cerebral cortex. The areas of the body that are required to move with great refinement are represented by a larger area in the cerebral cortex than those areas that require only gross control. The cerebral cortex is the initiator of all voluntary motion but is most intensely involved in the movements of the distal ends of limbs, and in movements of the face.

The cerebral cortex is critical in *fine* motor control. However, the cerebral cortex stimuli produce movement that is jerky and unsmooth. The learning of a new movement combination begins with new demands from the cerebral cortex. In the initial stages of motor learning, the movement frequently feels awkward and disjointed. This is the pyramidal system from the cerebral cortex at work, establishing new neural pathways. Once the other centers of motor learning catch up, performing their functions of grading through facilitation and inhibition, the movement begins to become smooth and refined. The extrapyramidal system produces gross movement that is refined by pyramidal control. Information about action and reaction is relayed to the cerebral cortex from the cerebellum via the thalamus. In this way the cerebral cortex can make adjustments to changing demands. The cerebellum also sends neurons to the spinal cord, influencing motor activity directly.

MIDBRAIN

Located in the midbrain is the primitive control center. All of the physiological correlates of emotional response are regulated in this region (sweating, vasoconstriction, vasodilation, etc.). Activation of movement by the midbrain is rhythmical and repetitive in nature. Actually, the word *activation* may be misleading, for the midbrain does not really activate motion but rather continues a pattern once it is established. True initiation is the role of the cerebral cortex. Control of the spinal-level reflexes and regulation of the gamma system are located in the midbrain. The reticular activating formation is thought to be the major factor controlling the gamma system. Beyond its regulatory role, the reticular formation is thought to amplify or attenuate certain impulses to and from the cerebral cortex. It serves as a screening device, determining the relative importance of the incessant barrage of sensory information being transmitted to the cerebral cortex. Research in the 1960s and 1970s identified the reticular activating formation as critical to focusing of conscious attention.

CEREBELLUM AND THALAMUS

The cerebellum and thalamus are located in the posterior portion of the brain (the hindbrain). The cerebellum and thalamus serve as the central switch-board of the nervous system. They do not have the ability to stimulate, but rather only to transmit. They serve in a regulatory, integrative, correlational capacity for all sensory input and motor output. Because they synthesize the information to be passed on to the cerebral cortex and midbrain regarding the status of the body, the cerebellum and thalamus are crucial in the maintenance of an upright posture, equilibrium, and a smooth, coordinated gait. Everyone has been shocked at one time or another by a "foul-up" of the thalamus and the cerebellum. For example, descending a flight of stairs requires adjustment of the contraction in the muscles of the torso and legs at the base of the stairs, when one shifts from descent to a normal gait. If the cerebellum receives the wrong information from the visual center or other centers, you can either miss the last step or continue the descent, depending on the nature of the misinformation. Likewise, when one sits on a chair that is lower than expected (the expectations come from a series of complex neural inputs to the cerebellum), one experiences a sensation of falling. What has actually happened is that the cerebellum and thalamus have signaled the centers of motor control to deactivate the extensor muscles too soon. Thus the sitter is left midair with no muscular support. Impairment in the function of the cerebellum and thalamus tells of their contribution to the neurological system. With dysfunction of the cerebellum and thalamus, movements become jerky and uncoordinated, starts and stops become imprecise, and rapid alternating movements are difficult. The cerebellum is also important in controlling the reciprocal relation between opposing muscles.

SPINAL LEVEL

Certain reactions to movement conditions are stimulated by activation at the spinal level. For example, the gamma system, which governs the stretch reflex is activated on the spinal level. While the stretch reflex occurs at the spinal level, there is also a relay of the information about what is happening sent to the cerebellum and to the midbrain and then relayed to the cerebral cortex. (The stretch reflex is one example of a spinal-level reflex, discussed below.)

Reflexive Control of Movement

SPINAL-LEVEL REFLEXES

The *stretch reflex* has been discussed at length in Chapter 7. It is dependent upon the muscle spindle and the status of the muscle fibers around the spindle (the extrafusal fibers). This reflex causes a contraction of muscle immediately after it has been stretched.

Reciprocal inhibition is a protective reflex to prevent muscle injury which may be caused by maximal contraction of the antagonistic muscle. When a muscle contracts maximally, it could tear the antagonistic muscle unless that antagonist is in a relaxed state. Fortunately, when a given muscle contracts maximally, the opposite muscle or muscles are reciprocally inhibited. That is, the stretch reflex is blocked in the opposite muscle. (This does not refer to *submaximal* co-contraction of agonist and antagonist muscles that is sometimes used to maintain control of position or action.) This reflex happens at the spinal level and is the result of activation of the inhibitory neuron that inhibits the stretch reflex. Reflexive reciprocal inhibition can be used to facilitate greater stretch and allow greater mobility. The reciprocal principle is used in the conditioning program in Chapter 19 as a guide for effective sequencing of exercises. In Chapter 19 there is also a section devoted to the use of reciprocal inhibition to facilitate greater stretch in various muscle groups.

Golgi tendon reflex is another protective reflex. The Golgi tendon organs are located at the musculotendinous junction (where the tendon and the contractile section of the muscle meet). They are sensitive to tension or pressure and are fully activated when the tendon is about to pull off the bone. When the Golgi tendon organs are activated in this way, they also depress the stretch reflex. However, in contrast to the reciprocal reflex, the Golgi tendon reflex depresses the stretch reflex more completely and for a longer period of time, resulting in a flaccid and totally relaxed muscle. In situations where the tension or pressure is submaximal, the Golgi tendon organs transmit proprioceptive feedback to the central nervous system.

Figure 14.7 shows a spinal-level reflex arc.

MASS BODY AND LIMB REFLEXES

In addition to the spinal-level reflexes discussed above, there are three facilitative reflexes which assist human movement. These reflexes occur because of neurological connections that facilitate actions of other muscles. These reflexes are primarily activated on the spinal level, but activation can be overridden by the cerebral cortex. The three facilitative reflexes are the flexor reflex, the extensor reflex, and the crossed-extensor reflex (natural opposition). The *flexor reflex* facilitates activation of all flexor muscles when one flexor muscle is powerfully activated. The *extensor reflex* facilitates activation of all extensor muscles when one extensor muscle is powerfully activated. The *crossed-extensor reflex* facilitates activation of the agonist of the diagonally opposite limb, facilitates the antagonistic muscles of the contralateral limb, and inhibits contralateral agonists. That is, when the right hip is powerfully flexed, the left hip will be extended, the right

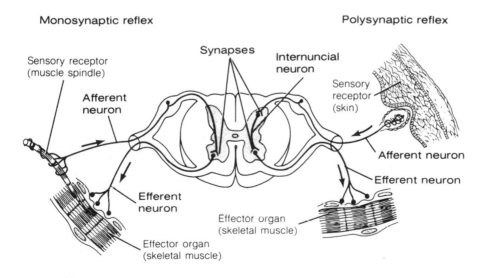

FIGURE 14.7. Schematic drawing of a spinal-level reflex arc

shoulder joint will be extended, and the left shoulder joint will be flexed. Propriospinal reflexes also contribute to natural opposition.

In each of these mass body and limb reflexes, the cerebral cortex can override the reflex and block it. This ability to override the mass reflexes is both a help and a hindrance to dancers. Sometimes blocking the reflex allows specific isolation of motion, but sometimes it causes awkward and uncoordinated movement.

Each of these mass body and limb reflexes has specific implications for dancers. The flexor reflex can be used to effectively increase the intensity of an abdominal contraction. Accompanying the abdominal contraction with a contraction of the flexors of the hands, feet, knees, elbows, etc., makes the contraction in the abdominal region more intense. In addition, awareness of the effect of the flexor reflex can explain why some powerful flexion actions are accompanied by unwanted flexion (called *overflow*) in other areas of the body.

The extensor reflex gives an explanation for the "bucking" which commonly occurs when beginners start to jump. Jumping requires powerful contraction of the extensors of the ankles, knees, and hips. The extensor reflex causes an overflow of neural activity to the extensors of the spine, which results in throwing the head and shoulders backward on a jump (bucking).

The crossed-extensor reflex is active in all balance and locomotion. It is the essential element in the natural tendency to spiral around the central axis. There are certainly implications here for dancers studying the Graham technique of modern dance, for the spiral is an important aspect of that technique. The most common example of a foul-up of the crossed-extensor reflex is seen when students are directed to pay conscious attention to the action of the arms on a skip. Usually, the most ridiculous flailing and flopping of the arms results. This is an example of the cerebral cortex overriding the spinal level crossed-extensor reflex. The wise teacher never even mentions the arms prior to sending the students across the floor in a skip combination. Rather, the teacher allows "the body to take over" and establish the crossed-extensor reflex as the normal pattern before calling attention to the arms.

Dancers often refer to "letting the body do it" or "getting out of their heads." Interestingly enough, these statements are not far from the truth. In order to smooth out a movement, to make it flow, and to give it the passion and the fire of dancing, activation must include the gamma system and the midbrain. Movements primarily activated by the cerebral cortex appear less fluid and fiery and do little to stimulate the kinesthetic sense of the viewer. Movement experiences designed to fortify the mass body and limb reflexes can intensify the role of the gamma system in motion.

RIGHTING REFLEXES

Balance is a major concern for the dancer. Four basic reflexes contribute to maintenance of an upright posture and perception of the vertical and horizontal coordinates: the *labyrinth righting reflex*, the *head and neck righting reflex*, the *bodily righting reflex*, and the *optic righting reflex*. Each of these reflexes has equal perceptual importance at birth, but the adult tends to depend most on the optic righting reflex. However, in dance this reflex is not always the most dependable; the dancer must draw information from all of the righting reflexes to perform the complicated balances, in odd positions, that are often called for.

Labyrinth righting reflexes. Stimulations from the vestibular system of the inner ear, particularly the semicircular canals, initiate the labyrinth righting reflexes. The semicircular canals are filled with a viscous fluid and the walls are lined with hairlike cilia which are stimulated by the shifting fluid according to the shifting position of the head. The labyrinth reflex works to keep the head vertical and is particularly sensitive to acceleration and deceleration. Coming to a quick stop when riding in an automobile causes the head to follow the thrust of the momentum in a forward direction. Then the labyrinth righting reflex takes over and the head is brought back to vertical by a contraction of the extensors. The reverse muscular action takes place on a quick start. The sense of continued motion that frequently occurs after long automobile trips or long periods on the water is also related to the function of the semicircular canals. The repetitious stimulation of the cilia becomes sensitized (sensation continues even after the actual stimuli have ceased), and there is a sense of continued motion (rocking or swaying) even after one is on solid ground. The important role of the semicircular canals in maintaining balance is pointed out dramatically when an individual has an inner-ear infection. There is a distortion of the feedback sent to the central nervous system, and loss of balance, staggering, and stumbling can result.

Head and neck righting reflexes. The head and neck reflexes serve to keep the body facing in the same direction as the head and neck. This is done by reflexive facilitation of contraction of specific groups of muscles. Divers and gymnasts are very aware of the effects of this reflexive system, and it is used to facilitate their twisting and spinning actions. It is thought that dancers may use the head and neck reflexes when they "spot" their turns. In spotting, the head turns very rapidly and thus activates the head and neck reflexes, which can facilitate the turn of the body. If this is true, the first turn of a sequence is not facilitated by the head and neck reflexes, and this first turn is frequently slower and characterized by a "getting started" quality. The subsequent turns, however, do utilize the head and neck reflexes and are usually smoother (as long as the dancer retains his or her sense of vertical). It should be noted that not all authorities agree with this theory.

Bodily righting reflexes. There are sensory receptors throughout the body which are sensitive to pressure. A discrepancy between the feedback received from the right foot and the left foot, for example, will cause a shift of the weight of the body to equalize the pressure and maintain an upright posture. The action causes the characteristic shift of body weight which occurs when one is walking across a hillside or up and down hills. Likewise, sitting on an uneven surface will cause an imbalance in the feedback from the two "cheeks" and will stimulate an adjustment of body position to equalize the input from both sides. This reflex gives the neurological system information about the verticality of the body in all positions because the sensory receptors are located throughout the body. Even in a prone or supine position, these receptors are activated, though the body is not vertical. Conscious awareness of these perceptions can be of great assistance to the dancer who, on stage under blinding lights, often cannot depend upon the optical righting reflexes. Increasing one's sensitivity to these receptors can be facilitated by performing first simple and then increasingly complex balance tasks with the eyes closed.

Optic righting reflexes. As stated before, adults depend mainly on the optical righting reflexes to maintain a vertical posture. The young child must develop a sense of absolute vertical and absolute horizontal, but once this awareness is developed the optical righting reflex usually becomes the most dominant of all the righting reflexes. Standing on one foot is a relatively simple balance task, but closing the eyes causes a profound sense of loss of balance. Even those who have excellent balance can have difficulty when the eyes are closed. In the process of learning to depend upon the visual righting reflexes, one has also lost awareness of the other reflexes. Actual activation of the visual righting reflexes is an attempt to keep the two eyes on horizontal. This reflex explains the difficulty that some dancers have with side tilts that also include a tilt of the head. As the body and head tilt to the side, the visual righting reflex will automatically bring the head back to vertical. Actually, tilts in any direction can cause similar difficulty, and turns with the head off center and not vertical are very difficult indeed, because of the visual righting reflexes.

The Kinesthetic Sense

The kinesthetic sense is forgotten in the traditional listing of the five senses: touch, taste, sight, hearing, and smell. It is indeed a sixth sense and intuition and psychic phenomena should be relabeled the seventh sense. The kinesthetic sense is literally the perception of motion. Actually, it is a perception of both motion and position.

The kinesthetic sense is dependent on the proprioceptors and the sensory organs involved in the righting reflexes. The proprioceptors are the muscle spindles, the Golgi tendon organs (both located within the muscle tissue), the pacinian corpuscles (located around joints and between muscles), and the joint capsule receptors. The proprioceptors provide feedback to the central nervous system regarding muscle contraction, relaxation, tension, and stretch as well as information about joint position and velocity of motion.[3] Accurate kinesthetic perception requires the integration of this information with the perception of spatial coordinates of motion, including horizontal, vertical, front, back, side, and many others. Try this little exercise. Close your eyes and then place your arm straight forward from your shoulder joint and parallel to the floor (horizontal). Then

3. However, some of this information (feedback) does not reach the conscious level. Only joint capsule receptors provide information for conscious awareness of position in space.

open your eyes and check the positioning of your arm. Was it accurate or was it slightly off the mark? It is the combined efforts of the proprioceptors which allow that action to be accurate. In postural kinesthesia, requiring a shift of the entire body rather than just a body segment, the proprioceptors are joined by the receptors of the righting reflexes to achieve accuracy.

Technically speaking, the kinesthetic sense is different from motor memory of a complex movement skill like riding a bicycle or diving off a board. The true motor memory is stored in the cerebral cortex and is assisted by the kinesthetic sense, but full motor memory goes beyond the scope of kinesthesia. Nevertheless, in common usage, the two are often thought of as one and lumped together under the term *kinesthetic sense*. This common use of the term *kinesthetic* includes perception and memory of motion, position, and motor coordination, and integration of sensory information.

Hemispheric Dominance

Up to about thirty-five years ago the term *hemispheric dominance* assumed a bilateral symmetry of the hemispheres of the forebrain. The symmetrical nature was assumed to apply to both the anatomical structure and the function of the two sides of the brain. Research showed us, however, that the two sides of the brain have very different capacities, related to each other but nevertheless distinct. Prior to that research breakthrough, studies of hemispheric dominance were related to laterality—handedness—and quantity of usage was assumed to be the primary discriminator between the right and left hemispheres. This discussion of hemispheric dominance will be divided into two sections. The first section will deal with traditional concepts of hemispheric dominance such as laterality, sidedness, and right/left discrimination. The second section will deal with the more recent investigation of the functional and qualitative differences between the two hemispheres in the processing of information.

LATERALITY

The newborn infant is assigned the perceptual task of discovering that he or she has two of many things: two hands, two arms, two feet, two legs, and so on. The next perceptual task is to discover that the two sides are alike in structure but can operate separately. The beginning of this perception is the foundation for the concept of *laterality*, or *sidedness*. Experience with the movement of the body yields an increasingly complex perception of the distinction between one side of the body and the other. The development of the concept of laterality progresses most naturally and easily for the strongly right-dominant child. The right hand is used for almost every movement task (reaching, throwing, eating, gesturing, scribbling, etc.), and the left hand is used for almost every holding task (holding to a base of support while gesturing, holding a teddy bear while building with blocks, holding the paper steady while scribbling, etc.). The differing sensory feedback received from the clear distinction of motor tasks provides a preconscious awareness of the fact that the two sides are different from each other. The strongly left-dominant child will have the same experiences and the same perceptions of differences, *if* the child is not confused by adults who try to force him or her to use the right hand for movement tasks. If the child is forced to use the right hand as the dominant hand some of the time and naturally uses the left as the dominant hand some of the time, the sensory distinction between the two sides is not so clear. The child with the greatest handicap in discriminating between the two sides of the body is the truly ambidextrous child. He or she simply uses the hand that is closest, or free at the time. This child presents the central nervous system with basically the same feedback from both sides of the body. There is little or no sensory basis for discriminating between the two sides. As this child grows to school age, it is very likely that he or she will have difficulty with reading and writing because the fundamental discrimination of letter shapes and integration of the reading process are very dependent on lateral discrimination. In order to correctly perform prereading tasks the child need not be able to label a side as right or left but must be able to discriminate between sides, both in the visual perception of letters and in the motor duplication of letters. Moreover, the reading process (going from left to right) requires a perception of differences between the two sides. (Otherwise, how does a child know where to start?) At this stage of the reading game, *right/left discrimination* (the ability to accurately label a body part as being right or left) is not really necessary. The development of this skill usually happens sometime around the age of five (give or take a year). However, sometimes this development is delayed or sidestepped entirely. Adults who have a major problem with right/left discrimination are not really uncommon. The ability to mirror motion performed by someone facing you is a complex application of the basic concepts of laterality and right/left discrimination. Re-education of a person who cannot discriminate between right and left should include simultaneous multisensory input (verbal identification, tactile stimulation, visual referencing systems, and kinesthetic feedback). In other words, the person should be directed to move one arm (for example) while the teacher is patting or rubbing that arm and saying over and over gain, "That is your right arm." Visual reference points can be easily added by putting a red dot on the right hand, or using some other visual referent. The teacher should not jump back and forth between one side of the body and the other. (The person is already confused; let's not add to it.) Instead, these experiences should focus on only one side of the body for an extended period of time—possibly weeks, depending on when the person begins to easily identify the right side of the body.

I am sure that my experiences in working with young children, both as a swimming teacher and as a teacher in the Early Childhood Unit of University Elementary School at the University of California, Los Angeles, are showing. I have included this rather lengthy discussion of laterality and right/left discrimination primarily because I believe it to be one strong argument in support of dance in elementary schools, and some dance educators may be able to use the information in a proposal. I share with all dance educators my dismay that we have to *prove* dance worthy of inclusion in the curriculum, but the fact remains that we must.

HEMISPHERIC ASYMMETRY

The two hemispheres of the brain are connected by the corpus collosum that lies between the right and left hemispheres of the cerebral cortex. In normal functioning, the connection provided by the corpus collosum allows for exchange of information. One way that the different information-processing functions of the two hemispheres was discovered was by studying individuals who had had the corpus collosum surgically severed for medical reasons. This gave brain researchers an opportunity to observe and document the variation in the modes of information processing used in the two hemispheres. Prior to this research, the left side of the brain was thought to be the dominant hemisphere for right-handed people because of the crossover that most of the neural tracts make at the level of the medulla. This means that the right hemisphere is the primary stimulator of action on the left side of the body and the left hemisphere is the primary stimulator of activity on the right side. It was assumed that the two hemispheres possessed the same abilities for processing information, but one side was simply used more than the other. With the relatively new research (which has been growing steadily since the early 1960s) on different functions of each of the hemispheres, it has been noted that the two hemispheres actually have qualitatively different ways of processing the same input. The dominant hemisphere, the left hemisphere for right-handed people, is said to process information in a linear, logical, and verbal mode, while the nondominant hemisphere processes information in a nonlinear, intuitive, and spatial mode. Further research shows that non-verbal representation such as drawing is more effectively performed by the nondominant hemisphere. For simplicity, the nondominant hemisphere will be referred to as the *right* hemisphere, and the dominant as the *left* hemisphere.

The right hemisphere is also crucial in the perceiving and remembering of spatial relationships, the representation of spatial relationships on maps or diagrams, the tactile discrimination necessary to recognize things by touch alone, the recognition of complex shapes for which there is no name, and the holistic processing of information.

The left hemisphere is more skilled at verbal processing and symbolic labeling of things and phenomena, establishing sequence (temporal order of occurrence), logical and analytical processing of information, and systematic analysis of internal and external stimuli.

In the normal brain, with the corpus collosum intact, the two hemispheres differ in their potential for processing information, but there is communication between the hemispheres via the corpus collosum. The left brain is the analyzer: it looks for minutia to support a proposition. The right brain is the holistic perceiver, looking for the overall picture. There may be some parallels to inductive and deductive logic buried in the split-brain information, but they are still to be researched.

Dancers, as a rule, tend to be more right-brain-oriented because of the spatial, nonverbal demands of the discipline. This does not mean that dancers are necessarily unskilled in verbal exchange, just that their primary mode is more likely to be nonverbal and right-brained. This tendency is my main reason for including so many illustrations in Sections II and III. To a dancer, one picture is worth a *million* words.

The educational journals are full of articles on the relative importance of the two hemispheres of the brain. It is being recognized that our educational system focuses primarily on left-brain skills, and some educators are calling for an expansion of the focus. For dance educators who are trying to justify the inclusion of dance in school curricula, the information on hemispheric dominance provides another powerful argument. "Readin', writin', and 'rithmetic" are all mainly left-brain skills. Where in the system is the education of the right brain to be accomplished if not in the arts?

This chapter has presented an obviously abbreviated discussion of three physiological systems and their contributions to motor learning, fitness, and motor control. There has been a Herculean effort to avoid any major errors in the process of simplification, but a few minor errors may have slipped through in my attempt to be concise. These systems simply are *not* concise. Their functioning is complex and confusing, even to those who are experienced in the field. Readers who are interested in the physiology of exercise and the mechanisms of motor control should refer to the references at the back of the book, and continue to study with more comprehensive sources.

CHAPTER *15*

Body Types

No two human bodies are exactly the same. Even though we all have the same basic equipment, there are many subtle and sometimes not-so-subtle differences. There have been many attempts to classify variations in human structure. One of these is *somatotyping* (body typing), first investigated by W. H. Sheldon and documented in his *Atlas of Men* (1954). Sheldon proposed three body types based on what he believed to be the predominant type of tissue: *ectomorph, mesomorph,* and *endomorph* (see Figure 15.1). According to Sheldon, the ectomorph has a predominance of nerve tissue, the mesomorph has a predominance of connective tissue and muscle, and the endomorph has a predominance of endocrine tissue. The relative proportion of tissue and the relative efficiency of functioning vary dramatically from one body type to another. In theory, these three somatotypes are separate and distinct, yet in practical application there is considerable overlapping. One seldom finds an individual who is a true ectomorph, mesomorph, or endomorph in the theoretical sense. It is much more common to find individuals who tend toward one body type but also have some characteristics of the other body types.

Information on somatotypes is of interest to dancers because it has direct implications for understanding capacities and limitations. Each body type has a proclivity for certain kinds of movement and certain movement limitations. Understanding body type can guide and direct the dancer's individual conditioning program. This information is certainly pertinent to teachers of dance, for it can assist in setting realistic expectations and individualizing instruction.

The information in this chapter is divided into two sections. The first discusses the shape, composition, and physiological functioning of the three body types. The second discusses the movement potential and limitations of the three types. Each tendency presents advantages and disadvantages, and an attempt is made to focus on both benefits and detriments.

Shape, Composition, and Physiology

The *ectomorph* has a long, narrow, lean, lithe body with a fragile bone structure. The hips tend to be wider than the shoulders, and excess weight

281

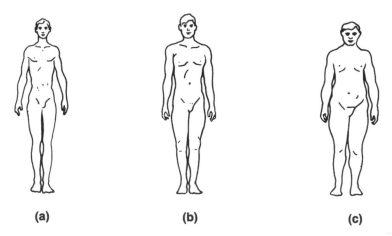

(a)   (b)   (c)

FIGURE 15.1. **Somatotypes or body types: (a) ectomorph, (b) mesomorph, and (c) en-**
domorph

will be carried in the hips and thighs. The bone tissue is actually less dense
and the long bones of the body are longer than the other two body types.
The ectomorph tends to mature late and (if a woman) experiences
menopause fairly early. The human skeletal system (particularly the long
bones) continues to grow approximately until puberty, and the ectomorph's delayed puberty allows the long bones to continue to grow for a
longer period of time. The ectomorph tends to be "loosely strung together," and this fact—combined with an inefficient muscular system—
leads to a tendency toward poor posture, but it also allows for greater mobility and flexibility. The cardiovascular system of the ectomorph is not
efficient. Specifically, there is a tendency to low blood pressure, poor vagal
tone, high heart rate, and, generally, poor circulation. The blood bed is not
efficient in adapting to differing demands, and therefore accommodations
in vasodilation and vasoconstriction are slower than for the other two
body types. These factors related to the cardiovascular system of the ectomorph lead to a tendency toward cold hands and feet, dizziness on standing up quickly, and poor endurance. In contrast to the cardiovascular system, the nervous system of the ectomorph is highly efficient. The
ectomorph is highly sensitive to stimuli, and the nervous system responds
rapidly. This higher sensitivity also means that the ectomorph is more sensitive to pain than the other two body types. The neural sensitivity of the
ectomorph also promotes a high level of neuromuscular tension. The digestive system is relatively inefficient. That is, the body does not absorb
nutrients as readily as the other two body types. This means that the ectomorph can eat like a horse and stay slim. But there is a disadvantage to
this: the low absorption rate makes the ectomorph susceptible to hypoglycemia (low blood sugar). The standard eating patterns in our culture
are not appropriate for the ectomorph. The long delay between meals allows the blood sugar to drop too low. A much more effective eating pattern
for the ectomorph is to eat six or seven smaller meals, spaced evenly

throughout the day. The ectomorph also has a tendency to be anemic (low hemoglobin count in the blood), and to have low levels of adrenaline in the bloodstream. The tendency to anemia contributes to the poor endurance of the ectomorph, because it is the hemoglobin that carries the oxygen necessary for resynthesis of lactic acid. Because of the narrowness of the body of the ectomorph, there is less space for the viscera (internal organs) and the belly tends to protrude, particularly after a large meal.

The *mesomorph* has a solid, square, muscled, athletic appearance. The shoulders tend to be broader than the hips, and the muscular system is well developed, giving a general appearance of width. Maturity comes relatively early for the mesomorph. Mesomorphs tend to excel at sports at an early age. The cardiovascular system and the muscular system are very efficient. When active, the mesomorph has average-to-low blood pressure and a low heart rate. However, with inactivity the blood pressure rises, as does the heart rate. This makes the mesomorph prone to hypertensive heart disease in later life when the activity level is lower. Vasoconstriction and vasodilation adapt rapidly to changing demands, and performing quick shifts in position seldom causes dizziness. Moreover, this efficiency of the mesomorph's circulatory system means that the mesomorph often can be out in shirtsleeves when the ectomorph is bundled up in three sweaters. The skeletal structure and connective tissue of the mesomorph are actually denser than those of the other two body types. The mesomorph is sturdy and tightly strung together. The strength of the musculature combined with the tight connective tissue and a strong stretch reflex make it difficult for the mesomorph to retain flexibility. On the other hand, the mesomorph excels at activities involving strength and endurance because of the efficiency of the muscular and cardiovascular systems. High levels of adrenaline give the mesomorph a high energy level, but the mesomorph can usually relax more easily than the ectomorph. The mesomorph has the best posture of the three body types because of the strength of the musculature and the density of the connective tissue. The digestive system and metabolism of the mesomorph are normal and, when active, the mesomorph can eat fairly large amounts without gaining weight. However, with inactivity the mesomorph must cut back on caloric intake. When the mesomorph puts on weight, it tends to localize in the center of the body; the classic "beer belly" is a perfect example of this tendency.

The *endomorph* has a rounded body contour with excessive amounts of fatty tissue. The shoulders tend to be slightly wider than the hips, but the excess weight tends to mask that difference. The weight is more evenly distributed than in the other two body types. Many of the physiological functions of the endomorph fall between those of the ectomorph and the mesomorph. The cardiovascular system and the muscular system are less efficient than the mesomorph's but more efficient than the ectomorph's. Posture also falls somewhere between that of the mesomorph and the ectomorph, with the endomorph having fairly good posture. The level of adrenaline is lower than in the mesomorph and higher than in the ectomorph. The endomorph is less flexible than the ectomorph, but more flexible than the mesomorph. For these reasons, the endomorph has a natural potential for strength, endurance, and flexibility. The endomorph defines the extreme when it comes to absorption of nutrients and relaxation, with a very efficient absorption of nutrients and an ability to relax totally at the drop of a hat. The endomorph must constantly diet to maintain an ideal weight because of the efficiency of the digestive system. This is often intensified by a low thyroid level (hypothyroidism) and low metabolism. Everything seems to be slowed down for the endomorph, including heart rate, blood pressure (surprisingly, it is low), the onset of puberty, and the onset of menopause. The endomorph is least sensitive to pain and other stimuli, which certainly contributes to the ability to relax. The major problem for the endomorph is weight management, and the problem becomes major if it is ignored. Overweight, ranging to obesity, is common for endomorphs.

Movement Capacities and Limitations

The ectomorph has a definite potential for quick, sudden movement facilitated by the efficiency of the nervous system and the mechanical relationship between different parts of the skeletal system. The inefficiency of the cardiovascular system, however, limits the duration of activity. Activities that require strength, muscular endurance, or cardiorespiratory endurance can be difficult for the ectomorph. With training, the ectomorph can improve in strength and endurance, but the levels achieved will not be equal to those of mesomorph or the endormorph in the same training program. Because high levels of neuromuscular tension are common in the ectomorph, some form of relaxation training is also necessary. Strength, endurance, and relaxation are the constant conditioning battles for the ectomorph. One day off, and the effects start to show. The ectomorph can maintain high levels of flexibility, however, with a minimum of effort.

The mesomorph excels at large, vigorous movements and can continue over long periods of time. Strength, endurance, and power are definitely capacities of the mesomorph. Compared with the amount of conditioning needed by the ectomorph to achieve strength and endurance, the mesomorph can maintain high levels of strength and endurance with a minimum of training. The mesomorph's Achilles' heel is inflexibility. One day away from stretching routines, and the mesomorph will show the effects. The mesomorph must work just as hard for mobility as the ectomorph works for strength and endurance.

The endomorph maintains strength, flexibility, and endurance rather well. The problem for the endomorph is, of course, weight control. One day without exercise, and the weight starts to climb. The best type of exercise for weight control is thought to be endurance exercises which continue over a long period of time.

IMPLICATIONS FOR DANCERS

Table 15.1 lists the information covered in this chapter regarding differences in capacities and limitations related to the three body types. A care-

TABLE 15.1 Movement Capacities and Needs

	Ectomorph	Mesomorph	Endomorph
PHYSIOLOGY AND STRUCTURE	Poor cardiovascular system Poor circulatory system Sensitive nervous system Inefficient absorption of nutrients Loose connective tissue Fragile bone structure Low adrenaline levels Poor posture Low blood pressure Poor vagal tone High heart rate	Excellent cardiovascular system Excellent muscular system Sturdy bone structure Strong stretch reflex Tightly strung together High adrenaline levels Average absorption of nutrients Excellent posture Low blood pressure Excellent vagal tone Low heart rate	Good cardiovascular system Good muscular system Medium-sturdy bone structure Good flexibility Medium adrenaline levels Excellent absorption of nutrients Good posture Low blood pressure Fair vagal tone Medium heart rate Low tension levels
MOVEMENT CAPACITIES	Speed for short duration Quick reaction time Bursts of energy Elasticity	Excellent strength Excellent muscular endurance Excellent cardiorespiratory endurance Good ability to relax Excels at medium-paced endurance activities Enjoys large, gross motor activity at a medium-fast pace	Excellent ability to relax Excels at slow rhythmical activities Good cardiorespiratory endurance Good muscular endurance Good strength Good flexibility
MOVEMENT LIMITATIONS	Strength Muscular endurance Cardiorespiratory endurance Relaxation	Flexibility Extremes of fast or slow	Weight control Fast movement
CONDITIONING NEEDS	Minimal conditioning to maintain capacities plus extreme focus on: Strength Muscular endurance Cardiorespiratory endurance Relaxation	Minimal conditioning to maintain capacities plus extreme focus on: Flexibility	Minimal conditioning to maintain capacities plus extreme focus on: Endurance (for weight control)

ful review of the table is encouraged. It may be helpful for the dancer to think of acquaintances who roughly fit into each of the body types and then think of the activities at which they excel.

This information is particularly helpful to mesomorphic dancers who think they are "evil" because they can't keep their hamstrings stretched, or to ectomorphic "huffers and puffers" who can't make it once across the floor without breathing hard. There are physiological explanations for these problems. They are not the punishment of the gods on wayward dancers. Dancers are noted for comparing their own bodies with the bodies of other dancers and measuring their abilities by looking at the abilities of others. This is truly self-defeating because capacities and limitations vary so remarkably. It is far better to focus attention on realistic appraisal of one's own capacities and limitations and work to maintain the capacities and reduce the limitations. But dancers tend to do what they excel at and what "feels good." Survey a dance studio before class begins and one will see mesomorphs jogging around the studio to warm up, and ectomorphs stretching to warm up. The needs of these body types are actually reversed. The mesomorph should be stretching and the ectomorph should be jogging if the focus is expansion of potential. Realizing that one tends to warm up with the activities that one does well, the dancer should balance the warm-up: something needed and something that feels good.

There are also some important implications for teachers of dance. What happens to a mesomorphic student dancer who takes a class from an ectomorphic teacher? Very likely the student will never feel warmed up and he or she will be demoralized (or injured) by the range of motion demanded in the class. If we switch the roles and send an ectomorphic student to a mesomorphic teacher, the student will be lucky to make it through class; and if he or she goes to class "cold" there may be an injury, or the student may constantly feel as if he or she is trying to "catch up." Understanding the natural tendencies of the different body types can do much to allow for differences in a class and to facilitate individually needed growth. The most horrendous words spoken by a teacher of dance are, "If I can do it, you can do it." Indeed that can be possible, but for the students who have a dramatically different body type, the effort must be awesome. Teachers should sometimes ask the impossible of students, but they ought to couple the request with sufficient preliminary training and adequate encouragement. Otherwise, the result is defeated students and a frustrated teacher. Basic information about the capacities and limitations of the three body types can guide the setting of realistic objectives. The information should be used not as a "cop-out" but rather for realistic, honest appraisal of capacities and limitations.

CHAPTER *16*

Movement Behavior

Qualitative differences in dance performance

Every dancer is aware of movement style at some level. Such words as *lyrical, sustained,* and *percussive* are used to describe different styles of movement. These terms are also used to classify dancers. The problem with analysis of movement style based on these words is that each term has a wide range of meaning and multiple connotations. Movement behavior analysis provides a system that focuses on the most basic elements of motion for distinguishing between movement styles.

The basic elements of any motion are time, space, and force. Every movement is initiated by a given amount of force, occupies a given amount of space, and continues over a given amount of time. There are two systems that focus attention on the analysis of an individual's or group's use of time, space, and force in motion.

Rudolf Laban, in the early to middle twentieth century, developed a whole new approach to the observation and analysis of human movement. His brilliant work formed the basis for the body of work currently known as *Laban Movement Analysis and Bartinieff Fundamentals.* Irmgard Bartinieff studied with Rudolf Laban and was the prime mover in bringing Labanotation and what was then known as *Effort/Shape Analysis* to the United States. Laban Movement Analysis is discussed at length in Chapter 17, in the sections by Madeleine Scott and Peggy Hockney. Irmgard Bartinieff's work centered in New York and spread through dance programs in the east.

Juanan de Laban, daughter of Rudolf Laban, traveled to the west coast and taught dance history at the University of California, Los Angeles, in the 1960s and 1970s. Dr. Valerie Hunt, a colleague of Juana de Laban's who taught dance kinesiology at UCLA, studied the written works of Rudolf Laban and developed a conceptual framework known as *Movement Behavior,* based on and growing out of Laban's work (Hunt, 1964). The present author served as Dr. Hunt's teaching and research assistant in the years 1966–1970. At that time, work in the Movement Behavior Laboratory focused on electromyographic (EMG) assessment of differences in movement behavior. EMG analysis of human movement yielded four distinct patterns of movement that are also observable without the use of EMG (Fitt, 1979b). These four patterns of neuromuscular activation (*Neuromuscular Excitation Patterns,* NEP) were called *burst, restrained, sustained,* and *undulate.* One of the major projects conducted by Dr. Hunt's reasearch team was EMG analysis of movement patterns before and after the Rolfing process (see the discussion of Rolfing in Chapter 17, in the section by Mary Bond). In an informal and unpublished electromyographic study of Laban's "Full Efforts," it was found that flick and dab used undulate NEP, press and wring used restrained NEP, punch and slash used burst NEP, and float and glide used sustained NEP (Fitt, 1970). These two systems—Laban Movement Analysis and Movement Behavior Analysis—have much in common but are different enough to warrant separate discussion.

Each of these two systems of movement analysis focuses on *style* or *quality* of motion. In contrast to kinesiology, which focuses on the identification of joint action and the muscles activated to produce that action, qualitative analysis of movement focuses on identification and analysis of the different possibilities of quality in performing the same action. Clearly, this information is of critical importance to dancers, choreographers, and dance educators, for it is this aspect of movement analysis which documents individual differences in performance quality and choreographic style. While both systems of quality analysis are of value to the dancer, students who have studied both systems have said that Movement Behavior Analysis, at least in its simple form, is easier to understand and requires less training for effective use. This chapter will present the very basic components of movement behavior theory and the use of simplified movement behavior analysis.

Definition and Purpose

Movement behavior is the analysis and identification of qualitative movement patterns characteristic of an individual or group. The focus is on the *style* of performance rather than on skill or effectiveness. A movement behavior specialist can observe an individual's use of time, space, and force in many different situations and consolidate these observations into a movement behavior profile that illustrates the individual's characteristic pattern (*central tendency*), the breadth of that pattern (*range*), and characteristic capacities and limitations.

Basic Assumptions

Four basic assumptions are involved in movement behavior analysis:

1. The human being operates as a functional whole: mind, body, and emotions are not separate functions but are integrated synergistically in human action and reaction.
2. Each individual has a characteristic and unique pattern of movement behavior.

3. There is a correlation between movement behavior and other modes of behavior such as personality, expression of emotions, patterns of cognitive information processing, and all aspects of behavior.
4. It is possible to expand the range of an individual's characteristic use of time, space, and force. (Fitt and Hanson, 1978.)

The Functional Whole

Throughout recorded history, and probably well before that, the human being has puzzled over the nature of the human species. The traditional approach, which assumes a split between mind and body, has served to alienate humans from their bodies, because many "base" or what were thought to be "evil" characteristics were attributed to the body. The "mind" (brain), on the other hand, symbolized higher purposes and was thought to be the seat of "godlike" qualities. However, as science has shed light on the intricate and complex interrelationships between the central nervous system (brain) and the periphery (body), this dichotomous concept is no longer appropriate. Feedback from the periphery is integral to the central processing of information. The concept of the reflex loop has replaced the concept of the reflex arc. Information processing is no longer a one-way street with the mind controlling and the body responding. Input from the body is as central to thought, imagination, and response as the brain. Human reception, processing, and response link brain and body into a functional whole. Consequently, a change in any one component of human behavior affects the entire system.

Characteristic Pattern of Movement Behavior

The human being is characterized by a complex set of behavior patterns, including personality, affective (emotional) behavior, cognitive behavior and many others. Movement behavior (the characteristic pattern of movement quality) is one component of human behavior and is a unique combination of elements, like a fingerprint or voice print. The exact nature of an individual's movement behavior pattern is determined by a merging of hereditary factors and experiential factors. Genetic coding provides the human with the basic parameters of movement, and the individual's movement experiences add coloring and texture to the basic outline. In movement behavior theory, it is thought that some stylistic characteristics are predetermined at conception. The fetus, in utero, exhibits a characteristic organization of expenditure of energy in movement. Some fetuses are kickers, some are rollers, and still others are relatively quiet. The effect of the mother's movement patterns while the fetus is in utero has not been fully investigated but is, nevertheless, fascinating. As the child grows into adulthood, and then into old age, the central tendencies of movement behavior patterns have continuity. New types of movement experiences can expand the movement potential, but the central pattern remains. I call this movement behavior core the *home base*, for it is the centerpoint for the patterning of movement style throughout life.

Correlation with Other Modes of Behavior

There have been any number of studies attempting to establish a correlation between movement and personality. Many of those studies proved inconclusive. Yet dancers and dance educators intuitively know that there is a connection between movement and personality. If one observes a person using fast time, small space, and strong force (a high-tension combination) the personality predictions are quite different from the predictions made if the mover uses slow time, large space, and weak force. Just this simple example points to an observable correlation between personality and movement behavior. Moreover, dancers or choreographers who wish to establish a character through movement are also aware of the correlation. Actors must consider the movement components of the character they are portraying, or the characterization falls short. Even though research may be well behind common knowledge in establishing a correlation between movement and personality, the fact remains that we do, in everyday life, observe movement and use it as a key to predictions about personality. The relation of movement behavior to patterns of emotional response and to patterns of cognitive processing of information is also a fascinating subject. Is there a characteristic movement pattern for a person who is right-brain-dominant? What is the expected movement behavior pattern for a person who is a linear, logical thinker? Is a person who exhibits a controlled and precise movement pattern more or less emotionally spontaneous than a person exhibiting low levels of tension and sudden explosions of action?

While research on the correlation of movement behavior with other modes of behavior is only in the early stages of development, practical observation of one's fellow human beings (and oneself) can leave little doubt that there is a correlation.

Expansion of Range

The assumption that expansion of range is possible forms the basis for all movement education programs. If expansion were not possible, there would be no point in offering physical education or dance classes. We in movement education assume that it is possible to expand an individual's range of movement patterns. Note that the word *expand* is used, not *change*. The central tendency (the home base of movement behavior) does not change. But training can add new dimensions to the existing patterns of movement behavior.

The Value System

A movement behavior specialist considers no movement pattern to be good or bad. All movement patterns have potential value to the mover in certain situations. However, the broader the range of possibilities, the greater the capacity to cope with differing demands. A broad range of movement behavior is definitely of value, while a limited range of movement behavior is thought to offer fewer options. The link between movement and perception raises an interesting question: If a person is limited to one characteristic movement behavior pattern, is that person also perceptually limited to the information admitted by that pattern? This is only one of the effects of a severely limited range of movement behavior.

As a movement specialist in the Early Childhood Unit of University Elementary School at the University of California, Los Angeles, I have had the opportunity to observe and identify the movement behavior patterns of hundreds of four- to six-year olds. Other members of the Early Childhood faculty made observations of the same children's affective behavior. Although we did not document our findings, a most interesting pattern was shown. The children who exhibited a unidimensional movement behavior pattern (limited to a narrow range) also had problems expressing emotions effectively. Following identification of these children, they were included in a program designed to expand the range of movement behavior. The changes that resulted were reflected in every aspect of the children's lives.

The perspective of any movement behavior program is to use systematic observation techniques to identify limitations in movement range and then design movement experiences to broaden the range of patterns used. It is thought that this approach to movement analysis can be of potential value to the dancer. Without a range of movement qualities to choose from, there is no possibility of choice. The dancer is limited to his or her characteristic pattern. In some cases this leads to the development of a very strong style, but versatility is blocked. In the training of young dancers it is essential that they experience all forms of motion, so that all possibilities of motion are available to them for use in the creative process. To repeat: no movement is considered good or bad, but a limited range of movement patterns locks the person into one mode of reception, response, and expression.

The Conceptual Model

The conceptual model of movement behavior is divided into three branches: observation and analysis of movement behavior; analysis of the relation between movement behavior and perceptual modes; and analysis of the relation between movement behavior and expressive styles. Table 16.1 illustrates the three branches of the conceptual model and identifies the components of each branch.

Observation of Time, Space, and Force

One chapter could never do justice to the material covered in the conceptual model of movement behavior laid out in Table 16.1. However, one segment of information is easily applicable: identification of characteristic patterns of quantitative use of time, space, and force. This cluster of information can be a powerful tool for identifying characteristic movement be-

Table 16.1   Concept Model of Movement Behavior

I. Observation and Identification of Characteristic Movement Patterns

Component	Quantitative Factors	Qualitative Factors
Time	Slow Medium Fast	Rhythm: regular or irregular Pace: accelerating, decelerating or steady

Personal space	Small
	Medium
	Large
		Use for both personal and
		    environmental space
		Direction: forward, backward, sideward,
		    diagonal, across the midline, upward,
		    downward, inward, outward

Environmental space	Small Medium Large	Path: curved or straight Body shape: curved or straight
Force*	Strong Medium Weak	Body focus: intense or diffuse Weight management: resistant or indulgent (passive or controlled)

Integrated patterns of energy expenditure:
   Neuromuscular excitation patterns (NEP)
      Burst
      Restrained
      Sustained
      Undulate (Hunt, 1970)
Integrated patterns of energy potential:
   Residual tension patterns
      Assistive
      Resistive
      Posturing
      Perceverating (Rathbone, 1943)

(continued on next page)

havior patterns. Simply focusing on the amount of time, space, and force used by an individual reveals patterns that can lead to activities that might expand the movement range of the individual. The first step is to simply begin observing.

OBSERVATION OF USE OF TIME

Possibly the easiest of the elements to observe is the time component. Ours is a time-oriented society and our perception of time is quite refined. A problem in observing an individual's use of time does arise: "How slow is slow?" and "How fast is fast?" These judgments are relative in two ways. First, judgment of relative speed is dependent on the human potential for the specific task. A run will move the person from place to place faster than a walk, but in movement behavior a run may be classified as slow and a walk may be classified as fast. This is possible because the movement behavior observer is focusing on the motion of the body itself, not the motion of the body through space. Each task must be observed in reference to the maximum and minimum possible speed of body parts for

TABLE 16.1   Concept Model of Movement Behavior (*Continued*)

II. Analysis of Relationship Between Movement and Other Modes of Behavior
   Body image
   Self-concept
   Figure/ground perception (field dependent and independent)
   Spatial orientation
      Vertical and horizontal
      Balance
      Centeredness (reliance on internal coordinates)
   Laterality
      Right/left discrimination
      Lateral dominance
      Mirroring
   Patterns of information processing such as:
      Hemispheric dominance (right/left brain)
      Inductive/deductive
   Patterns of expression such as:
      Direct/indirect
      Dynamic/passive
      Spontaneous/Controlled
   Patterns of interaction such as:
      Introversion/extroversion
      Dominant/submissive
      Rigid/flexible

III. Analysis of Movement Patterns and Relationship to Patterns of Expression
   Postural habits
   Gestural habits
   Patterns of spatial use
   Characteristic facial expressions
   Handwriting and graphics
   Tension patterns

---

* *Force* does not mean power or strength in movement behavior analysis. Rather, assessment of force reflects the relationship between amount of force used and minimum force required to accomplish a task.

that task. Second, judgment of the characteristic speed of a person's movement is also relative to the movement patterns of the observer. The observer's perception of motion is screened through his or her characteristic use of time. For example, a person who characteristically moves in a slow tempo may very well identify a movement of medium speed as fast. After all, it is fast compared with the observer's own patterns of movement.

The problems which arise for the observer in dealing with the relativity of judgments are most effectively dealt with in two ways. One, through experience the observer develops a frame of reference regarding the range of possibilities for different movement tasks. Two, the observer must become familiar with his or her own characteristic movement patterns and become aware of the biasing effect of those movement patterns on the objective observation of movement. (Note that these two precautions apply to observation of space and force as well as time.)

TABLE 16.2   Three Rating Scales for Observation of Time

A. Three-Point Scale
Task observed _____

Slow	
Medium	
Fast	

B. Five-Point Scale
Task observed _____

Very slow	
Moderately slow	
Medium	
Moderately fast	
Very fast	

C. Seven-Point Scale
Task observed_____

Extremely slow	
Much slower than average	
Somewhat slower than average	
Medium	
Somewhat faster than average	
Much faster than average	
Extremely fast	

TABLE 16.3 Identification of an Individual's Range in Time

Name _____

Task	Slow	Medium	Fast

Physical size is noted as a primary determiner of speed by some authorities. While there may be a relationship between physical size and speed (smaller bodies being able to move faster), movement behavior analysis does not focus on the *reasons* for certain tendencies, but rather focuses on *identification of the tendencies.*

If, as suggested, the new observer begins with the observation of time, the first step must be the analysis of his or her own characteristic use of time. From there, the observer moves on to begin observation of others. It is suggested that the person look at many different people performing the same task, in order to begin to develop a frame of reference. Once the frame of reference begins to emerge in the observer's perception, the observer can move on to observation of another task and again watch a variety of people performing it.

Very early in the process, the new observer will find that the three-point scale (slow, medium, and fast) is limiting and will naturally move on to a five-point scale or a seven-point scale as shown in Table 16.2. Each of the scales in Table 16.2 is designed to develop the observer's awareness of the range of possibilities. Each is designed to cover many people performing the same task. This is an important first step, for it lays a foundation for later judgments of speed. Once the observer has established that foundation, the next step is to look at one person in a number of different tasks in order to identify *range* and *central tendency* in use of time. Table 16.3 is a sample of a form that could be used for this purpose.

Observation of an individual for the purpose of identifying characteristic patterns of movement frequently leads to the question, "How do I know when I have observed enough?" There is no hard and fast rule, but generally, when a pattern begins to emerge and there are no surprises or variances from that pattern, the observer can be fairly confident that the established profile is representative.

From the results obtained through Table 16.3, the observer can begin to identify the *range* and *central tendency* of the person's use of time. For example, if the majority of the entries on the form are under one category such as "slow," the central tendency is clearly slow. The person characteristically moves slowly. If no entries appear in the "fast" column, there is a limitation in the person's range. However, all combinations are possible, and variances in range and central tendency become quite fascinating. For example, a person may move either very slowly or very fast with a range limitation in the midrange of speed. This profile is very different from that of an individual who has a wide range and uses each classification equally. Just looking at the raw data available from Table 16.3 gives movement specialists a clear sense of direction for the development of the full movement potential of the individual. It can also tell the movement specialist, who has identified the movement demands of specific tasks, which movement tasks will be easy for the individual and which will be difficult. The potential of systematic observation of movement behavior, even in this very simple format (focusing only on the quantitative aspects of a person's use of time, space, and force) is overwhelming.

To review: the observation process follows four steps: (1) the identification of one's own movement pattern; (2) observation of many different people performing the same task (subsequently repeated for many different tasks); (3) observation of one person in many different tasks; and (4) identification of a person's range and central tendency in the use of movement. Each of these steps should be completed for each of the components in the movement behavior model (time, space, and force). While the same process is used in the observation of space and force as in the observation of time, there are unique issues that arise in each of the two additional components of this simplified movement behavior analysis. For this reason, both space and force will be discussed, but you are reminded that the four steps of the observation process remain the same for each component.

OBSERVATION OF USE OF SPACE

Table 16.1 shows two categories of space: personal and environmental. *Personal space* is space through which one moves without using locomotion. Use of *environmental space* requires some form of locomotion, such as walking, running, rolling, leaping, or jumping. Separate recordings are required for each of these two categories, since they may or may not be similar. It is entirely possible to observe a person who uses vast amounts of personal space but very little environmental space, and vice versa.

Realizing that distinct observations must be made for personal and environmental space, the observation process follows the same steps as those outlined for observation of time. The dimension is size, and the three-point scale includes small, medium, and large. The actual size of the person is irrelevant. Judgments are based on the amount of space used by the movement. For example, if the arms are stretched wide and the legs spread as far as possible, the ranking would be "large" personal space. If, on the other hand, the appendages are drawn in close to the center of the body, use of personal space would be "small." Environmental space assessment focuses on use of the total environmental space available to the individual at the time. Because a person can be in only one place at one time, the assessment of environmental space usage must be done over a period of time, with judgments focusing on the use of the available space.

In observation of space usage, one must again take into account the maximum and minimum size possible for the particular movement task as well as one's own characteristic movement patterns, which can bias the observation.

OBSERVATION OF USE OF FORCE

Force is possibly the most difficult of the components to observe. In contemporary society, we have become highly sophisticated in our observation and identification of use of time and space. The clock and the ruler have seen to that. We are so sophisticated that we even transfer from one mode into the other in estimating distances. (How far is it from Los Angeles to Anaheim? About an hour.) The development of our perception of force and weight is much more embryonic. How much force do you need to move twenty pounds? How heavy is six ounces? We are much less sophisticated in our assessment of weight and force than we are with time and space. Kinesthetically, we do not lack the sophistication, for we can easily gauge the force required to push a piano or lift a folding chair. It is just that we have no constant feedback from a clearly defined measurement system such as inches or minutes. It is thought that lack of sophistication with measurement of weight and force is one of the reasons that new observers have difficulty identifying a movement as strong or weak. Another factor contributing to the difficulty with this component of movement behavior observations is that in movement behavior terms, *force* does not equal "potential power." That is, a physically strong person may or may not move with strong use of force. Force is assessed relative to the demands of the task. Using far more force than is required for a task is identified as "strong." Using the minimum amount of force possible to complete a task is identified as "weak." *Maximum* and *minimum* are the key words, and one must simultaneously assess the amount of force needed and the amount of force used. It is the ratio between these two factors that determines whether a movement is strong or weak.

Once again, experience with the observation process and awareness of one's own characteristic patterns are prerequisites to successful observation of an individual's use of force.

A Simplified Movement Behavior Profile

Combining the observations of an individual's characteristic patterns of use of time, space, and force yield a simplified movement behavior profile. Just the fact that observation of movement has been systematic yields a vast amount of information about the mover. For example, suppose the simplified profile showed that a person characteristically moved with fast time, strong force, and large personal space. How would that person differ in performing a dance combination from a person who characteristically moved with slow time, weak force, and small personal space? Clearly, the two people will approach every movement task very differently. Suppose those two people are cast in the same ensemble? Someone is going to have to modify his or her style if any semblance of unity is to be achieved. Most trained dancers have the necessary range of movement patterns to make these adaptations. But sometimes when a pattern is particularly predominant, problems will arise. These problems will be discussed at greater length below.

A warning: This simplified approach to movement behavior analysis is by no means complete. Referring back to Table 16.1 indicates that the simplified movement behavior profile encompasses only a very small part of the total movement behavior analysis. Qualitative components and the neuromuscular excitation patterns are not included here because specialized training is required for the observation and identification of them.

IMPLICATIONS FOR DANCERS

Information derived from systematic observation of characteristic use of time, space, and force can be applied in every process involved in dance. Students of dance, dance teachers, choreographers, performers, and accompanists can benefit from the knowledge gained through systematic movement behavior observations.

Students of dance often find that they have a "favorite" teacher, while other teachers make them "uncomfortable." If the movement style of the teacher is comparable to the movement style of the student, it is likely that the teacher might be listed in the "favorite" column. The combinations presented in class will reflect the movement style of the teacher, and if the student can easily perform within these stylistic requirements, he or she will be comfortable and successful. Conversely, a discrepancy between the movement style of the teacher and the student is quite likely to make the student uncomfortable and unsuccessful because of basic stylistic differences. Simply realizing that this stylistic compatibility or incompatibility exists can make the student more receptive to possible changes in his or her stylistic patterns of movement. Recognizing and acknowledging one possible source of discomfort in class may allow the student to deal effectively with that discomfort.

Certainly, this information is of equal or greater value to the teacher of dance. Systematic observation of students' patterns of movement can provide valuable information for the teacher who is planning course objectives for a given class. Moreover, a teacher who is aware of his or her own movement patterns can guard against presenting unidimensional classes, or, if a unidimensional class is in order, the information from simplified movement behavior analysis might produce greater unidimensionality. Most teachers of dance would agree that the current dance scene requires versatile dancers, not dancers who are limited to one style of movement. Simplified movement behavior analysis can do much to help the teacher build versatility in students.

Like teachers and students of dance who can benefit from systematic observation and identification of movement behavior, choreographers and performers also stand to benefit. A choreographer casting a particular dance work would be wise to evaluate the movement style of the auditioners in order to ensure that the final performance comes as close as possible to the intended choreography. Auditions certainly focus on movement style, but sometimes the evaluation of style is somewhat haphazard, depending upon the intuitive perceptions of the choreographer. Systematic observation and evaluation of the movement style of the auditioners, using the simplified movement behavior format, could mean more efficient selection of cast members.

The performer struggling with a difficult component of a given dance role might well be aided by movement behavior analysis of the role and his or her own movement potential. Movement behavior analysis might also suggest some approaches to the problem that might not otherwise be possible.

In all of the applications discussed above, there is one common factor. There is a shift from unconscious or subconscious awareness of movement style to conscious perception of movement style as a factor in dance. When one shifts to conscious awareness of a phenomenon, the awareness itself offers a sense of control. This does not mean that change is easy—it only means that desired change becomes definable. The student, the teacher, the performer, and the choreographer have a more refined perception of goals. This is one primary value of movement behavior analysis: to make the vague, intuitive perceptions of movement style definable.

Wellness
for Dancers

CHAPTER *17*

Somatics, Relaxation, and Efficiency

In the years since the first edition of *Dance Kinesiology*, there has been a remarkable growth of interest in what we used to call *relaxation techniques,* later called *body work,* and now call *somatics.* Accompanying the changes in wording has been a broadening of meaning.

When we spoke of *relaxation,* we were focused primarily on the neuro-muscular phenomenon of contraction and noncontraction. This focus dealt with the nature of neuromuscular tension and its role in life. It was in this context that the first edition presented concepts of relaxation techniques related to (1) management of tension, (2) reduction of extraneous (unnecessary) muscular contraction, and (3) promotion of greater efficiency in neuromuscular control. While relaxation is one effect of these systems, the full potential of the somatic systems is not represented by the word *relaxation.*

The term *body work* was presumably coined to imply the inclusion of more than reduction of neuromuscular tension in the various approaches. Efficiency and ease of movement gained importance, as did reduction of muscular armoring against the residual effects of a subject's painful past experiences. The concept that the body stores unresolved pain in the musculature became widely accepted. However, the term *body work* didn't last long. Almost before it was off the press, so to speak, practitioners became dissatisfied with it, since it implied that the work had impact on only the body. The term is now used primarily in fitness and sport magazines for the general public. Perhaps that is the case because the general public accepts the concept that somatic work focuses only on the body. Practitioners of the many somatic approaches, and dancers, know better. Changing or broadening the repertoire of movement patterns, postures, and gestures has far-reaching effects.

The first use of the term *somatics* in this context was by Thomas Hanna in 1976. Hanna referred to the "art and science of the inner-relational process between awareness, biological function, and environment, [with] all three factors [being] understood as a synergistic whole" (Hanna, 1976,

p. 30).[1] This definition presented a more holistic conceptualization than had been indicated by either *relaxation* or *body work*. Using the word *somatics* to represent all of the systems meant that body, mind, spirit, and environment were finally all represented in the name.

Somatic Approaches

The central objective of most somatic approaches is the encouragement of easeful, mindful, efficiency of motion which simultaneously promotes health, balance, and achievement of one's potential.

Another aspect of all somatic approaches is tapping into the inherent wisdom of the body. Learning to listen to that wisdom is one of the values of all somatics. It is within this context that the word *somatics* has been added to the title of this chapter. It is thought that *somatics*, with its multi-dimensional emphasis on body, mind, spirit, and environment, most accurately represents this domain, which includes Alexander Technique, Rolfing, Feldenkrais, Ideokinesis, Pilates-Based work, Cohen's Body-Mind Centering, Laban Movement Analysis, Bartinieff Movement Fundamentals, and others. A simplified definition of *somatics* might be "bodily based access to information about the whole system and its interactive patterns," or, very simply, knowing oneself from the inside out.

Somatic approaches do not neglect relaxation; there is still emphasis on awareness of stress, tension, equilibrium, and efficiency. But the sphere of influence has broadened to include more than the physical body. Each person is a functional whole, with every component of the whole linked to every other component. Just as droplets of ink dripped into a glass of water change the color of all of the water in the glass, bodily changes color the whole system, including, for example, the brain, mind,[2] body, personality, ego, soul, and spirit. *Somatics* implies this unified, interactive connection more explicitly than the earlier, previously used terms.

Basic Concepts: Tension, Efficiency, and Stress

Reviewing any contemporary publication on health, one would think that tension is the most evil culprit on the modern scene. Yet tension is a prerequisite for life. Without tension, there is no life. The question is, "How

---

1. According to Hanna himself. This was in the first issue of *Somatics*.
2. *Mind* in this context refers to more than the brain. As Hunt (1995) says, in reference to mind and brain, "They differ—one is a physical entity, and the other is something beyond the physical state" (p. 87). She also states that brain function is mechanical and thus predictable. Mind functions as a "field" and is thus unpredictable (p. 89). My use of *mind* in this chapter refers to the "mind field," not the brain.

much tension?" Each of us realizes that a certain level of physical tension ensures peak performance for our own individual functioning. The trick is to identify that tension level and learn how to maintain it. Going beyond one's optimal stress level serves only to reduce effectiveness. Yet a relaxed state does not produce maximum efficiency for work or for play. In an extremely relaxed state, one is so "spaced out" that simple functioning takes what seems to be extreme effort. Most of us have had the experience of participating in a relaxation session and being relatively nonfunctional afterward because of the low tension level achieved in the session. Relaxation is touted as a solution to many modern-day problems, but that assumption is categorically not true. Tension, in fact, is necessary, though not always at the high level maintained by modern society's men and women. Balance is the key: a balance between utilizing optimal tension levels when a task must be accomplished and using relaxation techniques to lower the tension level when leisure allows it. Conscious perception of tension levels is the first step toward effective tension management.

The goal of contemporary life seems to be "efficiency." Getting a lot of work done in a short period of time is respected and admired. It is interesting that the commonly accepted criterion for efficiency is time. Faster is better. To do some task slowly is not as respected as to complete it rapidly. Isn't it interesting that time is the criterion, not effort? Referring to the dictionary for a definition of *efficient* reveals that the word is defined as "producing the desired effect without waste." There is no specific reference to time, yet our common usage of the word connotes time. Why shouldn't we be as concerned with wasted force as we are with wasted time? In dance and movement in general, the word *efficient* often refers to *muscular* efficiency, or producing an action with *minimum effort*. This concept of *wasteless action* will be discussed at length below. At this point, you are encouraged to examine your concept of efficiency, focusing on the critical factor that is commonly used to assess efficiency, whether it be time, force, or some other criterion.

Another issue that must be considered in any discussion of tension, stress, efficiency, and relaxation is *sensory input*. The modern person is bombarded with complex sensory input. The sights, sounds, and smells of contemporary life are so intense and complex that it is all but impossible to maintain a balance of input and output. The human body is equipped with far more sensory nerves than motor nerves. It is quite common for modern individuals to be sedentary. This combination of sensory overload (input) and motor inactivity (output) may well be a major contributor to the high stress levels experienced in twentieth-century life. Balancing these two components requires increasing motor output and reducing sensory input.

For most dancers, who are very physically active, this input/output imbalance is not so critical as for their sedentary friends. Yet dancers also commonly experience high levels of neuromuscular tension. This must mean that maintaining optimum tension levels involves more than just balancing sensory input and motor output. There are certain individuals who are more susceptible to high levels of tension than others. This may be related to the body type of the individual, the movement behavior patterns of the individual, the demands placed on the individual by himself or herself or by society, or many other factors. Regardless of the source, the problem remains that excessive levels of neuromuscular tension are counterproductive and can actually play a major role in health problems. One solution is to learn effective techniques for the management of stress. This chapter will discuss a few of the variables that affect individual differences in tension levels, the nature of neuromuscular tension, the role of tension in motor learning and muscular efficiency, and finally will present a brief review of some of the techniques currently employed to effectively manage tension levels.

Tension, Stress, and the Dancer

Chapter 15 presented a brief review of some of the theories concerning body type. One factor is directly applicable here. Tension levels and abilities to relax vary markedly for the three body types. Reviewing: The ectomorph is thought to experience the highest level of tension and has the greatest difficulty achieving a relaxed state. The mesomorph falls somewhere in the midrange, with a moderate tension level and a good ability to relax. The endomorph operates on the lowest tension level of the three body types and is able to totally relax with what seems to be a mere flip of the switch. Because the dance world is populated by a majority of ectomorphs, with a few mesomorphs and hardly any endomorphs at all, high tension levels and inability to relax are quite common. Because dancers are so intensely aware of their bodies and bodily functioning, they have sought techniques for the reduction of tension. Nowhere in contemporary society is there a greater emphasis on relaxation techniques than in the dance world. Mature dancers are often quite sophisticated about the available relaxation techniques. In fact, those techniques may be the crucial factor allowing them to keep dancing as age advances. With ectomorphic tendencies predominating in dance, it is common to find dancers who are more sensitive to all kinds of stimuli, who have difficulty screening out excessive stimuli, who have a tendency to insomnia, and who seldom pause in their daily whirlwind of activities.

Body type is certainly a factor contributing to the high tension levels common in dance, but one must also look beyond body type to the characteristic patterns of dancers which lead to high tension levels. Physical patterns, social patterns, and nutritional patterns all contribute to the pressure-cooker atmosphere of the dance world.

Physically, the dancer constantly demands the utmost in bodily control. Any control of movement requires a high level of muscular tension. Thus the very nature of dance contributes to the high levels of tension in dancers. There are also a number of highly specialized tension areas in the body which are common in dance. Two of these tension areas are discussed in Chapter 13: pectoralis minor syndrome and tightness of the outward rotators of the hip joint. These two muscular imbalances are characterized by high levels of tension in particular muscles, and in each case that tension can cause pain and resultant tension in other areas of the body as well. Thus the specific physical demands of dance can contribute to the high level of neuromuscular tension common among dancers.

Socially, dancers are notably underpaid—if they are paid at all. It is quite common to find many dancers working at other jobs to "support their dance habit." Tight time schedules must accommodate to late-night rehearsals, work schedules, and pressures of performance or touring. These social patterns force the dancer to grab rest and nourishment at odd times of the day. Most dancers are constantly on the go, with schedules that leave precious little time for relaxation.

The nutritional patterns of dancers reflect the social patterns. Easily accessible food is often the primary nutrition for many dancers. Coffee, soft drinks, and such sugar products as candy bars are usually available and easy to tuck into a dance bag for a quick shot of energy. But the caffeine and sugar in these substances contribute to high levels of tension.

Looking at the whole picture of the dancer's life, including the body type, physical demands, social and nutritional patterns, it is not surprising to find that dancers operate on very high stress levels, experience high levels of physical tension, and find themselves in real need of relaxation techniques.

Neuromuscular Tension

Neuromuscular tension is an insidious condition; unless it becomes severe enough to produce pain, we don't even know it's there until it is gone. To put this another way: Gradual buildup of tension allows the neurological system to become accustomed to its presence. Until the tension is released in some way, we are not aware it was there. A common response of participants in a relaxation session is to exclaim with wonder, "I had no idea I was so tense." Of course, if muscle spasms accompany the tension, one is certainly aware of the tension because of the pain. But if the tension level is below the spasm-producing level, one just gets used to it.

Each individual has his or her own characteristic patterns of tension, and those patterns build high tension levels in certain areas of the body. Much has been written in the psychological literature about the meanings of high tension in certain areas of the body. It is not the purpose here to discuss the possible psychological causes and effects of tension. But it is important to acknowledge that each individual "stashes" tension selectively.

I call these areas of high tension "hot spots." The hot spots of tension for any person are the most difficult to release for three major reasons. First, there is the habitual postural pattern which contributes to the tension level of the hot spot. It is necessary to change the postural habit to reduce the buildup of tension in the area, and habits are hard to change. Second, the tension itself becomes an integral part of the expected feedback pattern of the body. Changing the tension level at the hot spot can cause a real sense of physical disorientation. In other words, the body image has incorporated the high levels of tension, and changing the tension levels results in a change of the body image that can be disturbing. Third, emotional or physical pain from past experiences is often masked by neuromuscular tension. Reducing the tension level allows one to perceive the pain, whether the specific cause of the pain is remembered or not. This can cause fear, often related to a perceived loss of control over the emotions.

A number of common effects can accompany the reduction of tension at a hot spot. Those effects may include nausea, disorientation, fear, weeping, exhaustion, flashbacks, and even hallucinations. Of course, it is possible to reduce tension without these effects, but when one finds a hot spot—a real center of tension—it is unusual to be able to reduce the tension in that area without at least one or two of these powerful effects. Understanding that these effects are common helps to neutralize the fear produced by a particular response. Anyone who works extensively with relaxation techniques is familiar with these effects and is usually not frightened by them. We learn to accept that, in the past, the body dealt with some pain by locking it up in tension. Reducing the tension allows access to the pain of the past, if the person wishes to deal with it, or sometimes even if the person doesn't wish to deal with it. This may be a primary reason why so many therapists use relaxation techniques to facilitate treatment.

Tension and Motor Learning

Learning any new movement skill requires the ability to physically focus movement on selected areas of the body. To do so, one must be able to inhibit undesired movements. In order to achieve control, the tension level goes up. In the initial stages of learning any new movement skill, the tension level is typically very high. One look at a beginners' dance class certainly supports this point. The observer is actually amazed that the students can move at all while utilizing such high levels of tension to perform relatively easy tasks.

In addition to generalized high tension levels, localized tension may be seen in the fingers, face, shoulders, and other areas. These are idiosyncratic positions which appear in the process of learning new, difficult motor patterns. "Beginner's paralysis," evidenced in many dance classes, diminishes as the skill level rises. Of course it returns with each new, difficult skill to be learned, but with practice the tension level is usually lowered. As new neurological patterns are imprinted in the repertoire of the individual, the amount of control required to prevent extraneous movement can be relaxed and the motion becomes more fluid. In this trial-and-error process of motor learning, the learner tries different combinations of muscles in different sequences of contraction to produce the desired movement.

Some movements seem to produce more difficulty for certain learners than other movement combinations. This may be due to specific weakness of the prime mover, inelasticity of the antagonistic muscles (kinesiological reasons); it may be due to variances in movement potential related to body type; or it may be due to stylistic blocks (movement behavior patterns). Analysis of the demands of the movement combination, combined with analysis of the movement potential of the individual, may speed up the learning process by identifying the critical blocked area of motor learning.

Muscular Efficiency

Muscular efficiency, as already noted, is a matter of using the minimum amount of effort to perform a given action. Working toward muscular efficiency involves reducing the number of active muscles to the bare minimum. It is, in effect, economy of motion (*wasteless motion*). Older professional dancers often exhibit economy of motion. They have to; it is a matter of survival. Aging bodies begin to show the effects of muscular overkill, and dancers who use far more effort than is necessary are frequently those who leave dance at an earlier age. Dancers still active in their forties and fifties characteristically have learned to economize—to use less effort to produce the same effect. If young dancers could form habits of efficient action early in their careers, their careers might last longer.

One approach to muscular efficiency is kinesiological analysis followed by carefully designed conditioning programs. Analysis of the desired movement combination reveals the specific muscles which are most efficient in producing the joint action. If these muscles are weak, compensatory muscular contraction is necessary. This builds neuromuscular patterns that are inefficient. If the dancer could analyze the action that is producing the problem, and specifically condition the muscles, which must be strong or elastic, there would be greater assurance of muscular efficiency. An even greater effect might be apparent if all teachers of dance were able to do such analysis. When students had difficulty with a combination, they could analyze the kinesiological requirements of that combination and then build the component strengths into lesson plans. This may be one of the greatest long-range benefits of studying kinesiology: more carefully planned classes designed to increase muscular efficiency with conscious attention to kinesiological factors.

Somatic Techniques

Active, Passive, and Combined Techniques

The need for somatic techniques is critical in dance. The social pressures placed on the dancer, combined with a natural tendency toward high tension levels, produce excruciatingly high levels of stress. There are so many approaches to somatics that to start looking at them without categorization is very confusing. I have classified the somatic techniques as *active*, *passive*, and *combined active and passive*. Active techniques are those in which the subject is an active participant; by his or her own action the subject increases awareness and lowers the tension level. Passive techniques are those which involve manipulation of the subject by a therapist or specialist. Combined techniques involve both.

Table 17.1 (p. 311) lists some active somatic techniques and gives brief descriptions. Table 17.2 (p. 312) lists some of the passive techniques. Table 17.3 (p. 312) lists some combinations of active and passive techniques.

Tables 17.1, 17.2, and 17.3 are by no means all of the possible somatic approaches to tension reduction, relaxation, increased awareness, and efficiency. There are many others being practiced throughout the country. The one objective all techniques have in common is to increase muscular efficiency and balance. As efficiency increases, the subject often experiences a relaxed sensation in the body and a "cleansing" of the mind. Different techniques appeal to different people. No single technique appeals to everyone. The imagery of Sweigard's techniques appeals to some, the quantitative approach of Jacobson's technique appeals to others, and the repetitive motion of the Feldenkrais technique appeals to still others. A person who is experiencing high levels of stress and accompanying physical tension should experiment with the different techniques to find the one that best meets the need.

Eight Leading Techniques

When I began working on this second edition, I was committed to one essential expansion: the inclusion of more comprehensive discussion of the somatic approaches that are popular with dancers. Out of respect for the specific training required of practitioners for each of the somatic approaches, I decided to ask practitioners of various approaches to write about the nature of their work and its particular value to dancers. Presented on the following pages are descriptions of the eight somatic approaches that seem to be the most popular in the dance world: (1) Pilates-Based Conditioning; (2) Rolfing; (3) Feldenkrais; (4) Alexander Technique; (5) Ideokinesis; (6) Body-Mind Centering; (7) Bartenieff Fundamentals; and (8) Laban Movement Analysis. The selection process is based on perceived level of interest in the various somatic approaches in the dance' community, and on availability of authors with expertise in the selected approaches. Certainly, the list could be expanded with the addition of yoga, Reflexology, Posturology, Applied/Educational Kinesiology, Trager Menastics, Postural Integration, and many others. But while the somatic approaches covered in this chapter are not all-inclusive, those currently most popular are represented. It is hoped that these descriptions will aid dancers and dance educators who wish to explore somatics but may not know where to begin.

TABLE 17.1   **Active Techniques**

Technique	Brief Description
Progressive Relaxation	This technique, developed by Edmund Jacobson, focuses on the amount of tension carried in each segment of the body. The body is approached segment by segment and usually the tension level is increased temporarily and then there is a systematic progressive relaxation of the musculature of that segment. *Conscious quantitative reduction of the tension level* is consistently used in this technique.
Constructive Rest Position (CRP) and Ideokinesis	Lulu Sweigard's approach to relaxation differs from Jacobson's in its *extensive use of imagery and imagined action (ideokinesis)*. Subjects assume the constructive rest position (CRP), lying on the back with knees bent, feet flat on the floor, and knees dropped together. The arms are wrapped across the chest (as if holding onto the opposite shoulders, but held in a relaxed fashion). While the subject is in the CRP, the instructor takes him or her through a series of imagined actions designed to facilitate a relaxed state and motional efficiency. Graphic images are the hallmark of Sweigard's work with relaxation.
Feldenkrais Group Sessions	The group work is directed by a practitioner (an extensive training program is required of all practitioners). This technique was developed by Moshe Feldenkrais. It is characterized by rocking, back-and-forth motions at a given joint. The motions are gentle; the tempo is slow at first, then accelerating, and finally slowing down again. Subjects are encouraged to do no more than is comfortable. After each exercise, the subject returns to a neutral position and is encouraged to compare the side of the body which participated in the exercise and the nonparticipating side. Usually there is a remarkable difference in the tension level. *Low-grade, repetitive motion is characteristic of this relaxation approach.*
Yoga	There are many different forms of Yoga which focus the attention of the participant on different bodily functions. The form most commonly taught to beginners is hatha yoga, in which the participant assumes positions designed to integrate his or her energy. Most of these positions place a number of muscle groups on stretch, and the positions are maintained for increasing periods of time. The positions themselves (such as the cobra or the plow) characterize this technique.
Meditation	One focus of any meditation technique is a clearing of the mind. In the process, there is a relaxation of the musculature which may or may not be the focus of a particular meditation exercise.

TABLE 17.2 **Passive Techniques**

Technique	Brief Description
Rolfing	Rolfing (developed by Ida Rolf) is a technique of *deep tissue massage* which includes ten one-hour sessions. Each session focuses on a specific body area. The massage is very deep, quite painful for some subjects, and reportedly effective in radically changing tension patterns. The change is so rapid that subjects frequently report physical disorientation. In order for the effects of Rolfing to last over a period of time, the subject (just as with other techniques) must invest time and energy in changing his or her habit patterns that caused the tension to build in the first place.
Applied Kinesiology Touch for Health Goodhardt Therapy	This technique is based on the theory of energy meridians (acupuncture/acupressure) and the linking of specific muscles and muscles groups with certain meridians. *Muscle testing for strength is followed by acupressure to increase the strength of weak muscles and decrease the strength of strong muscles* to create an evenly balanced muscular system. Holistic health is also a focus of this technique.
Posturology/Reflexology	Postural problems, health problems, and muscular imbalances are approached through *foot massage*. Practitioners of this technique base their work on the theory that all parts of the body are represented in specific areas of the foot.
Postural Integration	*Deep tissue massage* focuses on areas of high tension and muscular imbalance. Some say this technique is similar to Rolfing, but practitioners of the two techniques do not agree.

TABLE 17.3 **Active and Passive Techniques**

Technique	Brief Description
Alexander Technique	This technique is characterized by one-one-one therapy which focuses on increasing muscular efficiency. The practitioner calls the subject's attention to areas of tension through *touch and manipulation to facilitate lowering the tension level* used in everyday and specific actions.
Feldenkrais Individual Therapy	This technique uses the same principles as the Feldenkrais Group Sessions to repattern neural habits, but the work is done with individual subjects on a private basis.
Biofeedback	*Electromyographic equipment is used to give feedback* to the subject on the electrical activity of the musculature. The immediacy of feedback and the objectivity of the measure of tension are the outstanding features of biofeedback techniques.

The Pilates® Method
of Body Conditioning
Susan McLain

Joseph Pilates, born in Germany in 1880, was a frail child who suffered from asthma, rickets, and rheumatic fever. He pursued Yoga, gymnastics, and a variety of sports with the determination to overcome these childhood ailments, thus beginning a lifelong interest in body conditioning. While interned in England during World War I, he created exercises to aid rehabilitation of prisoners. He experimented by attaching springs to their hospital beds, allowing them to start exercising before they were able to get up. It was these makeshift mechanical designs that were the prototypes of the Pilates apparatus used today. After the war he returned to Germany, where he befriended Rudolf von Laban and influenced Laban with his body-building methods and teaching. The German government saw the importance of Joseph's teaching, and because of political pressure to train the new German Army he was motivated to immigrate to America. He met his wife, Clara, on the boat ride over. In 1926, he opened a studio in the same building that later housed the New York City Ballet, and from that moment his method of body conditioning caught the attention of the dance community. Over several decades, he created a conditioning method that embraced eastern disciplines and western physical training. Joseph Pilates was a visionary who's been quoted as saying, "My work is probably fifty years ahead of its time." How right he was.

Nearly 70 years after being introduced in the United States, the Pilates Method® of rehabilitation and conditioning techniques continues to provide a gratifying and essential adjunct to a dancer's training. Today, what was once an exercise regime for the dancer, the performer, and the elite athlete has now developed mass appeal for any individual interested in attaining optimum health and body beautification. Yes, the "underground" world of Pilates Method that has contributed to the training of such dance legends as Ted Shawn, Balanchine, Hanya Holm, Pearl Primus, and Jerome Robbins has now found its way to the mainstream public. In response to this growth of interest many dancers are seeking the Pilates Method, not only for their own conditioning and rehabilitative needs but also as a career opportunity: teacher certification in the Pilates Method has become a lucrative career transition for dancers. Many professional dancers will tell you that Pilates training is a "must" if they are to survive the rigorous demands of performing and teaching. If you are a student and are seriously pursuing a dance career, I highly recommend that you take an introductory course in this method. If you're wondering where to study the Pilates Method, most likely there is a studio near you or a university dance department that has augmented its curriculum with a Pilates Method program. To my knowledge, up until the early 1980s only four Pilates studios existed. Lately, owing to the Method's popularity, hundreds of studios are now in operation all over the world, with new ones opening monthly in such faraway places as Sydney, Singapore, and Warsaw.

Originally, this time-honored technique provided a rare, often only conditioning system outside the dance class that focused on range of motion and function peculiar only to dancers. Today, the Pilates Method is joined with other body therapies such as Gyrotonics, Alexander Technique, and Feldenkrais® in filling the void in "dancer specific" training, thus allowing dancers to augment their conditioning with movement integral to their profession. However, the true beauty of the Pilates Method lies in the fact that it can be tailor-made to fit anyone's level of physicality, which explains its current mass appeal. It is a sophisticated program yet one that can speak to a wide range of clientele in reference to technical proficiency, medical diagnosis, and physical fitness. Within the prescribed series of exercises, adaptations can, and should be, made by the trainer to accommodate and challenge the student's ability in reference to strength, joint range of action, muscular elasticity, skeletal alignment, coordination, and proprioception.

As with any technique, the Pilates Method is only as good as its instruction; therefore, close and knowledgeable supervision must be given to students if they are to receive the maximum result from this conditioning program. Most Pilates studios provide intimate, quiet environments conducive to deep concentration and undisturbed work, where instructors give one-on-one or small group instruction, gently correcting their clientele with verbal and tactile cues. Experts in this field will attest to the merit and accuracy of their training and the valued lineage with which they served their apprenticeship. Joseph Pilates was a man protective of his work, and he exercised caution in delegating teaching authority to his practitioners. Romana Kryzanowska, Carola Trier, Ron Fletcher, Kathleen Stanford-Grant, and the late Eve Gentry and Bruce King constitute "first generation" disciples whose long-standing apprenticeships have each carried on Joseph Pilate's legacy. Their disciples, in turn, continue to pass along the Pilates Method, and so on and so on, much like the game of "telephone." Direct disciples in this lineage feel it is their mission to maintain the technique's purity. Of course, how much license one should have in creatively interpreting and expanding upon the Pilates Method is an issue of considerable debate. Today, the direct descendant of Romana Kryzanowska is Sean Gallagher, who authoritatively owns the Pilates trademark and exercise system and is the director of the official "Pilates" studios that are increasingly being established throughout the country. It should be mentioned that other trainers not affiliated with this studio provide excellent instruction even though they legally are not copyrighted to use the official "Pilates Method" label. This legal glitch is, needless to say, problematic where those instructors not allowed to use the Pilates trademark are now forced to use a different name. A good example of this is the Dancemedicine Clinic associated with Saint Francis Memorial Hospital in San Francisco, California, where their form of conditioning is identified as Kinetic Activities. Here, a modified version of the Pilates equipment and system of exercises is being used but is creatively tailored and further developed for dance injury prevention and rehabilitation.

Wherever you decide to seek instruction, make sure you choose the studio that fits your particular needs by investigating thoroughly its reputation and training objective. If you're seeking to augment your dance training, a good question to ask is whether the studio's instructors have a thorough dance background with a sound kinesiological knowledge that can further meet your "dancer specific" needs. If you're seeking teacher certification, you should inquire as to its length and intensity, and better yet, how much it will cost. Investigate, and make sure you choose the studio that's right for you. Unfortunately, if your mode of research chooses a literary route, you'll most likely find it problematic to secure the Pilates Method instructional materials. Textual information, as it stands today, is limited owing to out-of-print materials, reluctance on the part of experts to document its theory, and legal complications in using the Pilates trademarks. Local newspapers and assorted magazines have frequently covered various Pilates training centers, only to provide a superficial overview and thrice-removed quotations on the merits of this conditioning method. Videos that show exercises performed on the mat and on the various pieces of apparatus, with Joseph Pilates himself seen on some of them, can be another source of information and are available through any of the official training centers.

Upon entering a Pilates studio, you will notice students gracefully gliding through exercises utilizing the mat and various kinds of apparatus that are specifically designed to address certain conditioning needs yet are versatile in their function. Each series of evolving exercises are dancelike in movement and are designed to lengthen and strengthen muscles and create trim and toned bodies. Joseph Pilates termed his technique "Contrology" in which the following six principles are the underpinnings to all movement: Control, Concentration, Centering, Precision, Flowing Movement, and Breathing. Joseph Pilates believed in working the body and mind in tandem where the guidance of one's energy produces quality of action integral to good health and vitality. "Contrology" strives to restore the body to true balance, and focuses on ease and economy of movement and on channeling one's flow of energy through mental and physical harmony. Exercises are performed as controlled movements with minimal repetitions to safeguard against mindless, automaton-like activity, which Joseph felt was detrimental to his goal of mind/body/spirit development. The quality of each movement is paramount where stressing attention to detail allows for the correction of postural problems, misalignments caused by imbalances, and neuromuscular patterning.

Most instructors will tell you that the heart of Joseph's work is based on the series of exercises performed on the mat. It is here that the student is introduced to the essence of the Pilates Method theory: the relationship of the body parts to the whole form. These introductory sessions often begin with basic movements like "Rolling Like a Ball," which is very fetal in nature, in order to facilitate the integration of abdominal control and spine articulation with breathing. The focus is very much on the torso, which Joseph Pilates felt was the "powerhouse" to all movement. Once abdominal strength, a supple spine, and pelvic stabilization are achieved, the student can then be further challenged with movements of the legs and arms. How the thoracic breath fuels the body to increase oxygen intake and the maintenance of abdominal support are both emphasized with every movement sequence. Much of the rolling and unrolling movement introduced at the mat and later performed on the apparatus is meant to restore the spine to its at-birth position; the feeling being that if your spine is stiff at any age, you will undoubtedly feel old.

As a instructor, I try to engage my new clients in mat activity prior to using the apparatus. Mind you, this is a bit of a tease and is much like telling children to eat their vegetables before desert. Why? Because the apparatus is very intriguing and looks like fun to perform on! Mat exercises tend to be thought of as the "grunt work" because of the intense nature of the abdominal series. They also lack the gratification of reciprocated motion that the apparatus provides. The entertaining challenge of any apparatus work lies in the relationship of human and machine, creating a point of reference with which to co-relate on one's journey of well-being; whereas the mat work provides the student with a solitary task of exercising that is rewarding but also lackluster. Dancers quickly realize, however, the importance of the mat work, and that the transportability of these exercises is of tremendous value for them if ever they're on the road away from the studio. As an interesting aside, permutations of these mat exercises can still be found in the warm-up of the Hanya Holm technique, stemming from her association with Joseph Pilates.

So what does the Pilates Method apparatus look like? It's been jokingly likened to medieval instruments of torture, but all would agree that Joseph's designs are aesthetically pleasing and mechanically brilliant. The most widely used piece of machinery is the "Reformer," which is the central part of the Pilates system. Hundreds of exercises can be performed on this horizontal, bedlike apparatus with a carriage that slides back and forth to accommodate a myriad of positions from lying to standing, sitting up, kneeling, piking, and even jumping. The carriage is tracked on metal runners where the exerciser has complete control of his/her movements by stabilizing, pulling, or pushing against a horizontal bar placed at the foot of the apparatus. Also attached are looped straps for one's arms and legs and four attachable springs hooked onto the carriage that determine the amount of resistance, which can be varied according to exercise and individual. This versatile apparatus, which utilizes spring tension attached to a pulley system, has the potential to work the entire body with isometric stabilization and isotonic resistive exercises that move through the range of motion.

The "plié series" is often first performed on the Reformer and has you lying supine with head elevated slightly on the headrest and feet propped up on the foot bar. This reclined position for the legwork section of the program—that is, demi and grande pliés, relevés, and jumps—avoids the pull of gravity on the lower extremities. This removal of force from the vertical axis allows the spine to stay aligned and helps to neutralize bad habits and tension. Other sections of the Reformer program focus on concentrated abdominal, torso isolation, upper body, and arms exercises that are integrated to total body movement. The Pilates Method principle of variable spring and weight-bearing resistance makes for a low-impact, therapeutic conditioning program, unlike that of weight training and aerobics. Here exercisers gently transform their bodies toward the "Balanced Ideal" and walk away feeling revitalized instead of exhausted. Today, the versatility and popularity of the Reformer is such that devotees are now purchasing collapsible, lightweight "Pilates Performers"™ or the Current Concepts Company's "Polstar Mini-Reformers" that can support a wide range of Pilates movement for their homes.

It would seem that, with the multitude of exercises performed on the Reformer, it would suffice in meeting most conditioning needs; and in many ways it does. For a dancer, who's continually challenged to move on various planes of motion, it's essential to provide a conditioning program that reinforces this spatial and positional awareness. That's where the next main piece of equipment, the "Trapeze Table" (a.k.a. The Cadillac), comes in. This four-poster bed can be designed to take on various configurations based on spring length attachments to bars that are positioned at different places on the bed frame. These exercises are similar to those performed on the mat and Reformer but exercisers are further challenged to encompass multidimensional movement; thus dancers are provided with complex neuromuscular patterning akin to their profession.

The Trapeze Table is greatly assessorized to enhance program versatility. The use of such props as foot plates, standing platforms, boxes, balls, nonskid pads, foam wedges, handle attachments, Velcro cuffs, disks, baby arc, etc., is designed and augmented to accommodate client ability while providing comfort and skeletal support. Once the client becomes well versed in his or her personalized routine, self-manipulation of machinery and handling of these assessories become second nature.

The "Wunda Chair" is another major piece of apparatus that looks like a boxed high chair that has a horizontal step with springs attached to it. The action of pressing down on this spring-tensioned step with one's hands or feet can be executed in varying body positions (seated, standing, squatting, lying down). This simple act of exerting pressure builds muscular strength but, more significantly, can be targeted to provide bilateral conditioning. The Wunda Chair can effectively correct imbalances to avoid one area of the body overcompensating for an injury, body weakness, or misalignment. The Wunda Chair exercises are also effective for closed-kinetic-chain work in vertical, standing position.

A well-stocked Pilates studio will also possess other pieces of equipment; including the Arm Chair, the High Barrel, the Small Barrel, the foot corrector, the spine corrector, the pedipole, and the wall unit. Each piece provides further exploration of movement but with greater specificity to certain muscle groups. Speaking in general terms, for example, the High Barrel supports a wide range of motion for the torso (extension, flexion, and lateral flexion) and can be used for many dance stretches. The Arm Chair facilitates further examination of arm movements similar to those done on the Reformer, thereby increasing awareness of the shoulder and scapula area. The Small Barrel, an auxiliary piece, addresses intense abdominal work done similarly at the mat, where torso and hip flexion are executed from a hyperextended spine, thus utilizing a more extreme range of motion. The exercisers experience "theme and variation" with each piece of apparatus, reinforcing and building upon movement information as they advance within their individualized program. Watching clients in a Pilates studio circulate from apparatus to apparatus is a ballet in itself.

The Pilates Method has often been referred to as the "thinking person's technique," where the disciplined mind governs the body to take ownership of one's conditioning and rehabilitative task. As a dance educator, I am always seeking to learn new ways to improve and strengthen technique and to bring consciousness to physical habits that jeopardize well-being. In this pursuit, I hope to help myself and others with the arduous challenge of surviving in the dance profession with health and graceful longevity. The Pilates Method has long satisfied this quest for me, and I encourage you to experience this technique, not only for its holistic benefits but also for its sheer aesthetic pleasure.

REFERENCES

"Fitness," *Lear's,* January, 1994.

FITT, S., STURMAN, J., AND MCLAIN-SMITH, S., The effects of a Pilates-based conditioning program on strength, alignment, and range of motion for ballet and modern dance majors at the University of Utah. *Kinesiology and Medicine for Dance.* 16:1: Fall-Winter 1993–1994, pp. 36–51.

FRIEDMAN, P., AND EISEN, G., *The Pilates Method of Physical and Mental Conditioning.* Warner Books Inc., New York, 1980.

PILATES, J., AND MILLER, W.J., *Return to Life Through Contrology.* J.J. Augustine Publisher, New York, 1945.

"Pilates Technique," *Dance Teacher Now,* November-December 1988.

FOR MORE INFORMATION CONTACT

For official Pilates Method training and equipment:

The Pilates® Studio, 2121 Broadway, Suite 201 New York, New York 10023
Phone: (212) 769-1423.

Other sources of related information:

Kinetic Activities, Elizabeth Larkam, Dancemedicine Clinic, St. Francis Memorial Hospital, 900 Hyde Street
San Francisco, California 94109

Current Concepts (for equipment based on the ideas and concepts of Joseph Pilates)
Ken Endelman
7500 14th Avenue, Suite 23
Sacramento, California 95820-3539
Phone: (916) 454-2838.

Note: Pilates® and the Pilates Studio® are Registered Trademarks of Pilates Incorporated of New York.

Rolfing: An Inquiry into the Human Structure
Mary Bond

> As in all matter organized into biological units, there is a pattern, an order, in human bodies. . . . Rolfers make a life study of relating bodies and their fields to the earth and its gravity field, and we so organize the body that the gravity field can reinforce the body's energy field.
> (Ida Rolf, in Feitis, 1990, p. 86)

THE NATURE OF ROLFING

All human movement is a dance with gravity. From the first time we reach for the breast to our final breath, gravity is our silent, unseen, and usually unacknowledged partner. The dancer magnifies this relationship, cloaking it in the myriad symbols of human life. As we watch dance performance, our own kinesthesia responds, and we are literally moved—however briefly or unconsciously—as the dancer evokes our own partnership with gravity.

Because the Rolf technique is concerned with organizing and refining the body's relationship with gravity, it's an ideal avenue of inquiry for the dancer. Ida P. Rolf, Ph.D., the founder of Structural Integration—or Rolfing, as it has become known—was not concerned, however, with the ability to create the illusion of effortlessness and grace on the stage. Her understanding was rather that an effortless and graceful relationship with gravity is the birthright of all human beings. In that sense she wanted to turn everyone into a dancer.

Dr. Rolf, formerly a biochemist with the Rockefeller Institute, developed her technique in the 1940s through her personal research into the relationship of human structure and function, studying, among other things, osteopathy and yoga.

Rolf's approach centered initially on the properties of fascia, or connective tissue. The collagenous tissue envelops the human body in a superficial layer just under the skin, wraps around each muscle and organ, and penetrates down to the cellular level. Fascia is so universal that if all other cells in a body could be removed, there would remain a recognizable human form.

Rolf observed that when the body falls out of alignment through trauma or habit, the fascia shortens and hardens to hold the misaligned parts in place. Over time, muscles in the involved area lose function, joints lose range of motion, and nerve and circulatory transmissions are impeded. The lack of motion can result in illness, injury, loss of sensation, or pain. And, because fascia is so pervasive throughout the body, distant areas compensate for loss of motion in the affected part, either by bracing or by becoming hypermobile. Rolf reasoned that since fascia is made of collagen, it should be plastic enough to recover elasticity through human touch.

Once she knew that human tissue was malleable, Rolf needed a template for balancing the human structure. She envisioned the ideal body as architecture organized around a central gravitational axis in the upright stance. Her manipulations of soft tissue addressed each individual's unique way of being out of true with the vertical. In assessing alignment, Rolf learned to look for balance between the front and the back of the body, releasing both the tendency to cringe or collapse and the tendency to overarch the spine. She looked for balance of right with left, upper with lower, and intrinsic with extrinsic. To explain this last, she used the analogy of a central "core" and a "sleeve." The larger, consciously controlled sleeve muscles were the structures of "doing," whereas the deep, usually unconsciously controlled core muscles were the structures of "being." For efficient and graceful doing, freedom of being is necessary. When all these aspects of balance were restored to a certain degree, Rolf considered that the structure was integrated.

The technique involved not just pressure but synchronous movement participation from the client as well. A client might be instructed to meet the Rolfer's pressure with his or her breath, to slowly move a limb, or to assume a certain posture on the table, on a bench, or standing up. The balanced shape of a Rolfed body is less a hallmark than its responsive, congruent movement quality. This is the result of a characteristic lengthening in the spine. When the inhibiting response of the antigravity muscles can itself be inhibited, the rest of the body is freed for congruent action. The structurally integrated body moves with the elegance one normally reserves to describe prize race horses or animals in the wild.

In Rolf's view, the more harmonious the body's relationship with the force of gravity, the healthier the individual became, holistically. With the Rolfer's help, gravity became the therapist for the total organism—body, mind, and spirit. This view came about because increasing numbers of clients reported emotional release and relief as the physical reorganization progressed.

As Dr. Rolf saw that her work could relieve not only physical but supressed mental suffering, she became increasingly interested in the relationship between the structural organization of the body and human behavior. She saw her goal as the evocation of human potential over and above the alleviation of physical symptoms. She believed Rolfing to represent humankind's first conscious attempt to assist its own evolution.

The first generation of Rolfers, those trained directly by Ida Rolf, were fascinated by the mechanics of Rolfing, by how it worked on the purely physical level. Dr. Rolf herself participated in several research projects in hopes of being acknowledged by the medical establishment. Although her work and its offshoots have spread around the globe, that acceptance is only marginally closer now than it was at her death in 1979.

A 1972 research project, headed by Dr. Valerie Hunt of the Department of Kinesiology at the University of California at Los Angeles, assisted by Larry Davis and Sally Fitt, showed that after ten sessions of Rolfing, body movements were smoother, larger, less constrained, and more energetic and involved less extraneous movement in performing specific tasks; and carriage was more erect, with less obvious strain to maintain positions (Hunt, 1972).

Research by John Cottingham, published in the *Journal of the American Physical Therapy Association* in 1988, showed that Rolfing improves parasympathetic activity, a neurological effect associated with a relaxed, nurturing state. In addition, measurements of the lumbar curve in these subjects showed increased low back flexibility (Cottingham, 1988).

Rolfers continue to quest for clinical and theoretic solutions as to how Rolfing achieves its results. Dr. Rolf's original thesis was that systematic stretching of the myofascia to reorganize the structure around the gravitational axis caused the nervous system to spontaneously reorganize toward a greater efficiency. An updated model by a German Rolfer, Robert Schleip (1991), proposes a neuro-myofascial loop in which the Rolfer's touch stimulates sensory receptors embedded in the myofascia, resulting in reorganization of the central nervous system. This model alters the intent of the Rolfer's touch so that the procedure is less an application of mechanical pressure to the fascia and more a communication with the client's nervous system.

While the Rolfer's application of pressure may occasionally be uncomfortable, *most clients experience this as pain being released rather than as pain being inflicted.* Moments of such intensity are brief and are manageable by relaxing and breathing into the area being worked on. An experienced Rolfer recognizes that a client cannot release tension in one part of the body if he or she is simultaneously bracing in another. The client knows when the pressure feels right, and the Rolfer modulates his or her touch accordingly. At its best, a Rolfing session feels like co-creation between client and practitioner—there is a sense of common rhythm, unity of purpose, and deep physical communication.

Although the Rolfing procedure is intended as a holistic reorganization of structure rather than as treatment for specific complaints, most clients report alleviation or eradication of physical symptoms. Clients commonly report relief from low back pain, sciatica, neck and shoulder pain, foot problems, scoliosis, carpal tunnel syndrome, and "TMJ" problems of the jaw. To refine their interventions for more accurate symptomatic treatment, some Rolfers have acquired osteopathic or physical therapy techniques.

Other Rolfers have become interested in reeducation of the client's movement patterns in conjunction with the mechanical intervention. Part of Dr. Rolf's legacy to her students was a set of exercises she had learned from an osteopath in the 1940s. These exercises became the foundation of an adjunctive motor retraining therapy called Rolfing Movement Integration. Because the slow, patterned movements had inherent reorganizing capability, clients could achieve structural improvement even if they had not experienced the deep tissue massage.

Eventually, Rolfing Movement Integration evolved to include assisted exploration of the client's internal body image, the proprioceptive sense of self. Through gentle touch, passive and active micro-movement, breathing work, and dialogue, Rolfing Movement Integration helps the client con-

nect with unconscious chronic tensions, renegotiate the emotions or be-
liefs associated with those tensions, and recover the ease of motion that
tension has overwhelmed. Work with various types of apparatus—large
gymnastic balls, balance boards, and the like—helps the client recognize
sensations of ease and stability in action and recruit those sensations in
performing the tasks of daily living.

Although many Rolfing clients report spontaneous reduction in mental
or emotional stress coincident with their Rolfing sessions, others seem to
need assistance with emotional processing. Rolfers have found that clients
whose bodies were unresponsive to the treatment were often those who
had done nothing to unravel their emotional entanglements. In order to be
able to assist clients in handling emotional expressions that may arise
from the physical release, some Rolfers have begun to specialize in the
body/mind aspect of the work. Some have studied dance or movement
therapy, or have received training in body oriented psychotherapeutic approaches such as Ron Kurtz's Hakomi (1990), Arnold Mindell's Process
Oriented Psychotherapy (1986), or Lizbeth Marcher's Bodynamics (un-
dated).

The Rolf Institute was founded in 1971 to carry on Dr. Rolf's work. Its
major purposes are to train Rolfers and Rolfing Movement teachers, to
carry on research, and to provide information to the public. Approximately 900 Certified Rolfers are listed in the Institute's directory, working
in the United States, Canada, Europe, Israel, South America, Australia,
and Japan. Over the years a number of Dr. Rolf's original students have
formed their own schools, notably Aston-Patterning, Hellerwork, and the
Guild for Structural Integration (see listing of schools at the end of this article). So, by now, Rolf-based bodyworkers probably number in the thousands, worldwide.

THE VALUE TO DANCERS

Rolfing has special benefits for dancers. All bodies have a particular shaping of fascia and muscle, and an individual timing of neural response that
evolves out of their histories of trauma, attitudes, and habits. This deep neu-
romyofascial pattern is at the heart of every action. It colors how we
breathe, how we embrace another, how we eat, walk, work, play, and dance.

When the deep pattern is "out of true" with gravity, every action has an
inherent imbalance that is usually too familiar to be noticeable. When
hours upon hours of rehearsal time are spent supporting movement from
this core imbalance, the deep structures become shorter and tougher, and
the concurrent nerve impulses more and more ingrained. This exacerbates
the pattern and often results in chronic pain or injury. But because dance
involves the creation of illusion, dancers may come to believe that effortlessness and grace are illusions that can be created only by inuring themselves to pain.

Because of refined coordination, a dancer usually has a well developed
sense of how the body functions at the extrinsic or "doing" level. But focus
on line and shape may exteriorize body awareness. Often awareness of the
deep imbalance is blocked or missing. And because release of that core

level of tension might initially interrupt familiar ways of mastering movement sequences, some dancers may be resistent to the core-level changes that must occur for the body—and the whole person—to find the ease and freedom of motion that can only occur when the core is released and responsive.

As mentioned earlier, the hallmark of this freedom of core is a spine that can lengthen in both directions, toward the earth and toward gravity's other pole, the sky. Most bodies have a proclivity for one pole or the other, or a pattern of compression that shrinks away from both poles. Fred Astaire is an example of a "skyward" dancer, while Gene Kelly is an "earth" type. To be versatile, a dancer must be able to respond equally well in both directions. For good elevation, a sky type must develop a sense of the downward direction in order to rebound into the air. By contrast, the earth type must learn to find the sky in order to have a destination for his or her leap. The dancer whose body is compressed into the center will be unable to move well at all until the core can relax and lengthen.

The sensorimotor education and myofascial massage of Rolfing help the dancer release the restrictions to bipolar responsiveness in the spine, as well as restore balance between right and left, front and back, and core and sleeve. When this has been accomplished, the dancer's effortlessness and grace are no longer an illusion, but an expression of true freedom of movement.

A NEW LOOK AT THE EFFECTIVENESS OF ROLFING

In an address at the annual convention of the Rolf Institute in 1994, Dr. Valerie Hunt suggested that the ultimate explanation for Rolfing's effectiveness is to be found in the field of biophysics rather than in biomechanics or neurology. According to her recent research, connective tissue is piezoelectric—it operates like an electrical system. Thus the fascia is the primary vehicle for the circulation of electromagnetic energy in the body. It is here that the acupuncture meridians and yogic chakras are to be found. What this means to Rolfing is that fascia is not just the soft tissue "guy wires" holding bony struts in place, nor merely a soft tissue bed whose release facilitates the transmission of nervous impulses. The Rolfer's intervention in the fascia is a major transaction in the client's energy field.

As biophysics uncovers more each year about the electromagnetic nature of cellular health, the implications for the fields of medicine, nutrition, and psychotherapy are enormous. According to Dr. Hunt (1995), body workers who intervene in the connective tissue system are working at the frontier of modern health—energy field facilitation. This transaction takes place at a molecular level, causing resonant interactions throughout the connective tissue matrix. Physicist Herbert Frohlich (1993) believes that such vibrations "communicate regulatory information responsible for the integration of function taking place at various levels within the organism" (p. 61).

More important than any specific bodywork technique is Dr. Rolf's initiation of the inquiry into the relationship of physical structure, mind, and energy. Whether through direct mechanical intervention into fascia; through gentle, indirect manipulation of joint capsules and sutures; through movement reeducation, body-oriented psychological counselling, or subtle energy transactions, Rolfing has enabled thousands of people to reclaim free, effortless, connected sensations of movement, and regain access to the calm state of mind that accompanies diminished physical strain.

REFERENCES

COTTINGHAM, JOHN. (1988). "Shifts in pelvic inclination angle and parasympathetic tone produced by Rolfing soft tissue manipulation." *Physical Therapy. 68:* 9, pp. 1364–70.

FEITIS, ROSEMARY (Ed). (1990). *Rolfing and Physical Reality.* Healing Arts Press, Rochester, VT.

FROHLICH, H., in OSCHMAN, JAMES L. (1993). "Matter, Energy, and the Living Matrix." *Rolf Lines* (The newsmagazine for Rolf Institute members) *21:* 3, (Oct.), p. 81.

HUNT, VALERIE V., et al. (1972). "A Study of Structural Integration from Neuromuscular, Energy Field, and Emotional Approaches." *Project Report, Rolf Institute.*

HUNT, VALERIE V. (1995). *The Infinite Mind.* Malibu Publishing Company, PO Box 4234, Malibu, CA 90265.

SCHLEIP, ROBERT. (1991). *Rolf Lines* (The newsmagazine for Rolf Institute members) *19:* 2, pp. 19–21.

SUGGESTED READINGS

BOND, MARY. (1993). *Rolfing Movement Integration: A Self-Help Approach to Balancing the Body.* Healing Arts Press, Rochester, VT.

ROLF, IDA P. (1990). *Rolfing and Physical Reality.* Healing Arts Press, Rochester, VT.

ROLF, IDA P. (1989). *Rolfing: Reestablishing the Natural Alignment and Structural Integration of the Human Body for Vitality and Well Being.* Healing Arts Press. Rochester, VT.

SCHOOLS OF STRUCTURAL INTEGRATION

The Rolf Institute. PO Box 1868. Boulder, CO 80306. (800) 530-8875

Guild for Structural Integration. PO Box 1559. Boulder, CO 80306. (800) 447-0150

Aston Patterning. PO Box 3568. Incline Village, NV 89450. (702) 831-8228

Hellerwork. 406 Berry Street. Mt. Shasta, CA 96067. (800) 392-3900

The Nature of the Feldenkrais Method®
and Its Value to Dancers
Carol Lessinger

INTRODUCTION

I remember being a dance student for many years. For over ten of those years, I received a specific correction from my teachers. I knew it had something to do with how I used my back, but in all honesty, I never truly understood what my teachers were asking of me. Undaunted by this lack of clarity, I tried to correct what I was doing. No matter what I did, there was no improvement and the correction would be repeated. I was frustrated and confused, and I felt inept.

Years later, while I was a student in a Feldenkrais Professional Training Program, we spent a few days doing variations of the classic Feldenkrais pelvic clock lesson. As always, after the floor work, we stood up and walked around to notice what had changed in our perception of ourselves. On this occasion, it was as though I'd been hit by a bolt of lightening with the realization, *"That's* what they were trying to tell me all those years!" Suddenly, I could sense separate movement in three adjacent vertebrae in my lumbar spine where, previously, I had sensed one solid block of movement. Three vertebrae, previously fused in my perception and function, had found their individuality. I could move in a new way, made available to me by the sensory communication link provided by the pelvic clock. Without this specific sensory awareness, there had been a "black hole" in the universe of my body. How could I have possibly changed something that was absent in my image of myself? In Moshe Feldenkrais's words, "You can't do what you want 'til you know what you are doing, and most of us don't know what we are doing" (Feldenkrais, 1980).

HISTORY OF THE FELDENKRAIS METHOD

Moshe Feldenkrais was the originator of the Feldenkrais Method® (FM). He was born in Russia in 1904. At the age of 15, he informed his parents that he was leaving, on foot, to go to Israel (then Palestine). Thus began the fascinating journey of one of the great Renaissance men of the twentieth century (Hanna, 1984–85). Besides developing his highly effective technique for self-improvement, he was a tutor of mathematics, land surveyor, mechanical engineer, physicist, researcher, inventor, cyberneticist, avid athlete, and martial artist. He possessed an insatiable hunger for learning in the fields of psychology, anthropology, anatomy, neurophysiology, child development, and human learning. He wrote books in Hebrew, French, and English, and had fluent command of Russian and some German. He received his doctorate in physics at the Sorbonne and went on to become a research assistant in the laboratory established by Madame Curie.

When the Nazis entered France, Dr. Feldenkrais escaped to Great Britain to assist with the war effort. At the request of the British Admiralty, he was stationed in Scotland, where he helped to develop sonar detection devices. The cold, damp weather in Scotland aggravated injuries that he had sustained in Palestine as a young athlete. Both knees were damaged severely when he was playing soccer. The pain in his knees made walking almost impossible, especially on slippery, rolling submarines. At that time, surgical techniques were not as sophisticated as they are today, and the prognosis for correction was very poor. As the story goes, Dr. Feldenkrais said something like, "I was born not knowing how to walk and I learned to walk on good knees. I'll learn to walk on these knees" (Feldenkrais, 1980). As he relearned how to move, he realized that he was recapitulating early childhood developmental movement patterns. This experience, combined with his knowledge of the laws of physics and the eastern principles of the martial arts, coalesced to form the basis of the Feldenkrais Method.

After World War II, Dr. Feldenkrais returned to Israel to take a position with the Ministry of Defense as the Director of its Electronics Department. He continued to teach movement classes that were later named Awareness Through Movement® and began to develop a hands-on technique that was later called Functional Integration®. He became very famous in Israel as the man who "cured" the prime minister's back problem. Students flocked to him, including a small group whom he agreed to train to teach the Feldenkrais Method. A growing number of people sought his help to correct problems with injuries and paralysis, and to improve performance in the arts and athletics. Therefore it became necessary to devote full time to his explorations in movement awareness and to his clinic that was growing in Tel Aviv.

Finally, in 1972, at the age of 68, Dr. Feldenkrais was "discovered" by Americans. He was given the opportunity to present a month-long intensive course at the Esalen Institute in California. Soon afterward, an American practitioners' training program was organized by Thomas Hanna. Later, the North American Feldenkrais Guild was established. There are now Feldenkrais practitioners, training programs, and Guilds worldwide. Dr. Feldenkrais continued to teach in Israel, Europe, and the United States, including another practitioner training program in Amherst, Massachusetts in 1980. He died in 1984, after publishing his final book, *The Elusive Obvious*. Dr. Bernard Lake, a distinguished Australian physician and writer, said of Dr. Feldenkrais that he gave us a system which "has as much potential for understanding the mind-body relationship as Einstein's general theory of relativity had for physics" (Lake, 1983, p. 13).

THE NATURE OF THE WORK

It is difficult to concretely describe the nature of the Feldenkrais Method in words because it is a nonverbal process. What it does, in movement, is to provide experiences whereby bodily information about movement patterns and habits gradually surfaces to allow examination and choice. It offers the sensorium a menu of beautiful little actions which allow the body to self-correct. There is a story of a young scholar who believed he could learn everything he needed to know from reading. As the story goes,

"He read many books about the stars and
   he became an astonomer.
He read many books about history and
   he became an historian.
He read many books about swimming and
   he drowned.
Some things you can only learn through direct experience,
   by rolling in the ocean and being tossed by the waves."
(Pfeffer, 1994, p. 25)

Awareness Through Movement classes (ATM) provide experiences of verbally guided sequences of movement. These are sometimes delicate, sometimes intricate, sometimes complex, sometimes simple; but they are always fascinating when the student allows his or her awareness to embrace the magnificent internal changes that occur in each shift of attention. The movement, by itself, does not create the changes that people experience; it is the quality of being in the here and now with awareness that provides the opportunity for new choices. In this timeless state, students are asked to relinquish the predictable ideas, the assumed outcomes, and the habits of thinking and doing that defined them. It is here, in the exploration of the unknown, that growth can occur.

WHAT YOU CAN EXPECT IN AN ATM CLASS

When participating in an ATM class, you can expect to be either lying on the floor, sitting, or standing. The movements and imagery explore small components of everyday human functions, like turning, reaching, sitting, or walking. Healthy people take these for granted, yet the habits inherent in these actions underlie everything else a person does. Students are encouraged to move slowly, smoothly, and in increments small enough to enable them to sense the relationships in the body that combine to actualize intention. Some parts of habitual movement are helping and some are actually interfering without our conscious knowledge of that interference. An example of the process of *shedding unnecessary interference* can be found in learning to ride a bicycle. When one first gets on the bike, movements are too intense and too jerky. Each extraneous motion needs another compensatory action (also extraneous) to regain balance. With increased skill, the ride becomes smoother. What actually happens is that the rider removes the unnecessary motion that inhibits good bike riding. The Feldenkrais Method acts in a similar fashion; it allows you to "know what you are doing" (Feldenkrais, 1980), so that you need only do the most efficient action.

Feldenkrais teachers encourage students to move as easily, gently, and lightly as possible to allow for more refined discernment of sensation. *When the effort is greater, the ability to feel diminishes.* For instance, if you were carrying a large stack of books, you wouldn't notice the weight of one raindrop landing on them, but you would notice the weight of that same raindrop falling on a feather carried gently between two fingers. *The lighter your movement, the easier it is to notice a small difference.* The idea is to become a more intelligent mover; therefore, the better you are at noticing small differences, the more kinesthetically intelligent you become.

When you move lightly, without the sensation of stretch or strain in your muscles, it is also easier to be aware of skeletal relationships than when moving with great strength. Try this for yourself by doing the "cat" pose from yoga (similar to the "Mad Cat" exercise in the Chapter 19 of this book, Figure 19.32). While on your hands and knees, move by pressing your back toward the ceiling and then down toward the floor. First do this action to your fullest stretch and feel the pleasant muscle sensations that it provides. Come to neutral and begin moving again, with one major change. Bring your awareness to the relationship of one vertebra to another, focusing on the bones. Notice which area of your spine allows the most motion and where you are restricted. Then match the entire action of your back to the most restricted area so that you are using a smaller range of movement. Proceed with the action softly and slowly, allowing yourself to feel the shifts in weight on your hands and knees. Also notice the different state of consciousness that you invoke when you shift your awareness from muscles to bones. You've heard the expression, "I feel it in my bones," when speaking about deep knowing. In this manner, you are organizing information for more even, cooperative, and fluid interactions throughout the spine. After you have explored these sensations for a short time, begin to enlarge your motion in small increments and notice if you have changed something in your perception of how to use your spine. *Movement from the bones is a way to learn what you are doing.* Sensory receptors in the joints feed direct information to the brain, often telegraphing messages that bypass belief systems and old habits which are difficult to access because they are so much a part of you.

The "cat" movement is a good example, because it typifies a common thread that runs through many ATM lessons. Many lessons ask for motion through the torso while maintaining relative stability in the limbs. This reverses the usual pattern of movement of the limbs while the torso is stabilized. The reversal of the information coming to the brain is out of the ordinary. The *novelty* provides more intense awareness, because it is different. It is novelty that provides the power for change.

An ATM class combines thinking and doing. A lesson can be done on one side of the body and imagined on the other side. Sometimes the imagined movement provides a greater degree of efficiency and change than that which occured on the side that was actually moved. This goes back to the idea of reducing the effort. It also indicates the power of awareness in the learning process. It shows that it is our perception of what we are doing that affects us more than our doing without noticing. By imagining what it would feel like to do a movement, we have an opportunity to "pretend" it with greater skill. This brings new possibilities into the connections between mind and movement. Another way to provide yourself with new choices is to have the freedom to make mistakes. An ATM class provides a safe environment to try things out, so that you can make choices based on your own experience rather than on someone else's opinion about what is "right." A Feldenkrais lesson can incorporate some options of motion that are less efficient so that students can feel them for comparison. Often these less-efficient options are drawn from what people are already doing in the class. *Through bringing an unconscious act to conscious awareness, choice becomes available.*

To do your best and to try hard are not the same thing. If you try very hard to do something, there is an inherent assumption that you are not good enough to accomplish it. Therefore, when learning something new, it is more efficient to do things in small increments, to introduce *ease* and *curiosity* rather than strain and self-recrimination. The unnecessary effort that occurs when you try hard causes extraneous motion and muscle tension that actually get in the way of learning. It is also important to point out that learning and doing are not the same thing. For example, when you are in performance, all the learning for that moment is already in place and your attention is on the performance, not the learning process that went before. The Feldenkrais Method is an *internal laboratory* for learning how to learn; it is foundation work.

There is another way to explore the Feldenkrais Method other than the class work. This is hands-on work and is called Functional Integration. All the principles are the same; the major differences are that you work one-to-one with the practitioner, you have the opportunity to experience passive movement, your needs are individually addressed, and the quality of touch is exquisite and healing.

THE VALUE TO DANCERS

The following is a summary of some reasons why dancers would benefit from including the Feldenkrais Method in their courses of study.

First, the Feldenkrais Method addresses fine-tuning of the kinesthetic sense. Improvement of alignment is best achieved through the kinesthetic sense rather than through visual assessment and mechanical forcing of corrections such as "shoulders back and stomach in." Paradoxically, dancers are often more visually acute than kinesthetically aware. This might be because enormous emphasis is placed on how a movement is expected to look. Mirrors in studios facilitate dependency on visual cues, sometimes to the point of ignoring kinesthetic cues.

Second, the professional dancer is entering a highly competitive field; therefore, there often is a high need for success. Even in technique class, where learning "how to" is appropriate, there is a drive to do it well. According to Dr. Feldenkrais, *"doing it well" inhibits the somatic experience* because it is difficult to have one's attention on achievement and simultaneously feel what one is doing. In a Feldenkrais class there is no pressure to do well; participants have the opportunity to feel what is being done and learn about optimum efficiency.

Third, beyond self-discovery, the Feldenkrais Method can be used as a very effective ingredient in a dancer's warm-up. Just as a musician would not think of playing without tuning his or her instrument, a dancer can "tune" his or her central nervous system by bringing a balanced tone to the body before class or performance.

Fourth, by sensing the connection of the limbs to the torso and by right use of power, the dancer can effectively prevent injury. *When one can more clearly feel what is being done, one increases the potential for accuracy in motion.* The Feldenkrais Method helps you to learn the right use of power by eliminating the excessive use of force and the unnecessary parasitic motions that interfere with the intended movement. Accidents often occur when attention is split, and the Feldenkrais Method helps to train attention. However, if an injury is sustained, it is valuable to know that a Certified Feldenkrais practitioner can often help in the recuperation process.

Fifth, for the professional dancer, performance and touring place high demands on the dancer's entire system. I remember Carol Warner, whose picture appeared on the dust cover of the first edition of this book, saying to me that the Feldenkrais Method was an invaluable tool in putting the pieces back together again when she was on tour. It is a way to take care of yourself and can be done alone in a small space if necessary.

Finally, while the Feldenkrais Method is not specifically a relaxation technique, one of its effects is to *facilitate relaxation*. A report I commonly hear after a class is that students feel simultaneously relaxed and alert. This is a wonderful feeling!

CONCLUSION

In summary, the Feldenkrais Method is a process of learning through the kinesthetic sense; it provides an environment where mistakes are accepted and questions are encouraged. The questions are asked primarily of oneself: "Do I need to do what I am doing in just this way?" "Is there another way?" "Which do I prefer?" "Which is most efficient?" In a culture where answers are more valued than questions, valuing the questions themselves is a novel idea. In the Feldenkrais Method, learning takes place via explorations of skeletal relationships. The idea is to notice what is being done and ask for different solutions to movement puzzles by making new choices. In doing the Feldenkrais Method, the student's curiosity is fostered, playful exploration is nurtured, and self-discovery is the key. This method is extremely effective for achieving proper alignment, for preventing injuries, for recuperation from fatigue, and for relaxation, but the heart of the method is that it links mind and body by making actions more harmonious and congruent with intentions.

REFERENCES

FELDENKRAIS, MOSHE. (1949). *Body and Mature Behavior: A Study of Anxiety, Sex, Gravitation, and Learning.* International Universities Press, Inc., New York.

FELDENKRAIS, MOSHE. (1972). *Awareness Through Movement.* Harper and Row, New York.

FELDENKRAIS, MOSHE. (1977). *The Case of Nora.* Harper and Row. New York.

FELDENKRAIS, MOSHE. (1980). *Class Quotations.* Feldenkrais Professional Training Program, Amherst, MA.

FELDENKRAIS, MOSHE. (1981). *The Illusive Obvious*. Meta Publications, Cupertino, CA.

FELDENKRAIS, MOSHE. (1984). *The Master Moves*. Meta Publications, Cupertino, CA.

FELDENKRAIS, MOSHE. (1985). *The Potent Self*. Harper and Row, New York.

Hanna, Thomas. (1984–85). "Moshe Feldenkrais: The Silent Heritage." *Somatics*. Vol. I, 1, pp. 22–30.

LAKE, BERNARD. (1983). "Functional Integration: A Literal Position Statement." *Somatics*, IV, 2, Spring/Summer, pp. 12–14.

PFEFFER, MYRIAM. (1994). "Souvenirs." *International Feldenkrais Journal*, 2, pp. 23–27.

OTHER RESOURCES

The Feldenkrais Guild®
PO Box 489
Albany, Oregon 97321-0143
1(800) 775-2118

Feldenkrais Resources
PO Box 2067
Berkeley, California 94720
1(800) 765-1907

Please indicate that you received this resource information from Carol Lessinger.

Carol Lessinger
Certified Feldenkrais Practitioner®
893 South McClelland
Salt Lake City, Utah 84102
(801) 363-1747

The Alexander Technique for Dancers
Jacque Lynn Bell

> He who knows that power is inborn . . . and so perceiving, throws
> himself unhesitatingly on his thought, instantly rights himself, stands
> in an erect position, commands his limbs, works miracles.
> —Emerson, *Self Reliance*. (1940c, 1968, p. 153)

As Descartes divorced mind from body, the Alexander Technique strives to reunite the two. Has there been success for dancers in marrying body to mind? F. M. Alexander might say flirtation . . . an affair perhaps . . . but certainly not a marriage.

The Alexander Technique confirms that the body has its own innate wisdom. It doesn't teach the learner anything new; the technique is an unlearning of that which is inefficiently habitual rather than natural. It teaches the student to get out of his or her own way so that the body's wisdom can manifest itself without interference. It is a means of letting go of old patterns and fixed opinions which are not useful in the present. Alexander's discoveries had a significant impact on some of the greatest minds of his time. The American educational philosopher John Dewey said, "Mr. Alexander created what may be truly called a physiology of the *living* organism" (Dewey, in Alexander, 1932, p. xiv). The scientist Nikolaas Tinbergen, in his acceptance speech for the Nobel Prize, asserted, "The Alexander Technique is based on exceptionally sophisticated observation, not only by means of vision, but to a surprising extent by using the sense of touch. Many types of underperformance and even ailments, both mental and physical, can be alleviated . . . by teaching the body musculature to function differently" (Tinbergen, 1974). Aldous Huxley, another advocate of the Alexander Technique, explained that, "together with improved physical and mental health I have found that the Alexander Technique has brought about a general heightening of consciousness on all levels" (Huxley, 1937, p. 259).

F. Matthias Alexander was born in Australia in 1869. He developed his technique in the last decade of the nineteenth century and taught it in England and in the United States until his death in 1955. Alexander, a stage actor, often lost his voice while performing. Having followed medical advice unsuccessfully, he solved his problem by carefully analyzing how he spoke on stage. In nine years of detailed self-observation, he discovered a reflex pattern which is universal in human beings. He noticed that when speaking or initiating movement he would tighten his neck muscles, pulling his head back and down, thereby compressing his spine. Eventually he found a means of bringing this reflex pattern to the conscious level and thus gained the possibility of choosing *not* to do it.

The Alexander Technique begins with thought. It enables one to use thought to make choices and create change in the body and the way it is used. F. M. Alexander developed a system of psychophysical education which enables a person first to become aware of how he or she misuses the body and then to learn an improved use of the body. Inhibition, a basic function of the nervous system, is understood in neurology as the elimination of unwanted activity. It naturally occurs at the unconscious or reflex level and helps to coordinate movement. Alexander discovered that by *inhibiting* the muscle tightening that leads to compression of the spine, the body is able to work more efficiently and with greater mechanical advantage. Bringing this important function of inhibition to the conscious level is what makes Alexander's work unique.

The importance of the head, leading the spine into length, as the organizer of all our movements was discovered by Alexander in his work on himself and with his students, and at the same time it was discovered by G. E. Coghill, a biologist researching animal organisms (1929). Its application is universal throughout the animal kingdom. Observe your own pet or animals at the zoo. Notice how the head leads the action, exerting a lengthening influence on the entire spine. Young children retain this ability. Even in the act of sitting, their heads are poised delicately atop their lengthening spines. Why do we lose effortless verticality? Why do dancers pull themselves up by muscular effort when a child does not have to? Alexander discovered that even dancers, if they release the muscular holding that is interfering with the body's natural organization, will go up effortlessly. It is their birthright.

When a dancer inhibits the tightening of the muscles at the back of the neck, the occiput is free to move upward, allowing the spine to follow. All of the body's joints then have more space and freedom. Following these principles, the dancer finds greater flexibility and an increased ability to use the body more fully. When the neck, head, and back are organized, postural reflexes and facilitating forces in the body are able to operate with greater biomechanical ease and efficiency. A balancing of the musculature occurs, and the body works synergistically instead of overusing particular muscles and joints. As a consequence, the dancer has greater power, strength, and freedom . . . not to mention freedom from injury.

The technique is not merely about changing the use of the musculature; it is a system of psychophysical reeducation in which the change occurs at a neuromuscular level. When this happens, lasting changes are the result. As people eliminate poor habits and begin to feel better in their bodies, their self-esteem increases, and, as a consequence, so does their level of performance.

Another benefit of the Alexander Technique is that it gives the dancer the ability to be more present with each moment. The dancer who is using Alexander principles is more riveting as a performer because his or her dancing is informed by consciousness, not habit. Alexander referred to this presence in the moment as "attending to the means whereby" rather than "end gaining." *Attending to the means whereby* means that the primary aim is to maintain good use, and it is secondary what end we bring about with this good use. Performing artists have found that when their attention is on the Alexander principles of good use, rather than on their dancing, acting, or playing, their artistic expression and technical ability increase (Caplan, 1987). Through my own exploration, teaching, and observation, I have found that dancers who apply the Alexander principles achieve the rare quality of being able to allow movement to unfold magically in the moment rather than proceeding with an intention programmed ahead of time. There is an undeniable freshness and beauty in this spontaneity.

Because the Alexander Technique is based on the premise of "letting go of knowing and embracing finding out," it gives the dancer valuable tools for performance, teaching, and choreography. The whole process of learning the technique is one of releasing what is familiar. This in itself leads to unknown territories and tremendous possibilities for creativity. Uncluttered by preformed expectations and habits, a student of the technique is taught to see exactly what is there. He or she then can *observe the doing*, not the presumptions and assumptions about the doing. The first step toward real change is simply looking at and accepting what *is*.

Study of the Alexander Technique eludes precise description because it involves a new experience . . . the experience of freeing oneself from the domination of fixed habits. The attempt to put this experience into words is necessarily limited, like trying to explain dancing to someone who has never danced. The only real way to understand the technique is by *guided practice with a trained instructor.*

The Alexander Technique is usually taught in private, in lessons lasting a half-hour to one hour. It is not a series of exercises or treatments. It is a *way of doing things,* rather than something new to do. With a teacher's gentle hands-on guidance, the student's kinesthetic sense is reeducated and the internal feedback system becomes more accurate. The student begins to understand, kinesthetically, how to stop interfering with the innate coordination of the body. Dancers can then dance with greater self-confidence and presence of mind. This newly gained practical skill helps them identify the destructive patterns of behavior that interfere with how they move. These destructive patterns can be consciously released, allowing for a greater utilization of the body's natural intelligence.

The Alexander Technique has been taught in a wide variety of academic settings. It is currently part of the dance curriculum at Ohio State University, the Juilliard School in New York City, and the London Academy of Music and Dramatic Art. It has been taught at the American Dance Festival as well as at dozens of other performing centers and institutions around the world.

As dancers are flirting with new ways of thinking and being in their bodies, they are overcoming the dualism that began with Descartes. Gaining the realization and tools to deal with the knowledge that the body and mind are indeed married, and have been all along, opens fresh and exciting possibilities for dance in the future.

REFERENCES

CAPLAN, D. (1987). *Back Trouble: A new approach to prevention and recovery based on the Alexander Technique.* Triad Publishing Company, Florida.

COGHILL, G.E. (1929). "Anatomy and the Problem of Behavior." London Lecture. Quoted in Alexander, F.M. (1941). *The Universal Constant in Living.* Centerline Press, Long Beach, CA., p. xxiv.

DEWEY, JOHN, in ALEXANDER, F.M. (1985). *The Use of the Self.* Centerline Press, Long Beach, CA., p. xiv.

EMERSON, RALPH WALDO. *Self Reliance.* (1940–1968). Random House, Inc., New York.

HUXLEY, ALDOUS. (1937). *Ends and Means,* 5th Ed. Harper, New York.

TINBERGEN, N. (1974). "Ethology and Stress Disease." *Science. 185:* 4175, p. 28.

SUGGESTED READINGS ON
THE ALEXANDER TECHNIQUE

If the following titles are not available at your local bookstore or library, many of them can be ordered from: Centerline Press, 2005 Palo Verde Avenue, Suite 325, Long Beach, CA 90815.

Alexander, F.M. (1985). *The Use of the Self.* Centerline Press, Long Beach, CA.

BARKER, S. (1978). *The Alexander Technique: The Revolutionary Way to Use Your Body for Total Energy.* Bantam Books, New York.

BARLOW, W. (1980). *The Alexander Technique.* Warner Books, New York.

CAPLAN, D. (1987). *Back Trouble: A New Approach to Prevention and Recovery Based on the Alexander Technique.* Triad Publishing, Florida.

GELB, M. (1987). *Body Learning: An Introduction to the Alexander Technique.* Henry Holt and Company, New York.

JONES, F.P. (1979). *Body Awareness in Action: A Study of the Alexander Technique.* Schocken Books, New York.

MAISEL, E. (Ed.) (1986). *The Resurrection of the Body: The Essential Writing of F.M. Alexander.* Shambhala, Boston.

STRANSKY, J., with STONE, R. (1981). *The Alexander Technique: Joy in the Life of Your Body.* Beaufort Books, New York.

Note: To find a certified instructor of the Alexander Technique in your area, call:

The American Center for the Alexander Technique at (212) 799-0468.

The Nature of Ideokinesis and Its Value for Dancers
Pamela Matt

As is emphasized repeatedly in this book and in other dance science literature, the dancer's posture or body alignment is central to the optimum performance of dance movement, both for aesthetic purposes and for the prevention of injury. However, it is often not readily understood that in order for alignment to be truly improved, the dancer must do more than engage in muscular holding patterns ("shoulders down," "stomach in," "neck long") which only momentarily make the body look more perfectly aligned. Rather, lasting improvements which center skeletal articulations and improve movement efficiency are more likely to occur when dancers undertake some form of kinesthetic reeducation. Ideokinesis is one such approach, which often improves the underlying neuromuscular habits from which posture is derived.

The notion of "neuromuscular habits" might best be understood by considering the development of the human infant. It is well known that reflex activity lays the foundation for the newborn's exploration of movement; voluntary control is learned through trial and error. Picture a baby with a toy just out of reach in his or her crib. The baby has a goal, the desire for the toy. With keen kinesthetic awareness, the baby explores various options (kicking, flailing, reaching, grasping) while improvising with aspects of timing, breath, initiation, and effort. When the best option is discovered (SUCCESS!!—baby makes toy jingle), it is repeated, facilitating a link between the goal and the most successful neuromuscular combination. With continued practice, the baby's movement becomes faster, smoother, and more efficient as a new neuromuscular habit for reaching for a toy is established. In the next play session, the new reaching strategy will be more readily available to the baby. There is no need to start from scratch—the baby will simply think of the goal, and the neuromuscular system will go into action to accomplish it.

Posture is a complex array of neuromuscular habits which maintain the relationships of the parts of the skeleton to each other and to a central mechanical axis. The neuromuscular habits which are persistently displayed as one's posture also have been formed in response to thinking about goals. It is extremely fortunate that the neuromuscular system develops habits in this manner. Imagine how difficult it would be to stand up from sitting if we had to consciously plan each muscular contraction involved in doing so. Instead, we simply think of the goal, and our well-rehearsed neuromuscular habits automatically and harmoniously go into action for us.

Fortunately, young children form postural habits largely without adult interference or instruction and emerge from their earliest movement explorations as inspiring examples of well-balanced posture. However, as they grow older, they continue to learn new neuromuscular habits. The kind of activities they engage in, the sort of furniture and clothing they use, and their daily stresses and emotions often subtly combine to negatively influence body alignment.

Another significant aspect of human development, the acquisition of language, seems to dull kinesthetic sensitivity. The experience of muscular ease around a joint which is transmitting weight through its mechanical center is a feeling the young child comes to know very well through experimentation with body balance. However, the language the child acquires from his or her family and the larger culture does not even attempt to describe experiences of this nature. Without the social reinforcement which language provides, the child's kinesthetic awareness begins to lose significance. Because the words he or she does learn about the body emphasize its appearance, the child becomes more aware of how the body looks from the outside than how it feels from the inside.

A preoccupation with how the body looks becomes one of the most influential factors in the continuing development of body alignment in adolescence and young adulthood. Images of rock stars and movie heroes made popular in print, film, and video become fashion mandates for impressionable youngsters who imitate the associated styles of clothing and hair. The body images of their idols are also very strongly internalized. Subtle nuances of gait and posture, which embody the attitudes teenagers admire, become goals that their neuromuscular systems endeavor to accomplish. The process of neuromuscular habituation is identical to that practiced in the early movement explorations of infancy. Unfortunately, the musculoskeletal adjustments which respond to these popular images, combined with the increasingly sedentary habits of emerging adulthood, often result in alignment which is tiring, inefficient, and ultimately injury-prone.

Fortunately, as we continue to grow toward greater maturity and personal responsibility, the flexible neuromuscular system can also be stimulated to form new, more mechanically efficient and aesthetically pleasing postural habits (or perhaps be reminded of old ones). This is the goal of Ideokinesis, an approach to kinesthetic reeducation which uses visualization of images as the corrective.

HISTORICAL BACKGROUND

The historical foundations of Ideokinesis can be traced back to 1906, when Mabel Elsworth Todd enrolled in the Emerson College of Oratory. In her study of voice there, Todd began to realize that problems with vocalization in singing and public speaking were often the result of poor habits of posture. Todd became convinced that a new concept of posture was needed, not only for orators but for the public at large. As she familiarized herself with the available research in the field, she learned to apply principles of mechanics to the analysis of posture, concluding that the condition of mechanical balance of the skeletal structure "implies freedom from strains, absence from stress, a readiness for action, a mobility—the opposite of fixity" (Todd, 1931, p. 244). Her insistence upon finding *balance*, rather than "imposing upon our bodies a fixed position of any part which we feel to be the 'right,' 'correct' or 'ideal' one" (Todd, 1931, p. 245), was unusual and separated her theory from other notions of posture generally accepted by physical educators of the day.

Along with her unique ideas about the attributes of good posture, Todd challenged the accepted notions of how to improve posture. Todd believed improvement could be made "by thinking continuously of a familiar motivating picture," (Todd, 1920–1934, p. 50) or visualizing images:

> Concentrating upon a picture involving movement results in such responses in the neuromusculature as are necessary to carry out specific movements with the least effort. In playing a part, the actor first forms a picture in his own mind of the character he is to depict and creates the impressions he wishes to give of that character largely through his bodily attitudes reacting automatically to the mental picture through the central reflexes. . . . In postural education we can take advantage of this fact. This psycho-physical process operates unerringly in forming better postural patterns in response to a concept of good anatomical adjustment based on clearly-defined mechanical principles. (pp. 49–50)

By the early 1920s Todd had established two private studios of "Natural Posture" in Boston and New York. As her reputation grew, she began teaching courses in universities and writing for medical and educational journals. Her books *The Thinking Body* (1937) and *The Hidden You* (1953) are classics of the field.

Dr. Lulu Sweigard, a student of Mabel Todd's, demonstrated in experimental studies that Todd's approach did produce measurable changes in body alignment in at least nine dimensions. Sweigard organized Todd's imagery and developed new ideas for visualization which specifically pertained to those nine dimensions of change. The nine lines of movement were listed as follows:

1. A line of movement to lengthen the spine downward.
2. A line of movement to shorten the distance between the mid-front of the pelvis and the twelfth thoracic vertebra.
3. A line of movement from the top of the sternum to the top of the spine.

4. A line of movement to narrow the rib-case.
5. A line of movement to widen across the back of the pelvis.
6. A line of movement to narrow across the front of the pelvis.
7. A line of movement from the center of the knee to the center of the femoral joint.
8. A line of movement from the big toe to the heel.
9. A line of movement to lengthen the central axis of the trunk upward (Sweigard, 1974, pp. 193–196).

Sweigard became particularly interested in the postural problems of dancers through her work at the Dance Division of the Julliard School, and the helpfulness of her teaching became well known among professional dancers in New York City. In 1974 she published *Human Movement Potential: Its Ideokinetic Facilitation.* In this anatomy and kinesiology text specifically designed for dancers, *ideokinesis* was suggested as an appropriate name for the approach. The specific movement education techniques Sweigard developed during her distinguished career are also presented and explained in this book.

Barbara Clark, another student of Mabel Todd's, was a pediatric nurse and nursery school teacher who initially related Todd's ideas and practices to motor development. Seeing the playful movement exploration of the child as nature's plan for building strong, well-aligned bodies, Clark utilized the visualization of simple images, along with the practice of developmental movement patterns such as rolling and crawling, to improve the body alignment of her young students and enhance their kinesthetic awareness. Later in her career, Clark also worked extensively with dancers and actors in New York and enlarged the literature of Ideokinetics immeasurably with the development of several manuals of image drawings and exercises. Her published and unpublished material is now available in a book entitled *A Kinesthetic Legacy: The Life and Works of Barbara Clark* (Matt, 1993).

THE IDEOKINETIC PROCESS

Although the literature of the founding teachers of Ideokinesis is relatively extensive, their methods have not been standardized. Indeed a codification of the approach for purposes of certification, or even posterity, seems antithetical to its nature as an evolving, creative endeavor. Although the educational process of Ideokinesis varies widely among teachers, perhaps a few common practices might be suggested and described.

Generally, teachers prepare students for experiences with the ideokinetic process by familiarizing them with the ideal mechanical balance of the human body. Most people have a very limited understanding of the design of the musculoskeletal system for balance and movement; this state of ignorance is, in itself, an impediment to the improvement of posture. In their early learning experiences, students come to appreciate the architecture of the skeleton as a framework for body support. They are encouraged to internalize this information by becoming aware of where key features of the skeleton actually exist in their own bodies. Knowledge of musculature is also developed in this preparation for ideokinetic learning. However, rather than focusing upon the identification of specific origins, insertions, and actions in kinesiological terms, students are encouraged to cultivate a general appreciation of muscular pathways as designs for action, stabilization, and release.

To provide further background for working ideokinetically, students also may learn about the typical manifestations of postural maladjustment. Discussion of the sorts of neuromuscular habits which are acquired in response to popular imagery, environmental and psychological stressors, time pressures, and notions of maleness and femaleness frequently proves to increase understanding of one's own posture and the factors which have influenced its development. Among dancers, the typical neuromuscular adjustments which take place in response to postural admonitions often repeated in dance classes should also be discussed. Hopefully, through these sorts of introductory activities, students learn that the musculoskeletal system is masterfully designed for balance and movement, that there are typical patterns of poor posture, and that no one perfect posture exists for all individuals.

In the course of building this conceptual framework, the imagination is often deliberately used as the avenue for learning. This paves the way for the concentrated use of visualization as a corrective means. The images used in ideokinetic practice describe aspects of musculoskeletal change toward a more ideal alignment, suggesting shifts of balance and subtle changes of coordination which will bring the body closer to the realization of mechanical efficiency. Simpler images describe specific locations for the flow of body weight and pathways of muscular release or initiation. More complex images describe imagined movements designed to "center" bony articulations or to encourage a more harmonious balance among various muscle groups. For instance, after an explanation of the importance of releasing tension from the erector spinae group for optimal balance of the pelvis, the following image might be suggested: imagine the sacral end of the spine sliding down through the open space between the two inominate bones in the back of the pelvis. The clarity of this image and its power as a picture for motivating change will be enhanced if the teaching targets the senses and appeals to a variety of learning styles. To increase their involvement with the image, students might be given the opportunity to manipulate bone models of the pelvis and spine to demonstrate the image as realistically as possible. Alternatively, simple drawings of the bones might be shown, with the direction of movement indicated by arrows. The triangular shape of the sacrum could be traced along the back of the student's pelvis to convey the actual location of the image. Then a downward direction could be given through touch in the sacral area to indicate the direction of the imagined movement. A casual, perhaps even playful, atmosphere should prevail in this period of exploration to encourage each student to internalize and embellish the imagery in his or her own way.

Individual visualization practice often begins in stillness, perhaps lying in the Constructive Rest Position (Todd, 1953; and later Sweigard, 1974) or in the standing, sitting, or crawling positions. The teacher or a partner might facilitate the experience by giving a tactile indication near the location of the imagined action, or the student might simply think of the image. The student is directed to think of each image intently and repeatedly but warned not to voluntarily direct the musculoskeletal system to respond in any foreseeable way. Rather, the student is encouraged to become sensitive to the kinesthetic responses which will develop spontaneously in response to the contemplation of the imagined action. If the student is patient and allows the body to respond naturally, sensations of muscular release and an enhanced awareness of the joints will begin to guide the inner exploration of improved balance. Concluding practice with journal writing or class discussion may be helpful in building confidence in this process, particularly as common experiences are shared.

Later, when students have developed some skill in the practice of contemplating imagery, movement might accompany visualization to provide another avenue for learning. For example:

> Sit in a chair that allows the knee ends of your thigh bones to be a little higher than the pelvic end of the bones. Your heels should rest on the floor. In your imagination, fit the sacral end of the spine down through the space in the back of the pelvis. Picture the image once again and raise your left thigh toward your head. Return to position.
>
> Again imagine the spine sliding downward through the open space in the back of the pelvis. Picture the image again as you raise your right thigh toward your head. Return to position. (Matt, 1993, p. 204)

or the image might be combined with breathing:

> Seeing the space the lower spine fills in the back of the pelvis also helps in breathing. Think down through the space as you easily exhale. Think up through the thigh sockets as you easily inhale. (Matt, 1993, p. 204)

As the students progress, learning new images and combining old images in new ways, each practice session becomes a new opportunity to traverse the fascinating kinesthetic landscape within. Often, the first felt discoveries are of the multiple ways in which muscular holding has been confused with bony support. Images which promote the release of tight, shortened musculature, combined with the awareness of new locations of muscular initiation, reveal the inefficiency of old patterns of muscular imbalance. As the exploration of imagery is continued, awareness of these poor habits is enlarged, tensions are discarded, and new possibilities for balancing are discovered. Gradually, joints relieved of the stresses caused by an inefficient balance of weights experience new freedom and ease. Greater endurance in maintaining upright positions becomes evident; there is a desire to move more vigorously through the improved neuromuscular patterns; breathing deepens and becomes better integrated with movement.

When students are highly motivated and willing to apply their new awareness not only in their lessons but throughout their daily lives, significant changes in body alignment do occur. Most noticeable might be an overall increase in height and decreased pelvic inclination (Sweigard,

1974, p. 191). Other, more subtle shifts of alignment also occur which bring "weight masses . . . closer to both the center and line of gravity" (Sweigard, 1974, p. 192). These changes in skeletal alignment, which bring the body into closer conformity with a state of mechanical balance, render the student less susceptible to overuse injuries caused by muscular imbalance and less encumbered by muscular tension. If the improved neuromuscular patterning is then practiced in vigorous exercise, the body becomes stronger and more efficient in the production of movement.

Although the benefits of Ideokinesis for dancers are undeniable, it is perhaps for the dancer that the process of kinesthetic discovery and re-learning may be the most difficult. Poor neuromuscular patterns developed through dance training are highly habituated. Often, elements of the dance aesthetic which have been poorly taught to dancers with significant anatomical limitations result in habits which break their bodies down. Even when dancers have become so riddled with injuries that dancing has become almost impossible, giving up familiar habits associated with the aesthetic mandates of the art form can be very difficult. For this reason, dancers studying Ideokinesis may be initially encouraged to work with their newly acquired kinesthetic awareness only in daily movement or in beginning-level dance classes. As the improved habits become better established, more advanced dance movement can be attempted. If the dance learning environment is supportive and encourages experimentation, great strides toward improved technique are possible. Informed by the ideokinetic process, dancers will assume greater responsibility for their dancing and come to know, "in their bones," the best path for their continuing development.

REFERENCES

MATT, PAMELA. (1993). *A Kinesthetic Legacy: The Life and Works of Barbara Clark.* CMT Press, Tempe, AZ..

SWEIGARD, LULU E. (1974). *Human Movement Potential: Its Ideokinetic Facilitation.* New York: Harper and Row.

TODD, MABEL ELSWORTH. (1920–1934). *Early Writings.* Dance Horizons, New York, 1977.

TODD, MABEL ELSWORTH. (1931). "Our strains and tensions." *Progressive Education, 8,* p. 244.

TODD, MABEL ELSWORTH. (1953). *The Hidden You.* Dance Horizons, New York.

TODD, MABEL ELSWORTH. (1972). *The Thinking Body.* Dance Horizons, New York.

ADDITIONAL SUGGESTED READINGS

BROWN, BEVERLY. (1979). "Training to dance with Eric Hawkins." In Lorber, Richard. (Ed.), *Eric Hawkins: Theory and Training.* American Dance Guild, Inc., New York.

DOWD, IRENE. (1981 and 1990.) *Taking Root to Fly.* Contact Editions. PO Box 603, Northampton, MA 01061.

ROLLAND, JOHN. (1984 and 1987.) *Inside Motion: An Ideokinetic Basis for Movement Education.* Contact Editions. PO Box 603. Northampton, MA 01061.

Introduction to Body-Mind Centering[3]
Bonnie Bainbridge Cohen

Body-Mind Centering™ (BMC) is an ongoing, experiential journey into the alive and changing territory of the body. The explorer is the mind—our thoughts, feelings, energy, soul and spirit. Through this journey we are led to an understanding of how the mind is expressed through the body in movement.

There is something in nature that forms patterns. We, as part of nature, also form patterns. The mind is like the wind, and the body like the sand: if you want to know how the wind is blowing, you can look at the sand.

Our body moves as our mind moves. The qualities of any movement are a manifestation of how mind is expressing through the body at that moment. Changes in movement qualities indicate that the mind has shifted focus in the body. Conversely, when we direct the mind or attention to different areas of the body and initiate movement from those areas, we change the quality of our movement. So we find that movement can be a way to observe the expression of mind through the body, and it can also be a way to affect changes in the body-mind relationship.

In BMC, "centering" is a process of balancing, not a place of arrival. This balancing is based on dialogue, and the dialogue is based on experience.

An important aspect of our journey in Body-Mind Centering is discovering the relationship between the smallest level of activity within the body and the largest movement of the body—aligning the inner cellular movement with the external expression of movement through space. This involves identifying, articulating, differentiating, and integrating the various tissues within the body, discovering the qualities they contribute to one's movement, how they have evolved in one's developmental process, and the role they play in the expression of mind.

The finer this alignment, the more efficiently we can function to accomplish our intentions. However, alignment itself is not a goal. It is a continual dialogue between awareness and action—becoming aware of the relationships that exist throughout our body/mind and acting from that awareness. This alignment creates a state of knowing. There are many ways of working toward this alignment such as through touch, through movement, visualization, somatization,[4] voice, art, music, meditation, through verbal dialogue, through open awareness, or by any other means.

---

3. This material is reprinted from *Sensing Feeling and Action* by Bonnie Bainbridge Cohen, published by Contact Editions, P.O. Box 603, Northampton, MA 01061, (413) 586-1181, and used with permission. ©1993 Bonnie Bainbridge Cohen. All rights reserved. For information about additional material by Bonnie Bainbridge Cohen, contact The School for Body-Mind Centering, 189 Pondview Drive, Amherst, MA 01002, (413) 256-8615.

4. I use this word *somatization* to engage the kinesthetic experience directly, in contrast to *visualization*, which utilizes visual imagery to evoke a kinesthetic experience. Through somatization the body cells are informing the brain as well as

After many years of pursuing this path of inquiry with students, clients, and colleagues, I founded The School for Body-Mind Centering in 1973 as a means to formalize and articulate the ongoing research, and as a vehicle for the continued exchange of information and discovery. At the school, techniques, applications and principles are discovered and used in many ways. Some people practice the techniques, and then out of their own experience the principles emerge. Others focus on the principles, and as they apply the principles in their lives, they develop the techniques. But the techniques and principles themselves are not the material—it is more the awareness and understanding of *how* and *when* to use them, or how to invent one's own. The important thing is for each person to learn how it is that they learn, to trust their own intuition, and to be open to the unique styles of others.

In BMC we are the material, our bodies and minds the medium of exploration. The research is experiential, as is the material. We are each the study, the student, the teacher. Out of this research, we are developing an empirical science—observing, contrasting, corroborating, and recording our experiences of embodying all of the body systems and the stages of human development.

For this science to have emerged, it has been essential to have many people involved in the exploration. Over the past twenty years, several thousand people have participated in the study and development of BMC, some briefly and a few for twenty years. The large number of people who have studied at the school have given the work its breadth. The approximately thirty people who have consistently collaborated with me over the past ten to twenty years have been essential in giving the work its depth. Their contribution to this body of work cannot be overemphasized. Together we have filtered through our differences toward a common experience which embraces all of our differences. The BMC principles are drawn from this collective experience. The universal has emerged out of the specific just as the specific has emerged out of the universal. This is part of the nature of the work. As we go from cellular experience to that of the body systems, to personal relationship, to family, to society, and eventually to culture and world community, we are always looking at how these principles travel along a continuum.

In BMC we use the maps of western medicine and science—anatomy, physiology, kinesiology, etc.—but Body-Mind Centering is being influenced by the philosophies of the east as well. It is a study coming out of

the brain informing the cells. I derived *somatization* from Thomas Hanna's use of *soma* to designate the experienced body in contrast to the objectified body. When the body is experienced from within, the body and mind are not separated but are experienced as a whole. While Tom spoke of this during the 1960s, his first book utilizing the term *soma* was *Bodies in Revolt*, which came out in 1970. Tom coined the term *somatics* in 1976 when he founded and named *The Somatics Magazine-Journal of the Bodily Arts and Sciences*. *Somatics* also names a field of study—the study of the body through the personal experiential perspective. Body-Mind Centering is a small part of this burgeoning field.

this time of east and west merging, so we are working with the concept of dualities blending, rather than sets of opposites conflicting. We are constantly looking at relationships and are always recognizing how opposite qualities modulate each other.

Though we use the western anatomical terminology and mapping, we are adding meaning to these terms through our experience. When we are talking about blood or lymph or any physical substances, we are not only talking about substances but about states of consciousness and processes inherent within them. We are relating our experiences to these maps, but the maps are not the experience.

The study of BMC includes both the cognitive and experiential learning of the body systems—skeleton, ligaments, muscles, fascia, fat, skin organs, endocrine glands, nerves, fluids; breathing and vocalization; the senses and the dynamics of perception; developmental movement (both human infant development and the evolutionary progression through the animal kingdom); and the art of touch and repatterning.

As a set of principles and an approach to movement and learning, BMC is currently being applied by people involved in many areas of interest, such as dance; athletics; bodywork; physical, occupational, movement and speech therapies; psychotherapy; medicine; child development; yoga; martial arts; and other body-mind disciplines.

While the basic material of Body-Mind Centering was well established by 1982, the principles continue to be elaborated on and refined, and changes made as new viewpoints arise.

As in any journey, what we perceive is influenced by what we have already experienced and therefore anticipate. Consequently, the BMC concepts are outgrowths of the personal histories, education, and experiences of the large number of individuals who have engaged in this exploration. As we analyze our experiences, the challenge is to continually allow our discoveries to pass into our unconscious and to approach each moment with trust and innocence.

The following are brief descriptions of tissue territories we have thus far mapped in 20 years of study at The School for Body-Mind Centering.

THE BODY SYSTEMS

Skeletal system: This system provides us with our basic supporting structure. It is composed of the bones and the joints. The bones lever us through space and support our weight in relationship to gravity. The shape of the joints defines the shape of our movements through space. The spaces within the joints give us the possibility of movement and provide the axes around which the movement occurs.

The skeletal system gives our body the basic form through which we can locomote through space, sculpt and create the energy forms in space that we call movement, and act on the environment, relating with the other forms around us.

Through embodying the skeletal system, the mind becomes structurally organized, providing the supporting ground for our thoughts, the leverage for our ideas, and the fulcrums of spaces between our ideas for the articulation and understanding of their relationships.

Ligamentous system: The ligaments set the boundaries of movement between the bones by holding the bones together, they guide muscular responses by directing the path of movement between the bones, and they suspend the organs within the thoracic and abdominal cavities.

This system provides specificity, clarity, and efficiency for the alignment and movement of the bones and organs. It is through the mind of the ligaments that we perceive and articulate clarity of focus and concentration to detail.

Muscular system: The muscles establish a tensile three-dimensional grid for the balanced support and movement of the skeletal structure by providing the elastic forces that move the bones through space. They provide the dynamic contents of the outer envelope of flesh encompassing the skeletal structure.

Through this system we embody our vitality, express our power, and engage in the dialogue of resistance and resolution.

Organ system: The organs carry on the functions of our internal survival—breathing, nourishment and elimination. They are the contents within the skeletal-flesh container.

They provide us with our sense of volume, full-bodiedness, and organic authenticity. Organs are the primary habitats or natural environments of our emotions, aspirations, and the memories of our inner reactions to our personal histories.

Endocrine system: The endocrine glands are the major chemical governing system of the body and are closely aligned to the nervous system. Their secretions pass directly into the bloodstream and their balance or imbalance influences all of the cells in the body.

This is the system of internal stillness, surges or explosions or chaos/balance and the crystallization of energy into archetypal experiences. The endocrine glands underlie intuition and the perceiving and understanding of universal mind.

Nervous system: The nervous system is the major electrical governing system of the body and is closely aligned with the endocrine system. It receives information and gives information to all the cells in the body. It coordinates this information in specific control or relay centers throughout the body, the spinal cord, and the brain.

The nervous system underlies alertness and thought, and gives precision to our coordination. This system establishes the perceptual base from which we view and interact with our internal and external worlds.

Fluid system: The fluids are the transportation system of the body. The major fluids are cellular, interstitial (intercellular), blood, lymph, synovial (joint fluid), and cerebrospinal.

Fluids are the system of liquidity of movement and mind. They underlie presence and transformation, and mediate the dynamics of flow between rest and activity.

Fascial system: Fascial connective tissue establishes a soft container for all the other structures of the body. It both divides and integrates all other tissues and provides them with semi-viscous lubricating surfaces so that they have independence of movement within established boundaries of the body as a whole.

It is through the fascia that the movement of our organs provides internal support for the movement of our skeleton through space, and the movement of our skeleton expresses in the outer world the inner movement of our organs. Through the fascial system we connect our inner feelings with our outer expression.

Fat: Fat is potential energy stored in the body. It provides heat insulation for the body and electrical insulation for the nerves. Fat synthesis, breakdown, storage, and mobilization are greatly controlled by the endocrine system.

Static fat is stored as repressed or unacknowledged potential power and creates a sense of heaviness and lethargy. Fat that is utilized expresses strong primordial power and a sense of peaceful fluidity. Fat that is embraced offers nurturing comfort.

Skin: Skin is our outermost layer, covering our body in its entirety and defining us as individuals by separating us from that which is not us.

Through our skin, we touch and are touched by the outer world. This outer boundary is our first line of defense and bonding. It sets our general tone of openness and closedness to being in the world—through our skin we are both invaded and protected, and we receive and make contact with others.

While each system makes its own separate contribution to the movement of body-mind, they are all interdependent, together providing a complete framework of support and expression. Certain systems are perceived as having natural affinities with others. However, those affinities vary among individuals, among groups, and among cultures. We discover their voices by consciously and unconsciously exploring them in different combinations.

DEVELOPMENTAL MOVEMENT

Underlying the forms of our expression through the body systems is the process of our movement development, both ontogenetic (human infant development) and phylogenetic (the evolutionary progression through the animal kingdom).

Development is not a linear process but occurs in overlapping waves, with each stage containing elements of all the others. Because each previous stage underlies and supports each successive stage, any skipping, interrupting, or failing to complete a stage of development can lead to alignment/movement problems, imbalances within the body systems, and problems in perception, sequencing, organization, memory, and creativity.

The developmental material includes primitive reflexes, righting reactions, equilibrium responses, and the Basic Neurological Patterns.[5] These

5. The Basic Neurological Patterns are sixteen primary movement patterns developed by Bonnie Bainbridge Cohen, based upon phylogenetic (animal) and ontogenetic (human) movement development.

are the automatic movement responses that underlie our volitional movement.

The reflexes, righting reactions and equilibrium responses are the fundamental elements, or the alphabet, of our movement. They combine to build the Basic Neurological Patterns, which are based upon pre-vertebrate and vertebrate movement patterns. The first of the four prevertebrate patterns is *cellular breathing* (the expanding/contracting process in breathing and movement in each and every cell of the body) which correlates to the movement of the one-celled animals. Cellular breathing underlies all other patterns of movement and postural tone.

Navel radiation (the relating the movement of all parts of the body via the navel), mouthing (movement of the body initiated by the mouth), and *pre-spinal movement* (soft sequential movements of the spine initiated via the interface between the spinal cord and the digestive tract) are the other three prevertebrate patterns.

The twelve vertebrate patterns are based upon: *spinal movement* (head-to-tail movement), which correlates to the movement of fish; *homologous movement* (symmetrical movement of two upper and/or two lower limbs simultaneously), which correlates to the movement of reptiles; and *contralateral movement* (diagonal) movement of one upper limb with the opposite lower limb), which correlates to the movement of mammals.

Development of the Basic Neurological Patterns establishes our basic movement patterns and corresponding perceptual relationships—including spatial orientation and body image—and the basic elements of learning and communication. In *spinal* movements, for example, we develop rolling, establish the horizontal plane, differentiate the front of our bodies from the back of our bodies, and gain the ability to attend.

In *homologous* movements we develop symmetrical movements such as push-ups and jumping with both feet, establish the sagittal plane, differentiate the upper part of our bodies from the lower part of our bodies, and gain the ability to act.

In *homolateral* movements we develop asymmetrical movements such as crawling on our bellies and hopping on one leg, establish the vertical plane, differentiate the right side of our bodies from the left, and gain the ability to intend.

In *contralateral* movements we develop diagonal movements such as creeping on our hands and forelegs, walking, running, and leaping; establish three-dimensional movement; differentiate the diagonal quadrants of our bodies; and gain the ability to integrate our attention, intention, and action.

The developmental movement-perceptual progression establishes a process-oriented framework for the dialogue of the body systems.

Aligning inner cellular awareness and movement with outer awareness and movement through space within the context of the developmental process can facilitate the evolution of our consciousness and alleviate body-mind problems at their root level. As we are more able to experience our consciousness at the cellular and the tissue level, we are better able to understand ourselves. As we increase our knowledge of ourselves, we increase in understanding and compassion for others. As we experience the uniqueness of cells within the context of tissue harmony, we learn about individuality within the context of community. As we gain awareness of our diverse tissues and the nature of their expression in the outer world, we expand our understanding of other cultures within the context of the earth as a whole and the awareness of our planet within the expanded consciousness of the universe.

THE DYNAMIC OF PERCEPTION

It is through our senses that we receive information from our internal environment (ourselves) and the external environment (others and the world). How we filter, modify, distort, accept, reject, and use that information is part of the act of perceiving.

When we choose to absorb information, we *bond* to that aspect of our environment. When we block out information, we *defend* against that aspect. *Learning* is the process by which we vary our responses to information based on the context of each situation.

In order to perceive clearly, our attention, concentration, motivation or desire must actively focus us on what it is we are to perceive. This aspect of perceiving we have named *active focusing*. It patterns our interpretation of sensory information, and without this active focusing our perception remains poorly organized.

Touch and movement are the first of the senses to develop. They establish the baseline for future perception through taste, smell, hearing, and vision. The mouth is the first extremity to grasp, release, measure, reach, and withdraw. It sets the foundation for the movement of the other extremities (hands, feet, and tail) and develops in close association with the nose. Movement of the head initiated from the mouth and nose underlies movement of the head initiated from the ears and eyes. Auditory tone, body postural tone, vibration, and movement are registered in the inner ear and are intimately related. Vision is dependent upon all the previous senses and, in turn helps to integrate them into more complex patterns.

Perception can be explored in terms of the interrelationship of the different senses and its relationship to the developmental process. Through exploring the perceptual process, we can expand our choices, in responding to ourselves, others, and the world in which we live.

BREATHING AND VOCALIZATION

Our ability to embody the structural and physiological processes underlying breathing and vocal production gives us another important way to establish our relationship to ourselves and to our environment.

Breathing is automatic. It is influenced by internal physiological and psychological states and by external environmental factors. The way we breathe also influences our behavior and physical functioning.

Breathing is internal movement. It underlies movement of the body through external space. Movement, in turn, alters our breathing process.

Breathing is organized in patterns. These patterns are influenced by emotional stimuli. They also evoke emotional responses. Our first breath, at birth, influences the pattern of our adult breathing.

Breathing can be consciously known. As the breathing process is sensed and felt, unconscious blocks can be released.

It is through the expressive qualities of our voice that we communicate to the outer world who we are. Our voice reflects the functioning of all of our bodily systems and the process of our developmental integration. Bringing kinesthetic and auditory consciousness to our vocal structures opens pathways of expression between our unconscious and our conscious mind and between ourselves and others.

THE ART OF TOUCH AND REPATTERNING

When we touch someone, they touch us equally. The subtle interplay between body and mind can be experienced clearly through touching others. The art of touch and repatterning is an exploration of communication through touch—the transmission and acceptance of flow of energy within ourselves and between ourselves and others.

In hands-on work, through touching in different rhythms, through placement of attention within specific layers of the body, through following existing lines of force and suggesting new ones, and through changes in the pressure and quality of our touch, we come into harmony with the different tissues and their associated qualities of mind. We begin with cellular presence (cellular breathing) and focus on the resonation and dialogue between client and practitioner. Each tissue of the client is explored from the corresponding tissues of the practitioner, i.e., bone from bone, organ from organ, fluid from fluid, etc. The initiation of intent, based upon what each person is perceiving, may be shared consciously and/or unconsciously by both people.

Acceptance and curiosity guide the inquiry. Through mutual resonance between client and practitioner, attention is given to discovering the primary tissues through which the clients express themselves and those tissues which are usually in shadow, so that the supporting tissues can be given voice and the articulating ones can be allowed to recuperate. This shifting of energy expression allows for more choices and expanded consciousness of body-mind for both the client/student and the practitioner/teacher.

POSTSCRIPT

My description of Body-Mind Centering would be incomplete without acknowledging my continual gratitude to all BMC teachers and students who have offered not only their experiences to the work but their thinking, articulation, and interpretations of those experiences. Beyond this, they have also given freely of their love and friendship through these many years.

And always by my side has been my husband Len. BMC could not have developed without his continual presence, penetrating questioning, steady guidance, and profound caring for me and all the people who have come to share in this ongoing journey.

Note: For further information on Body-Mind Centering™, contact Bonnie Bainbridge Cohen at:

The School for Body-Mind Centering
189 Pondview Drive
Amherst, MA 01002
(413) 256-8615

Making Connections Through Bartenieff Fundamentals^{sm}
Peggy Hackney

INTRODUCTION

As dancers we want to be able to communicate with our bodies effectively, speaking the core truths we experience as artists clearly so that our message reaches out to others. In other words, we want to *connect* across the footlights. In order to do this, we need to find means to connect inwardly both to what we want to say and to how all parts of the body relate to each other to support our artistic purpose. This ability to create relationships is a skill which begins "at home," within our own bodies.

So often in our training process in dance or sports we fragment work into isolated body segments. We do not acknowledge that artistry involves embodying the whole of who we are as sensing, feeling, thinking, spirited human beings. We assume that the integration will happen in the performance moment. I have come to believe that the *recognition of integration and wholeness needs to be present in movement training from the beginning.* I came to this realization through my thirty years of work with Laban Movement Analysis and Bartenieff Fundamentals. My major mentor in this area for nearly fifteen years was Irmgard Bartenieff.

IRMGARD BARTENIEFF

Irmgard Bartenieff (1900–1981) generated a new vision of possibilities for connectivity in human movement and movement training. This vision was forged from her various "lives" as a dancer, choreographer, student of Rudolf von Laban, physical therapist, research pioneer in cross-cultural dance style analysis, and prime mover in the field of Dance Therapy. Irmgard developed her major work in body training out of her experiences with Laban and her work as a physical therapist. This work eventually became known as *Bartenieff Fundamentals.*^{sm} She worked with many different types of patients, including dancers, and became fascinated with what she noticed was a major lack in most of them: they lacked the ability to *support from the internal core* of the body in order to *connect the lower body and the upper body for fluid muscular sequencing, weight shift, and full three-dimensional movement.* She felt that physical therapists in her time were mechanically oriented toward two-phasic repetitive movement (such as flexion and extension without movement on the other planes) for isolated muscle strengthening. She felt that they were not adequately using the connective possibilities of three-dimensional movement (particularly the rotary component), nor were they acknowledging the inner expressive life of the patient in the rehabilitation process. She felt that dance training was also overly mechanistic, with too much repetition of exercises approached from an external orientation toward "making shapes" and not enough understanding of the internal connective patterns (both physical and psychological) which initiate and give birth to those shapes.

Irmgard was well aware of what was known in her era about the neurophysiological aspects of development and movement control through the pyramidal and the extrapyramidal systems. (The pyramidal system includes basic reflexes, righting reactions and equilibrium responses which initiate action patterns; and the extra pyramidal is associated more with the qualitative aspects of action.) The specific experiences she used in the Fundamentals classroom to accomplish pure hip joint flexion or weight shift from the lowest connections of the legs into the pelvis, for example, were clearly based in this understanding. She was interested in the fluidity of movement which is so crucial to dancers and began to explore muscle sequencing in kinetic chains, particularly along diagonal pathways in the body. In this process she also utilized Laban's concepts of dynamism, which he called Effort; and his work with harmonic sequences in space, which teach clarity of Spatial Intent. In all her work she encouraged the student/patient to find a way to bring new discoveries to completion in phrases of movement that were personally motivated. It became clear that individual phrasing aided function as well as expression. As she worked, she realized that she was able to touch something that was very basic, very fundamental, to movement. She was helping people find *patterns of connection* in their bodies. Those connections were both developmentally and kinesiologically based, and were supported by an inner expressive life.

WHAT IS FUNDAMENTAL?

Irmgard encouraged me to continually ask, *"What is Fundamental?"* What underlies the ability to be both functional and expressive? The answer I came to after many years is this: *Patterning body connections is Fundamental.* I was helped along in this recognition also by the clarifying work of Bonnie Bainbridge Cohen, who was a student of Irmgard and me in the Laban Movement Analysis Certification Program. She has gone on to illuminate the underlying developmental process in rich detail in her Body-Mind Centering work. Recent work in Fundamentals has incorporated much of what Bonnie has elucidated in terms of recognizing the larger framework of sensory-motor development, both in relation to human development and in relation to other animal species in our world.

PATTERNS OF TOTAL BODY CONNECTIVITY

Below is a short list of patterns I work with in the Fundamentals class-room, which are based on the basic neurological patterns Bonnie has de-lineated, along with a brief sampling of what each pattern brings in terms of essential skills and knowledge. The names I use for the patterns are cho-sen because they reflect the historic vocabulary of Bartenieff Fundamen-tals rather than Body-Mind Centering. Bonnie's terms are in parentheses.

- *Breath*—includes both cellular and lung respiration and is a key to fluidity of movement, internal shaping, the experience of inner space as three-dimensional, and a basic sense of trust in Being.

- *Core-Distal Connectivity (Navel Radiation)*—includes developing In-ternal Core Support and the relationship of each limb to center core and through center core to the other limbs and out to the world.

- *Head-Tail Connectivity (Spinal)*—includes the ability to enjoy a flexi-ble sensuous spine in all three planes, particularly important for level change; and the ability to give attention as an individual.

- *Upper-Lower Connectivity (Homologous)*—builds grounding, strength, and intention through pushing into the earth. It patterns an ability to come from that grounded push to reach out into space and enable a pull without disconnecting from Core; relates to building a sense of personal power.

- *Body Half Connectivity (Homolateral)*—organizes the body to be able to work with one side stable while the other side is mobile; patterns sidedness functions in the brain; aids in clarifying issues.

- *Cross-Lateral Connectivity (Contralateral)*—develops full three-dimen-sionality and ability to spiral with complex level change and locomo-tion; prepares for multidimensional relational thinking and commit-ment to action.

Our neuromuscular system is constantly developing plans for executing movement sequences which become patterned. These patterns are habit-ual firings of muscular pathways that come into play to meet a need or fulfill an intent. Some patterns—such as the primitive reflexes, righting re-actions, and equilibrium responses, and the basic neurological patterns of development (breath through and including cross-laterality)—are built into our neuromuscular system. They are common to all human beings. We are physiologically mandated to fulfill certain physical developmental processes in order to be fully functional and expressive. When these pat-terns are not achieved and integrated, we can develop compensatory pat-terns that might not effectively support the next stage of development and may lead to either physical or psychological problems later on. But whether a pattern is maximally effective or not, patterning is always hap-pening as we grow and develop. Habitual ways of organizing the body to function in the world are being laid down in the neuromuscular system. It is also important to note that a part of our individual uniqueness as hu-man beings comes in the way we sequence and phrase these patterns to express ourselves. Each major developmental pattern of connectivity listed above (Breath through Cross-Laterality) is a primary level of experience. Each organizes a way of relating to the world and teaches skills that are needed for life functioning. Anyone who is training movers is dealing with patterning and could increase his or her effectiveness as a teacher by having a greater understanding of the fundamental patterns.

WHAT IS BARTENIEFF FUNDAMENTALS AND WHAT IS ITS GOAL?

Bartenieff Fundamentals is unique in the somatics/body therapies field because it is based in an understanding of the training process in movement that goes beyond simple body-level functioning. Most body therapies stress "awareness," "sensation," "release of excess tension," "ease of movement" and "efficient joint functioning." Most even acknowledge that the individual's ability to communicate expressively in the world is affected by body patterning. But very few systems provide a bridge in the actual training process for the student to grow to full potential in usage of three-dimensional space and make phrased movement statements that express a broad range of dynamic qualities and personal feelings. This leap from the body level to the expressive level is particularly important for the dancer who wants to both prolong performance lifetime by maximizing body function and "speak" effectively to an audience with his or her own unique voice.

BF is an approach to basic body training that deals with patterning connections in the body according to principles of efficient movement functioning within a context which encourages personal expression and full psychophysical involvement.

The goal of BF is to facilitate the lively interplay of inner connectivity for efficient body functioning with outer expressivity.

SIX PRIMARY METHODS USED IN BARTENIEFF FUNDAMENTALS

1. *Fundamentals works with connective patterns through the whole body, even when educating or rehabilitating a specific body area. Classes utilize the basic principle of Total Body Connectivity: The whole body is connected; all parts are in relationship.* By keeping this principle in mind we can make a major difference in our training process for dancers and other skilled movers or for any process of rehabilitation. For example, a problem in the lower back or a lack of range of motion in the hip joint might be addressed by dealing with patterning the entire connective pathway from the earth through the legs and spine to the head, with an emphasis on supporting from the internal core of the body. It is important to discover how the whole body is organizing to produce the movement even if what seems to be the focal point is the highly articulated parts. When learning or teaching one might ask, "What is the underlying pattern of total body connectivity which could support and organize the articulation I am seeking?" (See the list of patterns above.)

2. *Fundamentals utilizes the entire framework of Laban movement analysis to develop movement efficiency and expressiveness.* The interplay of Inner Connectivity and Outer Expressivity is facilitated in the classroom by approaching each new understanding of body function within phrases of movement which incorporate change in the relationship of *Body, Effort, Shape,* and *Space.*

Body aspects include all the basic patterns previously mentioned (Breath through Cross-Laterality) with particular emphasis on locating

- Breath and core support to engage internal musculature and minimize over-dependence on external muscles.
- Pure hip flexion and extension to prevent hip-hiking and/or substitution of low back usage for hip joint action,
- Pelvic shift in the sagittal and lateral (or frontal) planes for clarity of weight shift and ability to travel through space by connecting from the earth through into the lowest part of the pelvis.
- Body half for stabilizing one side of the body while the other side is moving.
- Diagonal connections through the body and graded rotation in the proximal joints to facilitate full three-dimensional movement.

In the classroom many different movement experiences are given. These could include the type of movement a baby might originally do in developing the targeted skill, as well as several adult versions including pedestrian, dance, or sports examples which break down the component parts of the skill into simple elements and then reintegrate those simple parts back into a complex sequence.

Effort aspects include the mover's attitude toward investing energy in the elements of Flow, Weight, Time, and Space. Effort provides an integrated statement from the feeling/emotion side which coordinates the entire being in a dynamic way. Engaging the mover from his or her own inner intent (perhaps from imagery, voice, or metaphor), prevents exercises from becoming montonious, which is deadening to artistic training. Imagine, for instance, using a sense of internal power to cast a spell with flowing, direct strength when working on the grounding necessary to stand firm.

Shape aspects stress the *process* of changing the form of the body. Every movement is an action of shape change from Closing to Opening, or Opening to Closing, even if the movement is very subtle. Fundamentals stresses investing in the changing shape from within as an expressive *process:* for instance, Sprea*d*in*g* as opposed to simply arriving at a wide shape. Awareness of this sort is particularly important for dancers who seem to get stuck in trying to make the "right shape" but are not connecting internally to enjoy the forming process itself.

Space aspects include, among other things, whether the movement is dimensional, planar, diagonal, or transverse spiraling. Spatial Intent organizes body connections by establishing a clear pathway/goal for the movement. These pathways are "alive highways" which the body can ride in both vertical and off-vertical movement. The clearer the spatial intent or goal of the movement, the more easily the neuromuscular system can accomplish the action in a fluid way. For instance, by clarifying that a fall to the floor "rides a diagonal highway" down forward to the left, the mover can grade the spatial change equally. The neuromuscular system can continually make adjustments in weight shift, using cross-lateral connectivity in the body along the pathway to prevent glitches in the muscular sequencing or difficulty in getting to the floor. A simpler example is intending to let the femur swing purely *forward* in the sagittal plane when walking. This encourages clarity in hip joint usage and diminishes hip-hiking.

3. *Fundamentals emphasizes phrasing.* This begins with internal preparation (through Body part, Effort, Shape, or Spatial intent). This preparation then organizes where the movement needs to initiate in the body in order to effectively fulfill the intent. *The moment and placement of initiation determine the entire process and path the movement will take. Once the movement is initiated, the action fulfills itself. Therefore, any training process in dance, sport, or rehabilitation must look at the entire phrase from the moment of the initiation if the training is to be effective.* By stressing phrasing in this way the Fundamentals approach is diagnostic as well as educational. Disturbances in developmental patterning and coordinated movement sequencing reveal themselves immediately and can be dealt with, whereas such problems in sequencing and phrasing might remain hidden in a traditional system of isolated "exercises."

4. *Fundamentals emphasizes sequencing of muscle groups in the context of the whole movement rather than simple muscle strength.* A focus on muscle strength, frequently seen in training for dance, sport, or rehabilitation, tends to fragment moving into isolated repetitive two-phasic movement, such as flexion-extension. Fundamentals builds function and strength through a variety of related experiences for a body part—not only for different roles of muscular action—using repetition, of course—but also for variation in dynamics, rhythm, shaping, and spatial pattern. This multifaceted training reflects the complexity of functioning in the world.

5. *Fundamentals stresses the interaction of stabilizing elements and mobilizing elements.* For both stability and mobility, Fundamentals concentrates on finding the active connections from the core of the body out into the limbs. These connections are then either activated for grounding (stability) or activated to move the body part (mobility). Fundamentals does not emphasize holding one part and moving another against it (for example, "Hold your shoulders down to move your arm"). The Fundamentals practitioner might say, "Stabilize by visualizing, or sensing, a connective relationship from your scapula to your coccyx. Mobilize by initiating your arm movement from the lowest border of your scapula."

6. *Fundamentals recognizes that any training in movement is a personal adventure.* There are basic patterns and principles of movement, but there

is no one pathway for all persons to achieve full functioning. Human beings pattern their movement responses in ways which they originally perceive will enable them to function in their environment, and each individual history is unique. Therefore, any training process must be done with an awareness of *personal contexting,* recognizing that personal history and motivation are operating continuously.

CONCLUSION

In summary, the Bartenieff Fundamentals practitioner is an avid observer of what is moving an individual at any given moment, where the movement is initiating, and how it is sequencing and following through the body in energy usage and in space. Fundamentals provides the tools to zero in on:

- What the individual is actually doing.
- How this may be different from what is desired.
- Numerous possible inroads for finding new patterns through Body connection/articulation, Effort and Shape motivation, and Spatial Intent.

Whether one is a dancer, an actor, an athlete or a business person, a fully functioning expressive body increases life's possibilities. Irmgard Bartenieff stated, "Body movement is not a symbol for expression, it is the expression." The functional and the expressive are in intimate relationship. Bartenieff Fundamentals activates connections to facilitate integration and enrich life.

REFERENCES

BARTENIEFF, IRMGARD. (1980). *Body Movement: Coping with the environment.* Gordon and Breach, New York.

HACKNEY, PEGGY. (1993). Remembering Irmgard. *Contact Quarterly.* Winter/Spring, pp. 13–20.

EDDY, MARTHA. (1995). "Holistic approaches to dance injury assessment and intervention." *Impulse* 3:1. Human Kinetics Publishers, Champaign, IL. In press.

RESOURCES

Peggy Hackney
439 NE Ravenna Blvd.
Seattle, WA 96115-6428
(206) 524-7343

Madeline Scott
School of Dance
The Ohio University
Athens, Ohio 45701
(614) 593-1828

Martha Eddy
Moving on Center

School for Participatory
Arts and Research
San Francisco, CA 94123
(415) 267-4823

Note: For information regarding certification programs or a listing of
Certified Movement Analysts in your area, contact:

The Laban/Bartenieff Institute of Movement Studies
11 East Fourth Street
New York, New York 10003
(212) 477-4299

Laban Movement Analysis and Bartenieff Fundamentals[sm]
Madeleine Scott

INTRODUCTION

To the dancer who relishes the immediate experience of movement, the
analytic study of movement and its components can seem altogether pal-
lid, overly detailed, and even fussy in comparison with the actual event.
Something gets lost in translation from the doing to the describing. The
richness of the moving experience seems diminished by reducing it to a
dry listing of what body parts went where and when. We are confronted
with a classic example of the sum of the parts not equalling the experience
of the whole.

However, Laban Movement Analysis (LMA) offers a great deal to the
dancer through enhancing the capacity to refine movement perception
and train more efficiently to meet a wide variety of movement challenges.
LMA values the embodied experience of the mover as a richly expressive
being.

HISTORICAL BACKGROUND

Rudolph Laban (1879–1958), born in the Austro-Hungarian Empire, was
an artist, philosopher, dancer, author, educator, and researcher into the
nature of movement. His early training included theater, painting and
drawing, architecture, dance, and military studies, but the study of movement and its role in human lives proved to be the primary devotion of his
life. Laban's choreography for his company and movement choirs for large
community events (performed primarily in Germany, Italy, Yugoslavia,
and Austria) gave artistic expression and outlet to this passion. His work
with his dance company included explorations with movement theory that
later formed an integral part of what became LMA (Groff, 1990).

In 1937 he left Germany and moved to England, where, with F.C.
Lawrence and later with Warren Lamb, he expanded his studies of move-

ment to the workplace. His approach to work-based movement embraced a more humane view of the worker as an individual with specific movement predilections and capacities that could be enlisted to support the worker in his or her tasks. For example, he was able to train women working in wartime factories to phrase movement more efficiently so that they could handle heavier loads with less fatigue.

He directed the development of a comprehensive system of movement notation, Labanotation, with Albrecht Knust and, later, Ann Hutchinson Guest. He wrote extensively on theories of movement and dance, including *Choreutics, Modern Educational Dance, Effort, Mastery of Movement,* and *A Vision of Dynamic Space,* to name a few.

Laban guided many others in their studies of and development in movement fields. Among these was Irmgard Bartenieff (1900–1981). Born in Germany, Bartenieff studied with Laban in Berlin and England. She eventually emigrated to the United States, where she founded the Laban Institute of Movement Studies (LIMS). As a dancer turned physical therapist, Bartenieff contributed to LMA her development of what Laban called the "body aspect" of movement study. Her name is most frequently associated with Bartenieff Fundamentals[sm], but she was also instrumental in bringing Laban's work to the United States. To honor the significance of her contributions to Laban Studies, the Institute was renamed the Laban/Bartenieff Institute of Movement Studies at the time of her death in 1981.

The legacy of Laban and Bartenieff is reflected in the dynamic vitality of their pioneering and visionary efforts. Hundreds of Certified Movement Analysts (CMA's) have taken the original work into applications such as sports and fitness training, theater, movement therapy, physical therapy, education, communication, as well as dance. The Institute offers coursework and programs of study in Laban Movement Analysis (which includes Bartenieff Fundamentals) that lead to certification as a Laban Movement Analyst.

DESCRIPTION OF LABAN MOVEMENT ANALYSIS (LMA) AND BARTENIEFF FUNDAMENTALS (BF)

LMA is a system of movement study that recognizes movement as our primary language. Yet this language can be frustratingly evanescent, disappearing even as it happens (Moore and Yamamoto, 1963, p. 63). Although videotaping records a map of the movement event, it cannot seem to capture the qualitative essence and spatial complexity of the movement. LMA provides a means, through standardized terminology and symbols, to define and identify the ephemeral aspects of this nonverbal language. This is LMA's descriptive function. It also has a prescriptive function to facilitate movement training.

LMA defines categories which serve as lenses through which to observe and sharpen the focus of movement experiences. The analysis stands in relation to the movement event like a prism refracting a rainbow spectrum from a white light source. It delineates many features of movement and contributes to an understanding of the whole movement experience. This, in turn, can increase the mover's capacity to clarify and further refine the movement experience, itself. *LMA identifies four categories in movement: body, effort, shape, and space. All movement represents a composite chording, or complex layering, of these four categories.*

BODY[6]

"Body" relates to how the body organizes itself, the relationship of body parts to each other, the location and quality of movement inititation, and the phrasing of body use (sequential, simultaneous, or successive).

Irmgard Bartenieff drew on her background as a physical therapist, as well as on her training with Laban, to develop what is now known as Bartenieff Fundamentals (BF). With BF, Laban's belief in movement as an expression of personal identity takes on a practical, body-level application. Indeed, the goal of BF is to "facilitate the lively interplay of inner connectivity and efficient body function with our outer expressivity" (Hackney, 1987). Two keys of BF are: (1) *promotion of efficient movement function grounded in anatomical principles* and (2) *keen appreciation for the integral role that expressivity plays in the training process.* Basic concepts which BF addresses are: *inner connectivity, breath support, phrasing, initiation, grounding,* and *core support.*

BF facilitates movement training through a series of specific movement sequences that expand upon these key concepts. The best-known of the sequences are called the *Basic Six:* (1) "heel rocking" to establish the body's vertical line; (2) "femoral flexion" (hip flexion) or "thigh lift" to refine the femoral-pelvic rhythm; (3) sagittal and lateral pelvic shifts to prepare for weight shifting; (4) "body half" to enhance the sense of the vertical midline and the orchestration of the upper and lower units of the body; (5) "knee drop or reach" to prepare for contralaterality, which is necessary to walking; and (6) arm circle sequences to emphasize the diagonal connections between the upper and lower units and to facilitate initiation in the upper body with support from the lower body.

The Basic Six are supplemented by a wide variety of additional materials tailored to the movement issues of a particular individual. BF meets the mover as an individual, acknowledging expressive preferences while guiding him or her toward the desired movement skill. A movement issue, such as increasing breath support, can be addressed in a variety of ways. It could be encouraged through vocal work in "sounding exercises" (a Basic Six preparatory exercise) to help the mover gain a more volumetric sense of body cavities. It could be facilitated through hands-on work to increase a perception of holding patterns that work against accessing breath support. Or it could be explored through an improvisation on breath-initiated and breath-phrased movement as a means to help the mover identify and value the contribution of breath to the development of a rich and varied movement palette. BF, therefore, offers a myriad of personalized approaches and solutions to movement skill development, each of which physicalizes and implements Laban's concepts of body, effort, shape, and space.

6. Also see Hackney's discussion of Bartenieff Fundamentals.

Effort is what we experience as the dynamics of expressive movement, the inner energy that drives our movement. It is an essential and omnipresent feature of our expressive movement life. It is reflected in our voices, facial expressions, and everyday movement. The implications of effort go beyond a simple energetic mobilization of muscle power. Rather, its contribution lies in the fact that it is the *motivation to move*. Before there is movement, there must be an intention to move. Effort is that motivation. Effort is the intentionality that orchestrates the complex events of movement.

Consider the following examples of how effort can coordinate movement. A woman, lounging on a sofa, sees her child begin to fall forward. She recognizes instantly that the toddler will hit his head on a sharp table edge. She nearly levitates as she moves into action. One arm reaches forward to grab him. The other arm helps mobilize a shift in her center of gravity as she launches herself from the sofa to her feet and forward to snatch the child from the jaws of disaster.

There is a great deal happening very quickly in this example. Indeed, powerful bursting contractions of muscle groups help to mobilize the woman, but her motivation, her intent, helps her orchestrate and coordinate their effective use to support her objective. Thus, we see her direct her attention toward the toddler and reach for him with alarm. With great urgency, she pushes herself off the sofa, using enough force to rise and hurl herself forward as she seeks to prevent the impending accident.

We can utilize this scenario to further illustrate the effort category of LMA. There are four basic efforts which combine in a variety of ways to describe movement qualitatively. These basic efforts are: *space, time, weight*, and *flow*. Each is assessed on a continuum ranging from one extreme to another. *Space effort* corresponds to a quality of attention which ranges from *direct to indirect focus*. In the mother/toddler example, the mother's space effort is direct as she focuses on the threatened toddler. *Time effort* describes an attitude toward *pace*, either increasing pace with a sense of urgency or decreasing it with sustainment. The mother in our scenario begins with a more sustained attitude toward time as she lounges on the sofa, but is launched into action with urgency as she races to catch her child. Pushing herself off the sofa, she engages her *weight effort*, employing her *strength* as she increases pressure and pushes herself to her feet, overcoming the pull of gravity on her body mass. *Lightness*, the opposite of strength in the weight effort, would be evident in movement with decreasing pressure. The remaining effort is *flow*, in which varying tension levels are expressed as either *bound* or *free*. Returning to our scenario, we can see that the mother hurls herself with free flow toward the child. The mother's intent is not to control or bind the flow of her movement; it is to propel herself toward her objective without restriction.

While single effort factors were identified in the example, it is apparent that other effort factors were active as well. Effort factors appear in combinations of two, called *states;* and combinations of three, called *drives*. Experience with states and drives which focuses on how they inform and clarify movement intent offers the dancer a rich resource as a performer.

Indeed, effort explorations can help build a personal lexicon of movement experiences on which to draw for enriching performance, creating new work, refreshing old work with a new approach, and stimulating new approaches to the solution of movement problems.

SHAPE

For dancers, the capacity to identify and change shape is one of the basic skills developed in early training. We often learn movement by registering the shapes and then linking them to create movement sequences. This is a sort of "connect-the-dots" approach to movement. As proficiency is gained, experiencing the moving arc of the phrase, the designs created in space by limbs, and the changing volume of the space inside and around the body becomes more apparent. In short, we see the movement in the movement.[7] LMA distinguishes these differences through analysis of the shape category.

"Shape" includes (1) *basic shapes* the body can assume (such as ball, wall, pin, and screw), (2) *descriptive terms* that identify how the body changes its shape, and (3) the *process* it undergoes to rearrange itself. The process of changing shape can be *internal* or *external*. Internal changes can be represented by the changes that accompany breathing, which contribute to a growing and shrinking quality as the volume changes. Young dancers who "forget to breathe" often look like frozen blocks because this inner shaping is absent. An example of externally focused shape change might focus on how one reaches toward an object or how one conforms to accommodate to the shape of another person or object.

Changing shape also has a qualitative component. A few examples might help to clarify this concept. A sharp intake of breath in a moment of delight, surprise, or anticipation might be accompanied by a rising and spreading change of shape. A dancer, after taking a bow, might move toward the audience while spreading and rising to receive and acknowledge applause. A parent might change shape by enclosing protectively around a babe in arms. These are only a few examples of shape change; they are not meant to be all-inclusive but rather are intended to give the reader a general sense of the shape element of LMA.

SPACE

Body, effort, and shape concerns merge and blend in the demands "space" places on the mover to integrate and coordinate movement. The space category includes direction, pathway, location, and general and personal space. The personal space we maintain around us is known as the *kinesphere*. *Size* of the kinesphere may alter, expanding to fill a large performance space or shrinking to fit in a crowded elevator. Size is only one component of LMA consideration of space. Another is *space harmony*. It is

7. This might ring a bell for students of kinesiology who have grappled with the "how" and "what" of movement demonstrations, asking, "Do I analyze specific muscles for the starting position (shape), the ending position (shape), or the joint action between positions (movement)?"

through Laban's work in space harmony that his genius as an observer of movement is most clearly seen.

Laban said, "Space is a hidden feature of movement and movement is a visible aspect of space" (1966, p. 4). In developing space harmony, he built upon the three dimensions (sagittal, vertical, and horizontal) to further explore movement in the three planes using polyhedral forms, such as the cube, octahedron, and icosahedron. He created movement scales for each polyhedral form which, like musical scales based on intervals of tone, are based on an ordered progression of points illustrating intervals in space. A musician practices scales to gain skills that broaden the expressive choices available. Movement scales can serve the same purpose. In both, one practices the accuracy and expressivity of the note or point in space, and the intervals between them. The intervals in movement scales are the paths of motion between two points. These require subtle and specific gradations in the use of the body, effort intent, and shaping response as one progresses through the spatial arrangement of points on the scale. Movement scales offer an opportunity to rehearse full expressivity within functionally supported movement.

IMPLICATIONS FOR DANCERS

The need for integrated body use. Too often dancers conceive of the body as an assemblage of parts, as if it comprised only gears and levers, systems of pulleys, cords, cogs, and wheels. Approaches to training and conditioning the body easily reveal the effects of such a mechanistic viewpoint. We target an objective, identify the area of the body needing work, and apply correctives to it as if the part addressed had no relation to the rest of the body. For example, dancers often do more abdominal curls to support centering, push-ups to connect the arms, or intensive stretching to increase the height of an extension. Certainly, these exercises will endow the body part with additional capacities, but they will not necessarily improve the objective the dancer has in mind. The objectives (centering, connecting, and supporting) are more about *integrated use of the body part in relationship to the whole* than they are about the discrete functions of the abdominals, shoulder muscles, or hamstrings.

The very structure of many technique classes reiterates this separation of the body into units. Classes that move through an orderly progression of combinations designed to focus on a specific area such as legs, feet, upper back, arms, spine, and so on, are intended to train use of these parts. And they accomplish the goal. But it is assumed that the dancer will find a way to connect this patchwork of parts into a whole body. Even notions about alignment, when approached principally as stacking and bracing parts, reinforce a "part versus whole" ideation.

Attention to the whole. The dancer is not an assemblage of intricately trained parts. The beauty of an eloquent performance is more than the sum of its parts. It is the harmonious and dynamic relationships within the body that draw attention, and *awareness of inner connectivity supporting outer expressivity* that engages the imagination of the viewer. Laban

Movement Analysis and Bartenieff Fundamentals address the wholeness of the mover and facilitate training toward this objective.

BREATH

"Begin with the breath," Bartenieff urged. *Breath is elemental to feeling connections—both the connections among parts and the connection of the whole to the environment.* The dancer is encouraged to experience breath as a centering activity that enhances support to and from the body core. The LMA/BF approach also guides explorations of breath as the expressive underpinning of movement phrasing, and as a means to create emotional resonance in performance. Breath enlivens and supports the full expressivity of the dancer; without it a dancer is wooden.

RELATIONSHIP OF PARTS TO THE WHOLE

Arm circles, one of the Basic Six that helps clarify carriage of the arms, are performed with an intent to establish a diagonal connection between upper and lower quadrants of the body (Bartenieff, 1980). They help the dancer to gradate rotation in the gleno-humeral joint (shoulder joint) and facilitate a secure connection between the arm and torso. A fully expressive use of the arm is characterized by the harmonious relationship of the part to the whole in a constellation of body, effort, shape, and space concerns. A dancer could be coached to find the scapula anchoring, clear spatial intent, responsive shaping in the torso, and an awareness of the kinesphere as possible features of this constellation.

Increasing the height of leg "extensions" to the front does indeed require flexibility of the hamstrings, but it also demands the orchestration of clear spatial intent in the pathway of the gesturing leg, a secure sense of grounding through the standing leg and its relationship to the pelvic girdle, and the capacity to stabilize through the torso without a counterproductive increase in tension. But a high leg extension is a mere pyrotechnical trick unless the dancer claims its expressive value, feels its expansive use of space, reveals the eloquence of its changing shape, and embodies the musicality of its effort phrasing.

CONCLUSION

Clearly, the functional issues that concern the dancer cannot be viewed as merely mechanical. They are uniquely expressive representations of the body, effort, shape, and space issues of the individual. LMA/BF affords a means of addressing functional and expressive issues in an ongoing process of change and enrichment that engages the whole being of the dancer. Experience with an approach to movement training as a harmonious integration of the body and mind of the mover must happen in the doing, for it is here that synthesis occurs and the sum is greater than all its parts. It is here that, as Laban (1984) said, "It becomes possible to grasp with our intellect that old prophetic dream of mankind, the unity of the body and mind" (p. 39).

REFERENCES

GROFF, EDWIN E. (1990). *Laban Movement Analysis: An Historical, Philosophical, and Theoretical Perspective.* Unpublished MFA Thesis. Connecticut College, New London.

BARTENIEFF, IRMGARD. (1980). *Body Movement: Coping with the Environment.* Gordon and Breach, New York.

HACKNEY, PEGGY. (1987). Unpublished class notes for intensive CMA program. Seattle, WA.

LABAN, RUDOLPH (Ed. Lisa Ulman). (1966). *Choreutics.* MacDonald and Evans, London.

LABAN, RUDOLPH (Ed. Lisa Ulman). (1984). *A Vision of Dynamic Space.* The Falmer Press, London.

LABAN, RUDOLPH, and LAWRENCE, F.C. (1947). *Effort.* MacDonald and Evans, London.

MOORE, CAROL-LYNNE, and YAMAMOTO, KAORU. (1988). *Beyond Words.* Gordon and Breach, New York.

Note: For information regarding certification programs or a listing of Certified Movement Analysts in your area, contact:

The Laban/Bartenieff Institute of Movement Studies
11 East Fourth
New York, New York 10003
(212) 477-4299

Somatics and the Dance Major Curriculum[8]
Sally Fitt

Dance major programs have come a long way since the first programs made their way into institutions of higher education. Gradually, new areas have been added, as concepts of the necessary artistic, intellectual, physical, and psychological components of dance training expanded. I personally remember conducting a questionnaire in 1973 (sent to all institutions that then offered a four-year dance major program) which focused on assessing the perceived need for teachers of dance kinesiology. It should be noted that at that time the term *dance kinesiology* itself was new, and most classes that dealt with it were called Movement Analysis, or some other equally vague

8. I am indebted to Silvie Fortin for her ideas on this subject, which made me realize that these concepts needed to be put into writing at this time, when so many dance departments are including, or thinking about including some form of somatics in their curricula. Dr. Fortin has written an article on this topic from a different perspective than mine. It was scheduled for publication in the academic year 1995–1996 in the journal *Impulse,* which is published by Human Kinetics Publishers.

title. Of the thirty-three responses received from four-year dance major programs, seventeen offered *no* dance kinesiology! That was a little more than twenty years ago. Today, it is clear from the inclusion of dance kinesiology in the National Accreditation Standards for Schools of Dance (CODA, 1973; NASD, 1986) that the curricula of dance major programs continues to grow and develop and reflects the directions taken by leaders in the field of dance.

A Call for Change

If there is one thing I have learned from more than thirty years in higher education, it is that *change takes time*. That doesn't mean that I have learned patience with the process, only that I recognize the nature of the beast.

I have personally been involved in pushing for a number of curricular changes over the years. Four are related to dance kinesiology: (1) naming the classes I taught *dance kinesiology;* (2) the addition of conditioning classes that were separate from the technique classes; (3) the addition of Pilates-based conditioning for majors; (4) the addition of a quarter of other somatics work to the undergraduate curriculum. Our undergraduate program in the Modern Dance Department at the University of Utah now includes one quarter each of the following: conditioning for dancers; some somatic approach, such as Feldenkrais Method, Alexander Technique, or Bartinieff Fundamentals; the "Dancer Specific" program (Sturman, 1993); on the New Concepts Reformer; dance kinesiology; and applied dance kinesiology. Some of these changes happened as easily as putting on a different shirt, but others required a long-drawn-out process of education and lobbying for change.

Changes that only have to label attitudes and perspectives that already exist are easy to make. Those that require a change in the fundamental attitudes of "change makers," may take a frustratingly long time to accomplish. Changing the name of the classes I taught is an example of the first type of change; it was easy. Getting approval for the addition of extra conditioning classes for dance majors took a long, long time. At UCLA it took five years. Then I moved to Utah and had to start lobbying for change all over again. At Utah it took four years for me to get approval for the addition of the conditioning class. A number of the research projects that I have done on dance conditioning were done for the sole purpose of showing the value of additional conditioning for the dancer. I include this explanation for the benefit of dance educators and future dance educators to again emphasize the point that change takes time.

It is hoped that the addition of somatic approaches to dance curricula will be one of the easy changes, reflecting general acceptance of the value of somatics by dance educators. Basic to the necessary attitude of acceptance is the concept that *the body possesses an inherent wisdom that is accessible only through the body*. If change makers agree with this assumption, the change should be relatively easy. If not, addition of somatics to the curriculum will take more time. In the process of doing therapeutic massage for students, I have often said, "My hands are smarter than my head. My head is not stupid, but my hands are smarter." I believe, whole-heartedly, that *the wisdom of the body is more important, more viable, and more soul-satisfying than intellectual "word" wisdom*. That may surprise some of you, coming from the author of a dance science book, but it is my strong belief that the body is far smarter than the brain. The brain only processes information, the information that it receives from the body. It is only when the brain and the body are treated as a unified whole that the mind (the totality of the person and the surrounding energy systems) can reach its full potential. In keeping with this belief, I believe that somatics, whatever the specific system, is of great value to the dancer. Somatic approaches open doorways to (1) clearer understanding of individual differences, (2) the broadening of one's movement repertoire, (3) performance enhancement, and (4) increasing one's sensitivity to body wisdom. These are just a few of the benefits I have seen from the inclusion of somatics in the curriculum. While some individuals seem to be naturally "body smart," others seem to need a bit of a nudge or a reminder in order to connect with the wisdom of the body.

Being Body-Smart

Being "body-smart" is far more than having a technically proficient, physically well-trained body. Being "body-smart" means *respecting the body* as a self-correcting mechanism. It means acknowledging in word and deed the information that the body supplies for everyday living and the achievement of one's potential. It means *listening to the body with all of the inner ears of the body,* (for example, the one that hears muscles complaining of overwork, the one that hears the body's nonverbal messages about nutrition and rest patterns, or the one that hears the joyful expression of the body as it moves with commitment and passion). It means *loving the body* for the magnificence of its capacities. It means *caring for the body* when repair and rehabilitation are needed. Finally it means *revering the body* for the mysterious doorway it opens to the essential meaning of life and living.

Technique classes do not teach us to be *fully* body smart; nor does kinesiology; nor does conditioning. Each of these areas of study provides only a portion of the full dimension of *being body smart*. Somatics approaches have, I believe, the potential to take us closer to the full dimensionality of being body smart. For this reason, I believe it is time, perhaps even past time, for dance educators to add somatics to the curriculum.

In Conclusion

Somatics, regardless of the approach, cannot be reduced to verbal descriptions. Each system begins and ends in nonverbal awarenesses of information provided by the body in sensory, tactile, and kinesthetic forms. Words are ultimately inadequate to describe the dimensions and ramifications of the work. Synthesis and application of nonverbal sensations and perceptions have the potential to take the participant far beyond the words used to describe the experiences. Even so, one thing becomes very clear after reading the descriptions of the somatic techniques included above. While the tools, the techniques, and the vocabularies may vary, the ultimate purpose of all of these approaches is the same.

Each approach encourages the participant to treat the human body with care, respect, and awe. Each leads the participant to a fuller realization that the body offers more than mechanical and muscular efficiency, more than motional capacity, and more than physical health. *The body is the tangible reflection of the soul and spirit within each of us. Moreover, the body is our first and most profoundly relevant teacher.*

Young children are sensitive to the messages from this wise teacher, but we adults must relearn to listen to the messages the body conveys. Each somatic approach, in its own way, provides a pathway that leads to reconnecting with the wisdom of the body. The reawakened awareness of the exquisite beauty and powerful wisdom of the body is both the meeting point and the purpose of all somatic approaches.

CHAPTER 18

Prevention of Dance Injuries

It has been only since the late 1970s that dancers have come to the attention of orthopedic surgeons and sport medicine specialists. The appearance of articles in journals and in the press on dance injuries, their prevention and care, is most encouraging. Previously, little attention was given to dancers, even though dancers are as active, and as susceptible to athletic injuries, as almost any group. The dancer is, indeed, an athlete and deserving of the specific attention of the medical profession.

Dancers and Doctors

In the past, dancers were practically forced to treat themselves because medical professionals simply were not conversant with the physical demands placed on the dancer, nor were they familiar with the psychology of the dancer. Many dancers heard the all-too-frequent advice, "Just stay off of it," or even worse, "Just don't dance any more." Fortunately, there are a growing number of physicians who understand that the dancer is as committed to dance as any athlete is committed to sport. As understanding grows, the dancer is receiving better medical advice than ever before, if he or she is able to find a specialist who is interested in dance. The dancer looking for a doctor (particularly if on tour or in an unfamiliar city) must have sufficient knowledge to screen doctors before selecting one. One of the best leads is to find a physician recommended by the local athletic teams. If there are professional or university teams in the city, a call to the team trainer can frequently yield valuable advice.

The Psychology of the Injured Dancer

The injured dancer is as fanatical about getting back to activity as any athlete. If the dancer is faced with an upcoming performance, the pressure is even more intense. Almost all dancers subscribe to the old adage "The show must go on," no matter what the consequences. At the time of the injury, sound advice can do much to prevent reinjury and, possibly, very serious consequences. The more information dancers have about the nature of injuries and the possible problems resulting from the injuries, the more effectively they can make the difficult decisions that can drastically affect their future as dancers.

It has been my experience that dancers are incredibly impatient with the healing process and rehabilitation. Sometimes that works to the advantage of the dancer, but sometimes not. Dancers tend to want it all, *yesterday*. If one repetition of exercises is good, ten must be ten times as good. When this attitude is applied immediately following an injury, the dancer may be taking the chance of making the condition more serious. The injured dancer must ask sufficient questions of the attending physician to make the most effective treatment possible.

Dancers have often been intimidated by doctors, fearing to ask the questions necessary to clarify what the problem is, and how to deal with it. I have repeatedly advised my students to continue asking questions until they are perfectly clear about the condition and the recommended treatment. The dancer must also ask the important questions about possible consequences if the advice is not followed, since it is quite common to find a dancer nodding in agreement in the physician's office and then proceeding *not* to follow the advice. Both short- and long-term consequences should be considered.

The young dancer lives in the rosy glow of what I call the "indestructo" phenomenon, having only lived in a young body. There is a basic assumption that one's body will be resilient, quick to heal, and mobile *forever*. Mature dancers know better. The old injuries come back to haunt the aging dancer, and there are the inevitable *"ifs."* (*If* I had only stayed off the injury for a few weeks . . . *if* I had religiously done the exercises . . . *if* I hadn't performed on the injury.) The ifs are valuable only when the dancer *considers them at the time of the injury*. Good advice at the time of the injury, focusing on possible consequences (whether it comes from a doctor, a friend, a teacher, or oneself), is the most effective medicine. The dancer may ignore the advice and continue dancing, but at least he or she does so with an understanding of the possible effects.

Pain

Dancers have a remarkable ability to dance through pain. The performance "high" often overshadows immediate pain. Yet it is important for dancers to recognize that pain is actually valuable information about the status of the body. Pain is a valuable warning signal, and the wise dancer pays attention to pain. For that reason, analgesic balms, or any forms of anesthetic, cut the dancer off from the valuable information available from pain. If the injury or condition is so painful that performance is impossible without an anesthetic, the dancer has no business performing. Common sense and an understanding of the difference between good pain and bad pain are essential to the dancer.

Good Pain and Bad Pain

Obviously, no pain feels good. But certain pains are good because they lead to increased capacity. "The burnies" are a perfect example of good pain. In conditioning the muscular system for increased muscular endurance or strength, a person reaches the point when the muscles start to burn. That very burning is a key to conditioning; it says that the muscle is working beyond previous capacities. The human body responds positively to the stress caused by working beyond one's capacity, providing that the stress is not so extreme as to cause spasm or other major problems. Stretching out after a heavy workout of a given muscle group (always wise) brings the dancer face to face with another good pain: "the stretchies." Stretching out a tight muscle gives the sensation of warm, generalized prickling.

Good pain—that which accompanies an increase in capacity—is generalized and rather dull. In contrast, bad pain is sharp, piercing, highly localized, and sometimes shooting to other parts of the body. Bad pain should not be ignored. It may be the localized pain of tendonitis, in which case treatment is necessary. It may be the sharp pinching sensation (*impingement*) caused by bone contacting bone in a mobility exercise, in which case the dancer knows that he or she has reached the bony limitation of movement. Any sharp, shooting, bad pain should cause the dancer to pause and investigate its possible causes. This type of pain is a warning signal from the body, and dancers simply *must listen to their bodies.* Pain accompanying an injury is the result of three factors: the injured tissue itself, the spasm of muscles around the site of the injury, and the swelling which immediately follows and puts pressure on surrounding nerve endings. There is immediate vasodilation at the site of an injury. The swelling which results can be increased by damage to the blood vessels in the area, and by the increased metabolism at the site of the injury. Reduction of swelling through rest, ice, compression, and elevation (RICE) not only serves to reduce pain but also reduces excessive buildup of scar tissue. *Gentle* stretching can reduce muscle spasm around the injury.

Muscle Soreness

Another type of pain common among dancers is muscle soreness lasting a day or two after a heavy exercise bout. The peak of muscle soreness occurs twenty-four to forty-eight hours after exercise. *Stretching out immediately following exercise* seems to reduce muscle soreness for many people. Delaying the stretch until soreness peaks is less effective, but still helps.

Three steps can be taken to reduce muscle soreness.

1. *Identify the sore muscle by analysis and exploration:* Where does it hurt? What muscles are located in that area? What action causes pain? What muscle(s) perform that action or are stretched by that action? Is the pain a "stretch" pain, or a "contraction" pain? From the answers to these questions, identify the sore muscle.

2. *Identify the joint actions performed by the sore muscle.*

3. *Do a gentle long sustained stretch of the muscle* by assuming a position opposite to the joint action performed by the muscle and releasing into the stretch for at least one minute.

It is hoped that you will be able to identify the muscle and its attachments without consulting a book. Whether you consult a book or not, the technique is very effective in reducing normal muscle soreness resulting from a heavy exercise bout. It is even better if the dancer is aware, *at the time of the exercise*, that there has been excessive stress on a muscle or muscle group and stretches it (them) out before stopping for the day. Careful selection of stretches during the cool-down period can do much to reduce muscle soreness.

Causes of Injury

We all know the primary causes of injury: ignorance and stupidity.[1] The only difference among causes of injury is the point at which stupidity occurs. Ignoring misalignments can lead to chronic aches and pains due to muscular imbalance. Dancing on a hard surface can lead to shin splints or stress fractures. Dancing when one is out of shape can lead to a galaxy of injuries. Dancing in excessive heat without paying attention to dehydration and the depletion of body salts can lead to muscle spasms and more serious consequences. Poor health habits (for example, unbalanced eating habits, lack of sleep, or use of drugs) can lead to injury. Trying to perform a combination that is beyond one's ability often leads to injury. Ignoring one's own warning signals of fatigue increases the likelihood of injury. Maintaining a body weight that is higher than ideal puts extra stress on weight-bearing joints. Being underweight for a dancer is just as serious as being overweight, for the body is less able to fight off disease and heal itself. Dancing when one is under severe emotional or psychological stress can reduce concentration and increase the chance of injury. Dancing without proper preparatory conditioning (such as strength, endurance, or warm-up) often leads to injury.[2]

Prevention of Injury

The smart dancer pays careful attention to environmental conditions (floors, heat, cold, altitude, hazards, etc.); takes particular care to condition the body effectively; is aware of his or her strengths and weaknesses and allows for them; concentrates with great intensity; maintains a consis-

---

1. There is no such thing as a smart injury. One may be unaware of potential problems (ignorance) or may disregard warning signals (stupidity).
2. All the causes of injury listed above are, in one way or another, stupid. Don't be offended. No one is immune to occasionally doing "dumb stuff." The critical issue becomes "How often do we do the same dumb stuff?"

tent ideal body weight; tries to get enough rest; eats well; recognizes his or her own warning signals of fatigue; and cuts back on the activity or intensity that caused the fatigue. Yet even the smartest dancer can be injured. The cause of injury then shifts from stupidity to bad luck. One simply cannot prevent bad luck. There are times when even the "smartest" dancer has the misfortune to be injured. However, attending to the factors listed above can certainly reduce the likelihood of injuries. When an injury does occur, whether because of stupidity or bad luck, it is important for the dancer to be aware of the types of injury in order to make decisions about seeking medical assistance or not and continuing activity or not.

Types of Injury

The usual classification of injuries has two categories: traumatic or acute injuries and chronic injuries. Traumatic injuries happen suddenly and often involve a fall or some other sudden accident. Chronic conditions are those which recur over time and are more usually due to misalignment, overuse, poor training habits, or compensation for performance errors. Systemic conditions must also be considered.

Traumatic Injuries

Traumatic injuries include such conditions as fractures, sprains, strains, bruises and contusions, concussions, cuts, lacerations and punctures, dislocations and subluxations, and other results of accidents. Each type of traumatic injury deserves definition and discussion.

Fractures. All fractures are destruction of the structural integrity of bone tissue caused by the application of force. A fracture may be classified as simple or compound, or as greenstick, spiral, or stress. It is not true that one *cannot* move the body part if there *is* a fracture, but *can* move the body part if there *is not* a fracture. The only way to conclusively rule out the possibility of a fracture is by x-ray, and even then it is difficult to identify some greenstick fractures and stress fractures. A bone scan (considerably more expensive than an x-ray) is more reliable for identifying stress fractures than the x-ray. Clearly, whenever there is any possibility of a fracture, the dancer should see a physician.

Sprains. A sprain is a consequence of overmovement of a joint that results in injury to connective tissue (ligaments or joint capsule) and may also include a strain or injury to surrounding soft tissue (blood vessels, muscle tissue, and nerves). Common locations of sprains include the ankle/tarsus region, the knee, and the low back. Improper mechanics and misalignment are the most common causes of sprains. Depending on the severity of the sprain, it may require total or partial immobilization. It is wise to have severe sprains x-rayed to rule out the possibility of fracture.

Strains. The term *strain* is limited to injury of the soft tissue, and the term is most usually related to muscle tears. A strain often accompanies a sprain because overmovement of a joint frequently results in muscle tears.

It is also possible to incur a strain when antagonistic muscles are powerfully and simultaneously contracted. Tears to the hamstring muscle are perhaps the most frequent strains, followed closely by the strains of the groin (pectineus, iliopsoas, sartorius, rectus femoris, adductor brevis, adductor longus, or adductor magnus). The pain resulting from a relatively minor strain can often be relieved with gentle stretching, but severe strains should be examined by a doctor.

Bruises and contusions. These are common in dance. (Perhaps there is some truth to the idea that dancers are clumsy, except in performance.) A bruise is the result of a blow to or a tearing of blood vessels. The blood then flows into the surrounding area, and the "pooling" of blood and other fluids can cause swelling and pressure on nerves, in turn causing pain. In severe cases, the bruise may need to be aspirated (drained) by a physician to reduce the swelling.

Concussions. A concussion is really a bruise to the head, inside the skull. Because of the sensitivity of the brain tissue to pressure, a concussion can have very serious consequences. Symptoms of concussions include headache, nausea, dizziness, inequality of pupil size, sleepiness, and general disorientation. A dancer incurring a blow to the head should be carefully watched for these symptoms, and should see a physician if these symptoms appear.

Cuts, lacerations, and punctures. These should be treated according to first aid procedures, using gloves and other necessary protection. Bleeding should be stopped, and the wound should be carefully cleaned and bandaged to prevent reopening. The area of the wound should be kept sterile to prevent infection. A tetanus shot and stitches may be necessary in severe cases.

Dislocations and subluxations. These are the injuries that result in loss of joint integrity. If the bones of the joint return to the normal position after joint integrity is disturbed, it is called a *subluxation*. If the bones remain disarticulated, it is a true *dislocation*. These injuries are very painful and are accompanied by strains and sprains of surrounding tissue. In addition, the muscles around the joint will often spasm. It takes training and knowledge to relocate a joint, and amateurs should not try. The injured dancer should see a physician immediately. The first few days after a dislocation or subluxation are critical. Any movement of the joint can result in reinjury because of the injury to all of the supporting tissue around the joint. Rest and immobilization of the injured joint should be judiciously observed.

Chronic Conditions

The suffix *-itis* refers to inflammation. Inflammation of tissue at areas of high stress is common in chronic conditions. Misalignment, inadequate conditioning, and muscular imbalances are the most common causes of chronic conditions such as tendonitis, bursitis, myositis and fascitis.

Tendonitis. Inflammation of the tendon and the tendon sheath is called *tendonitis*. With tendonitis, the dancer will experience pain on contraction of the muscle, tenderness of the area around the tendon, and crepitus (creaking and crunching in the area of the tendon on movement of the joint). Ice and rest are the first lines of defense for tendonitis. Mild stretching of the muscle may also relieve some of the pain, at least in the very early stages of the condition. Ignoring tendonitis is the worst possible treatment. Early and careful attention is essential. The condition will seldom go away by itself. Aspirin (an anti-inflammatory drug) may be helpful in reducing inflammation, if the dancer's stomach will tolerate aspirin. If these treatments do not reduce the pain, a physician may prescribe a heavy-duty anti-inflammatory drug. The most common locations of tendonitis in dancers are the Achilles tendon, the tendon of the biceps brachii, and the tendon of the flexor hallucis longus. If immediate attention (ice, rest, gentle stretching) is given at the first sign of tendonitis, the dancer may avoid a severe case that requires total rest, anti-inflammatory drugs, and an extended time away from dancing.

Bursitis. Bursae are the ball bearings of the body. They are fluid-filled sacs located at points of high friction in the body. Undue stress at a given area may cause an irritation of the bursa, resulting in an inflamed condition and tenderness. Often there is the sensation of a hot spot, and swelling may be quite localized. Doing a lot of knee work (in a kneeling position, without knee pads) may cause an inflammation of the bursae of the knee. Two other locations that are common sites for bursitis are just beneath the anterior deltoid muscle of the shoulder, and just beneath the tendon of the iliopsoas where it crosses the anterior rim of the pelvis. As with tendonitis, the first lines of defense for bursitis are rest, ice, and aspirin. Severe cases of bursitis are often treated with cortisone. Cortisone is an effective anti-inflammatory drug, and cortisone shots can effectively pinpoint the location of the inflammation; but these should be used only as a last resort because of possible side effects. There are some situations in which a cortisone shot is not appropriate. Consult a physician and ask questions about possible consequences before using cortisone.

Myositis and fasciitis. Both myositis and fasciitis are conditions of generalized inflammation. Myositis is an inflammation of muscle tissue and fasciitis an inflammation of the fascia. Both conditions result in generalized soreness and spasm in a broad area surrounding the inflamed tissue. Sometimes massage is an effective way to reduce the muscle spasm, but it should be accompanied by the standard treatment for all inflammation: application of cold. In extreme cases, it may be necessary to take a general muscle relaxant to relieve the spasm. The dancer experiencing either of these conditions should carefully analyze his or her alignment, for it is very likely that there is major misalignment contributing to the condition.

Systemic Conditions

In addition to traumatic and chronic conditions, there are a number of systemic conditions to be considered in a discussion of dance injury. Examples of these conditions include shock, hyperventilation, salt deficiency, anemia, and hypoglycemia, but these are not the only systemic conditions to have an effect on dancers.

Shock. Shock is a very serious systemic condition and may accompany any traumatic injury. Symptoms of shock include cold, paleness, light-headedness, nausea, and a shallow, weak, rapid pulse. The injured dancer should be encouraged to lie down with the feet and legs slightly higher than the head (unless the injury prohibits this position), and body temperature should be kept as close to normal as possible. An injury severe enough to cause shock will almost always require medical attention. To be on the safe side, always call for medical help.

Hyperventilation. Hyperventilation is, literally, breathing *too much*, resulting in the presence of more oxygen in the system than needed. Symptoms of hyperventilation include deep, panicky breathing, accompanied by weakness, dizziness, and nausea. In extreme cases, the dancer may lose consciousness. Standard first aid for hyperventilation involves rebreathing the expired air, which is higher in carbon dioxide concentration. This process serves to equalize the oxygen and carbon dioxide present in the system. Having the hyperventilating dancer breathe into a paper bag is the most common technique, but if a paper bag is not available, cupping one's hands over the nose and mouth can be a relatively effective technique. Hyperventilation can have serious consequences, and the dancer should always see a physician after hyperventilating.

Salt deficiency, anemia, and hypoglycemia. Systemic deficiencies can have a drastic effect on the performance of the dancer, whether the deficiency is in salt, iron, or blood sugar. Each of these deficiencies will result in weakness and fatigue. There may be other accompanying conditions such as muscle spasm, nausea, or dizziness, depending on the deficiency. Dancing when the temperature is high can quickly lead to dehydration. The best fluid replacement is plain (tap) water. Drinks with caffeine (coffee, tea, or soft drinks) do not replace body fluids as effectively as plain water and should be avoided. A dance studio that operates in the hot months should replace the soft drink machine with a water cooler.

Salt and potassium deficiency can also result from extreme perspiration. Normally, dietary intake is sufficient to make up the loss, but occasionally salt tablets may be an appropriate addition to the regular diet.

Both iron deficiency anemia and low blood sugar (hypoglycemia) result in fatigue, but for different reasons. Iron has a critical role in the formation of hemoglobin, the element in the blood which carries oxygen. Depletion of iron lowers the hemoglobin count of the blood, thus making the system less efficient in transporting oxygen. Blood sugar (glycogen) is necessary for the resynthesis of lactic acid. If blood sugar is low, the resynthesis rate is lowered. Both of these conditions contribute to systemic fatigue. Food intake—both the substances ingested and the timing of meals throughout the day—can have an effect on these deficiencies. The dancer who is prone to any of these deficiencies should consult a physician and take particular care with his or her eating habits.

Tissue Repair

The human body has a remarkable capacity to repair itself while continuing some level of activity. Of course, the more serious the injury the greater the need for rest and recuperation.

Scar Tissue

Tissue repair is accomplished by the formation of scar tissue at the site of the injury. Fibroblasts are the human body's cellular unit of repair. They are always present in the system but congregate at the site of an injury as the presence of body fluids (swelling) increases. The fibroblasts, specialized in some cases to repair specific tissue types, form a fibrous network at the site of the injury which eventually becomes scar tissue. Scar tissue is seldom as sound as the original tissue; thus the ideal healing process involves a minimum of scar tissue. However, *when it comes to scar tissue, the body is a lot like a four-year-old gluing: the puddle of glue far exceeds the amount needed.* Likewise, the body tends to overproduce scar tissue at an injury site, and this is one of the reasons for trying to minimize swelling. It is thought that by keeping swelling down, less scar tissue is produced. Scar tissue is inelastic and has no circulation and thus it cannot perform the function of normal muscle tissue. Scar tissue is extremely strong and inelastic. The collagen fibers are laid every which way, rather than parallel to the fibers of the injured muscle. The muscle is readily reinjured in approximately the same spot because the muscle fibers tear away at the "seam" of the scar tissue "patch." It is often recommended that very mild stretching be begun early in the rehabilitation process because it encourages the collagen fibers to be laid parallel to the muscle fibers and thus interferes less with the muscle's capacity for stretch.

While scar tissue is certainly necessary at the site of an injury, it is essential to keep scar tissue to a minimum. This concept guides the immediate care of an injury.

Immediate Care of an Injury

The first decision the dancer must make on incurring an injury is whether it requires medical attention. Excessive pain, swelling, or both clearly warrant medical attention. If there is a possibility of a fracture, medical attention is needed. If there may be major damage to ligamentous tissue, medical attention is needed. While these few guidelines may be helpful, they certainly do not represent a hard and fast rule. The ultimate decision is the dancer's, but if there is any doubt, see a doctor.

It is essential to minimize swelling at the injury site until the swelling subsides (at least 72 hours following the injury). Four techniques are commonly accepted for reducing the swelling that accompanies an injury.

1. Icing or application of cold
2. Elevation of the injured area

3. Compression on the injured area
4. Immobilization or rest of the injured area

The application of ice should include some form of insulation so that the ice is not placed directly on body tissue. Periods of cold application should not exceed 20 minutes at a time. Frostbite can occur if ice is applied directly to the injured area or if application of cold continues for more than 20 minutes. Compression to the area can take many forms, but the most common is an elastic bandage applied to the injured area. Elevation of the injured area also decreases swelling. Rest and immobilization are self-explanatory, but dancers tend to keep "testing" an injury to see if it still hurts. The dancer should avoid this tendency. Rest means just that: don't move the injured area any more than is absolutely necessary.

Long-Range Care

The long-range care of an injury actually begins as soon as the swelling at the injury site subsides. This may seem early to begin the rehabilitation process, but the more immediately a carefully designed exercise program is begun, the better. There are two separate types of care required. First, one certainly must consider the rehabilitation of the injured area. Second, one must consider the maintenance of conditioning in unaffected areas. The approaches for the injured area and the unaffected area are quite different. One must be patient, gentle, and careful with the injured area. However, one can be quite demanding of the unaffected areas. Often the injured dancer thinks that rest and recuperation applies right across the board. In most cases, there is no reason why a strenuous exercise program cannot be maintained in unaffected areas of the body as long as stress is not placed on the injured area.

Care of injured areas. As soon as the swelling goes down, the injured dancer should take inventory. One must first get the "go ahead" from the physician; then the dancer can gently check for range of motion and strength. A certain amount of atrophy (weakening of the musculature) is certainly to be expected, and so is a limitation of the normal range of movement. Musculature around the injury can be gently stretched by moving through the range of motion. A mild form of strength conditioning may begin, using very low resistance. It is critical for the dancer to check with the doctor prior to even these mild exercises, for in some conditions, such as dislocations, even mild exercise may be contraindicated. Careful analysis of the condition of the injured area and a patient approach to reconditioning are essential. The distinction between good pain and bad pain can be a powerful aid to the dancer trying to recondition an injury. If it hurts (bad pain), don't do it. One certainly cannot expect to jump back into activity at the same level that had been attained prior to the injury. One must start slowly and carefully and take real care to monitor the injured body part constantly. Remember, pain is an ally in the rehabilitation process. The level of pain is an accurate indicator of "how much is enough." For this reason, it is my opinion that painkillers should not be used during the rehabilitation process. The injured dancer needs the valuable information provided by pain. Without pain, the dancer may seriously reinjure the area. In the most conservative rehabilitation, one waits until the pain disappears before returning to class or rehearsals. But dancers are an impatient lot, and they often return before the pain has disappeared. Willingness to risk reinjury can be dangerous, but the danger can be lessened if the injured dancer approaches class or rehearsal with *common sense*. Careful analysis of the demands of class or rehearsal and choosing activities which place little or no stress on the injured area make sense. For example, after an ankle sprain a dancer would be wise to "sit out" during the "across the floor work" and not perform on *relevé* or on *pointe*. Again, the pain will make it very clear when one is doing too much. When it hurts, stop. *Returning to full use of the injured area should be postponed until preinjury strength is regained and exceeded.* To really prevent reinjury, one needs *greater* strength than that which existed at the time of the injury.

Care of uninjured areas. The fact that one area of the body is injured is no reason to let the whole system turn to sand. It is essential to maintain condition in the unaffected areas of the body. Strength, mobility, muscular endurance, and cardiorespiratory endurance can all be maintained with a creative approach to conditioning. Injured dancers often have more time than usual because they are not attending classes or rehearsals. In addition to maintaining normal conditioning, it is even possible to do some specialized conditioning for muscular imbalances or misalignments which have been previously ignored. One can actually use the time to great advantage if one is aware of conditioning needs and is knowledgeable about the principles of conditioning. Doing so would also help the psychological condition of the dancer.

Review of Common Injuries

Dancers are very aware of every sensation received from their bodies. Often, even a relatively minor condition can cause distress and worry. While some conditions certainly make worrying justified, there are some conditions that occur with relative frequency for dancers but are not terribly serious. One very valuable ability for the dancer is to be able to distinguish which are the "big worry" conditions and which are the temporary nuisances. Table 18.1 lists some common dance injuries, symptoms, and one approach to treatment. It is hoped that the chart will be valuable in assessing injuries, but if there is any doubt at all, the dancer should see a physician. Table 18.2 presents one system for dealing with a problem common among modern dancers, the split callus.

Table 18.3 (later in this chapter) presents some general guidelines for dealing with dancers' everyday aches and pains. Dancers regularly encounter aches and pains that are not sufficiently severe to need a physician, but are a source of irritation and distraction and can become a major problem if ignored. Some of these aches and pains recur often enough

TABLE 18.1 **Conditions and Injuries: Symptoms and Care**

Body Area	Injury or Condition	Symptoms	Care
Foot	Calluses and splits	Buildup of hardened superficial tissue, which can split and become very painful.	Bob Small's technique for care of calluses (Table 18.2).
	Tendonitis of flexor hallux longus	Pain on flexion of big toe against resistance. Pain on *relevé* or on *pointe*. Pain on locomotor pushoffs.	Standard treatment for tendonitis: ice, rest, aspirin, gentle stretching. (If pain persists, see a physician.)
	Flat feet	Ligamentous looseness on plantar surface of foot.	Strengthen the intrinsic muscles which flex the toes and support the arch.
	Muscle cramps in toes	Weakness of intrinsic muscles which flex the toes.	Grip toes forcefully while dorsiflexing the ankle and gripping the hands to fortify the flexor reflex. Repeat three or four times a day.
	Pronated feet	Weakness of the supinator muscles that also plantar-flex the ankle, often accompanied by a tendency to supinate in *relevé* and non-weight-bearing positions.	Strengthen the supinators and plantar flexors. Also strengthen pronators and plantar flexors.
	Morton's neuroma	Localized point of pain which feels similar to a stone bruise. Actually, it is an irritation of a nerve ending that can be caused by ill-fitting shoes or some other pressure.	Rest and ice. Sometimes gentle massage can relieve the pain somewhat.
	Stone bruise	Single point of tenderness on the sole of the foot. Most often occurs on calcaneous and on head of second metatarsal when one has Morton short toe.	Rest, ice, and application of "doughnut pad." Doughnut pad: Cut chiropodist's felt in shape of small doughnut. Tape over the bruise so the doughnut hole is directly over the most tender point.
	Sesamoiditis	Tenderness of the sesamoid bones beneath the head of the first metatarsal.	Treat like stone bruise, but if pain persists, consider the possibility of a stress fracture.
	Bunions and bone spurs	Bony scar tissue develops on the foot at point of high stress. The area is tender, inflamed (red) and usually swollen.	Examine weight-bearing mechanics for misalignment and correct any habitual misalignment.

(continued)

TABLE 18.1 Conditions and Injuries: Symptoms and Care (*Continued*)

Body Area	Injury or Condition	Symptoms	Care
Ankle and Lower leg	Ankle sprains	Pain, with swelling, bruising, or both, of the ankle region after a fall.	See a physician. Apply cold compression and elevate to reduce swelling. Rest. When no longer painful to move, begin conditioning the musculature around the sprain to increase stability. Use some form of support such as adhesive taping (not an elastic bandage) to provide extra support in first phases of weight-bearing on the injured ankle.
	Shin splints	Muscle soreness in the lower leg caused by excessive demands on musculature (frequently caused by dancing on concrete or improper landings from jumps, etc.). Common muscles affected are tibialis anterior, tibialis posterior, and peroneal muscles.	Gentle stretching, ice and rest. If pain continues for more than two weeks, consider the possibility of a stress fracture.
	Achilles tendonitis	Pain in Achilles tendon on *pointe*, *plié*, *relevé*, pushoff, and landing. Often accompanied by creaking and crunching in the area.	General treatment for tendonitis (see flexor hallucis longus tendonitis). See physician if condition persists. A consistent pattern of stretching out the Achilles tendon after class and rehearsals is the best prevention of Achilles tendonitis.
	Ankle impingement syndrome (anterior or posterior)	Bony restriction of plantar flexion or dorsiflexion. The sensation of bony contact is different from muscular restriction.	Generally, be content with a restricted range of motion unless the restriction is quite severe, in which case surgery can be considered to remove the obstruction.
	Torn plantaris	Plantaris muscle is most frequently torn when one is making sudden starts, stops, and direction changes. The rupturing of the plantaris is frequently accompanied by a loud snap and immediate pain in the calf.	See a physician. Rest, ice, and elevation are the first treatments. After a period of rest, gentle stretching is appropriate (dorsiflexed ankle with extended knee) to maintain a normal range of motion at the ankle joint.

Knee	Ligamentous tears	Pain, swelling, and sense of instability of the knee joint.	See a physician immediately, preferably an orthopedic surgeon specializing in knees.
	Meniscus tears	Pain, pinching on flexion or extension, a feeling that the knee is "catching."	Immediately following injury, apply ice, elevate, and stay off it. See a physician.
	Inflammation of subpatellar fat pad	Pain underneath the patellar ligament accompanying extreme extension of the knee.	Ice, rest, aspirin. If pain persists, see a physician.
	Bursitis	Localized swelling, pain and inflammation.	Ice, rest, and aspirin are the first line of defense. If pain persists, see a physician.
	Dislocation of patella	Lateral or medial displacement of the patella out of the patella notch of the femur.	See a physician immediately.
	Condromalacia of patella	Erosion of the underneath side of the patella due to misaligned patella. Movement of the knee is usually accompanied by creaking and crunching.	Strengthen the quadriceps muscles, particularly the vasti.
	Strain of popliteus or tearing of popliteal ligament	Caused by rapid forcible extension of the knee. Taping to prevent full extension of the knee may be wise.	Ice, rest, and avoidance of extension of the knee for a few days to facilitate healing.
Hip	Sciatica	Pain in dimple of buttocks and radiating down the leg following the path of the biceps femoris and peroneus longus and brevis, and sometimes involving the lateral muscles of the foot.	Check with a physician to make sure no bone tissue is pressing on the sciatic nerve. Stretch and deep massage of the six deep rotators will give immediate relief, if the pressure on nerve is only muscular.
	Anterior snapping hip or tendonitis in one of the hip flexors (rectusfemoris, sartorius, or iliopsoas)	Localized pain accompanying hip flexion. Creaking or popping may accompany the pain with flexion (anterior snapping hip).	Ice, rest, aspirin. Stretch the hip flexors. When pain subsides, build strength in the hip flexors and continue stretching.
	Lateral snapping hip	Loud clunking snap of the hip (deep) on *grand ronde jambe* and on return from dance "extension."	Stretch and strengthen the abductors of the hip joint.

(continued)

TABLE 18.1 Conditions and Injuries: Symptoms and Care (Continued)

Body Area	Injury or Condition	Symptoms	Care
Hip	Tight hip flexors	See low back pain below and anterior snapping hip above.	
	Hamstring strains	Pain, spasm, or both of the hamstring muscles. Frequently isolated to either medial hamstrings (semitendonosis or semimembranosis) or lateral hamstrings (biceps femoris).	Identify which hamstrings are affected and stretch accordingly. To stretch biceps: flex, adduct, and inwardly rotate. To stretch semis: flex, abduct, and outwardly rotate
Spine (low back)	Spondylolisthesis	Displacement of the fifth lumbar vertebra on the sacrum, frequently accompanied by muscle spasms due to pressure on nerves.	See a physician.
	Sacroiliac condition	Slight movement of the usually immobile sacroiliac joints can cause sharp pain in the area of the sacrum.	See a physician.
	Herniated disk	Unequal pressure between two adjacent vertebrae can cause the intervertebral disk to "pooch out" from its normal placement. When this happens, there may be pressure on a nerve which can cause muscle spasm.	See a physician.
	Low back pain can be a result of a number of different causes, including:		
	Tight hip flexors	Lumbar lordosis, low back pain. Increased pelvic inclination.	Stretch the hip flexors
	Tight latissimus dorsi and quadratus lumborum	Pain is more lateral on the low back.	Stretch the latissimus dorsi and use deep message on the quadratus lumborum.
	Fasciitis	Generalized muscle spasm across the low back.	Deep message is painful but can sometimes reduce the muscle spasm. Moist heat can sometimes relieve a muscle spasm.

Spine (upper back and neck)	Rib "catch"	Spasm or tightness of one or more of the fibers of the deep posterior muscles can pull on a rib and cause a slight displacement of the rib at its articulation with the vertebrae. When this happens, there can be a sharp "catching" pain accompanying deep breathing.	Stretch the deep posterior muscles with mild rotation back and forth. If pain persists, see a physician.
	Pectoralis minor syndrome (stiff neck)	Spasm in levator scapula, upper trapezius, or rhomboids.	Deep massage and stretch of pectoralis minor will give delayed relief (about 2 to 3 hours later) if the pectoralis minor is the cause of the pain. If not, see a physician.
	Spasm in lower or middle trapezius	Pain in midback, at level of lower ribs and below.	Stretch out the trapezius with the water ski stretch (holding onto doorknobs on either side of door and contracting abdominals to press back into the trapezius).
	Tension headaches	Often caused by muscular tension in the muscles of the neck.	Do the neck stretch series in Chapter 19.
Shoulder	Most shoulder injuries to dancers are the direct result of inadequate shoulder conditioning. When demands are placed on the weak musculature, injuries result.		
	Bicipital tendonitis	Pain and tenderness on the anterior of the shoulder right at the bicipital groove.	Ice, rest, aspirin. Gentle stretching of the muscle. When back to normal, condition for strength, muscular endurance and then stretch out.
	Bursitis below anterior deltoid.	Hot spot, about the size of a quarter, just below the spot where the anterior deltoid crosses over the pectoralis major.	Ice, rest, aspirin.

(continued)

TABLE 18.1 **Conditions and Injuries: Symptoms and Care** *(Continued)*

Body Area	Injury or Condition	Symptoms	Care
Shoulder	Dislocation or subluxation of shoulder	Most frequently occurs in a handstand position or bearing a weight above the head, because the lower, posterior segment of the shoulder joint is only supported by muscle (no bony restriction). Musculature must be strong to support weight. Preconditioning prior to strenuous shoulder activities is the best prevention. Severe pain and distortion of the normal shape of the shoulder are symptoms of dislocation.	See a physician immediately and *follow* the instructions for rest and immobilization.
Arm and hand	Dancers seldom complain of injuries to the arm and hand because weight is seldom borne on the upper extremity. However, if the arms are expected to bear the weight of the body, preconditioning is essential.		

TABLE 18.2 Robert Small's procedure for taping feet to alleviate splitting*

Items needed:
1. Dr. Scholl's callus reducer with stainless steel head
2. Johnson & Johnson *Elasticon* stretch elastic surgical tape
3. Foot cream with lanolin
4. Scissors
5. A & D ointment or equivalent

Step 1. Soak feet while in bath or shower. At end of bath or shower, sit comfortably in tub or on side. Leave some water in tub to keep soaking feet and to rinse out reducer.
Step 2. Clip away all flaps of skin from splits with surgical or sharp scissors.
Step 3. With callus reducer, gently scrape callused areas of foot.
Caution: Stay away from uncallused skin, as callus reducer will scratch tender areas. Use criss-cross pattern and circular motion to evenly scrape down calluses. In case of split, try to scrape and even out all areas. Scrape along line of split, not across, to prevent additional tissue splitting.
Caution: If you have not been using a callus reducer regularly, work on thick calluses for several sessions. Do not try to scrape all callus away until you find optimum amount of callus you need for protection of your feet.
Step 4. Dry feet completely with towel around all toes and then let air dry for several minutes.
Step 5. Cut circle of tape that will cover problem area by about one-fourth inch around all edges.
Caution: Remove all corners from tape patches, or they will catch and the tape will roll. Tape should be cut so that stretch will go across foot to allow for expansion. Across splits to allow for expansion.
Step 6. Place tape patch on dry callus and press down along edge of tape with fingernail to ensure adhesion.
Step 7. Put moisturizing cream on other parts of feet to keep skin moist and pliable. Place A & D ointment directly under toes to keep that skin pliable.
Step 8. If taping in morning, put on socks so heat of foot and compression will allow patches to adhere. Take socks off with care so as not to pull patches off if tape sticks slightly to them.

Special applications: Tape patches can be put on any part of foot.
1. Floor burns can be covered by this method. However, *do not* use callus reducer on top of foot. Wash and dry the area thoroughly, put a bit of A & D ointment on burn, place a piece of tissue or Kleenex on floor burn. Then put a patch over area with one-fourth inch of clearance on all sides.
2. If tape comes off during the day, wipe off all excess dirt and tape. Wash foot, and place another patch on area. Rub the patch in some dust to set it or put on a pair of socks for a few minutes.
3. Cracks under toes. Cut a strip of tape one-half inch wide and long enough to wrap fully around the toe. Along one edge, cut several short notches into the tape.

If split is still raw, put a bit of ointment in the crack. Apply the tape with the notches toward the back of the foot to allow for stretch. One-half of the tape should be on the toe, and the other half on the soft part of the foot. Split should be completely covered and tape replaced almost every day.
To remove tape patches, carefully peel away along line of split, not across it. There will be some excess adhesive that can be removed by rubbing with moisturizing cream and tissue. Do not use the callus remover to take off the excess adhesive, as it will clog the reducer.
Replace patches when needed, usually every two days.
Once you have your calluses reduced, light scraping every other day or so should maintain proper depth of callus.
If you have no splits, but are susceptible to the condition, try to anticipate when you might be on a sticky floor and put tape patches over problem areas.
In the winter particularly, put cream on feet in morning and night to keep the skin elastic.
Sounds like a lot of time and work, but if you get into a plan of treatment, it takes very little time and will cut down a good percentage of your splits.

---

*I was remiss in the first edition, in that I made no reference to Robert Small other than to include his taping procedure. Robert is Artistic Director of The Small Dance Company and teaches modern dance in guest residencies across the country.

TABLE 18.3 Procedures for self-diagnosis of everyday aches and pains

I. Analysis of Symptoms
    A. *Where does it hurt?* Location
        1. What muscles are in the area?
        2. What other structures are in that area (bones, ligaments, fascia, cartilage, etc.)?
        3. List the possible sources of pain, based on location.
    B. *How does it hurt?* Nature of pain
        1. Is the pain localized or general?
        2. Is the pain sharp and shooting or diffuse and spread out?
        3. If it is a muscle pain, is it a "contraction pain" or a "stretching pain"?
        4. Is there any "point tenderness?" Where? (This is indicative of a possible bone fracture, a flareup of bursitis, or some other point-specific condition.)
        5. Is there any radiating pain? From where to where? This may indicate that something (muscle, bone, or other body tissues) is pressing on a nerve, which is called an *impingement syndrome.*
    C. *When does it hurt?* Function
        1. What joint position or action causes or intensifies the pain?
        2. What muscles are involved in that position or action?
        3. What changes in the daily routine immediately preceded the onset of the pain?

II. Correction
    A. *Do you think it is a muscular problem?*
        1. What muscles?
        2. What muscles are antagonistic to the hurting muscles?
        3. Try gentle stretching and/or massage of muscles listed in (1) and (2).
            a. Does gentle stretching cause an increase in the pain? Does it feel like "good pain?"
            b. If it does feel like good pain, proceed with slightly more intense stretches. Let your body tell you how much is enough.
            c. Repeat steps a and b, using gentle massage, increasing the pressure if it "feels right."
            d. If your body tells you "no!" see a physician.
    B. *If it seems to be a bone, ligament, or nerve problem, see a physician.*

III. Tracking down the cause and planning rehabilitation
    A. *Why did it happen?*
        1. Overuse—the muscles were not strong or elastic enough to meet the demands placed on them.
        2. Misuse—there is a pattern of misalignment and/or muscular inefficiency.
        3. Undue situational or environmental stress—such as fatigue, bad floors, demanding classes or rehearsals
    B. *Analysis of relative strength, endurance, and elasticity of agonist and antagonist* to identify imbalances which might contribute to the problem.
    C. *Design a rehabilitation program based on the findings in A and B.*
        1. Build muscular capacity through specific exercises based on the analysis above. Strengthen weak muscles; stretch tight muscles; and increase endurance for muscles that cannot continue to contract over time.
        2. Review neuromuscular patterns and, if necessary, establish new, more efficient patterns that increase the use of the prime movers.
        3. Review alignment patterns and, if necessary, establish new, better alignment habits to avoid misuse and stress.
        4. *In rehabilitation, it is essential to condition beyond the capacity level that was present when the injury occurred before returning to activity.*

that the dancer develops a standard set of exercises to alleviate them. However, new "naggers" (as we call them in class) seem to crop up, and then new corrective procedures must be developed. Table 18.3 is a handout that I developed for my students to use once they were familiar with the material in the preceding sections of the book. I include it here in the hope that it will help other dancers identify the specific nature of everyday aches and pains so that major problems might be avoided.

In addition to dealing with everyday aches and pains that appear periodically, it is wise to review patterns of activity that contribute to those problems. Analysis of habitual patterns that contribute to injuries or chronic conditions can be as simple and informal as remembering overexertion on the day before, or as complex and systematic as the assessment of alignment and muscular imbalances presented in Chapter 13. However formal or informal the analysis is, the secret to prevention is *awareness*, and *awareness comes through knowledgeable observation.*

Martha Eddy (1995) has written an article on the use of somatic approaches (Bartenieff Fundamentals, Laban Movement Analysis, Body-Mind Centering, and Somatic Movement Therapy) for injury assessment and intervention. The article calls for skilled observation by teachers of dance, and concludes by stating, "Increasing teachers' observational skills could both drive the curriculum and contribute to the reduction of unsafe practices" (Eddy, 1995, p. 7).[3]

There are many approaches to the prevention of injuries, but perhaps the most crucial skills and attitudes for the individual dancer are *common sense, respect for the body,* and the *ability to listen to messages the body transmits.* One of the messages is pain. Pain is an *ally,* not an enemy, in the process of treating and preventing injury. Little nagging pains are the first signs. It is important to listen for those naggers and care for them immediately so that they don't mushroom into major problems. The information in this book can be used to identify and treat minor aches and pains. Doing so may extend your longevity as a dancer. You have made a major investment in your body: an investment of time, energy, and even money. Treat it with care and respect so that it will continue to serve you well into your advanced years.

---

3. I had hoped to include this article in its entirety, but it was not in its final form when the manuscript for the second edition was submitted. The article is well worth reading.

CHAPTER 19

Conditioning for Dancers

The basic principles of conditioning for dance are not much different from the basic principles of conditioning for athletics. However, the specific demands of dance distinguish physical conditioning for dance, somewhat, from other exercise programs. In any conditioning program, there are four fundamental objectives, but in dance there are three additional, specialized areas. The "big four" of conditioning are strength, flexibility, muscular endurance, and cardiorespiratory endurance. The three additional categories of conditioning for dance are conditioning for alignment, neuromuscular coordination, and relaxation. *Rehabilitative conditioning*, following an injury, utilizes these objectives differently depending on the loss of condition caused by the injury. *Corrective* or *preventive conditioning* involves analysis of capacities and limitations and remediation before the injury occurs.

Technique classes vary dramatically with respect to the relative emphasis placed on the different categories of conditioning, but all technique classes focus intensively on neuromuscular coordination, as they should. After all, technique is the craft of dance performance and, as such, is a foundation for the art of dance. Technique classes are normally an hour and a half in length, and that period of time simply does not allow for meeting all of the conditioning needs of dancers. The artistic expectations in a technique class often preempt time needed for building strength and muscular endurance. The usual structure of a technique class (warm-up, floor work, center floor, and across-the-floor work), like the stop-and-go nature of the class itself, prevents effective conditioning for cardiorespiratory endurance. Technique classes may focus quite intensively on exercises for muscular endurance or flexibility, but this varies from teacher to teacher. It becomes quite clear that for efficient and optimal development of dance skills, conditioning work above and beyond daily technique classes is needed.

This chapter has three purposes. The first is to outline the most effective ways of increasing capacity in each of the four major categories of conditioning. It is hoped that this information will be applied by technique teachers to increase the efficiency of conditioning in their classes.

The second purpose is to outline a basic program of conditioning for dance to be used outside of the technique class. The program is based on a study that was the foundation of an article in *Dance Research Journal* (Fitt,

1981–1982). The study showed a significant improvement in strength, range of motion, and cardiorespiratory endurance for experimental subjects in twenty-two out of twenty-seven tests. The control group showed significant improvement in only three of the twenty-seven tests. All of the experimental and control subjects were simultaneously taking technique class. The changes for the experimental group were observable and positive as reported by the technique teachers. These findings clearly call for conditioning for dancers beyond the conditioning received in technique class. The basic program is designed to meet the critical needs of dancers. Any conditioning program must take into account the relative age and fitness of the target population. This particular program is designed for healthy, relatively fit, adult or young adult dancers. Modification of the program may be appropriate for different age and fitness groups.

The third purpose of this chapter is to outline mini-programs for specific problems that often occur in dance. The mini-programs are designed to correct misalignments and muscular imbalances and to provide the specialized strengths required in dance.

General Principles of Conditioning

Before proceeding to the discussion of the techniques for increasing strength, flexibility, muscular endurance, and cardiorespiratory endurance, five general principles of conditioning must be presented.

Warm Up and Cool Down

The first principle involves *warming up* and *cooling down*. At the beginning of any exercise bout it is important to prepare the body for the stress to come. That preparation is normally called a *warm-up*. Warm-ups vary from individual to individual. The mesomorph, for example, is often seen jumping or jogging around the studio to warm up; the ectomorph is often seen stretching; the endomorph is often seen doing slow, rhythmical repetitions. Whether these apparently preferred warm-up techniques are the most effective in preparing the dancer for exercise is sometimes questionable. The last thing an ectomorph needs is stretching. A mesomorph really needs the stretching far more than the big-muscle warm-up of jogging or jumping. Yet the selection of warm-up activities seems to be based primarily on what "feels good."

There is one camp of exercise physiologists who maintain that warm-up is primarily psychological; it works if the mover thinks it works. Other authorities note a need for literal warm-up: raising the temperature of active body parts. But although the value of warm-up is questioned by some authorities, it seems simply foolish to begin an exercise bout without gradually preparing the body for the demands to come.

Cool-down is as important as warm-up, and possibly far more important. At the end of an exercise bout it is important to keep moving, while gradually decreasing the intensity of the exercise (slowing down, decreasing resistance, etc.) to prevent the blood from pooling in the active areas. When the blood pools (owing to cessation of muscular contraction, which provides a pumping action in the active areas) the likelihood of delayed muscle soreness can increase and immediate muscle spasms may result. In addition to a gradual slowdown after an exercise bout, the cool-down process should include "stretching out" of the muscles which were intensively active in the preceding exercises. Dancers who have studied dance kinesiology are encouraged to "custom design" the cool-down and stretching out specifically to the active muscle groups. Careful cool-down can do much to prevent muscle soreness and chronic conditions.

Use It or Lose It

The second principle is *use it or lose it*. The human body responds to stress by a buildup of capacity. It responds to inactivity with a loss of capacity. Anyone who has had a cast removed knows the horrifying atrophy (loss of muscle mass) that results from inactivity. Likewise, a dancer who takes a vacation from dance must rebuild the system when he or she returns. How fast capacity is lost does seem to vary, and that may be related to body type or movement behavior. The mesomorph loses flexibility faster than the ectomorph, but the ectomorph loses strength and endurance faster than the mesomorph. Each dancer should develop a "survival" conditioning program for those periods when he or she is not dancing regularly, to prevent "losing it" during layoffs.

Develop Progressive Overload

The third principle has to do with *progressive overload*. To continue to increase the capacity of the human body, the stress level must continually be increased. This progressive overload means that for strength one must continue to increase the resistance; for muscular endurance, the repetitions must be increased; for flexibility, the range of the exercise must be increased; and for cardiorespiratory endurance, the time or the target heart rate must be raised. Of course, the continual cycle of increasing stress, building capacity, and increasing stress again must stop somewhere. The ultimate acceptable level of conditioning must be set by the dancer after taking into account the demands on his or her physical system.

Work in Mechanically Efficient Positions

The fourth principle involves *mechanically efficient positions*. Conditioning can actually cause problems if the positioning for the exercises is habitually misaligned. Joint stress may result in degenerative arthritis, stress fractures, or other symptoms. It is essential that the dancer who participates in a conditioning program take exceptional care to ensure proper alignment throughout the program. It is not unusual for alignment to deteriorate under the influence of fatigue. The dancer should persistently guard against the misalignments that come with fatigue. It is better to cut the exercise program short than to continue in a misaligned position.

Sequence the Exercises Effectively

Of all of the principles of conditioning, the most frequently overlooked is the fifth, *effective sequencing*. There are effective ways to sequence an exercise set. There are also ineffective techniques which can block or delay optimal conditioning. Sequencing is in turn based on five "sub-principles," which are used consistently in the conditioning program included later in this chapter. First, *start gently and gradually build to more vigorous activity*. This principle may be achieved by doing an all-over warm-up at the beginning of the set, or by approaching each muscle group with a gentle "wake up" exercise before asking the maximum of that muscle group. Second, *after an exercise that really stresses a muscle group, take time to undo the bad effects or note the good effects*. For example, after a maximal contraction for strength building, do an exercise that goes in the opposite direction in order to facilitate stretching out. After a heavy-duty stretch, take some time to reassemble. Often a major stretch will leave the dancer slightly disoriented at the joint involved. Taking a moment to recover is time well spent. It also offers the dancer time to process new information about joint positions and to assess the effects of the stretch. Third, *before doing a major stretch, "set up" the stretch by doing a maximal contraction of the opposite muscle group* (if muscle mass is equal) to block the stretch reflex (reciprocal inhibition). Fourth, *use the information on possible joint actions and specific muscle actions to pinpoint the exact muscle or muscles that need to be strengthened or stretched*. For example, to strengthen the rectus femoris (flexor of the hip), it is best to flex the hip with neutral rotation and neutral ab/adduction, and remember to extend the knee. Or, in stretching the hamstrings, either stretch in a parallel, neutral ab/adducted position, or be sure to stretch both the medial and the lateral hamstrings. (Medial: by abducting, flexing, and outwardly rotating the hip and extending the knee. Lateral: by adducting, flexing, and inwardly rotating the hip and extending the knee.) Finally, *the most important principle of sequencing is to listen to your body*. When your body is crying for a particular action, it is sheer foolishness to ignore it. Don't be afraid to follow the directions given by your body, even if that means changing the sequence. It has long been my contention that kinesthetically wise movers do this automatically. Our internal signals are the most valid; we must listen to them.

Fundamental Areas of Conditioning

To repeat, the four fundamental areas on objectives of conditioning are (1) strength, (2) flexibility, (3) muscular endurance, and (4) cardiorespiratory endurance.

Strength

Strength is usually defined as the ability to exert tension against resistance. Strength is primarily a neurological phenomenon, requiring the firing of more motor units which contribute to the performance of a given motor task.

Strength is relatively easy to increase, if one follows some fundamental guidelines. *To build strength, one uses relatively few repetitions (5 to 10) and maximal resistance.* Moving *through the range of motion* against resistance (isotonic) is thought to be more effective than *static contractions* against resistance (isometric) because strength builds "specifically." When one performs a strength exercise in a single position, strength increases, but almost exclusively for that position and not for other positions. To build strength in the flexors and outward rotators of the hip one must be in a position of flexion and outward rotation during the exercise. For this reason most of the strength exercises in the basic program require movement through the full range of motion to ensure the buildup of strength at all joint angles. In addition, most of the strength exercises in the basic program involve slow movement through the range of motion. It is thought that the momentum created by fast repetitions allows the dancer to skip over the weak spots in the range of motion. Moving slowly allows for the identification of particularly weak areas in the range of motion, and focusing on them in the exercise allows the dancer to equalize strength through the full range of motion. However, strength conditioning is also specific to velocity of contraction. Therefore, it is recommended that once a certain level of strength has been built through the full range of motion by slow contractions, faster contractions should then be added.

Flexibility

Achieving extreme flexibility is a fetish of the dancer. It would seem that even the most elastic of dancers wishes to increase his or her range of motion even further. While flexibility and muscular elasticity have certain advantages for the dancer, there can be a point of diminishing returns. This is particularly true if the dancer does not pay equal attention to building strength to facilitate management of the increased flexibility. As mobility increases, stability decreases and vice versa. The dancer needs both stability and mobility. Consequently, to increase mobility without increasing strength to control that mobility is counterproductive. Given the need for *both* flexibility and strength, there are some basic guidelines for increasing mobility.

Increasing mobility is really a matter of increasing muscular elasticity. A dancer who wants to stretch the ligaments is unwise. The ligaments provide joint stability, which is a prerequisite for efficient action. The elongation of ligaments decreases joint stability, increases the likelihood of injury, and thus is undesirable. However, when a joint action is restricted, stretching the musculotendinous units can often increase range of motion without jeopardizing joint stability. The ultimate limit to flexibility is either the ligamentous restriction or the bony restriction. When one begins an intensive program to increase range of motion at a given joint, one must take into account the natural restrictions for that joint, and all individual differences that might contribute to a limited range of motion. To work beyond one's bony and ligamentous limitations is foolhardy. Yet a wisely designed program to increase muscular elasticity can increase range of motion. The assumption that all dancers should be able to achieve the same range of motion is simply false. Differences in body type may require different amounts of time for each stretch to achieve the elasticity desired. It is thought that mesomorphs may need to increase the time spent in a stretch to at least 1 minute, while ectomorphs and endomorphs may be able to achieve the desired results with stretches that last for only 15 to 30 seconds.

The enemy of the dancer trying to increase muscular elasticity is the *stretch reflex,* a protective reflex that results in contraction of a muscle immediately following the stretch of that muscle. Consequently, the muscle doesn't get a chance to stretch fully. There are a number of techniques for reducing the effect of the stretch reflex that can be used to increase muscular elasticity.

While the stretch reflex operates on the spinal level, there is also constant information being sent to the higher centers regarding the status of the musculature. The cerebral cortex has the ability to override the stretch reflex in slow action. Conscious control is required to remain in a stretch position without succumbing to the stretch reflex.

The *long sustained stretch* is the best example of the cerebral cortex overriding the stretch reflex. In a long sustained stretch, the individual assumes a position in which gravity increases the stretch and then consciously blocks the stretch reflex, which would otherwise be automatic. This position is maintained for at least 30 seconds, constantly increasing the stretch with each exhalation. In the long sustained stretch, slight shifts in position can reveal the specific muscle fibers that need extra stretching. These shifts in position are called "nudging around." This technique works the stretch to its maximum.

Reciprocal inhibition is another way to temporarily reduce the stretch reflex. Reciprocal inhibition is another reflexive action to protect the body, in which a maximal contraction of a given muscle will temporarily block the stretch reflex of the opposite muscle, providing the two muscles (or groups) are of approximately equal muscle mass. The steps for designing a reciprocal setup for a stretch are given in Table 19.1. Number six has been included because the most common error in designing a reciprocal is to maximally contract and then try to stretch the same muscle. The residual contraction that follows a maximal contraction of a muscle means that the person is then trying to stretch a muscle that is in a state of contraction.

The optimal stretch reduces muscular contraction (the connection between the actin and myosin in the sarcomere of the myofibril) to allow a full stretch of the sarcolemma. Any contraction of the muscle will reduce the effectiveness of the stretch and may actually produce microscopic

TABLE 19.1   Designing a Reciprocal Stretch

1. Determine which muscle is to be stretched (the target muscle).
2. Identify the joint action of that muscle.
3. Reverse the actions and identify which muscle performs those exact antagonistic actions (the opposite muscle).
4. Maximally contract the opposite muscle, in the midrange of motion, against resistance, for approximately 10 to 20 seconds.
5. Follow the maximal contraction immediately with a long sustained stretch of the target muscle for at least 30 seconds.
6. Remember, the maximal contraction and the stretch both go in the *same direction.*

---

tearing of the musculature. For this reason, if the objective is increased elasticity, *bouncing stretches are ineffective and produce muscle soreness.* In the hard-driving, bouncing stretch so common in dance classes a few years ago, the muscle is stretched, then contracted (because of the stretch reflex), and then vigorously stretched again. The results of bouncing stretches are increased muscle soreness and far less muscular elasticity than is achieved with the long sustained stretch or reciprocal stretches. However, a distinction must be made between bouncing stretches and pulsing stretches. The primary distinctions are the amount of force used and the time factor. A bouncing stretch uses strong force and fast time, pounding into the muscle to be stretched. A pulsing stretch uses weak force and medium-slow speed, with a regular repetitive rhythm. A pulsing stretch is far more gentle than a bouncing stretch, and the regular, repetitive rhythm has a tendency to fatigue the gamma system, which is the controlling system for the stretch reflex. Thus, pulsing stretches may be another effective way to increase muscular elasticity, *if one takes care to reduce the force to a minimum.*

Generally speaking, the reciprocal stretch is the most effective way to stretch, if the target muscle and the opposite muscle are of approximately equal muscle mass. If not, as in the case of the gastrocnemius and soleus (the muscle mass of the dorsiflexors of the ankle is nowhere near the mass of the plantar flexors), the long sustained stretch is the most effective technique. A positive by-product of the reciprocal technique of stretching is the strength gained in the opposite muscle as a result of the maximal contraction. For these reasons, the reciprocal techniques of increasing muscular elasticity are highly recommended.

Muscular Endurance

Muscular endurance can be defined as the ability of a muscle to continue to contract over a period of time. *Conditioning for muscular endurance requires many repetitions with relatively light resistance.* Stating the principle for building muscular endurance is an easy matter, yet actually building muscular endurance requires Herculean self-discipline because the number of repetitions required makes endurance conditioning boring. However, if one stays with the conditioning program, the muscular endurance exercises eventually can become a meditation exercise of sorts, and the quietude of repeating an exercise over and over can become quite pleasing. In the initial phases of muscular endurance training it is wise to build some kind of interest, or do the exercises with a friend to ward off the initial boredom. The question asked more than any other involves the number of repetitions: How many is enough? The answer is that listening to the body can provide the key. When a muscle has been contracted over a period of time, it begins to produce a burning sensation. Five repetitions past the onset of the "burnies" is an effective rule of thumb for increasing muscular endurance.

Cardiorespiratory Endurance

Cardiorespiratory endurance is the ability to continue aerobic activity over a period of time. As in conditioning for muscular endurance, there are many repetitions, boredom is a factor, and self discipline is essential.

There are special guidelines for improving cardiorespiratory endurance which involve some preliminary calculations. Before beginning the actual exercise program, it is necessary to calculate "target heart rate." *In cardiorespiratory conditioning, exercise that maintains the target heart rate is continued for at least fifteen minutes.* There are a number of techniques for calculating target heart rate, which vary in complexity. The simplest is to subtract one's age from 220 and take 60 percent of that figure as the target heart rate. If one is in good-to-excellent condition, 60 percent or slightly higher is appropriate. If one is in terrible condition, a lower percentage is safer (DeRenne, 1984, p. 2). A healthy heart is essential to cardiorespiratory conditioning. If there is any question about the health of one's heart, a stress EKG is warranted. Exercise should then be monitored by a physician. A more complicated formula for the calculation of target heart rate is included in Table 19.2. Another formula is included in Chapter 14.

Aerobic activity maintains the target heart rate for approximately 20 to 30 minutes and will build cardiorespiratory endurance. Activities which, by their very nature, are aerobic include fast walking, jogging, running, biking, swimming, and cross-country skiing. The critical feature of aerobic activity is continuous activity. Certain aerobic activities are more appropriate for dancers than others. For example, if a dancer has alignment problems of the leg (knock-knees, pronated feet, or others), running is less advisable than walking, biking, or swimming. Jogging on a mini-trampoline causes less stress on the joints than running on hard surfaces. Swimming is an excellent aerobic activity, but the muscle tone developed by

TABLE 19.2 Calculation of the Target Heart Rate

Maximum heart rate = 220 − age
Heart rate reserve = maximum heart rate − resting heart rate
Resting heart rate = heart rate per minute, taken before rising after a night's sleep
Training heart rate (target heart rate) = resting heart rate + 60 to 75 percent of heart rate
   reserve, depending on relative condition

working out in a relatively lower gravitational situation may be different from that developed in the dance studio. An exercise bike or a regular bike will provide an aerobic workout, but care should be taken to maintain proper foot and leg alignment or chronic conditions can be aggravated.

Whether *aerobic dance* can be considered dance depends on one's definition of *dance*. Characteristically, aerobic dance classes are intended to incorporate fun and camaraderie into maintenance of cardiorespiratory fitness. The usual pattern includes learning a "routine," or following the instructor through a series of vigorous exercises for the duration of the class. These activities are most frequently accompanied by recordings of popular music. The variety of exercises offered and the music make these classes more satisfying to some people than repetitive exercise like jogging or swimming. Continuous activity for approximately an hour certainly does increase cardiorespiratory fitness; however, harmful results may come from improper training. It is not unusual to find participants plunged into intense activity with little or no introduction to minimal precautions. Nor is it unusual to find untrained, though well-meaning, individuals teaching the classes. Consequently, there should be a real concern for the health and safety of participants in aerobic dance.

One of the major problems is that the type of injury which can result from improper training in aerobic dance classes does not always appear immediately. Insidious injuries often surface some time later.

There are some potential benefits from aerobic dance, but care must be taken in selecting a class. Because there is no certification for teachers of aerobic dance, the buyer must beware. Answering four simple questions can help assess the quality of the class.

1. Is an adequate warm-up given?
2. Does the instructor check for proper alignment and make individual corrections?
3. Does the instructor exhibit a sincere concern for the students' well-being?
4. Is a cool-down period included at the end of class?

These four questions can assist the consumer who is searching for a safe aerobic dance class. The dancer with a background in dance kinesiology will certainly be able to assess the safety and soundness of any class with more sophistication than these questions represent. The questions represent the minimum standards of safety.

Interrelationship Among Types of Conditioning

Each of these four types or areas of conditioning is vital to the dancer—and, as might be expected, there is a relationship among strength, flexibility, muscular endurance, and cardiorespiratory endurance.

Strength and muscular endurance are related in a number of ways. If a muscle is strong, it will take fewer motor units to perform a given task. Therefore, the muscle can continue activity longer; thus strength has a positive effect on muscular endurance. In the process of conditioning for muscular endurance, the fatigue level rises and the last few repetitions can actually be "maximal" in nature. Thus, muscular endurance training can serve to build strength, but not in the most efficient way.

The relationship between strength and flexibility is one of facilitation. When the muscles are elastic and stretched out, it takes less strength to perform a given action because one is not contracting against the inelasticity of the opposing musculature. Likewise, and for the same reason, muscular endurance is increased with an increase in flexibility. Another facilitative relationship between strength and flexibility shows up when one does a reciprocal stretch. If the opposite muscle is strong, it seems easier to activate the reciprocal inhibition mechanism.

Understanding the relationship between cardiorespiratory endurance training and other categories of conditioning requires a review of changes that occur with increased aerobic capacity. As aerobic capacity increases, general metabolism rises, muscle metabolism is enhanced, hemoglobin rises, buffers in the bloodstream increase, venous return is improved, stroke volume is improved, and the blood bed becomes more able to adapt readily to varying demands. Each of these results of cardiorespiratory conditioning will have a direct positive effect on muscular endurance, and an indirect effect on strength and flexibility.

This discussion has been very brief. For fuller explanations, you are directed to the literature related to exercise physiology.

Myths of Dance Conditioning

It is only within the last thirty to forty years that dancers have systematically studied the science of human motion. Prior to that, tradition was the sole director of dance training. Therefore, it is not surprising to find myths thriving in dance studios where teachers have not been trained in the science of human motion. It is hoped that this book will help to reduce the propagation of those myths. Table 19.3 lists both general and specific myths of dance conditioning.

The Basic Exercise Program

The basic exercise program includes a set of exercises that can be done every day, and three alternative plans that focus on different areas of the body.[1] The core program is a segment of the conditioning program. It focuses on torso strength and mobility. The torso is critical for dancers be-

---

1. This exercise program was designed to build the strengths needed by dancers, while maintaining and increasing mobility. It is *not* designed for the general public because some of the exercises require specialized capacities common in dance. Moreover, if any of the exercises causes undue stress, even the dancer should approach that exercise with caution or possibly exclude it.

TABLE 19.3   Myths of Dance Conditioning

General myths
   All dancers have the same potential.
   More is always better.
   Pain is good.
   All bodies need the same kind of warm-up.
Myths about strength
   Building strength always builds excessive bulk.
   Dancers should never use weights.
   If dancers build strength, they lose mobility.
   A tight muscle is a strong muscle.
   All dancers have the same potential for strength.
Myths about flexibility
   A dancer can never be too flexible.
   Increasing range of motion in one direction of joint action reduces range of motion in
     the opposite direction.
   All dancers have the same potential for flexibility.
Myths about muscular endurance
   Endurance equals strength.
   All dancers have the same potential for muscular endurance.
Myths about cardiorespiratory endurance
   Technique class and rehearsals are adequate to build cardiorespiratory endurance.
   Dancers, as a group, are in great shape.
   All dancers have the same potential for cardiovascular endurance.

TABLE 19.4   The Core Exercise Program and Three Alternative Plans

Primary conditioning objective (in parentheses) follows each exercise
Core Program
  1. Knee-overs (warm up abdominals)
  2. Abdominal curls (strengthen abdominals)
  3. Arches (strengthen extensors of the spine)
  4. Curl (stretch out extensors of the spine)
  5. Abdominal curls (reciprocal "set-up" for the plow)
  6. Plow (stretch hamstrings and spine extensors)
  7. Spine assembler (recovery and "reassembling" after major stretch)
  8. Supine leg swings (warm-up for ab/adductors of the hip and lateral flexors of the
     spine)
  9. Side leg lifts and side torso lifts (strengthen ab/adductors of the hip and lateral
     flexors of the spine)
 10. Stretch out: use any combination of the following
     a. C-curve stretch (stretch lateral flexors of torso and abductors of hip)
     b. Lunge stretch (stretch abductors of the hip)
     c. Leg-over stretch (multipurpose stretch—hips, torso, shoulder)
     d. Yoga sit stretch (stretch outward rotators of hip)
     e. Latissimus stretch (stretch of latissimus dorsi, quadratus lumborum, and lateral
       flexors of torso)

First alternative plan: For legs, feet, and cardiorespiratory fitness
11. Heel presses (strengthen quadriceps and hip flexors)
12. Toe gripper (strengthen intrinsic muscles of the foot)
13. Seated leg lifts (strengthen hip flexors—both parallel and outward rotated)
14. TV stretch (stretch hip flexors and quadriceps)
15. Ankle/tarsus series (strengthen ankle/tarsus muscles)
16. Ankle circles (stretch ankle/tarsus muscles)
17. Shin-splint stretch (stretch dorsiflexors of ankle)
18. Standing foot wobble (kinesthetic centering on feet)
19. One-legged demi-pliés (strengthen all antigravity muscles of leg and hip)
20. Slow prances (utilize new alignment in motion)
21. Wind sprints/walk it out (cardiorespiratory endurance and cool-down)
22. Stretch gastrocnemius and soleus (stretch plantar flexors of ankle)
23. Standing reciprocal stretch for hamstrings (stretch hamstrings)
24. Stork stretch (stretch hip flexors)
25. Wallpaper stretch/finish and reassemble (stretch hamstrings and spine extensors and take time for recovery)

Second alternative plan: For arms, shoulders, and neck
26. Seated reciprocal stretch for hamstrings (stretch hamstrings)
27. Iliopsoas isolator (isolate and strengthen iliopsoas)
28. Seated arm circles (strengthen shoulder muscles and torso stabilizers)
29   Shoulder sequence (strengthen shoulder muscles and torso stabilizers)
30. Stretching curl (stretch shoulder muscles)
31. Wing stretch (stretch shoulder muscles)
32. Mad cat (use strength and mobility in motion)
33. Scapula push-ups (strengthen abductors of scapula)
34. Parallel bar press (strengthen depressors of scapula)
35. Flagman presses (strengthen adductors of scapula and horizontal extensors and outward rotators of shoulder)
36. Arm-over stretch (stretch shoulder and scapula muscles)
37. Shoulder flop (relax shoulder and scapula muscles)
38. Neck stretches and neck circles (stretch neck muscles)
39. Reciprocals for pectoralis major (stretch pectoralis major—strengthen antagonists)
40. Doorjamb hang and deep massage for pectoralis minor (stretch pectoralis minor)
41. Deep massage for the pectoralis minor (release tension in pectoralis minor)

Third alternative plan: For hips
42. Supine leg lifts (strengthen hip flexors and outward rotators that flex)
43. Prone leg lifts (strengthen hip extensors and outward rotators that extend)
44. Lying hip flexor stretch (stretch hip flexors)
45. Supine hamstring stretch (stretch hamstrings)
46. Seated frog press and stretch of inward rotators (stretch inward rotators that also extend and strengthen outward rotators)
47. Lying knee press and stretch of outward rotators (stretch outward rotators)
48. Lying frog press and stretch of inward rotators (strengthen outward rotators that also extend and stretch inward rotators that also flex)
49. Yoga sit stretch (stretch outward rotators that also extend)
50. Hip greaser (use new mobility in motion)
51. Hip flop (relax hip muscles)
52. Pyramidalis isolator (reinforce use of pyramidalis before standing)

cause each movement of the limbs requires stabilization of the torso. Moreover, many dance combinations require the initiation to come from the center of the body, and thus the "center" must be strong. The three alternative plans, each of which is designed to *follow* the core program, focus on other critical needs of the dancer. The first alternative plan focuses on legs, feet, and cardiorespiratory endurance (Figs. 19.11–19.25); the second focuses on arms, shoulders, neck, and upper back (Figs. 19.26–19.41); and the third focuses on hips (Figs. 19.42–19.52). Table 19.4 lists the exercises; Table 19.5 defines the positions used in the exercise program. Following the tables are the exercise descriptions, with illustrations.

TABLE 19.5   Description of Positions

1. *Hook lying position.* Lying on the back with the knees bent and the feet on the floor aligned with the hip joint.
2. *Prone position.* Lying on the stomach.
3. *Supine position.* Lying on the back.
4. *Side lying position.* Lying on the side with the torso straight and the hip extended.
5. *Frog sit position.* Sitting with the soles of the feet together and the weight up on the sit bones.
6. *Seated second position.* Sitting with the weight up on the sit bones, the torso vertical, and the legs spread as far to the sides as possible (abducted and outward-rotated), with knees extended.
7. *Long sit position.* Sitting with the legs extended out in front (parallel) and the weight up on the sit bones.
8. *Tailor sit position.* Sitting with the legs crossed.
9. *Push-up position.* With the weight supported on the hands and feet (shoulders directly above hands), and the torso maintained in a straight position.
10. *Lunge position.* With one foot in front and one behind, in parallel, the weight is forward and the front leg is bent at the knee and the back leg is straight.
11. *Lying frog position.* Lying on the back with the soles of the feet together and the knees flexed and dropped out to the side. The lower back should not be hyperextended.

Exercise Descriptions

The Core Program

FIGURE 19.1.   Knee-overs.
BEGINNING IN HOOK LYING POSITION, DROP THE KNEES TO THE RIGHT. USE ABDOMINAL CONTRACTION TO INITIATE BRINGING THE KNEES BACK UP TO VERTICAL. REPEAT TO LEFT. REPEAT SEQUENCE ABOUT 8 TO 10 TIMES, GRADUALLY INCREASING TEMPO. AS STRENGTH INCREASES, DRAW THE BENT KNEES TOWARD THE CHEST AND DO THE SEQUENCE WITH THE FEET OFF THE FLOOR.

FIGURE 19.2.   Abdominal curl.
IN HOOK LYING POSITION, WITH THE ARMS *AT THE SIDES,* SLOWLY CURL UP TO A POSITION JUST SHORT OF A VERTICAL SITTING POSITION OR JUST BEFORE FLEXION OF THE HIPS BEGINS. SLOWLY CURL DOWN TO A POSITION JUST SHORT OF CONTACTING THE FLOOR. REPEAT 2 OR 3 TIMES, THEN ADD ROTATION TO THE CURL-UP, STARTING THE ROTATION AS EARLY IN THE CURL-UP AS POSSIBLE AND PROLONGING IT AS LONG AS POSSIBLE IN THE CURL-DOWN. DO ROTATING CURL TO RIGHT AND LEFT 2 OR 3 TIMES TO EACH SIDE. AS STRENGTH INCREASES, INCREASE REPETITIONS; MOVE HANDS TO SHOULDERS; THEN BEHIND THE NECK.

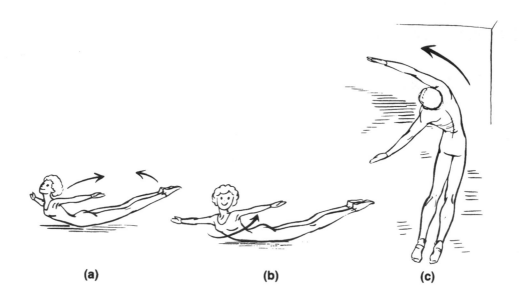

FIGURE 19.3.   Arches.
(A) BEGINNING IN A PRONE POSITION WITH THE ARMS OUT TO THE SIDES, LIFT THE HEAD, ARMS, TORSO, AND LEGS OFF THE FLOOR AS HIGH AS POSSIBLE. (B) TWIST TO THE LEFT, RO-TATING AROUND THE CENTRAL SPINAL AXIS WITH NO LATERAL FLEXION AND LIFT THE RIGHT LEG HIGHER WITHOUT ABDUCTING AT THE RIGHT HIP. RETURN TO CENTER AND REPEAT TO RIGHT. REPEAT SEQUENCE 2 TO 3 TIMES, RETURNING TO CENTER ARCH POSITION. (C) LATERALLY FLEX THE TORSO TO THE LEFT, REACHING THE RIGHT ARM ACROSS THE MIDLINE AND KEEPING THE PELVIS LEVEL ON THE FLOOR. RETURN TO CENTER AND THEN REPEAT TO RIGHT. DO 2 TO 3 REPETITIONS OF SEQUENCE. AS STRENGTH INCREASES, INCREASE REPETI-TIONS OR ADD WEIGHTS IN HANDS AND ON FEET.

FIGURE 19.4.   Curl.
FROM A PRONE POSITION, SUCK THE KNEES UP UNDER TORSO WITH BUTTOCKS DOWN ON HEELS. CONTRACT ABDOMINALS AND PRESS INTO AREAS OF SPINE THAT ARE TIGHTENED FROM THE ARCHES.

FIGURE 19.5. Abdominal curl.
REPEAT ABDOMINAL CURL A FEW TIMES (2 OR 3) TO SERVE AS A RECIPROCAL SETUP FOR THE PLOW (BELOW). GO IMMEDIATELY FROM LAST CURL INTO THE PLOW.

(a) **(b)**

FIGURE 19.6. Plow.
FROM A SUPINE POSITION, BEND THE KNEES AND BRING THE LEGS OVER THE HEAD UNTIL THE TOES TOUCH THE FLOOR ABOVE THE HEAD. (A) FLEX THE FEET, EXTEND THE KNEES, AND MAXIMIZE THE HIP FLEXION BY LOWERING MORE OF THE SPINE TO THE FLOOR. HOLD FOR AT LEAST 30 SECONDS, WORKING THE STRETCH. THIS FOCUSES ON STRETCHING THE HAMSTRINGS. (B) EASE THE KNEES (FLEX THEM) AND RAISE MOST OF THE SPINE OFF THE FLOOR, TIPPING WAY OVER. CONTRACT THE ABDOMINALS TO PRESS GENTLY INTO THE INFLEXIBLE AREAS OF THE SPINE. SLOWLY RETURN TO A HOOK LYING POSITION, LOWERING ONE VERTEBRA AT A TIME TO THE FLOOR. THIS FOCUSES ON STRETCHING THE EXTENSORS OF THE SPINE.

FIGURE 19.7. Spine assembler.
IN HOOK LYING POSITION PRESS THE FEET TO THE FLOOR AND LET THE BACK OF THE WAIST DESCEND TO THE FLOOR, WITHOUT LIFTING THE BUTTOCKS OFF THE FLOOR. RELEASE AND LET THE WAIST RISE FROM THE FLOOR. REPEAT THE "PRESS AND RELEASE" SEQUENCE IN A REGULAR RHYTHM, ALLOWING EACH REPETITION TO WAVE FARTHER UP THE SPINE, FINALLY ALLOWING THE HEAD TO MOVE ALONG WITH THE MOVEMENT OF THE SPINE. THIS EXERCISE IS VERY GENTLE AND SMOOTH.

FIGURE 19.8.   Supine leg swings.
FROM A SUPINE POSITION, SPREAD THE LEGS AS FAR APART AS POSSIBLE WITHOUT HYPER-EX-
TENDING THE LUMBAR SPINE. WHILE STABILIZING THE PELVIS ON THE FLOOR AND WITHOUT
LIFTING THE LEGS OFF THE FLOOR, SWING THE RIGHT LEG OVER TO THE LEFT LEG (IT PROBA-
BLY WON'T GO ALL THE WAY AT FIRST), THEN SWING THE RIGHT LEG BACK TO THE RIGHT.
REPEAT THE SEQUENCE WITH THE LEFT LEG SWINGING TO THE RIGHT LEG. REPEAT 6 TO 8
TIMES, REMEMBERING TO KEEP THE PELVIS STABILIZED.

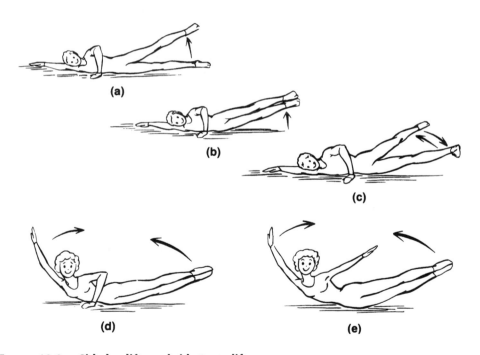

FIGURE 19.9.   Side leg lifts and side torso lift.
(A) WITH THE LEGS EXTENDED, ROLL TO THE RIGHT SIDE, FLEX THE FEET, AND KEEP THE HIPS
IN PARALLEL POSITION WHILE RAISING THE LEFT LEG TO THE SIDE (WITHOUT FLEXION OF THE
HIP OR HYPEREXTENSION OF THE SPINE), TAKING 4 COUNTS TO RAISE THE LEG AND 4 COUNTS
TO LOWER IT. (B) ON THE FOURTH REPETITION, HOLD THE LEFT LEG IN THE ABDUCTED POSI-
TION AND THEN RAISE THE RIGHT LEG TO IT TAKING 4 COUNTS UP AND 4 COUNTS DOWN.
REPEAT 4 TIMES. (C) HOLDING BOTH LEGS OFF THE FLOOR, TAKE TOP LEG FORWARD AND
BOTTOM LEG BACK. REVERSE DIRECTION AND REPEAT SEQUENCE. (D) AND (E) THEN RAISE THE
TORSO OFF THE FLOOR, CONTRACTING THE LEFT LATERAL FLEXORS OF THE TORSO AND AS-
SISTING WITH THE LEFT HAND AT FIRST. REPEAT THE ENTIRE SEQUENCE ON THE OTHER SIDE.
AS STRENGTH INCREASES, INCREASE THE REPETITIONS, OR INCREASE THE NUMBER OF COUNTS
TO EIGHT, AND THEN ADD WEIGHTS.

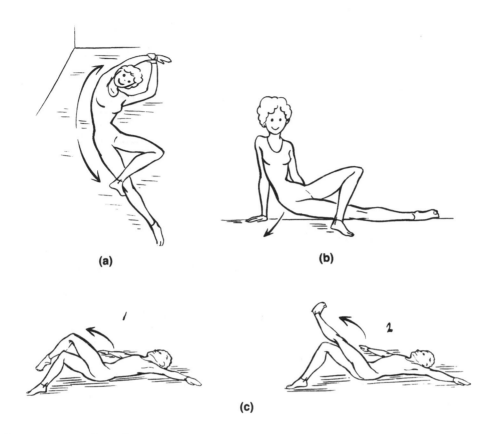

FIGURE 19.10. Stretch out.

(A) *C-CURVE* (TO STRETCH ABDUCTORS OF THE HIP AND LATERAL FLEXORS OF THE TORSO). IN A SUPINE POSITION, EXTEND THE RIGHT ARM AND RIGHT LEG LONG ON THE FLOOR. LATERALLY FLEX THE TORSO TO THE LEFT AND ADDUCT THE RIGHT HIP. FLEX THE LEFT HIP AND PLACE THE LEFT FOOT LATERAL TO THE RIGHT KNEE. WITH THE LEFT HAND TAKE HOLD OF THE RIGHT WRIST AND PULL THE RIGHT ARM LONG AND ACROSS ABOVE THE HEAD, THUS INCREASING THE LATERAL FLEXION TO THE LEFT. CONTRACT THE ABDOMINALS AND PRESS THE LOWER BACK TO THE FLOOR IN ORDER TO MAINTAIN AN EXTENDED HIP ON THE RIGHT SIDE. HOLD THE STRETCH FOR AT LEAST 30 SECONDS. REPEAT THE STRETCH ON THE OTHER SIDE.

(B) *LUNGE STRETCH.* STARTING IN A PUSH-UP POSITION WITH THE WEIGHT ON THE HANDS AND FEET, BRING THE LEFT FOOT FORWARD INTO A LUNGE POSITION. TURN TO THE LEFT SO THAT THE RIGHT HIP IS TOWARD THE FLOOR AND THE WEIGHT IS HELD ON THE RIGHT HAND AND THE SIDE OF THE RIGHT FOOT, WITH SOME SUPPORT FROM THE LEFT FOOT. ALLOW GRAVITY TO INCREASE THE ADDUCTION OF THE RIGHT HIP. HOLD THE STRETCH FOR AT LEAST 30 SECONDS. REPEAT ON THE OTHER SIDE.

(C) *LEG-OVER STRETCH* (TO STRETCH POSTERIOR ABDUCTORS OF THE HIP AND THE LATERAL FLEXORS AND ROTATORS OF THE TORSO). IN A SUPINE POSITION, DRAW THE LEFT KNEE TO THE CHEST, PULLING IT CLOSE WITH THE HANDS. KEEPING THE LEFT SIDE OF THE POSTERIOR RIB CAGE ON THE FLOOR, PULL THE LEFT KNEE ACROSS THE MIDLINE OF THE BODY, FEELING THE STRETCH IN THE LEFT BUTTOCKS. AFTER STRETCHING IN THIS POSITION FOR AT LEAST 30 SECONDS, FLEX THE LEFT FOOT; EXTEND THE LEFT KNEE WHILE KEEPING THE LEFT POSTERIOR RIB CAGE ON THE FLOOR. AFTER STRETCHING IN THIS POSITION FOR AT LEAST 30 SECONDS, ALLOW THE RIB CAGE TO RISE OFF THE FLOOR WHILE KEEPING THE LEFT SHOULDER ON THE FLOOR AND LET THE STRETCH GO INTO THE LEFT SIDE OF THE TORSO. REPEAT ON OTHER SIDE. (*CONTINUED*)

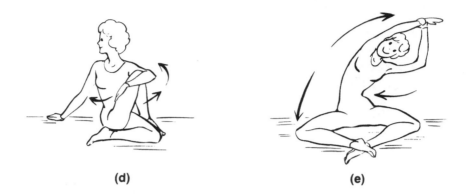

(d)   **(e)**

FIGURE 19.10.   Stretch out (*Continued*).

(D) *YOGA SIT STRETCH* (TO STRETCH THE SIX DEEP ROTATORS). SITTING IN TAILOR SIT POSITION, FLEX AND INWARDLY ROTATE THE RIGHT HIP. TAKE HOLD OF THE RIGHT KNEE WITH THE LEFT HAND AND INCREASE THE INWARD ROTATION OF THE RIGHT HIP. ALLOW THE RIGHT FOOT TO REST ON THE FLOOR. LIFT THE RIGHT BUTTOCK OFF THE FLOOR, INCREASE THE FLEXION OF THAT HIP, AND REPLACE THE RIGHT BUTTOCK ON THE FLOOR, FARTHER AWAY FROM THE LEFT HEEL. HOLD STRETCH FOR AT LEAST 30 SECONDS. REPEAT ON OTHER SIDE.

(E) *LATISSIMUS STRETCH.* IN A TAILOR SIT POSITION, RAISE THE RIGHT ARM ABOVE THE HEAD. WITH THE LEFT HAND, GRASP THE RIGHT WRIST AND PULL THE RIGHT ARM AS LONG AS POSSIBLE. LATERALLY FLEX THE THORACIC SPINE TO THE LEFT AND ROTATE SLIGHTLY TO THE LEFT, PRESSING THE RIB CAGE OUT TO THE BACK RIGHT SIDE. HOLD STRETCH FOR AT LEAST 30 SECONDS. REPEAT ON THE OTHER SIDE.

First Alternative Plan: For Legs, Feet, and Cardiorespiratory Endurance

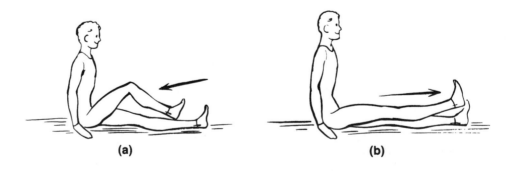

(a)   **(b)**

FIGURE 19.11.   Heel presses.

(A) SITTING IN LONG SIT POSITION, FLEX THE FEET AND DRAW THE RIGHT HEEL BACK TOWARD THE BUTTOCKS WITH THE HEEL ONE OR TWO INCHES OFF THE FLOOR. (B) THEN PRESS THE HEEL AWAY FROM THE BUTTOCKS, FULLY EXTENDING THE KNEE AND "SETTING THE QUADS" WITH THE HEEL HELD OFF THE FLOOR. REPEAT ABOUT 4 TO 5 REPETITIONS PAST THE "BURNIES." REPEAT ON THE OTHER SIDE.

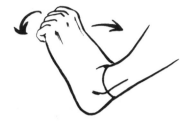

FIGURE 19.12. Toe gripper.
FROM LONG SIT POSITION, FLEX THE KNEES SLIGHTLY, FLEX THE FEET, AND GRIP THE TOES AS HARD AS POSSIBLE. FORTIFY THE CONTRACTION BY CONTRACTING THE ABDOMINALS AND CLENCHING THE FISTS. HOLD THE CONTRACTION FOR ABOUT 15 TO 20 SECONDS, BUT NOT TO THE POINT OF SPASM. RELEASE AND REPEAT.

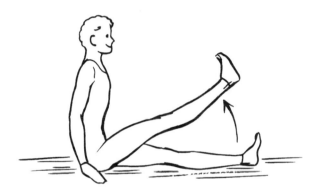

FIGURE 19.13. Seated leg lifts.
IN A LONG SIT POSITION, KEEPING THE KNEES EXTENDED, RAISE THE RIGHT LEG OFF THE FLOOR IN PARALLEL AND LOWER IT BACK TO THE FLOOR. REPEAT 8 TO 10 TIMES. TURN RIGHT LEG OUT AT THE HIP JOINT AND DO 8 TO 10 LIFTS IN THE TURNED-OUT POSITION. REPEAT SEQUENCE WITH THE LEFT LEG. AS STRENGTH INCREASES, INCREASE REPETITIONS AND ADD WEIGHTS.

FIGURE 19.14. TV stretch.
LYING ON THE RIGHT SIDE WITH THE HIPS EXTENDED, FLEX THE RIGHT KNEE SO THE HEEL COMES UP TOWARD THE BUTTOCKS. TAKE HOLD OF THE RIGHT ANKLE WITH THE LEFT HAND WITHOUT RELEASING THE LOWER BACK (HYPEREXTENDING). SIMULTANEOUSLY PULL ON THE RIGHT FOOT WITH THE LEFT HAND AND CONTRACT THE ABDOMINALS. HOLD THE STRETCH AT LEAST 30 SECONDS. REPEAT ON THE LEFT SIDE WITH THE LEFT LEG BENT AND HELD BY THE RIGHT HAND. THIS EXERCISE WAS "INVENTED" WHILE I WAS LYING IN FRONT OF THE TV ONE NIGHT; HENCE THE NAME.

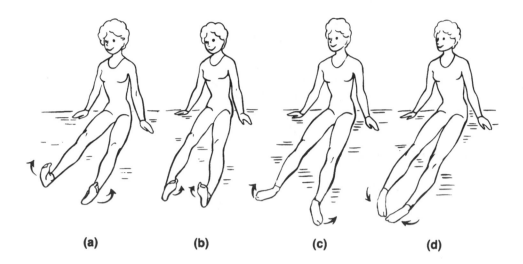

(a)   (b)   (c)   (d)

FIGURE 19.15.   Ankle/tarsus series.
THIS SERIES CAN BE DONE IN LONG SIT POSITION OR SUPINE POSITION. DORSIFLEX THE ANKLE JOINT. (*A*) PRESS THE SOLES OF THE FEET OUT TO THE SIDES (PRONATION) WITHOUT IN-WARDLY ROTATING AT THE HIP JOINT. (*B*) PRESS THE SOLES OF THE FEET INWARD (SUPINATION) WITHOUT OUTWARDLY ROTATING THE HIP JOINT. ALTERNATE IN AND OUT ACTION IN DORSI-FLEXED POSITION, REPEATING AT LEAST 10 TO 15 TIMES. (*C*) AND (*D*) REPEAT THE SAME SE-QUENCE WITH THE ANKLES IN A PLANTAR-FLEXED POSITION. AS STRENGTH INCREASES, ADD A CUT CROSS-SECTION OF INNER TUBE (LIKE A BIG RUBBER BAND) AROUND THE FOOT AT THE METATARSAL-PHALANGEAL JOINT, AND PRONATE AND SUPINATE AGAINST THE RESISTANCE OF THE INNER TUBE.

FIGURE 19.16.   Ankle circles.
SITTING WITH THE KNEES FLEXED AND THE ARMS WRAPPED AROUND THE THIGHS, CIRCLE THE FEET FIRST IN ONE DIRECTION AND THEN IN THE OTHER DIRECTION AT LEAST 6 TO 8 TIMES IN EACH DIRECTION.

FIGURE 19.17.   Shin-splint stretch.
KNEEL AND SIT BACK ON HEELS. PLACE HANDS TO THE SIDES OF THE KNEES. TAKE THE
WEIGHT ON THE HANDS AND ON THE TOPS OF THE FEET, ALLOWING GRAVITY TO INCREASE
THE PLANTAR FLEXION OF THE ANKLE JOINT. BE SURE THAT THE TARSUS IS IN A NEUTRAL POSI-
TION. HOLD THE POSITION FOR AT LEAST 30 SECONDS.

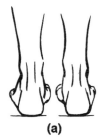
(a)

(b)

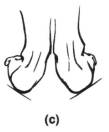
(c)

FIGURE 19.18.   Standing foot wobble.
(*A*) IN A PARALLEL STANDING POSITION WITH THE FEET HIP WIDTH APART, (*B*) SHIFT THE
WEIGHT TO THE LATERAL BORDER OF THE FOOT. (*C*) THEN SHIFT THE WEIGHT TO THE MEDIAL
BORDER OF THE FOOT. WOBBLE BACK AND FORTH FROM ONE EXTREME POSITION TO THE
OTHER, GRADUALLY DECREASING THE AMOUNT OF DEVIATION UNTIL THE FOOT STOPS IN A
CENTERED POSITION

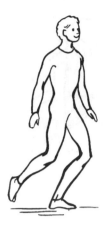

FIGURE 19.19.   One-legged *demipliés.*
Utilizing the centered position established in the previous exercise, put all of the weight on one foot and slowly *demiplié* down and up. (This exercise doubles the weight load and thus is an effective strength builder.) Repeat on other foot. Do this exercise in parallel and in turned-out position, taking great care to keep feet, knees, and hips aligned.

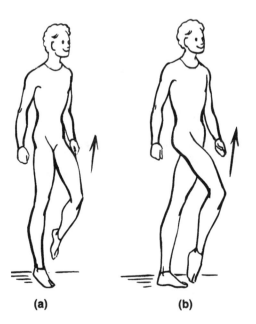

(a)   **(b)**

FIGURE 19.20.   Slow prances.
(*a*) Standing with the weight on both feet, in parallel position, slowly roll the left foot up onto the heads of the metatarsals (the ball of the foot); continue rolling the foot through the toes until the foot leaves the floor. Slowly return to standing, rolling through the whole foot on the way. (*b*) Repeat with the other foot. On the initial repetitions, carefully check the foot alignment to maintain the centered position established in Figure 19.18.

FIGURE 19.21.   Wind sprints.

Proceeding directly from the slow prances, gradually increase the tempo until more time is spent in the air than on the ground. Stay at an easy tempo for about 15 seconds; then up the tempo to very fast prances and maintain for 15 seconds. Alternate fast and slow prances for at least 2 to 3 minutes, ending with slow and then slowing even more so that more time is spent on the floor than in the air. WF: Alignment tends to go out the window as speed is increased. Take particular care to check alignment at the higher speeds.

Walk it out. After the wind sprints (Figure 19.21) have slowed—walk it out. Walk around the room until the respiratory rate returns to normal. Be sure to maintain a centered position of each foot in the walking.

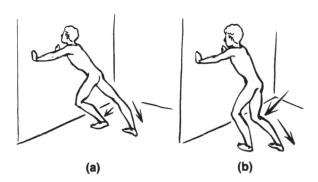

(a)   (b)

FIGURE 19.22.   Gastrocnemius and soleus stretch.

(A) Assume a parallel lunge position with the left leg forward and the hands against a wall. Keeping the right knee straight and the right heel on the floor, press forward farther onto the left leg, taking more weight on the hands. Hold this position for at least 30 seconds. (B) Then ease the right knee, keeping the right heel on the floor, and hold for at least 30 seconds. Repeat the sequence with the right foot forward and the left foot back.

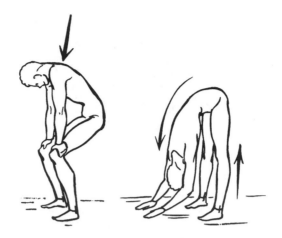

FIGURE 19.23.   Standing reciprocal stretch for the hamstrings.
(A) STANDING IN PARALLEL POSITION WITH THE FEET HIP WIDTH APART, BEND THE KNEES SLIGHTLY AND PLACE THE HANDS ON THE THIGHS ABOVE THE KNEES. KEEPING THE ARMS STRAIGHT, CONTRACT THE ABDOMINALS AND THE HIP FLEXORS IN A MAXIMAL, ISOMETRIC CONTRACTION, *REMEMBERING TO BREATHE,* AND HOLD THE CONTRACTION FOR ABOUT 15 TO 20 SECONDS. (B) RELEASE THE CONTRACTION AND DROP OVER INTO A HAMSTRING STRETCH, KEEPING THE KNEES EXTENDED. MAINTAIN THE LONG SUSTAINED STRETCH FOR AT LEAST 1 MINUTE.

FIGURE 19.24.   Stork stretch.
STANDING WITH THE WEIGHT ON THE LEFT LEG, FLEX THE RIGHT KNEE AND TAKE HOLD OF THE RIGHT ANKLE WITH THE RIGHT HAND. CONTRACT THE ABDOMINALS AND PULL BACK WITH THE HAND TO STRETCH THE HIP FLEXORS. BE SURE TO KEEP THE RIGHT LOWER LEG ALIGNED WITH THE THIGH. HOLD THE STRETCH FOR AT LEAST 30 SECONDS. REPEAT ON THE OTHER LEG.

FIGURE 19.25. **Wallpaper stretch.**
STANDING FACING A WALL, BEND AT THE HIP AS IF TO STRETCH THE HAMSTRINGS. INCH THE
FEET UP CLOSER TO THE WALL UNTIL THE BACK IS AGAINST THE WALL. EXTEND THE KNEES
AND STRETCH THE HAMSTRINGS. NUDGING AROUND BY CONTRACTING THE ABDOMINALS,
THE STRETCH CAN BE REFOCUSED TOWARD THE SPINE. MAINTAIN THE POSITION FOR AT LEAST
30 SECONDS.
FINISH AND REASSEMBLE. COME TO STANDING POSITION, WALK EASY, FOCUSNG ATTENTION
ON ALIGNMENT OF THE FEET, KNEES, HIPS, AND SPINE.

Second Alternative Plan: For Arms, Shoulders, Neck, and Upper Back

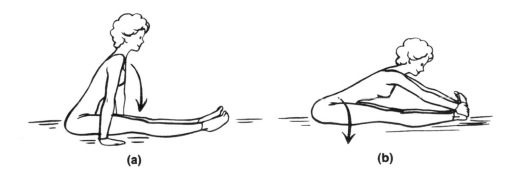

(a)   (b)

FIGURE 19.26. **Seated reciprocal hamstring stretch.**
(A) IN THE LONG SIT POSITION, PLACE THE HANDS ON THE FLOOR OUTSIDE THE LEGS AP-
PROXIMATELY HALFWAY UP THE THIGH. KEEPING THE ARMS STRAIGHT, CONTRACT THE AB-
DOMINALS AND THE HIP FLEXORS AND PRESS THE HANDS INTO THE FLOOR. (REMEMBER TO
BREATHE ON ALL MAXIMAL CONTRACTIONS.) HOLD THE CONTRACTION FOR 15 TO 20 SEC-
ONDS. (B) THEN IMMEDIATELY DROP OVER THE LEGS TO STRETCH THE HAMSTRINGS.
CONCENTRATE ON INCREASING THE HIP FLEXION BY PRESSING THE ANTERIOR SUPERIOR
SPINES OF THE ILIUM TOWARD THE TOPS OF THE THIGHS. HOLD THE LONG SUSTAINED
STRETCH FOR AT LEAST 30 SECONDS.

(a)   **(b)**

FIGURE 19.27.   Iliopsoas isolator.
(A) FROM THE LONG SIT POSITION DRAW THE FEET UP TOWARD THE BUTTOCKS AND PLACE
THE HANDS ON THE OUTSIDE OF THE KNEES. (B) KEEPING THE SHOULDERS, UPPER BACK, AND
LEGS STEADY AND UPRIGHT, FLEX AT THE HIP AND HYPEREXTEND AT THE LUMBAR SPINE,
ROCKING THE PELVIS FORWARD. RELEASE AND LET THE PELVIS ROCK BACK TO THE STARTING
POSITION. REPEAT 10 TO 15 TIMES.

FIGURE 19.28.   Seated arm circles.
IN THE LONG SIT POSITION, UP ON THE SIT BONES, ABDUCT AT THE SHOULDER JOINT SO
THAT THE ARMS ARE STRAIGHT OUT TO THE SIDES WITH THE HANDS CLENCHED IN FISTS.
START BY MAKING SMALL CIRCLES BACKWARDS WHILE KEEPING THE TORSO ABSOLUTELY VERTI-
CAL. (THIS IS TOUGH BECAUSE THERE IS A NATURAL FORWARD-AND-BACKWARD ROCKING AC-
TION WHICH MUST BE COUNTERACTED.) DO ABOUT 10 SMALL CIRCLES, AND THEN INCREASE
THE SIZE TO MEDIUM CIRCLES THAT ARE SLIGHTLY FASTER. DO 10 OF THESE MEDIUM CIRCLES.
THEN INCREASE THE SIZE TO LARGE AND THE TEMPO TO FAST AND DO 10 MORE. ALL OF
THESE CIRCLES ARE DONE WITH THE TORSO STABILIZED AGAINST THE ROCKING ACTION. DO
10 MORE MEDIUM AND 10 MORE SMALL CIRCLES, BACKWARD. THEN REVERSE THE DIRECTION
AND DO THE WHOLE SEQUENCE FORWARD (10 SMALL, 10 MEDIUM, 10 LARGE, 10 MEDIUM,
AND 10 SMALL) WHILE STABILIZING THE TORSO. LET THE ARMS STOP, STILL IN THE ABDUCTED
POSITION. THEN SLOWLY LOWER THE ARMS TO THE FLOOR WHILE LENGTHENING THE SPINE.
SIT TALL FOR A FEW SECONDS TO ESTABLISH THE NEW POSITION OF VERTICAL WHICH ACCOM-
PANIES THE INTENSE STABILIZATION OF THE TORSO. THEN RELEASE INTO THE SPINE AND SHAKE
OUT THE SHOULDERS.

FIGURE 19.29. **Shoulder sequence.**

(A) Start in push-up position; take 4 counts to lower the belly toward the floor while raising the head, keeping the shoulders down, and sticking the chin out toward the ceiling. Take 4 counts to return to the push-up position, pulling the belly back up. Take 4 counts to press the hips up into the air, head down, and heels down to the floor; 4 counts back to push-up position. Repeat at least 3 times. Increase the counts to 8 as strength increases. (B) Balancing on one hand and both feet with the right side toward the floor, take 4 counts to sag down toward the floor, 4 counts to return to level, and 4 counts to press high. Repeat 3 times. Shift hand position to take the stress off the wrist. Hang in there . . . this is a toughie, but it really strengthens the adductors of the shoulder joint and the lateral flexors of the torso. Do only one repetition to start and gradually increase to 3. Then increase the counts. (C) Roll over so that the back is toward the floor with the weight supported with both hands and both feet with pelvis high, knees bent, and abdominals contracted. Shift weight from side to side. Eventually, after strength has built, put the weight on the right hand and the left foot only, still keeping the pelvis up. Then switch to the opposite hand and foot. When you are really adventurous, try balancing on the right hand and right foot with the pelvis up. Then switch to the other side. Repeat (B) on the left side. (*Continued*)

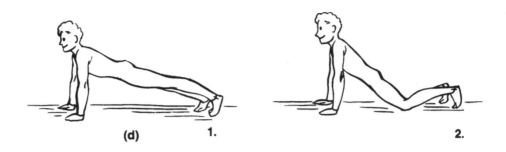

(d)   **1.**   **2.**

FIGURE 19.29. **Shoulder sequence (*continued*).**
(*D*) ROLL TO THE FRONT PUSH-UP POSITION AND DO AS MANY PUSH-UPS AS POSSIBLE. WHEN DOING PUSH-UPS GO CLEAR DOWN TO THE FLOOR (NOT LYING DOWN, OF COURSE) AND PUSH UP FROM THERE. OTHERWISE THERE IS A WHOLE RANGE OF JOINT MOTION THAT IS IGNORED. IF YOU ARE TOO WEAK TO DO PUSH-UPS FROM THE REGULAR PUSH-UP POSITION AT FIRST, DO THEM FROM THE KNEES TO START. THEN SHIFT TO THE TOES AS SOON AS POSSIBLE.

FIGURE 19.30. **Stretching curl.**
FROM THE CURL POSITION, REACH THE ARMS OUT AS FAR FROM THE SHOULDERS AS POSSIBLE (IN A POSITION OF EXTENSION ABOVE THE HEAD). PRESS THE RIBS TO ONE SIDE TO STRETCH THE LATISSIMUS AND TERES MAJOR ON THAT SIDE. THEN PRESS THE RIBS TO THE OTHER SIDE AND STRETCH. HOLD THE STRETCH FOR AT LEAST 30 SECONDS. TO ACCENTUATE THE STRETCH, SLIDE THE ARMS TO THE RIGHT SIDE (KEEPING THEM ON THE FLOOR) AND PRESS THE LEFT HIP BACK FARTHER BEHIND THE HEEL. THEN REPEAT ON THE OTHER SIDE, WITH THE ARMS GOING TO THE LEFT AND THE RIGHT HIP PRESSING BACK.

FIGURE 19.31. **Wing stretch.**
STILL IN THE KNEELING CURL POSITION, CLASP THE HANDS BEHIND THE BACK, TURNING THE PALMS AWAY FROM THE BUTTOCKS. BEND OVER SO THE FOREHEAD IS CLOSE TO THE FLOOR AND PRESS THE HANDS BACK UP OVER THE HEAD. HOLD THE STRETCH FOR AT LEAST 30 SECONDS.

FIGURE 19.32. Mad cat.
(A) FROM A POSITION ON THE HANDS AND KNEES, (B) LIFT THE HEAD AND ARCH THE BACK; (C) KEEPING THE SPINE AND NECK HYPEREXTENDED, PUSH THE WEIGHT BACK TOWARD THE HEELS; (D) LOWER THE BUTTOCKS AND HEAD; (E) CONTRACT THE ABDOMINALS AND FLEX THE SPINE; (F) SWING THE WEIGHT FORWARD ONTO THE HANDS; AND (G) RETURN TO THE STARTING POSITION. REPEAT THIS CIRCLE ABOUT 3 TIMES AND THEN CHANGE THE DIRECTION OF THE CIRCLE AND REPEAT 3 MORE TIMES.

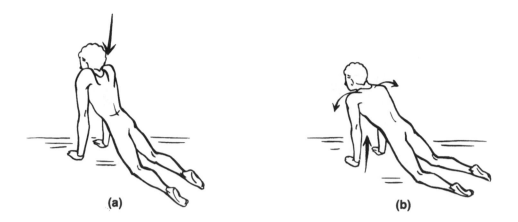

(a)   (b)

FIGURE 19.33.   Scapula push-ups.
(A) FROM THE PUSH-UP POSITION, EITHER FROM THE FEET OR FROM THE KNEES, KEEP THE EL-
BOWS EXTENDED AND ALLOW THE CHEST TO SAG DOWN BETWEEN THE SHOULDERS (WITH
THE SCAPULA ADDUCTING); (B) THEN PRESS THE THORACIC SPINE UP AND AWAY FROM THE
SHOULDERS. REPEAT ABOUT 10 TIMES. AS STRENGTH INCREASES, SHIFT FROM KNEES TO FOOT
PUSH-UP POSITION.

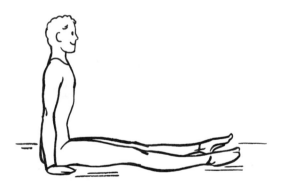

FIGURE 19.34.   Parallel bar press.
IN THE LONG SIT POSITION, PLACE THE HANDS ON EITHER SIDE OF THE BUTTOCKS. PUT THE
WEIGHT ON THE HANDS AND DEPRESS THE SCAPULA, SO THAT THE HEAD RISES HIGHER. IF
THE ARMS ARE SHORT, IT MAY BE NECESSARY TO PUT BOOKS UNDER THE HANDS. THIS EXER-
CISE CAN (OBVIOUSLY) BE DONE ON PARALLEL BARS, OR ON TWO STURDY CHAIRS PLACED
BACK TO BACK, OR ON STAIRWAY BANNISTERS. THE ACTION IS FOCUSED AT THE SCAPULA
WITH ELEVATION AND DEPRESSION OF THE SCAPULA. THE ELBOWS REMAIN EXTENDED
THROUGHOUT THE EXERCISE.

FIGURE 19.35.   Flagman presses.
LYING SUPINE, PLACE THE ARMS IN "FLAGMAN POSITION." PRESS THE BACKS OF THE HANDS ONTO THE FLOOR. HOLD THE CONTRACTION FOR ABOUT 10 SECONDS AND THEN RELEASE. REPEAT 5 TO 10 TIMES. NEXT, PRESS THE ELBOWS BACK ONTO THE FLOOR. HOLD FOR ABOUT 10 SECONDS AND THEN RELEASE. REPEAT 5 TO 10 TIMES.

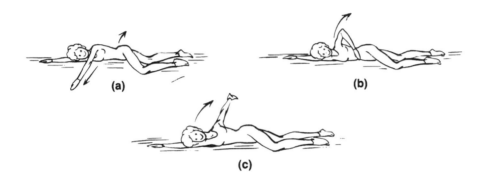

FIGURE 19.36.   Arm-over stretch.
(*A*) LYING ON THE RIGHT SIDE WITH THE KNEES AND HIPS COMFORTABLY FLEXED, REACH THE LEFT HAND OUT IN FRONT OF THE TORSO AS FAR AS POSSIBLE, USING THE FRICTION OF THE FINGERS ON THE FLOOR TO INCREASE THE STRETCH. (*B*) EASE THE ELBOW, AND DRAW THE ELBOW DIRECTLY OVER THE SHOULDER UNTIL THE HUMERUS IS BACK BEHIND THE BODY AT RIGHT ANGLES TO THE TORSO. (*C*) EXTEND THE ELBOW, PALM TO THE CEILING AND ARMPIT OPEN TO THE CEILING (NO FORWARD TILT TO SCAPULA), AND ALLOW GRAVITY TO PULL THE ARM CLOSER TO THE FLOOR. HOLD THIS POSITION FOR AT LEAST 30 SECONDS. EASE THE ELBOW AND STRETCH TO THE FRONT. REPEAT THE WHOLE SEQUENCE 2 OR 3 TIMES. FINALLY, LET THE WEIGHT OF THE ARM TAKE YOU OVER ONTO YOUR BACK. REPEAT ON THE OTHER SIDE.

FIGURE 19.37.   Shoulder flop.
LYING ON THE FLOOR IN A SUPINE POSITION, LIFT THE RIGHT SHOULDER OFF THE FLOOR AND LET IT FLOP DOWN TO THE FLOOR. REPEAT THE LIFT AND FLOP SEQUENCE ON THE RIGHT SHOULDER, GRADUALLY INCREASING THE TEMPO UNTIL YOU ARE GOING AS FAST AS POSSIBLE WITH VERY LITTLE EFFORT, ESPECIALLY ON THE FLOP. GRADUALLY SLOW DOWN UNTIL YOU COME TO A STOP, AND THEN REST A MOMENT BEFORE STARTING THE SAME SEQUENCE WITH THE LEFT SHOULDER.[2]

2. Fitt modification of a Feldenkrais exercise.

FIGURE 19.38.   Neck stretches and neck circles.

(A) SITTING IN THE TAILOR POSITION, RAISE THE RIGHT ARM TO VERTICAL, THEN BEND THE ELBOW AND PLACE THE RIGHT HAND OVER THE LEFT EAR. PLACE THE LEFT HAND UNDER THE LEFT BUTTOCK. ALLOW THE WEIGHT OF THE RIGHT ARM TO PULL THE HEAD TO THE RIGHT SIDE STRETCHING THE LEFT LATERAL FLEXORS OF THE NECK (THE LEFT HAND UNDER THE BUTTOCK HOLDS THE LEFT SHOULDER DOWN PASSIVELY). HOLD THE STRETCH POSITION FOR AT LEAST 30 SECONDS. RELEASE SLOWLY. REPEAT EXERCISE (A) TO THE OPPOSITE SIDE. RELEASE SLOWLY. (B) IN THE SAME STARTING POSITION, RAISE THE LEFT ARM ON THE FRONT LEFT DIAGONAL (FLEXION AND ABDUCTION). BEND THE ELBOW AND PLACE THE LEFT HAND ON THE RIGHT, SIDE, BACK OF THE HEAD. THE RIGHT HAND IS PLACED UNDER THE RIGHT BUTTOCK TO PASSIVELY HOLD THE RIGHT SHOULDER DOWN. LET THE WEIGHT OF THE LEFT ARM PULL THE HEAD FORWARD AND TO THE SIDE, STRETCHING THE EXTENSORS AND LATERAL FLEXORS ON THE RIGHT SIDE OF THE NECK. HOLD THE STRETCH AT LEAST 30 SECONDS. RELEASE SLOWLY. REPEAT (B) TO THE OPPOSITE SIDE. RELEASE SLOWLY. (C) IN THE SAME TAILOR SIT STARTING POSITION, RAISE BOTH HANDS IN FRONT OF THE FACE, PALMS TOWARD THE FACE. REACH UP OVER THE HEAD AND PLACE THE PALMS OF THE HANDS ON THE CROWN OF THE HEAD. ALLOW THE WEIGHT OF THE ARMS TO PULL THE HEAD FORWARD TO STRETCH THE EXTENSORS. ALLOW THE NECK AND UPPER BACK TO FLEX TO INCREASE THE STRETCH, BUT DO NOT ALLOW FLEXION AT THE HIP JOINTS. HOLD THE STRETCH FOR AT LEAST 30 SECONDS. RELEASE SLOWLY. (D) IN THE TAILOR SIT POSITION, WITH THE ARMS TO THE SIDES AND THE HANDS ON THE FLOOR FOR SUPPORT, STICK THE CHIN OUT TOWARD THE WALL IN FRONT. IMAGINING A PENCIL POINT ON THE CHIN, DRAW A LINE UP THE OPPOSITE WALL AND ACROSS THE CEILING AS FAR AS POSSIBLE, EXTENDING AND HYPEREXTENDING THE NECK TO STRETCH THE FLEXORS OF THE NECK. HOLD THE FINAL POSITION FOR AT LEAST 30 SECONDS. RELEASE SLOWLY. (E) IN THE TAILOR SIT POSITION WITH THE HANDS TO EITHER SIDE OF THE BUTTOCKS, ALLOW THE HEAD TO FLEX FORWARD, THEN TO THE RIGHT DIAGONAL, THEN TO THE RIGHT SIDE, THEN TO THE RIGHT BACK DIAGONAL, THEN STRAIGHT BACK, THEN TO THE LEFT BACK DIAGONAL, THEN STRAIGHT TO THE LEFT, THEN TO THE LEFT FRONT DIAGONAL, AND BACK TO FLEXION. THIS SEQUENCE IS DONE IN A CONTINUOUS, *VERY SLOW* MOTION WITH MAXIMAL STRETCH IN EACH DIRECTION. REPEAT ABOUT 3 TIMES. THEN REVERSE THE DIRECTION OF THE CIRCLES AND SLOWLY REPEAT 3 TIMES. WHEN THE CIRCLES ARE FINISHED, RETURN THE HEAD TO VERTICAL.

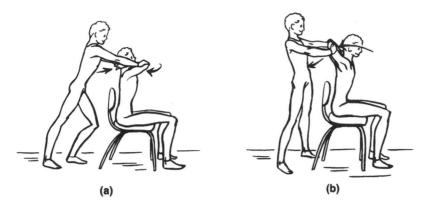

(a)   (b)

FIGURE 19.39. Reciprocal stretch for pectoralis major.

A PARTNER IS NEEDED FOR THIS STRETCH. (*A*) ONE PARTNER IS SEATED ON A CHAIR, AND THE
OTHER PARTNER STANDS BEHIND THE CHAIR. THE SEATED PARTNER CLASPS THE HANDS BEHIND
THE NECK AND HOLDS THE ARMS ON THE FORWARD DIAGONAL (FLEXED AND ABDUCTED). THE
STANDING PARTNER PLACES HIS OR HER HANDS ON THE BACK OF THE ELBOWS OF THE SEATED
PARTNER. THE SEATED PARTNER PRESSES BACK (HORIZONTAL EXTENSION) WITH THE ELBOWS
AGAINST THE RESISTANCE PROVIDED BY THE STANDING PARTNER. THE CONTRACTION IS HELD FOR
ABOUT 20 SECONDS. (*B*) IMMEDIATELY FOLLOWING THE CONTRACTION, THE STANDING PARTNER
REPLACES HIS OR HER HANDS ON THE FRONT OF THE SEATED PARTNER'S ELBOWS AND *GENTLY*
PULLS THE SEATED PARTNER'S ELBOWS BACK TOWARD HORIZONTAL EXTENSION. IF THE SEATED
PARTNER POWERFULLY EXHALES, THE STRETCH WILL BE INCREASED BECAUSE OF THE DEPRESSION
OF THE RIB CAGE ON EXHALATION. HOLD THE STRETCH POSITION FOR AT LEAST 30 SECONDS.
VERBAL COMMUNICATION BETWEEN PARTNERS IS ESSENTIAL TO MAXIMIZE THE STRETCH WITHOUT
GOING TOO FAR. RELEASE SLOWLY AND GENTLY. (IT IS POSSIBLE TO DO THIS STRETCH ALONE BY
STANDING IN A CORNER WITH THE BACK TO THE CORNER AND PRESSING THE ELBOWS BACK
AGAINST THE INTERSECTING WALLS. AFTER THE CONTRACTION, TURN TO FACE INTO THE CORNER
AND USE THE WALLS TO HELP THE STRETCH TOWARD HORIZONTAL EXTENSION.)

FIGURE 19.40. Doorjamb hang.

STAND IN A DOORWAY AND HOLD THE DOORJAMB AT SHOULDER HEIGHT WITH THE THUMB
UP. STEP FORWARD FAR ENOUGH TO ALLOW THE ELBOW TO EXTEND. TURN THE HIPS AND
TORSO AWAY FROM THE HAND HOLDING THE DOORJAMB, KEEPING THE ELBOW STRAIGHT.
HOLD THE STRETCH FOR AT LEAST 30 SECONDS; THEN REACH UP WITH THE OPPOSITE HAND
AND MASSAGE THE PECTORALIS MINOR IN A CIRCULAR MOTION. HOLD THE STRETCH AN-
OTHER 15 TO 30 SECONDS. RELEASE SLOWLY. REPEAT ON THE OTHER SIDE.

FIGURE 19.41.   Deep massage.
TO MASSAGE THE RIGHT PECTORALIS MINOR, REACH UP WITH THE LEFT HAND AND FEEL AROUND UNDER THE CLAVICLE TO ISOLATE THE CORACOID PROCESS. USING DEEP, CIRCULAR MOTIONS MASSAGE AROUND THE CORACOID PROCESS. THEN FOLLOW THE PATH OF THE MUSCLE DOWN TO THE THIRD, FOURTH, AND FIFTH RIBS, USING DEEP, CIRCULAR PRESSURE. REPEAT ON THE OTHER SIDE.

Third Alternative Plan: For Hips

FIGURE 19.42.   Supine leg lifts.
IN A SUPINE POSITION WITH THE LEGS STRAIGHT AND IN PARALLEL POSITION, CONTRACT THE ABDOMINALS AND LIFT THE RIGHT LEG TO ABOUT 45 DEGREES FLEXION OF THE HIP, KEEPING THE KNEE EXTENDED. REPEAT AT LEAST 10 TIMES. TURN OUT AT THE RIGHT HIP AND DO 10 LEG LIFTS IN THIS POSITION. REPEAT PARALLEL AND TURNED-OUT LEG LIFTS WITH THE LEFT HIP. MAINTAIN CONTRACTION OF THE ABDOMINALS AND PYRAMIDALIS THROUGHOUT THE SEQUENCE. *DO NOT DO DOUBLE LEG LIFTS.* THEY PUT EXTREME STRESS ON THE LOWER BACK BECAUSE OF THE ATTACHMENT OF THE ILIOPSOAS TO THE LUMBAR SPINE. INSTEAD, DO AB-DOMINAL CURLS TO DIRECTLY STRENGTHEN THE ABDOMINALS OR ADD WEIGHTS TO THE LEG LIFTS DESCRIBED HERE TO INCREASE STRENGTH OF THE HIP FLEXORS. NOT ONLY ARE DOUBLE LEG LIFTS A POTENTIAL STRAIN ON THE LOWER BACK; THEY ARE ALSO NOT THE MOST EFFEC-TIVE WAY TO BUILD STRENGTH IN EITHER ABDOMINALS OR HIP FLEXORS.

FIGURE 19.43.   Prone leg lifts.
IN A PRONE, PARALLEL POSITION WITH THE KNEE EXTENDED AND THE ANKLE PLANTAR-FLEXED, LIFT THE LEFT LEG AS HIGH AS POSSIBLE OFF THE FLOOR AND RETURN TO STARTING POSITION. REPEAT AT LEAST 10 TIMES. THEN TURN OUT AT THE HIP JOINT AND DO 10 REPETITIONS IN THE NEW POSITION. REPEAT THE SEQUENCE ON THE RIGHT SIDE. (A SET OF 10 REPETITIONS MAY ALSO BE DONE WITH AN INWARDLY ROTATED HIP JOINT TO STRENGTHEN INWARD ROTA-TORS AND EXTENSORS.) AS STRENGTH INCREASES, ADD ANKLE WEIGHTS.

FIGURE 19.44. Lying hip flexor stretch.

TO BE DONE IMMEDIATELY FOLLOWING THE PRONE LEG LIFTS. IN A PRONE POSITION, BEND THE KNEES SO THE HEELS ARE DIRECTLY BEHIND THE BUTTOCKS AND THE LOWER LEG IS ALIGNED WITH THE THIGH. GRASP THE ANKLES WITH THE HANDS, CONTRACT THE ABDOMINALS, AND PULL WITH THE HANDS TO STRETCH THE HIP FLEXORS. *DO NOT CONTRACT* THE HAMSTRINGS TO EXTEND THE HIP, SINCE THIS ACTION IS LIKELY TO CAUSE A SPASM IN THE HAMSTRINGS. INSTEAD, PULL WITH ONLY THE HANDS AND THE ABDOMINAL MUSCLES. HOLD THE STRETCH FOR AT LEAST 30 SECONDS. (*NOTE:* IF THE RECTUS FEMORIS IS VERY TIGHT AND INELASTIC, THE FIRST SENSATION IS PRESSURE ON THE KNEE. AS LONG AS THE TIBIA AND FEMUR ARE ALIGNED WITH EACH OTHER—NO TORQUE—THIS WILL NOT HURT THE KNEE. AS ELASTICITY INCREASES, THE STRETCH WILL BE FELT PRIMARILY IN THE MIDTHIGH. THEN, FINALLY, AS THE RECTUS FEMORIS IS STRETCHED, THE DEEP HIP FLEXORS OF THE GROIN WILL BE STRETCHED. WHEN THIS FINAL PHASE IS REACHED, THE DANCER MAY WISH TO SPREAD THE KNEES APART, IN PARALLEL POSITION, KEEPING THE HEELS AT THE BUTTOCKS AND THE UPPER AND LOWER LEG ALIGNED, IN ORDER TO FACILITATE THE STRETCH OF THE DEEP HIP FLEXORS.)

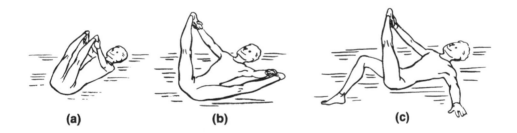

(a)   (b)   (c)

FIGURE 19.45. Supine hamstring stretch.

ILLUSTRATIONS (*A*) AND (*B*) SHOW THE EXERCISE BEING PERFORMED WITH BOTH LEGS SIMULTANEOUSLY, BUT IT SHOULD FIRST BE PRACTICED WITH ONE LEG AT A TIME. (*A*) IN THE SUPINE POSITION, BEND THE LEFT KNEE, TAKE HOLD OF THE LEFT FOOT WITH THE LEFT HAND, AND SLOWLY EXTEND THE KNEE AND DORSIFLEX THE ANKLE. HOLD THIS STRETCH POSITION AT LEAST 30 SECONDS. (*B*) THEN ABDUCT AND TURN OUT AT THE LEFT HIP TO INCREASE THE STRETCH OF THE SEMITENDINOSUS AND SEMIMEMBRANOSUS. HOLD THE NEW POSITION AT LEAST 30 SECONDS. (*C*) FINALLY, TAKE HOLD OF THE LEFT FOOT WITH THE RIGHT HAND AND ADDUCT AND INWARDLY ROTATE THE LEFT HIP, MAXIMIZING THE STRETCH ON THE BICEPS FEMORIS. THIS FINAL STRETCH IS THE MOST DIFFICULT FOR DANCERS, FOR DANCE TECHNIQUES SELDOM STRETCH THE BICEPS SPECIFICALLY. HOLD THE STRETCH AT LEAST 30 SECONDS. REPEAT THE SERIES OF 3 STRETCHES WITH THE RIGHT LEG.

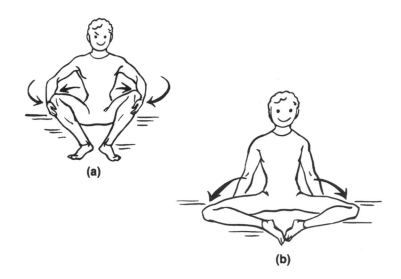

FIGURE 19.46.   Seated frog press (reciprocal for inward rotators).

(A) IN THE FROG SIT POSITION, WITH THE SOLES OF THE FEET TOGETHER, PLACE THE ARMS AROUND THE OUTSIDE OF THE THIGHS SO THE FOREARMS ARE CONTACTING THE LATERAL SURFACE OF THE THIGH AND CALF. PRESS OUT WITH THE KNEES AGAINST THE RESISTANCE PROVIDED BY THE ARMS. HOLD THE CONTRACTION ABOUT 20 SECONDS, REMEMBERING TO BREATHE. (B) THEN RELEASE THE ARMS AND LET THE KNEES OUTWARDLY ROTATE TOWARD THE FLOOR. HOLD THE STRETCH POSITION FOR AT LEAST 30 SECONDS.

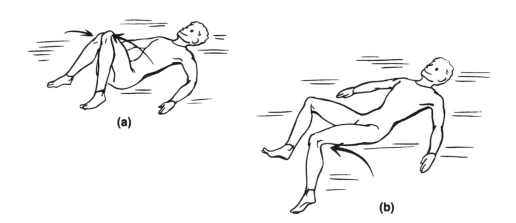

FIGURE 19.47.   Lying knee press (reciprocal for outward rotators).

(A) IN THE HOOK LYING POSITION, MOVE THE FEET *SLIGHTLY* FARTHER APART AND ALLOW THE KNEES TO DROP TOWARD EACH OTHER UNTIL CONTACT IS MADE. PRESS THE KNEES TOGETHER AS HARD AS POSSIBLE, REMEMBERING TO BREATHE. HOLD THE CONTRACTION FOR ABOUT 20 SECONDS. (B) THEN FOCUS ON THE LEFT KNEE AND HIP, ALLOWING THEM TO ROTATE IN-WARD AND EXTEND. IF STRESS IS FELT IN THE KNEE, IT CAN BE REDUCED BY DORSIFLEXING THE ANKLE. HOLD THE STRETCH POSITION (INWARD ROTATION AND EXTENSION) FOR AT LEAST 30 SECONDS. REPEAT THE KNEE PRESS AND REPEAT THE INWARD ROTATION STRETCH OF THE OUTWARD ROTATORS WITH THE RIGHT LEG.

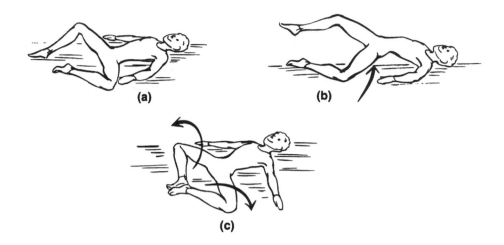

FIGURE 19.48.   Lying frog press (reciprocal for inward rotators).
(A) FROM THE HOOK LYING POSITION, DROP THE LEFT KNEE OUT TO THE SIDE, WITH THE
KNEE STILL FLEXED. (B) PUTTING THE WEIGHT ON THE OUTSIDE OF THE LEFT KNEE AND BOTH
SHOULDERS, LIFT THE HIPS, BUTTOCKS, AND SPINE OFF THE FLOOR WITH A CONTRACTION OF
THE EXTENSORS, ABDUCTORS, AND OUTWARD ROTATORS. LIFT RIGHT FOOT OFF THE FLOOR.
HOLD THE LIFT FOR ABOUT 20 SECONDS, REMEMBERING TO BREATHE. (C) THEN LOWER THE
PELVIS TO THE FLOOR AND LET THE RIGHT KNEE DROP DOWN TOWARD THE FLOOR, INCREAS-
ING THE OUTWARD ROTATION. MAINTAIN THE STRETCH POSITION FOR AT LEAST 30 SEC-
ONDS. REPEAT THE SEQUENCE WITH THE RIGHT LEG.

FIGURE 19.49.   Yoga sit stretch.
IN THE TAILOR POSITION, FLEX AND INWARDLY ROTATE THE RIGHT HIP. TAKE HOLD OF THE
RIGHT KNEE WITH THE LEFT HAND AND PULL TO INCREASE THE INWARD ROTATION OF THE
RIGHT HIP. ALLOW THE RIGHT FOOT TO REST ON THE FLOOR. LIFT THE RIGHT BUTTOCK OFF
THE FLOOR, INCREASE THE FLEXION OF THE RIGHT HIP, AND REPLACE THE RIGHT BUTTOCK ON
THE FLOOR, FARTHER AWAY FROM THE LEFT HEEL THAN IT WAS AT THE BEGINNING OF THE EX-
ERCISE. HOLD THE STRETCH POSITION (NUDGING AROUND) FOR AT LEAST 30 SECONDS.
REPEAT WITH THE LEFT SIDE.

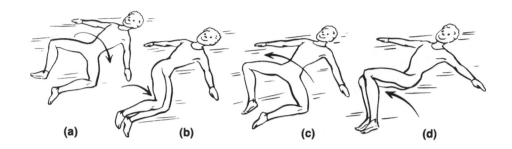

(a)   (b)   (c)   (d)

FIGURE 19.50.   Hip greaser.
(*A*) IN THE HOOK LYING POSITION, ALLOW THE LEFT LEG TO DROP OUT TO THE SIDE, KEEPING THE KNEE FLEXED. (*B*) ALLOW THE RIGHT LEG TO RESPOND (VIA THE STRETCH REFLEX OF THE ADDUCTORS OF THE LEFT HIP) AND FOLLOW THE LEFT LEG OVER TO THE LEFT SIDE. (*C*) ALLOW THE RIGHT LEG TO REBOUND (STRETCH REFLEX AGAIN) AND SWING BACK OVER TO THE RIGHT SIDE. (*D*) ALLOW THE LEFT LEG TO FOLLOW. ALLOW THIS CHAIN REACTION TO CONTINUE, TRYING TO "DO" AS LITTLE AS POSSIBLE. PASSIVITY IS THE KEY TO THE HIP GREASER. GRADUALLY ACCELERATE THE ACTION SLIGHTLY, KEEPING THE EFFORT AT A MINIMUM. THEN GRADUALLY SLOW DOWN AGAIN AND COME TO REST. RELAX AND COLLECT FOR A MOMENT.[3]

FIGURE 19.51.   Hip flop.
IN A SUPINE POSITION, FOCUS THE ATTENTION ON THE RIGHT HIP. WITH A VERY SMALL ACTION, PRESS THE RIGHT HIP (THE CENTER OF THE JOINT) UP TOWARD THE CEILING, AND THEN *DROP* IT BACK TO THE FLOOR, WITH A COMPLETE RELEASE OF THE CONTRACTION. REPEAT THIS SMALL PRESS-AND-DROP ACTION, GRADUALLY ACCELERATING THE TEMPO, THEN DECELERATING THE TEMPO AND COMING TO REST. AS ALWAYS, IT IS INTERESTING TO COMPARE THE "FEEL" OF THE TWO SIDES BEFORE DOING THE SEQUENCE WITH THE LEFT HIP.[4]

3. Fitt modification of a Feldenkrais exercise.
4. Fitt modification of a Feldenkrais exercise.

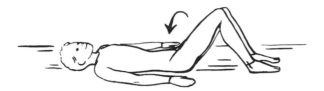

FIGURE 19.52. Pyramidalis isolator.

IN THE HOOK LYING POSITION WITH THE HANDS RESTING ON THE LOWER ABDOMEN BE-TWEEN THE UMBILICUS (BELLY BUTTON) AND THE SYMPHASIS PUBIS, IMAGINE THAT YOU ARE URINATING AND YOU MUST STOP THE PROCESS. FEEL THE CONTRACTION OF THE LOWER AB-DOMINALS AS YOU STOP THE IMAGINARY STREAM OF URINE. (THIS IS THE BEST WAY I HAVE FOUND TO ISOLATE THE PYRAMIDALIS MUSCLE.) USE THE HANDS ON THE LOWER ABDOMINAL REGION TO GET FEEDBACK ABOUT THE LEVEL AND NATURE OF THE CONTRACTION. THEN RE-MOVE THE HANDS AND JUST CONTRACT THE PYRAMIDALIS.

STAND TO CHECK OUT NEW ALIGNMENT. EXPLORE MOTION OF THE HIP JOINT WITH *DEMI-PLIÉS,* EASY WALKS, LEG SWINGS, AND THE LIKE. COME TO A STANDING POSITION IN PARAL-LEL. CONTRACT THE PYRAMIDALIS AND FEEL THE SENSE OF READINESS TO MOVE AT THE HIP JOINTS. WHEN THE HIP FLEXORS HAVE BEEN STRETCHED, THE PELVIS EASILY SHIFTS INTO AN IDEAL ALIGNMENT AND THE SLIGHT CONTRACTION OF THE PYRAMIDALIS IS SUFFICIENT TO MAINTAIN THAT ALIGNMENT. THIS IS WHAT MANY DANCE TEACHERS MEAN WHEN THEY TALK OF "BEING *ON* THE LEGS." IT IS CERTAINLY EASIER TO STRETCH THE HIP FLEXORS AND ENGAGE THE PYRAMIDALIS THAN IT IS TO CONTRACT THE GLUTEUS MAXIMUS (FOR HIP EXTENSION), THE QUADRICEPS (TO PREVENT KNEE FLEXION THAT ACCOMPANIES THE HIP EXTENSION), AND ALL OF THE ABDOMINALS (TO HOLD UP THE FRONT RIM OF THE PELVIS). THE MOST COMMON EXCLAMATION I HEAR AT THIS POINT IS, "BUT IT'S TOO EASY." EXACTLY.

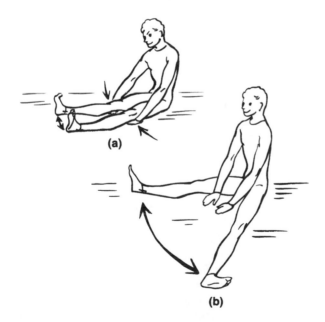

(a)

(b)

FIGURE 19.53. Seated reciprocals for adductors.

STARTING IN LONG SIT POSITION, PLACE THE HANDS ON THE FLOOR ON EITHER SIDE OF THE LEGS. PRESS THE LEGS OUT AGAINST THE RESISTANCE OF THE HANDS. HOLD THE CONTRAC-TION FOR 10 TO 15 SECONDS. THEN MOVE THE HANDS AND LET THE LEGS SPREAD WIDE, STRETCHING THE ADDUCTORS OF THE HIP.

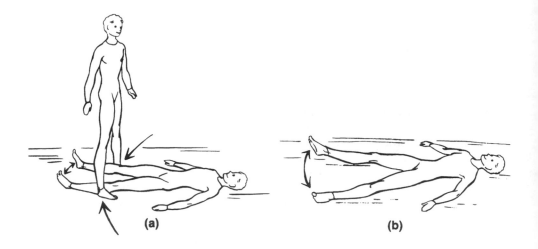

FIGURE 19.54.   Supine reciprocals for adductors.

IN A SUPINE POSITION, WITH A PARTNER STANDING WITH FEET OUTSIDE YOUR LEGS, PRESS OUT AGAINST THE RESISTANCE OF THE PARTNER'S ANKLES. HOLD THE CONTRACTION FOR 10 TO 15 SECONDS. THEN RELEASE AND ALLOW THE LEGS TO SPREAD WIDE, STRETCHING THE ADDUCTORS OF THE HIP.

Additional Exercises

PELVIC CLOCK[5]

Beginning in a hook lying position with the feet hip-width apart, press the feet down into the floor and roll the back of the waist down to the floor at the same time, without allowing the sacrum to lose contact with the floor. This "waist to the floor" position is then defined as 12 o'clock. Allow the waist to rise from the floor so that the tailbone (coccyx) is the only part of the lower spine contacting the floor. This position is defined as 6 o'clock. Gently and easily change the pelvic position from 6 to 12 and back approximately 4 or 5 times. Then, in your mind, locate 3 o'clock and 9 o'clock. (Assume that your clock is lying with its back on the floor so that 9 o'clock is to your right and 3 o'clock is to your left.) Without allowing the back of the pelvis to lose contact with the floor, shift the pelvis so that the point of contact with the floor is at 3 o'clock. In this position, the posterior of your pelvis on the left side is contacting the floor and the right side is slightly lifted off the floor. Now switch to 9 o'clock, with the weight shifting to the back of the right side of the pelvis. Alternate back and forth between 3 o'clock and 9 o'clock 4 or 5 times. Having established the four reference points on your pelvic clock, go back to 12 o'clock and then proceed gently and smoothly clockwise through 1, 2, 3, 4, 5, 6, 7, 8, 9, 10, 11, and back to 12 o'clock. (You will probably find certain zones on your clock that are kinesthetically blurry. On subsequent passes of these blank zones, you should pay particular attention to moving through them with conscious

5. Modification of a Feldenkrais exercise.

attention.) Repeat the clockwise trip around the pelvic clock at least three or four times (more may be necessary if you discover serious "snags" in a particular region). Then change direction and go counterclockwise. (You may find that different zones are "blank" or filled with "snags" when you change direction.) Repeat the counterclockwise trip at least 3 or 4 times, and more if you feel it is necessary. Return to the original hook lying position and allow a moment to process the kinetic information you have gained from the exercise. Then, one leg at a time, stretch your legs out into a straight-leg supine position, and once again take a moment or two to process new sensations.

SHOULDER CLOCK[6]

Lie on the right side in a loose fetal position, with the right arm in a comfortable position and the left arm lying easily on the side of the body. Focus your attention on the tip of the left shoulder. Take the shoulder up toward the ear. That is 12 o'clock. Take the shoulder down away from the ear, past your starting position. That is 6 o'clock. Gently and easily shift back and forth between 12 o'clock and 6 o'clock 4 or 5 times. Locate 3 o'clock and 9 o'clock. (Assume that 9 o'clock is in front of you and 3 o'clock is behind you.) Take the shoulder tip forward to 9 o'clock and then back to 3 o'clock. Gently and easily shift between 9 and 3 about 4 or 5 times. Then take the shoulder tip to 12 o'clock and, moving clockwise, take the tip of the shoulder through all positions on the face of the clock: 1, 2, 3, 4, 5, 6, 7, 8, 9, 10, 11, and back to 12 o'clock. Do not rush. Take time to work through zones that are unfamiliar and zones that have "snags." Then return to 12 o'clock and reverse the direction to move counterclockwise around the face of your shoulder clock. Repeat the counterclockwise trip at least 4 or 5 times. Then return to the neutral starting position with your shoulder tip in the center of your clock face. Pause here for a moment to process any new sensations that you may have encountered. Then roll onto your back and sense the difference between the two shoulders. Take a moment for conscious processing of this difference, as the contrast between sides provides valuable kinesthetic information about tension and nontension in the shoulder region. After your processing and comparison time, roll to the left side and repeat the exercise with the right shoulder moving. When you finish the right shoulder, again take time to process any new kinesthetic information.

THORACIC CLOCK[7]

In hook lying position, with the feet hip-width apart, focus your attention on your rib cage. Sense the contact between the back of the rib cage and the floor and tune into the changes in its contact with the floor as you take

6. Modification of a Feldenkrais exercise.
7. Although I "invented" this exercise, the concept clearly originated with Feldenkrais. I didn't specifically learn it in a Feldenkrais session, but that does not make the "clock" concept mine. Somehow I am sure that Feldenkrais did this exercise well before I thought of it.

a few deep breaths. Having focused your attention on the shifting contact with the floor, inhale deeply and lift the lower portion of the rib cage so that the upper thoracic region of the spine is the primary contact with the floor. This is 12 o'clock. Then exhale deeply, allowing the upper portion of the rib cage to lift off the floor as the lower ribs become the primary contact with the floor. This is 6 o'clock. Gently and easily, in coordination with your breathing pattern, switch back and forth from 12 to 6 o'clock about 4 or 5 times. Locate 3 o'clock and 9 o'clock. (Assume that 9 o'clock is to your right and 3 o'clock is to your left.) Inhale and shift the primary contact with the floor to 9 o'clock, and then exhale and return to neutral. Inhale again and shift to 3 o'clock, returning to neutral on your exhalation. Then, breathing easily, shift back and forth from 3 to 9 o'clock about 4 or 5 times. Beginning at 12 o'clock, gently and easily proceed clockwise around the clock face, taking time to work through "snags" and smooth out the rough spots. Repeat the clockwise circling about 4 or 5 times. Then shift to a counterclockwise direction and once again work through the snags and rough spots. Repeat the counterclockwise rotation about 4 or 5 times. Then return to the neutral center position and process the new kinesthetic information this exercise provided.

WATER SKI STRETCH

Stand facing the edge of an open door and take hold of the two doorknobs, one in each hand. Straighten the arms and stand an arm's length from the edge of the door. Bend the knees and move the feet slightly closer to the edge of the door so that you are in demiplié with your feet between the vertical line of your spine and the edge of the door. Slowly ease the knees closer and closer to the edge of the door (without moving the feet) and allow the spine to go into a flexed position. (As the knees get closer to the edge of the door, you will feel the stretch move slightly higher into the upper thoracic region, stretching the middle trapezius and the rhomboids. As your knees move away from the edge of the door, the focus of the stretch moves downward in the spine toward the upper lumbar region, stretching the lower trapezius.) Crossing each hand to the doorknob on the opposite side increases the stretch. This stretch can be further increased by pulling one hip back away from the edge of the door and working the stretch on the same side of the spine as the shifted hip. Then shift the other hip back and stretch the other side of the back. This hip-shift section tends to focus on stretch of the latissimus dorsi and, with patience, the quadratus lumborum.

A New Approach to Releasing Muscular Tension[8]

For the last ten years, I have been using a technique to release neuromuscular tension which I call, very simply, *lifts*. In this technique the subject is

8. This approach is based on a Feldenkrais principle and was developed after a conversation with Carol Lessinger, Feldenkrais practitioner. Trager Menastics seems to use a similar releasing technique, as do some other hands-on somatic approaches.

passively manipulated by a partner. The technique is very effective, immediately releasing tension for many people who have tried it.

While I have not researched these lifts, I do have some theories about what is happening. I think that the lifts are really a method to assist the subject in learning how to *deactivate* the musculature. This is done by a partner who lifts the subject's body parts, supporting the whole weight until the subject has relaxed the muscular control of a part or given up control of the weight. Then the body part is put down on the floor, and the subject experiences a profound change in the residual tension patterns. I realize that this technique is not new; various approaches to body therapy have been using the basic technique for some time. However, the ease with which subjects are able to release tension is so remarkable that I must include a description of the various lifts I have designed.

The lifts, like the general conditioning program, reflect the particular needs of dancers. Areas of high tension for dancers are found in the hip region, the upper back and neck, and the lower back. The lifts are designed to reduce tension in these areas.

There are six general principles for doing the lifts. *First,* the manipulator must be aware that he or she is responsible for the subject's safety during the lifts. The manipulator must move the subject gently in order to facilitate release of tension. Trust is an essential component of the relationship between the manipulator and the subject. *Second,* when the lifts are being done on the appendages, only one side can be done at a time. If the subject has a particular problem with one side, it is recommended that the manipulator begin with the "good" side and do the problem side second. This utilizes bilateral transfer, which seems to occur in the lifts. That is, the second side learns from the first and the release is more complete on the second side. *Third,* when the lifts are done on the appendages, there must be processing time between the first and second side. When the subject is "half-baked," so to speak, there is a massive amount of information about the nature of tension readily available upon examination of the contrast between the two sides. *Fourth,* before progressing to the second side, the subject should be instructed to try to achieve the same level of release in the "undone" as in the "done" side. In this way the subject learns sensory techniques for tension identification and release which is not dependent upon a manipulator. *Fifth,* the subject should be encouraged to resist the natural impulse to move the body part immediately after the lift. There is, apparently, a real need to reestablish tension patterns. This may be related to the need to maintain the familiar neuro-feedback which is a part of the subject's body image. By resisting the impulse to move following the lifts, the subject is giving the body a chance to accommodate to a new, realigned position. *Sixth,* subjects will sometimes experience a sense of disassociation (or even fear) at the loss of habitual tension patterns. The manipulator should be prepared to reassure the subject, primarily through touch, if there is any evidence of fear.

The following list of the seven existing lifts includes procedures for those lifts.

1. *Hip flexor lift* (to reduce tension in the hip flexors). The subject lies on his or her back on the floor with the legs straight. From the side, the manipulator places one hand under the subject's knee and the other hand under the subject's ankle. Cradling the weight of the subject's leg, the manipulator moves the leg into flexion, back into extension, through inward and outward rotation, and through abduction and adduction while constantly giving verbal feedback to the subject about the weight of the leg. As the subject begins to give up control of the leg, the leg will feel heavier to the manipulator. When the leg feels very heavy to the manipulator, the leg is pulled long into extension of the knee and hip and is then gently placed down on the floor. After a pause, the manipulator instructs the subject to try to release the "undone" side to match the "done" side through conscious relaxation. When the subject has relaxed the undone side as much as possible, the manipulator repeats the lift on the second side. It is frequently necessary to go back to the first side for a brief additional lift to balance the two sides, since the second side will frequently release more completely than the first. Apparently the second side learns from the first side and thus relaxes more completely. After a period of internal processing of the new alignment of the hip allowed by release of tension in the hip flexors, the subject is instructed to imagine some simple actions, utilizing the new alignment. Eventually the subject is instructed to stand, activate the pyramidalis to lift the front rim of the pelvis, and experience the new alignment in the standing position. The immediate change in pelvic alignment caused by the release of tension in the hip flexors is frequently quite profound, but the subject may find that habitual patterns are strong and that tension returns. Daily repetition of the lift is recommended in the early phases of realignment.

2. *Shoulder lift* (to reduce tension in the elevators of the scapula). The subject is instructed to sit in an armless chair with his or her arms hanging easily to the sides. The manipulator stands to the side of the subject and cups both hands firmly under the subject's armpit. The shoulder is then lifted, and the subject is instructed to give all the weight to the manipulator. The shoulder is moved up, down, forward, and back by the manipulator. Once again verbal feedback about the relative weight felt by the manipulator can help the subject release control of the weight. When the shoulder is very heavy to the manipulator, it is slowly lowered to its new resting position. Comparison of the two sides at this point often shows a remarkable difference in the height of the two shoulders. Time should be taken between shoulders for the subject to process information about the difference between the two sides, and to "go inside" and try to release the "undone" side to match the "done" side. When the subject is ready, the manipulator repeats the procedure on the second side. It may be necessary to return to the first side to balance the release in the two shoulders.

3. *Low back lift* (to reduce tension in the lower back). The subject lies in the hook lying position with the knees bent. The manipulator stands straddling the subject and places his or her forearms under the knees of the subject. The manipulator rests his or her elbows on the front of his or her own thigh and then lifts the weight of the subject's low back and buttocks

with the legs. (Do not try to do this lift using the back muscles, as back strain could result. Also, the subject and the manipulator should be approximately the same size.) As the manipulator lifts the subject's back and hips from the floor, it is helpful for the manipulator to swing the weight from side to side and to step backward with the swinging to stretch the subject's spine longer. After the subject has released control of the weight, the feet are lowered to the floor, and the manipulator supports the legs while extending the knees of the subject to allow the subject to assume a long supine position.

4. *Scapula lift* (to reduce tension in the pectoralis minor and other abductors of the scapula). The subject is instructed to lie in a supine position. The manipulator squats near one shoulder of the subject and cups the hands under the shoulder. The shoulder is lifted off the floor, and the subject is instructed to give all of the shoulder weight to the manipulator. When the shoulder is very heavy, the manipulator manually adducts and depresses the subject's scapula by pushing the scapula in toward the spine and down toward the waist. (This action is very much like tucking the blankets under the mattress when making a bed.) The scapula is literally tucked in and down. Process time is allowed between sides, and the subject is instructed to try to match the undone side with the done side. When the subject has lowered tension in the undone side as much as possible, the process is repeated on the second side. The subject is then instructed to imagine some simple actions of the arms utilizing the new alignment. Following the imagined action the subject is instructed to stand and allow the shoulders to hang gently to the sides.

5. *Head lift* (to reduce tension in the neck). The subject is instructed to lie supine on the floor. The manipulator sits behind the subject's head. The manipulator's fingers are cupped under the base of the subject's skull, and the head is gently lifted off the floor. The manipulator's fingers should be spread wide so there is a maximum amount of support for the subject's head. The head is moved in order to flex, laterally flex, and rotate the subject's cervical spine. When the head feels very heavy to the manipulator, it is very gently placed back down on the floor. The manipulator's hands should remain on either side of the subject's head for a while after the head is put down, to support the head as it rests on the floor and to prevent rolling from side to side. This lift should be followed by the neck lift.

6. *Neck lift* (to reduce tension in the neck). In the same position as the head lift, the manipulator cups his or her hands behind the neck of the subject. The neck is gently lifted, allowing the head to rock back and remain on the floor. The movement of the manipulator's hands is quite small on this lift, while raising and lowering the neck. When the neck feels heavy to the manipulator, it is lowered to the floor, the hands are shifted up to cup the base of the subject's skull, and the head is gently pulled away from the spine in order to lengthen the neck. The neck is released, with the manipulator's hands staying in contact with the subject for a brief period to provide lateral support.

7. *Outward rotator lift* (to reduce tension in the outward rotators of the hip). The subject is instructed to lie on one side with the top hip and knee

flexed so the knee is in front of the subject. The manipulator places one hand under the subject's knee and one hand under the subject's ankle. The leg is then lifted into an abducted and outwardly rotated position. The subject is instructed to give up control of the weight. The leg is moved into flexion, extension, abduction, adduction, inward rotation, and outward rotation. When the leg feels very heavy to the manipulator, it is gently lowered to the floor. The subject is then given time to process the difference in the two sides. After a short time, the subject is instructed to roll over onto his or her back and lie with the legs extended to compare the rotation of the two hips. The process is then repeated on the second side.

Each of the lifts described above can be used by itself to facilitate the reduction of neuromuscular tension in the subject. The lifts also can be used to accompany other exercises for a particular problem. The specialized exercise programs, which follow, include the lifts.

Mini-Programs for Specialized Problems

The following mini-programs have been designed to meet specialized needs of dancers. The numbered lists refer the reader back to the figure number of the exercise in the basic program. If the exercise is new, a description of the exercise is given.

Pronated feet, flat feet, weak feet and ankles, or rehabilitation after ankle sprain. For each of these problems, it is important to increase the strength of the musculature of the foot, tarsus, and ankles. The following program is designed to build strength and to stretch out after the strength exercises.

1. Ankle/tarsus series (Figure 19.15). As strength builds, use the added resistance of a circle of elastic or cross-section of inner tube around the feet to further build strength.
2. Toe gripper (Figure 19.12)
3. Standing foot wobble (Figure 19.18)
4. Stairstep full *relevé*. Standing on a stairstep with the balls of the feet on the edge of the step and the heels unsupported, allow the heels to slowly descend as far as possible, keeping the tarsus in a neutral position. Maintaining the neutral tarsus throughout the exercise, rise from the lowest position, through a normal standing position and on to a full *relevé* position. Then return to the starting position and repeat the exercise 3 times "past the burnies." When strength has reached the point that 30 repetitions are easy, do this exercise with all of the weight on one foot. The number of repetitions will be reduced considerably when the weight is doubled. Do a series on both feet when only one foot is being exercised at a time.
5. Gastrocnemius and soleus stretch (Figure 19.22)
6. Shin-splint stretch (Figure 19.17)
7. Ankle circles (Figure 19.16)

Limited range of motion at the ankle joint. A study by a graduate student (Tye, 1982) has shown that the total range of ankle action is more important to jump height than the depth of the *demiplié*. Thus, it is thought that increasing the full range of plantar and dorsiflexion of the ankle joint is a feasible goal.

1. Heel presses (Figure 19.11)
2. Toe gripper (Figure 19.12)
3. Mouth. Using a cross-section of inner tube around the balls of the feet, place the right heel on the anterior aspect of the ankle joint of the left foot. Working against the resistance of the inner tube, dorsi-flex the right ankle and plantar-flex the left. Repeat at least 5 times "past the burnies." Repeat with the left foot on top.
4. Stairstep full *relevé*. Standing on a stairstep with the balls of the feet on the edge of the step and the heels unsupported, allow the heels to slowly descend as far as possible, keeping the tarsus in a neutral po-sition. Maintaining the neutral tarsus throughout the exercise, rise from the lowest position, through a normal standing position and on to a full *relevé* position. Then return to the starting position and repeat the exercise 3 times "past the burnies." When strength has reached the point that 30 repetitions are easy, do this exercise with all of the weight on one foot. The number of repetitions will be re-duced considerably when the weight is doubled. Do a series on both feet when only one foot is being exercised at a time.
5. Shin-splint stretch (Figure 19.17)
6. Manual stretches. In the tailor sit position, manually press the foot into a plantar-flexed position of the ankle and swing from side to side, pronating and supinating in the plantar-flexed position. Dorsi-flex the ankle, pulling the toes up into hyperextension, and use the hands to manually work the ankle and tarsus into pronation and supination. Repeat on the other side.
7. Ankle circles (Figure 19.16)

Shin splints. You are reminded that true shin splints are a muscular phenomenon and thus should decrease considerably within two or three weeks, at least. If shin splints continue longer than that, the dancer should be checked for a possible stress fracture. True shin splints are actually a microscopic tearing of the musculature of the lower leg, particularly those muscles that attach directly to the periosteum (bone covering) such as the tibialis anterior, the tibialis posterior, and the peroneals. Ice and gentle stretch are the best treatments for true shin splints. For shin splints on the anterior side:

1. Shin-splint stretch (Figure 19.17)
2. Manual stretches. In the tailor sit position, manually press the foot into a plantar-flexed position of the ankle and swing from side to side, pronating and supinating in the plantar-flexed position. Dorsi-flex the ankle, pulling the toes up into hyperextension and use the

hands to manually work the ankle and tarsus into pronation and supination. Repeat on the other side.

3. Ankle circles (Figure 19.16)

For shin splints on the posterior side:

1. Gastrocnemius and soleus stretch (particularly the soleus stretch) (Figure 19.22)
2. Manual stretches (same as number 2, above)
3. Ankle circles (Figure 19.16)
4. Supine hamstring stretch (Figure 19.45)

Once the immediate pain of the shin splints has diminished, the dancer should do the pronated-feet series to build strength in the musculature to prevent recurrence.

Chondromalacia of the patella. The basic approach to chondromalacia of the patella is to strengthen the vasti muscles of the thigh. Ideally one would primarily strengthen the medial vasti if the patella was displaced laterally and strengthen the lateral vasti if the patella was displaced medially (the latter is less common). However, because it is difficult to selectively strengthen the individual vasti muscles, the conditioning approach is to strengthen the vasti generally.

1. Heel presses (Figure 19.11)
2. Seated leg lifts (Figure 19.13). Adding ankle weights as strength increases.
3. One-legged *demipliés* (Figure 19.19)
4. TV stretch (Figure 19.14) or stork stretch (Figure 19.24) to stretch out the vasti.

Rehabilitation of the knee after an injury and a physician has approved exercise. In this case, both the flexors and the extensors of the knee are strengthened to add stability to the knee joint.

1. Heel presses (Figure 19.11)
2. Seated leg lifts (Figure 19.13). Adding ankle weights as strength increases.
3. TV stretch (Figure 19.14)
4. Weighted knee flexion. Standing in parallel with the feet hip-width apart, wearing ankle weights (start with lighter weights and increase weight as strength increases), flex the right knee slowly to 90 degrees and slowly lower, repeating 5 repetitions "past the burnies." Repeat with left leg.
5. Standing reciprocal for hamstrings (Figure 19.23)
6. One-legged *demipliés* (Figure 19.19)
7. Stork stretch (Figure 19.24)
8. Gastrocnemius and soleus stretch (Figure 19.22)

Tight hip flexors, lumbar lordosis, anterior snapping hip. Since all of the conditions listed above may be related to tight hip flexors, many of the same exercises can be used for each of the conditions. Since abdominal strength is needed to hold up the front rim of the pelvis once the hip flexors have been stretched, strengthening exercises for the abdominals are included.

1. Knee-overs (Figure 19.1)
2. Abdominal curls (Figure 19.2)
3. Arches (Figure 19.3)
4. Prone leg lifts (Figure 19.43)
5. Lying hip flexor stretch (Figure 19.44)
6. TV stretch (Figure 19.14)
7. Spine assembler (Figure 19.7)
8. Hip flop (Figure 19.51)
9. Pyramidalis isolator (Figure 19.52)
10. *Hip flexor lift*

Lateral snapping hip. Lateral snapping hip, evidenced by the greater trochanter slipping out to the side when the hip is adducted, is caused by tight and weak abductors of the hip joint. The approach to reducing the snapping is to stretch and strengthen the abductors.

1. Supine leg swings (Figure 19.8)
2. Side leg lifts (Figure 19.9)
3. Reciprocals to stretch adductors and strengthen abductors (Figures 19.53 and 19.54).
4. C-curve (Figure 19.10a). Isolate the abductors of the hip by stabilizing the torso. That is, if stretching the left abductors, the left lateral flexors of the lumbar spine (particularly quadratus lumborum and internal oblique) are activated to pull up on the left side of the pelvis.
5. Leg-over stretch (Figure 19.10c). Focus this stretch on the hip joint by keeping the rib cage (on the same side as the leg being stretched) on the floor.
6. Lunge stretch (Figure 19.10b)
7. Yoga sit (Figure 19.10d)
8. Hip greaser (Figure 19.50)

Sciatic syndrome. Sciatic syndrome can be a nagging nuisance or flaming agony. For preventive maintenance or when the pain is light, do all of the exercises listed below. However, when the pain is intense, radiating (and possibly even spasmodic) down the entire lateral side of the leg, do exercises 3 through 9, below, which are the stretching and releasing exercises.

1. Frog press and stretch (Figure 19.46 and Figure 19.48)
2. Lying knee press and stretch (Figure 19.47)
3. Hip greaser (Figure 19.50)
4. Leg-over stretch (Figure 19.10c)

5. Supine hamstring stretch (Figure 19.45)
6. Repeat hip greaser (Figure 19.50)
7. *Outward rotator lift*
8. Deep massage (requires a partner). Lying on the side with the "bad" hip toward the ceiling, flex the top hip and knee and allow the knee to drop to the floor. The partner, standing above the person with sciatic syndrome, massages deep in the gluteal dimple, finding the tight musculature and working at those muscles with deep pressure.
9. Repeat *outward rotator lift*

Exercises to increase dance "extension" (flexion of the hip with extended knee). Limitation of dance "extensions" can come from weakness of the hip flexors or from tightness of the hip extensors, notably the hamstrings. Because the abdominals play an essential role in the stabilization of the pelvis to allow efficient hip flexion, the abdominals must also be strengthened.

1. Knee-overs (Figure 19.1)
2. Abdominal curls (Figure 19.2)
3. Pyramidalis isolator (Figure 19.52)
4. Supine leg lifts (Figure 19.42). Add weights as strength increases.
5. Supine hamstring stretch (Figure 19.45)
6. Seated leg lifts (Figure 19.13)
7. Seated reciprocal hamstring stretch (Figure 19.26)
8. TV stretch (Figure 19.14)
9. Standing reciprocal stretch for hamstrings (Figure 19.23)

Exercises to increase the height of the arabesque. Torso strength and hip strength combine with mobility of the hip flexors to facilitate a higher arabesque. A dancer with a short torso, and less space between the lower ribs and the iliac crest, will naturally have a lower arabesque because the ribs actually contact the crest of the ilium in the arabesque position. If, however, there is no bony obstruction, these exercises will build strength in muscles critical to the arabesque.

1. Knee-overs (Figure 19.1)
2. Abdominal curls (Figure 19.2)
3. Arches (Figure 19.3)
4. Curl (Figure 19.4)
5. Prone leg lifts (Figure 19.43). Add ankle weights as strength increases.
6. Lying hip flexor stretch (Figure 19.44)
7. TV stretch (Figure 19.14)
8. Supine hamstring stretch (Figure 19.45)

Exercises to increase torso strength and mobility. In observing dancers in my conditioning classes, I have noted a patterned relationship between hamstring elasticity and torso mobility. Dancers with flexible spines often have tight hamstrings, while dancers with extreme hamstring stretch have less mobility in the spine. This may be due to the nature of dance stretches: they combine spine and hamstring stretches. In these combined stretches, the dancer utilizes existing mobility without necessarily stretching the immobile area. For this reason, careful attention to the relative flexion of the specific joints involved must be given in each stretch.

1. Knee-overs (Figure 19.1)
2. Abdominal curls (Figure 19.2)
3. Arches (Figure 19.3)
4. Curl (Figure 19.4)
5. Mad cat (Figure 19.32)
6. Abdominal curls (Figure 19.5)
7. Plow (Figure 19.6)
8. Spine assembler (Figure 19.7)
9. Seated arm circles (Figure 19.28)
10. Shoulder sequence (Figure 19.29). Without the pushups at the end.
11. C-curve stretch (Figure 19.10a)
12. Leg-over stretch (Figure 19.10c)
13. Yoga sit stretch (Figure 19.10d)
14. Wallpaper stretch (Figure 19.25)
15. Water ski stretch. Standing near an open door with solid hinges, take hold of the two doorknobs; stand in parallel position with the feet about six inches from the door. Bend the knees and allow the weight of the torso to hang from the doorknobs, while pressing the knees in toward the edge of the door. Nudge around in this position to find areas of needed stretch. Twisting the pelvis to the right and left may identify such areas.

Exercises for pectoralis minor syndrome.

1. Scapula push-ups (Figure 19.33)
2. Prone arm lifts. Lying in a prone position with the arms out to the sides, lift the arms off the floor while adducting the scapula. Repeat 10 to 20 times and add weights in the hands as strength increases.
3. Flagman presses (Figure 19.35)
4. Reciprocal stretch for pectoralis major (Figure 19.39)
5. Doorjamb hang (Figure 19.40)
6. Water ski stretch. Standing near an open door with solid hinges, take hold of the two doorknobs; stand in parallel position with the feet about six inches from the door. Bend the knees and allow the weight of the torso to hang from the doorknobs, while pressing the knees in toward the edge of the door. Nudge around in this position to find areas of needed stretch. Twisting the pelvis to the right and left may identify areas of needed stretch.
7. Arm-over stretch (Figure 19.36)

8. Shoulder flop (Figure 19.37)
9. Shoulder clock. Lying on the right side with the knees and hips comfortably flexed and the top arm lying comfortably on the side of the body, move the left shoulder toward the ear and identify that position as 12 o'clock. Then move the shoulder down away from the ear as far as possible and identify that position as 6 o'clock. Next move the left shoulder forward as far as possible and identify that position as 9 o'clock. From 9 o'clock move the shoulder backward as far as possible and identify that as 3 o'clock. Return to 12 o'clock and then go in sequence through 1, 2, 3, and so on, back to 12 o'clock. Repeat the circle slowly 3 or 4 times or until the shoulder moves through the full circle with ease. Reverse the direction and repeat 3 or 4 times in the new direction. Repeat on the other side with the right shoulder.
10. *Scapula lift*

Exercises for kyphosis (excessive flexion of the thoracic spine).

1. Prone arm lifts. Lying in a prone position with the arms out to the sides, lift the arms off the floor while adducting the scapula. Repeat 10 to 20 times and add weights in the hands as strength increases.
2. Arches (Figure 19.3)
3. Flagman presses (Figure 19.35)
4. Reciprocal stretch for pectoralis major (Figure 19.39)
5. Rowing on a rowing machine
6. Scapula push-ups (Figure 19.33)
7. Arm-over stretch (Figure 19.36)
8. Water ski stretch. Standing near an open door with solid hinges, take hold of the two doorknobs; stand in parallel position with the feet about six inches from the door. Bend the knees and allow the weight of the torso to hang from the doorknobs, while pressing the knees in toward the edge of the door. Nudge around in this position to find areas of needed stretch. Twisting the pelvis to the right and left may identify such areas.
9. Latissimus stretch (Figure 19.10e)

Exercises for shoulder, upper back, and neck tension.

1. Water ski stretch. Standing near an open door with solid hinges, take hold of the two doorknobs; stand in parallel position with the feet about six inches from the door. Bend the knees and allow the weight of the torso to hang from the doorknobs, while pressing the knees in toward the edge of the door. Nudge around in this position to find areas of needed stretch. Twisting the pelvis to the right and left may identify such areas.
2. Latissimus stretch (Figure 19.10e)
3. Neck stretches and neck circles (Figure 19.38)
4. Arm-over stretch (Figure 19.36)

5. Shoulder clock. Lying on the right side with the knees and hips comfortably flexed and the top arm lying comfortably on the side of the body, move the left shoulder toward the ear and identify that position as 12 o'clock. Then move the shoulder down away from the ear as far as possible and identify that position as 6 o'clock. Next move the left shoulder forward as far as possible and identify that position as 9 o'clock. From 9 o'clock move the shoulder backward as far as possible and identify that as 3 o'clock. Return to 12 o'clock and then go in sequence through 1, 2, 3, and so on, back to 12 o'clock. Repeat the circle slowly 3 or 4 times or until the shoulder moves through the full circle with ease. Reverse the direction and repeat 3 or 4 times in the new direction. Repeat on the other side with the right shoulder.
6. Shoulder flop (Figure 19.37)
7. *Shoulder lift*
8. *Head lift* and *neck lift*
9. *Scapula lift*

Exercises for scoliosis. Scoliosis is a complex phenomenon. It includes both lateral flexion and rotation of the spine. Theoretical analysis of the tight muscles and the weak muscles can become incredibly complex. Luckily, the body gives a very simple clue to its needs by comparing the relative ease of strength and mobility exercises on the two sides. The general prescription for balancing strength and mobility is actually quite simple. When a strength producing exercise is harder on one side, do more repetitions on that side. When a mobility exercise (a stretch) is more difficult on one side, stay with that stretch for a longer period of time. (For extreme case of scoliosis, be sure to consult a physician.) *Exercises for strength:*

1. Abdominal curls (Figure 19.2)
2. Arches (Figure 19.3)
3. Side torso lifts (Figure 19.9)
4. Shoulder sequence (Figure 19.29)

Exercises for mobility.

1. Latissimus stretch (Figure 19.10e)
2. Long C-curve (Figure 19.10a)
3. Leg-over stretch (Figure 19.10c)
4. Water ski stretch.
5. Plow (Figure 19.6). Do this with a twist, first taking the feet off to the right and pressing the rib cage to the left and then taking the feet to the left and pressing the rib cage to the right.

Exercises to reduce the frequency of foot cramps. When dancers return to the studio after a layoff, they frequently experience foot cramps in the initial phases of reconditioning. Effective use of the feet demands both strength and mobility.

1. Towel pulling. Place a towel on the floor and use the toes in a flexion action to pull the towel toward the heel.
2. Toe gripper (Figure 19.12)
3. Ankle/tarsus series (Figure 19.15)
4. Tennis ball roller. Place a tennis ball on the floor and place one foot on top of it. Placing some of the body weight on the foot, roll the tennis ball back and forth to massage the plantar surface of the foot.
5. Deep massage. Manually massage the entire foot, pressing deeply into the tender areas to relieve the tension spots.
6. Gastrocnemius and soleus stretch (Figure 19.22)
7. Ankle circles (Figure 19.16)
8. Shin-splint stretch (Figure 19.17)

Exercises for reducing forward head. Often forward head is accompanied by (or caused by?) tightness of the flexors of the cervical spine. An exercise program for this problem should include strengthening the extensors and stretching the flexors of the cervical spine.

1. Arches (Figure 19.3)
2. Prone lying head raise. From a prone position, lift the head as high as possible off the floor. Repeat 5 repetitions "past the burnies."
3. Neck stretches and neck circles (Figure 19.38)
4. *Neck lift*
5. *Head lift*

In Conclusion

This chapter has covered a lot of territory, from basic principles of conditioning through specific applications of those principles. Many exercises have been included, but you should not think that these are the only exercises for the specific conditions listed. There certainly may be many other exercises that meet the specific needs of dancers. You are encouraged to experiment with different exercise programs to correct problems, increase capacities, reduce limitations, and increase efficiency. The keys to effective conditioning are practicing systematically, noting the effects of particular exercises, and modifying sequences and exercises accordingly. Kinesiological analysis of most problems can identify the muscles that need strength and those that need elasticity in a given action. At this point, you should have the skills necessary to design your own programs to meet specific needs. Application of the principles of conditioning in this chapter should guide the design, after you have identified the changes desired.

CHAPTER *20*

Weight Management

Dancers are one of the groups most susceptible to nutritional fads and crash diets. There is no place to hide a few extra pounds in a leotard. Both internal and external pressures are placed on the dancer to maintain a thin body. These pressures lead the serious dancer to diet patterns that may not be appropriate. The appeal of a ten-pound weight loss in one week may be strong, but the nutritional consequences may be quite serious. Nowhere is the need for sound, rational eating habits more necessary than in the dancer's world. Realistically, it may be difficult to find time for sensible meals, and yet the physical demands placed on the dancer make adequate nutrition an absolute necessity.

One of the biggest fallacies of weight management is the assumption that what works for one person works for all. No single dietary approach is effective for all. There are simply too many variations in body composition, absorption rates, and metabolism to make a single approach appropriate for all dancers. Each dancer must select a plan that is individually effective.

This chapter is not written from the perspective of a nutritional expert, but rather from the perspective of one who has battled excessive weight all her life and who has advised students in the same battle. Rather than presenting the standard approach to nutrition, I will focus on some of the relationships between individual differences and the dancer's maintenance of an ideal weight. I will share attitudes, rather than facts, about nutrition.[1]

Overweight and Underweight

The dangers of overweight for the dancer are relatively clear. An overweight body is placed under high stress, physiologically, biomechanically, psychologically, and aesthetically. Physiological dangers include excessive stress on the heart, circulatory system, and muscular system. Biomechanical dangers include greater stress on the weight-bearing joints. When one is overweight, any misalignment can result in a serious injury. Because of the increased pounds per square inch carried by the weight-bearing joints,

---

1. For a more detailed discussion, the reader is referred to: Chmelar and Fitt. *Diet* (Dancing at Your Peak Series). Princeton Book Company, Pennington, N.J., 1990.

443

what might be a minor injury can be amplified into a very serious injury. Psychological dangers have a direct effect on performance. When one is overweight, one hesitates to appear before an audience, and, after all, that is the essence of dance performance. Aesthetic dangers relate to getting jobs. Choreographers are reluctant to hire fat dancers. That is the reality of the matter. A fat dancer, no matter how beautifully he or she dances, will seldom be taken into a company or recruited by a choreographer. Thus the dangers of being overweight place many pressures on the dancer to remain thin.

At the other end of the scale is the underweight dancer, who is in just as much danger as the overweight dancer. Two psychological disorders—*anorexia nervosa* and *bulemia*—have called attention to the serious, and sometimes fatal, consequences of excessive dieting. Commonly recognized symptoms of anorexia nervosa include a distorted body image (seeing one's body as fat when in actuality it is very thin); extreme eating habits such as fasting, binging, and purging (forced vomiting, excessive use of laxatives, or both); and a deep-seated sense of insecurity. The ultimate danger of anorexia nervosa and bulimia is, quite simply, starvation and death. The contributory dangers along the way include malnutrition, loss of hair, loss of fingernails, loss of teeth, and many other effects of nutritional deprivation. Anorexic and bulimic individuals often speak of a "sense of control" that is gained from the manipulation of nutritional intake. Anyone who has exercised enough willpower to lose weight has experienced that sense of control. Yet for anorexics, the sense of control becomes an obsession distorted by insecurity. It is the rare anorexic who independently changes eating habits to a more normal pattern. Far more frequently, the anorexic needs support and guidance from a specialist who deals with the problem on a regular basis. The anorexic must be assisted in developing a realistic body image, in controlling erratic and dangerous eating habits, and in identifying and facing the deep-seated causes of the problem.

Dieting Effectively

Compared with the possible consequences of anorexia nervosa, the problems of the overweight dancer are quite inconsequential. But that knowledge still doesn't make weight loss an easy task. There is no getting around it: dieting is a drag. There are, however, some approaches to dieting that seem to be more effective than others. Those approaches will be divided into four categories for discussion: systematic self-assessment, choosing a dietary approach, adopting effective eating habits, and changing attitudes.

Systematic Self-Assessment

Any systematic approach to change begins with an assessment of present conditions. Losing weight is no different. The first step is to identify the present conditions. There are a number of components to the process of realistic self-assessment preceding an effective weight-loss program.

First, one must look at *body type, body composition, and body proportions.* Some people are more heavily muscled than others and will naturally carry more weight. For example, the ideal weight of a mesomorph and an ectomorph of the same height may be quite different. Frame size, which is a popular assessment mode, is only one of the indications of variance in body composition. Hydrostatic weighing is the most accurate measure of body composition developed to date. The trusty tape measure offers another perspective to the data on existing conditions, but it is not as sound as the hydrostatic weighing, which gives the prospective dieter information about the percent of body fat he or she carries. A preliminary assessment should include identification of body type, identification of present weight and ideal weight, percent of body fat as measured by hydrostatic weighing, and body measurements taken by a tape measure. These figures objectively identify existing conditions.

The next step is analysis of *eating habits.* Self-delusion is very easy when one is looking at one's own eating habits. It is very easy to say "Oh, I don't eat much" when no record has been kept of actual intake. For this reason it is essential to keep a running record of all nutrients ingested to facilitate intensive analysis of eating patterns. A record of when food is eaten, why it is eaten, and what physical and emotional effects it has can offer profound insights about one's eating habits. Table 20.1 is an example of the kind of record that is most helpful in analyzing eating habits. Please note that this table includes more than the usual record of what is eaten. It also includes time of day, nutritional content of the food, reasons for eating, and immediate and long-term effects of the food.

Careful record keeping gives one a clear picture of one's eating habits and the effects of these habits. Highs and lows of blood sugar may often be traced back to eating simple sugars or some other particular food. However, no matter how carefully the record is kept, it can do no good if there is no analysis of eating patterns and modification following the analysis.

As just noted, Table 20.1 gives the prospective dieter information about eating habits and their effects. The time when food is eaten is recorded. Some people eat earlier in the day, some eat later in the day. This relates to the metabolism of the individual and the periods of the day when the person is most active. For some, a big breakfast is essential. For others, it makes them sluggish and logy throughout the morning. Attention to time of day is important because one can bring these eating patterns to conscious attention. The nutritional content of the food eaten is recorded to assist in analysis of the effects of varying types of food on one's system. Simple sugars are known to raise the blood sugar fast and then drop it like a hot potato. Proteins tend to raise the blood sugar more slowly, but the effects last longer.[2] Table 20.1 can illustrate to the potential dieter these types of effects. Careful analysis can also lead to awareness of the potential for hypoglycemia and other problems. By looking at the record kept over a period of time, one can begin to identify those foods to which one

---

2. Proteins also tend to contain high levels of fat. Therefore, moderation is called for.

TABLE 20.1   Record of Food Intake

	Eating Record			Analysis of Eating (same day)		Immediate Effects (next day)		Long-Term Effects	
Date	Weight	Time of Day	Food Eaten and Amount	Reason for Eating	Nutritional Content of Food Eaten	Immediate Physical Effects	Immediate Emotional Effects	Long-Term Physical Effects	Long-Term Emotional Effects
	1		2	3	4	5	6		

1. Weigh yourself at the same time every day. Weighing daily gives a clear picture of what is going on.
2. Record everything: meals, snacks, water, coffee, and everything else that goes into your mouth.
3. There are many reasons for eating other than hunger. Boredom, frustration, depression, and celebration are only a few.
4. Proteins, fats, carbohydrates, etc. (record whether the carbohydrate is simple sugar, fructose, or complex carbohydrate).
5. Record sensations: sleepy, sluggish, twitchy, and the like.
6. Record feelings such as depressed, excited, lethargic, and the like.

may be addicted, such as refined sugar, milk products, caffeine, etc. Careful analysis of reasons for eating can be a real eye-opener. One may be unaware of some of the excuses used to rationalize eating more than is needed, but one's record, if kept accurately and carefully, won't lie. Charting the physical and emotional effects of foods can yield valuable information about which foods are long-lasting, which provide a quick lift, and which will guarantee return of hunger in a short period. If a running record of weight is also kept in the time period in which the eating record is kept, the effects of certain foods on one's weight can be noted. People have different absorption rates for different types of foods. Thus, it is necessary to keep a record such as the one shown in Table 20.1 to identify those patterns. Whether or not the chart is an exact replica of the one in Table 20.1 is irrelevant. The point is to keep track, note patterns, and systematically analyze the effects of ingestion. Any diet undertaken without this kind of analysis will result in, at best, only a temporary loss of weight. For long-term change, one must change habits. Before one can change habits, one must know what the habits are.

Choosing a Dietary Approach

The words, "I'm on a diet" are a sure sign that the person will not keep the weight off once it is lost. "I'm on a diet" implies that it is a temporary condition, and that there is another state: "not dieting." One must change eating habits to lose weight and keep it off permanently. On-and-off dieting is typified by all of the "crash diets" one can find in almost every popular magazine. Crash dieting is just that: crash, it comes off; crash, it goes back on. The roller coaster cycle of crash dieting is a real threat to the effective functioning of the body. Moreover, ups and downs of weight make it difficult to build dance skills. Changes in weight change the balancing of the body, and even five pounds can make a difference to the skilled dancer's performance. Instead of going on a diet, the dancer who is serious about weight loss should think in terms of *dietary approach*. This implies a lifetime commitment to the approach which will ensure a more permanent weight loss than crash dieting.

In choosing a dietary approach, one must take into account all of the information available about the effects of different foods, the natural tendencies of one's own body, and the demands one places on that body in dance. Consultation with a nutrition specialist can add considerable information. To repeat: No single dietary approach will work for everybody; there are too many individual differences in metabolism, absorption rates, and eating patterns to make any approach effective for all. Thus, one must systematically analyze dietary patterns on an individual basis. What works? What doesn't?

Effective Eating Habits

The next step is to adopt *effective eating habits*. The first phase, in turn, of changing eating habits is sensory awareness. What does it feel like to be truly hungry? What does it feel like to be full? What is the sensory difference between hunger and thirst? These types of questions are essential to adopting effective eating habits. A second phase is analytical. One must distinguish between eating because one is truly hungry and eating because one is bored, frustrated, excited, or angry. All too often, eating is an escape: something to take the mind off other matters. When this is the case, we often do not pay attention to eating itself. It is an escape, a release, or a substitute rather than a physical necessity to fuel the system. Becoming aware of eating in sensory and motivational terms is essential to the adoption of effective eating habits. First, eat only when truly hungry. Find other activities to ward off boredom, frustration, and other feelings. Second, eat slowly. Many studies of overeaters have shown that eating fast is a characteristic of overweight individuals. Apparently there is a neurological delay in the satiation (fullness) signal. Eating slowly allows the signal to be processed before we wolf down another helping. Third, while eating, monitor the sensations carefully and stop, even if the fork is midway to the mouth, as soon as you feel full.

The body tells us when to eat and how much to eat if we only will learn to listen to the signals. Just as we must learn to pay attention to the body to achieve high-skill levels, we must also listen to the body to achieve ideal weight. Listening to the body carefully is the single most important eating habit one can acquire.

Changing Attitudes

Many parents raise their children using food as a positive or negative reinforcer. That is, food is used as a reward ("Have a cookie") when the child is good, and food is withheld ("You'll go to bed without your dinner") when the child is bad. These emotional connotations become inextricably linked with food as we grow up. In adulthood, vestiges of those childhood reinforcers can still control our lives, if we let them. Habits instilled early in our lives continue to influence us in adulthood ("Clean your plate," "Don't waste food," "Eat what's put in front of you"). Looking carefully at the psychology of eating patterns often reveals that food is eaten as a replacement for love, acceptance, or success. Analyzing deep-seated attitudes about food is crucial in changing one's psychological dependence on food.

It has been said that fat people live to eat while thin people eat to live. This sums up the difference between a fat attitude and a thin attitude. Hardly before a fat person is finished with a meal, he or she is thinking of the next meal, much as a travel addict starts to plan the next trip on the first day home, or as an alcoholic thinks of the next drink. Food becomes a fetish, a recreational activity, and a means of showing and getting affection. A shift in attitude from fat to thin requires a modification of this attitude.

Food is a means, not an end in itself. Food is essential to survival, but one must constantly ask, How much? How often? Food is not an antidote to boredom, satisfying activity is. Food is not a solution for frustration; removing the irritant is. Likewise food is not a salve to spread on wounded feelings, nor is it a means to calm one's fears. Yet we tend to use food in all of these ways at one time or another. Recognizing the tendency to believe that eating has all of these restorative powers is a way to start shifting one's attitude toward food. The attitude shift is not easy, but it must be made if a person is to lose weight and keep it off.

The new attitude is a lifetime change, not one that lasts two weeks and then is discarded, particularly for those with a real tendency to be overweight. One can afford to be patient. A lifetime change means that one small slip does not negate all effort; there is no real hurry when one shifts into the lifetime attitude. The panicky rush occurs only when a person puts himself or herself in the pressure-packed position of having to lose a certain amount of weight within a certain time. Then a slip is perceived as total failure.

Nothing is more important to weight loss and weight management than a healthy attitude, and nothing can sabotage the most sincere efforts as thoroughly as the wrong attitude. Think of a weight loss plan as a performance. No dancer would think of stopping a performance because of one small slip. One doughnut, a candy bar, a cookie or sweet roll shouldn't be the signal to give up either. In weight management, as in performance, the show must go on.

These four elements are critical to effective weight management: realistic self-assessment, choosing a dietary approach, adopting effective eating habits, and changing one's attitude toward food. Each is equally important to a person who is trying to lose weight, but the most essential ingredient is the desire to lose weight. Without that, none of these techniques will have any effect at all.

Aerobic Exercise and Weight Loss

Increasing exercise is also important when one is attempting to lose weight. Most dancers think they get plenty of exercise, but most of their activity is anaerobic. Aerobic activity (see Chapter 19) is known to raise the metabolic rate (the body's rate of burning calories) and thus should be added to the daily routine of the dancer. Whatever the form of aerobic exercise, it is essential to both weight loss and general good health. Aerobic activity is particularly essential in the first few weeks of a weight-loss program. When caloric intake is reduced, the body responds with an automatic lowering of the metabolic rate. It is thought that this response is the body's protective mechanism against starvation. This response can be somewhat counterbalanced by the addition of aerobic exercise, which raises the metabolic rate.

A Note on Ideal Weight

While this chapter has dealt mostly with losing weight, the problems of underweight must also be considered by the dancer. Each dancer should identify a range of ideal weight. For beginning dancers, the range is frequently broader than for the professional who has narrowed the range that is ideal for performance to within three to five pounds. A drop below ideal weight is as serious to the dancer as a rise above ideal weight. Constant monitoring of weight is important so that small losses or gains can be dealt with immediately.

Conclusion and Applications

CHAPTER 21

Enhancing Performance

Performance is an integral component of dance, but because judgment of quality of performance in dance is so subjective, little research has been done on the factors which promote optimal performance. This does not mean that research in this area is impossible; it is just difficult. A truly brilliant dance performance is easily recognizable, but the criteria for assessment of performance often remain unidentified. This is part of the mystery and magic of the art form. Nevertheless, the question arises: If a majority of observers (the audience) agree that a given performance is brilliant, what is it that they are all seeing? Even as I write this, there is a glimmer of hesitation at even raising the question, for I am not sure that I wish to see the magic and mystery of the performance moment dissected and analyzed. However, from the performer's perspective, attention to factors that contribute to optimal performance (often defined as consistently performing at or close to the highest level possible) must be given attention. Sometimes that attention is sporadic and haphazard, but when preparation is systematic, the performer reduces the likelihood of errors that spring up in the unpredictability of the performance moment. The goal of all performance preparation is to find what some authors call the *zone* and others call *transcendence;* whatever it is called, it is the achievement of magical and seamless performance, when all the details disappear and the soul of the dancer emerges to embody the vision of the choreographer.

Every seasoned performer has a pre-performance ritual. Performers have found that certain foods, rest patterns, and warm-up activities "work." Even though there is no guarantee that a brilliant performance will result from the pre-performance ritual, it is practiced because the dancer feels that it increases the likelihood of an optimal performance. So, even though we may not wish to dissect the magic for the audience, performers may indeed benefit from awareness of some accepted techniques of enhancing performance.

Preparation for the performance moment can be divided into three general areas: *physical, psychological,* and *spiritual.* Kinesiology can add much to the normal rehearsal process: physical preparation. Sport psychology offers valuable insights into psychological preparation. Spiritual preparation is up to the individual dancer.

Physical Preparation

Rehearsals are the first venue for physical preparation for performance. In a rehearsal, the dancer learns the "steps" or movement combinations which make up a dance. Of course the rehearsal process also requires that dancers find a way to harness their passion and give more to the work than simple performance of steps, but first the steps must be learned. As the dancer learns the work, certain gaps in physical capacity may be exposed. For example, a given movement combination may require more strength, flexibility, or endurance than the dancer can muster. It is then the responsibility of the dancer to build the deficient capacity in order to meet the demands of the dance work. Muscular analysis, as practiced in Section III of this book, can pinpoint the prime movers in a given combination. Principles of conditioning can then be utilized to plan a conditioning program to increase capacity. If the work presents a cardiorespiratory challenge, the dancer may wish to engage in additional aerobic workouts. If the work puts an inordinate stress on a particular part of the body, a preventive program of strengthening and/or stretching may serve to prevent overuse injuries.

Psychological Preparation

Physical preparation for the performance moment is a necessary, but not a sufficient, condition for optimal performance. Psychological preparation is also necessary.

Sport psychologists have researched factors which contribute to optimal performance, aided by the fact that most sports have some kind of objective criteria such as scores, times, and distances. A few years ago, I took a class in Sport Psychology taught by Keith Henschen at the University of Utah. The content seemed to me to transfer directly to dance performance. On the basis of lectures, readings, and discussions in that class, I formulated an outline of factors in optimal performance. I do not pretend to be an expert in sport psychology, but feel that the information is so relevant to dance performance that it warrants brief discussion here.

Four major psychological factors contribute to optimal performance: (1) attention, (2) arousal, (3) motivation, and (4) self-confidence. Remember that these are psychological factors and that they come into play once the physical preparation for a performance has been done. The following discussion of these factors is not intended to be comprehensive. Rather, it is hoped that it will stimulate thought and discussion by dancers.

Attention

Attention can be active or passive. *Active* attention tends to focus on individual components of a task and is effective and appropriate for learning new skills. *Passive* attention is more responsive to the moment and is often likened to putting the body on "automatic pilot," or being in the "zone." The difference between "thinking" and "doing" relates to active and passive attention: thinking contributes to active attention, and passive attention contributes to doing. Dancers often speak of "getting out of their heads" in order to find the essence of a movement. This is the first step toward passive attention.

Different types of *cues* capture the attention of the performer. *Task-relevant cues* point to specific components of the performance that require attention. These cues are very individual in nature and are most effective when they are kinesthetically linked to specific performance demands. In the rehearsal process, the dancer might discover a particular image (kinesthetic, visual, or verbal) that enhances the performance of a particular movement combination. For example, sensing roots burrowing into the earth might provide a kinesthetic image to enhance balance; the wide sweep of an arm might be enhanced by the visual image of a mountaintop vista; or a word cue like "prickly" or "charge!" might provide an underlying motional sense. These are only examples. Each role demands that the dancer develop specific task-relevant cues. *Distractors* are cues which take attention away from task-relevant cues. In dance, problems with costumes and missed music cues are just two examples of possible distractors. The seasoned performer is able to deal with such distractions and return quickly to task-relevant cues. *Outcome cues* take the attention of the performer out of the moment and project attention into the future with thoughts that often begin "What if . . . ?" Examples of outcome cues include negative *self-talk:* What if I stumble? What if I miss the balance? What if my friends and family think I look foolish? Outcome cues are insidious saboteurs of optimal performance, for they take the attention of the performer away from the performance moment. Of these three types of attention cues, task-relevant cues are the most appropriate for the achievement of optimal performance.

Arousal

Arousal is a term used to indicate general internal feelings of energy and excitement on one end of a waking continuum and distress and anxiety on the other end of the continuum. Each performer has his or her own *optimal range of arousal.* *Sensory* (not mental) identification of that optimal range, along with knowing ways to raise or lower one's own arousal level, is thought to contribute to optimal performance.

Motivation

Motivation is an extraordinarily complex topic. Individual motivational patterns form the foundation of incentives which direct human action. Examination of motivational patterns reveals *why* we do things in the first place. In this very brief discussion, only a few motivational factors will be presented as examples of effects on performance.

Motivation patterns can be *extrinsic* (seeking external rewards or praise) or *intrinsic* (seeking some component of self-satisfaction); they can be oriented toward *fulfillment of deficiencies, preservation of safety,* or *the need for growth and change;* they can be *process-oriented* or *product-oriented.* A young dancer is encouraged to ask the questions: Why do I dance? What do I expect to achieve by dancing? Who decides if I am dancing well? The answers will lead the dancer to a clearer understanding of his or her motivational patterns.

The multidimensional motivational patterns of an individual have a direct effect upon his or her attitudes. Certain attitudes, reflecting motivational patterns, have a powerful effect on performance. A performer might be a *"success seeker"* or a *"failure avoider."* While these two attitudes may seem at first to have the same goal, in application they are very different. Every performer engages in self-talk, but is it positive or negative? The difference in attitude can be quite remarkable.

No discussion of motivation would be complete without acknowledgement of the role of *fear*. Common fears include fear of failure, fear of success, fear of the unknown, fear of rejection, fear of want, fear of change, fear of abandonment, and many others. Fear creates energy and arousal, but too much fear creates panic and immobilization. The first step to channeling the energy of fear is learning to manage one's own arousal level. It is when the individual faces his or her fears that *risk* enters the picture. How willing are you to take a risk, to dare, to go where you have never been?

Self-Confidence

Self-confidence is the fourth psychological factor affecting performance. *Self-confidence* is difficult to define, but I think it is evidenced by "doing," by being in the moment, and by daring to do new things that might result in failure. When I taught very young children (ages 3–6), one of our primary objectives was development of self-confidence—the attitude that "I can do it." It was then that I began to think that self-confidence comes from repeated survival of failure and subsequent growth from it. I discovered that self-confidence bloomed most gloriously when a child was able to make something positive out of what initially appeared to be a failure. Persistence despite frustration seemed to be another indicator of self-confidence—again, an "I can" attitude. But with children and adults alike, the basis of self-confidence always seems to be *self-acceptance* and *self-love*.

In the cluster of characteristics of self-confidence, "trying" contrasts sharply with "doing." People who "try" tend to focus on deficiencies, make value judgments of themselves and others, and make excuses for mistakes and failures. People who "do" tend to evaluate themselves honestly, take responsibility for mistakes or failures, and learn from those mistakes and failures. These contrasting concepts—"doing" and "trying"—come from Tom Kubistant's book *Performing Your Best*. Kubistant includes a wonderful list illustrating a shift from stubborn negativity and fear to positive accomplishment:

I won't
I can't

I don't know how
I wish I could
I want to
I think I might
I might
I think I can
I can
I will
I did!!
    (Kubistant, 1986, p. 25).

There is no neatly packaged formula for excellent performance, for there is none that would apply for all dancers. Each dancer must consider the factors which seem important, and then experiment with those factors to optimize performance.

In Conclusion

This chapter has covered many elements of preparation for performance in dance, including physical and psychological preparation for the performance moment. But the heart and soul of performance simply cannot be reduced to perfect technique, wise conditioning, and psychological maturity. It is more; much, much more.

There is a real danger in assuming that excellent performance can be ensured by kinesiological or psychological analysis. When the art form of dance performance is approached from the perspective of the sciences, the core—the heart and soul—of dance performance may well be neglected. Exquisite technique and physical skill is only a part of performance—and perhaps not even the most important part!

The heart of performance includes intense presence, vulnerability, and mystery. The intent of this chapter is not to reduce the mystery of the performance moment, but rather to allow preparation that may serve to facilitate the birth, growth, and full blooming of the mystery and magic of performance.

CHAPTER *22*

Applications of Dance Kinesiology

This book has presented information about the structure and function of the human body as it specifically relates to dance. Applications of the basic information have been noted throughout the preceding chapters. However, a general review focusing attention on the potential uses of dance kinesiology may be of value to you. There are three general categories into which these potential uses fall: self-awareness; use of specific information and principles to promote growth; and maintenance of health. These three applications apply equally to students and teachers of dance, but it may be helpful to identify some of the specialized applications for each group.

Uses by Students

The first and foremost application for students of dance is heightening *awareness of one's own capacities and limitations.* Realistic and objective self-appraisal is essential to understanding one's own performance. The sometimes subtle, sometimes not-so-subtle change that occurs concurrently with objective self-assessment is accompanied by a shift in attitude toward growth and change. The objectivity of the data seems to make change more attainable. Perhaps it is the specificity of the information that contributes to the change; perhaps it is being forced to look honestly at one's capacities and limitations. Whatever the reason, change becomes possible if the dancer is willing to work at it. One also identifies those features that are not changeable and, if wise, one quits worrying about them. After all, Morton short toe, tibial torsion, or knock-knees cannot be changed. A much wiser investment of energy is to focus on changeable weaknesses. Knowing what to work on, after systematic evaluation, the dancer can design an equally systematic conditioning program.

Effective conditioning techniques and teachers who focus on those techniques can speed up the growth process. At some point, it is hoped that self-acceptance will filter into the self-perception of the student dancer. The dancer can then develop techniques to minimize the aesthetic and physical effects of problematic characteristics: learning to "fake it with class." Envy of other dancers and self-flagellation for unchangeable features are futile and waste valuable time and energy. Knowing one's own capacities and limitations is crucial to achieving excellence in dance. But possibly most important of all, a dancer must learn to *listen to the body*. The intensive focus on specific body regions in kinesiology class can serve to heighten the perceptual awareness of bodily sensations, warning signals, and fatigue indicators. That heightened perception will serve the dancer very well in the quest for excellence.

The second application of dance kinesiology for the student dancer is *acceleration of progress along the path to excellence*. The simple fact is that the student who consistently uses kinesiological principles can *get better, faster*. Muscular analysis can provide information about the specific nature of a limitation. The principles of conditioning, when carefully applied, can increase strength, flexibility, and endurance quite rapidly. The habit of systematic self-evaluation allows the dancer to choose an exercise program to meet his or her needs. Knowing what the needs are, the dancer can then use dance kinesiology to help evaluate possible teachers. Different teachers focus on different components of dance. Data from the observation of prospective teachers can be compared with one's own needs to make selection an individual prescription rather than blind luck. This can further contribute to the acceleration of growth.

Speeding up the growth process is an obvious advantage when one considers the brevity of a dancer's performing time. Techniques that speed up the training process also serve to lengthen the dancer's time as a performer. Efficient, well-trained dancers tend to stay in the performance arena longer than those who consistently employ muscular "overkill." Dance kinesiology can help the student dancer move with greater efficiency. That is, he or she can perform the same combinations as before, but using less effort. Learning to move with minimum effort, without sacrificing performance level, is essential to the longevity of the dancer.

The third application of dance kinesiology for the student dancer is *maintenance of a healthy body*. The potential applications of dance kinesiology to prevention of injury have been discussed at length. Proper alignment and a balance of strength, flexibility, and endurance are the primary means of prevention. The dancer who consciously works toward these goals reduces the likelihood of injury. Another safeguard against injury is the ability to distinguish between good pain and bad pain.[1] Knowing the difference between these two types of pain can prevent injury or at least reduce the severity of injuries when they do occur. When injuries occur, the dancer with a background in dance kinesiology has a strong foundation upon which to base evaluation and decisions and can more easily understand the physician's diagnosis than the dancer with no science background. The terminology used by the physician will not be foreign, and questions can be phrased in the physician's language. A dance kinesiology background can even assist in the selection of a physician who will provide the most effective treatment and care. All of the decisions made at the time of an injury are potentially strengthened by a sound dance kinesiol-

---

1. Defined and discussed in Chapter 18.

ogy background. All components of health maintenance can also be improved through a knowledge of dance kinesiology.

The three classes of potential applications of dance kinesiology present a very brief and deceptively simple view of the value of dance kinesiology to the student dancer. But what can possibly be more important than self-awareness, accelerated growth in the development of dance skills, and maintenance of health?

Uses by Teachers

As might be expected, the teacher's uses of dance kinesiology build upon and expand the uses for the student. They follow the same pattern: awareness of individual differences, specificity of training based on kinesiological information, and promotion and protection of the students' health.

Just as the student must be aware of his or her capacities and limitations, the dance educator must be *aware of the range of individual differences in the class.* Information which contributes to this heightened awareness includes conscious or intuitive assessment of body type, movement behavior, range of conditioning levels in the class, and students' capacities and needs. Most of the best teachers of dance use evaluation of this sort. Those who have had no kinesiological training usually undertake the process intuitively. While an intuitive approach to assessing individual differences is better than ignoring the issue, it is not nearly as effective as conscious assessment. Dance kinesiology can serve as a valuable guide for conscious assessment of differences and can further guide the teacher in developing class sequences that focus on specific needs.

Specificity of training is the second application of dance kinesiology for teachers of dance. Identification of students' needs is useless if one does not follow through with movement experiences to meet those needs. The advantage of teaching from a kinesiological base is that once needs have been identified, there are specific techniques for meeting them. For example, the mere identification of weakness of the torso muscles will not correct the problem. The teacher must have the knowledge to design specific exercises to strengthen the weak musculature, using principles for building strength. Stretching, no matter how valuable, will not increase strength. Fifty-seven repetitions with no resistance will not be the most effective way to build strength. Dance kinesiology allows the teacher to pinpoint a problem and then "nail it" with a specifically designed combination.

Another component of specificity of training is kinesiological logic. Effective sequencing of a dance class requires the application of kinesiological logic to achieve optimal growth. Essential kinesthetic concepts should be built into the beginnings of the class, should be developed throughout the class, and should reach fruition with the final combinations. Thinking "backward" is often helpful in planning the sequence of a class. Starting with the motional objective, whatever it may be, the teacher can easily design a terminal combination that focuses on that objective. The problem is that, all too often, the component skills are not presented individually; this reduces the likelihood the student will achieve excellence at the combination. Using dance kinesiology to identify the components of the terminal objective and then planning backward, integrating the component skills into the early part of the class, is the foundation for kinesiologically sound sequencing (kinesiological logic). Teaching is, after all, a process of ensuring that students can do more at the end of the class than they could do at the beginning, and perhaps even more than they thought possible. Kinesiology can be an extraordinarily valuable tool in the process of ensuring students' growth.

Kinesiology can also assist the teacher in feedback and criticism. The statement, "That's good" may be a psychological shot in the arm for students, but it doesn't ensure repetition of the desired performance nearly as well as a compliment that specifically identifies why the performance was good ("That was good *because* you kept the knee extended and the hip turned out"). Likewise, a specific criticism is far more valuable than a general one. It gives the student specific information about the needed changes. A kinesiological background can give the teacher a vocabulary for feedback—certainly not the only vocabulary, but nevertheless a valuable one. The apparent objectivity of kinesiologically based criticism sometimes makes the comment seem less personally threatening, and may make it easier for the student to internalize the content.

The third use of kinesiology for the teacher of dance is the *promotion and preservation of students' health*. The teacher must be hawk-eyed to spot misalignment and misperformance. Kinesiology can help to develop that eye. Once a misalignment or misperformance has been identified, the teacher has an ethical obligation to call it to the attention of the student. Ignoring the problem could aggravate it and result in serious injury, either in class or later in performance. It is the teacher's responsibility to give as much feedback (verbal and physical information) as possible to the student and then insist upon accuracy of performance.

The timing of demands is another factor in the promotion and protection of students' health. Decisions regarding when demands are made should take into account the status of the students (physical, emotional, and psychological) as well as checking to make sure that adequate preparation has been done to allow for success in meeting the demands. Dance kinesiology can be fundamental to the preparation of demands. The use of specific muscular analysis of movement expectations can give a clear view of needed strength, flexibility, and endurance. Dance kinesiology can also aid the teacher in assessing a student's status by making the teacher more attuned to changes in the physical ramifications of fatigue, depression, and other states. Ill-timed demands can actually produce injury instead of producing the intended growth. The teacher's antennae must be constantly attuned to changes in students' status.

All of the applications of dance kinesiology revolve around three major functions:

1. Learning to work *with* the body, *not* against it
2. Being highly specific about training procedures

3. Listening to the signals given by the body and having the knowledge to interpret these signals

These three central applications form the core of all dance kinesiology classes.

A FINAL WARNING

Growth is a risky business. One cannot stay safe and grow. To grow means that one must take chances and push oneself beyond yesterday's limits. Throughout this book a great deal of time has been spent on the need for care and safety. Dance kinesiology can provide the dancer with many reasons why a given skill is impossible. The serious dancer says, "I don't care about that," and proceeds to achieve the impossible. That's growth. That's risk. And that is what dance is made of. Dance kinesiology can give dancers knowledge about when it is appropriate to push for the impossible and when it is not appropriate. Kinesiology is not, however, an excuse for failure. To dance, one must dare to go beyond the limits.

References

Alkire, Helen, "Standards for Dance Major Programs." Council of Dance Administrators' Publication. Ohio State University Dance Department, 1979.

Annarino, Anthony, *Developmental Conditioning for Men and Women.* C.V. Mosby, St. Louis, 1976.

Arnheim, Daniel, *Dance Injuries: Their Prevention and Care,* 2nd ed. C.V. Mosby, St. Louis, 1980.

Barham, Jerry, and Thomas, William L., *Anatomical Kinesiology.* Macmillan Publishing Company, New York, 1969.

Barham, Jerry, and Wooten, Edna, *Structural Kinesiology.* Macmillan Publishing Company, New York, 1973.

Basmajian, John V., *Primary Anatomy,* 8th ed. Williams & Wilkins, Baltimore, 1982.

Beck, Ernest W., *Mosby's Atlas of Functional Human Anatomy.* C.V. Mosby, St. Louis, 1982.

Benson, Herbert, *The Relaxation Response.* Avon, New York, 1975.

Bliss, P.M., and Lane, K.L., "Musculoskeletal Injuries in Dance Majors at Arizona State University." Unpublished, Arizona State University, 1980.

Brooks, George A., and Fahey, Thomas D., *Exercise Physiology: Human Bioenergetics and Its Applications.* John Wiley & Sons, New York, 1984.

Brown, Barbara, *New Mind, New Body.* Bantam Books, New York, 1974.

Brunnstrom, Signe, *Clinical Kinesiology.* F.A. Davis, Philadelphia, 1966.

Cannon, Walter B., *The Wisdom of the Body.* Norton, New York, 1932.

Cantu, Robert, and Gillespie, William, *Sports Medicine and Sports Science: Bridging the Gap.* Collamore Press, Lexington, Mass., 1982.

Chmelar, Robin and Fitt, Sally. *Diet* (Dancing at Your Peak Series). Princeton Book Company. Pennington, N.J., 1990.

Clark, Ronald G., *Essentials of Clinical Neuroanatomy and Neurophysiology,* 5th ed. F.A. Davis, Philadelphia, 1975.

Clarke, H. Harrison, *Muscular Strength and Endurance in Man.* Prentice-Hall, Englewood Cliffs, N.J., 1966.

Crafts, Roger C., *A Textbook of Human Anatomy.* Ronald Press, New York, 1966.

Crouch, James E., *Functional Human Anatomy.* Lea and Febiger, Philadelphia, 1978.

De Renne, C., "Exercise RX." *Highlights.* Southeast District, American Alliance of Health, Physical Education, Recreation, and Dance, February 1984.

De Vries, Herbert, *Physiology of Exercise for Physical Education and Athletics.* Wm. C. Brown, Dubuque, 1966.

Diamond, John, *Behavioral Kinesiology.* Harper & Row, New York, 1979.

Dolan, Joseph, and Holladay, Lloyd, *First-Aid Management: Athletics, Physical Education and Recreation,* 4th ed. Interstate Printers, Danville, Ill., 1974.

Dolan, Joseph, and Holladay, Lloyd, *Treatment and Prevention of Athletic Injuries,* 3rd ed. Interstate Printers and Publishers, Danville, Ill., 1967.

Downie, Patricia, *Cash's Textbook of Neurology for Physiotherapists.* Lippincott, New York, 1982.

Edington, D.W., and Edgerton, V.R., *The Biology of Physical Activity.* Houghton Mifflin, Boston, 1976.

Eddy, Martha, Holistic approaches to dance injury assessment and intervention. *Impulse.* Champaign, Ill., Human Kinetics Publishers, 1995 (in press).

Featherstone, D.F., *Dancing Without Danger,* 2nd ed. A.S. Barnes, New York, 1977.

Feldenkrais, Moshe, *Awareness Through Movement.* Harper & Row, New York, 1972.

Feldenkrais, Moshe, *Body and Mature Behavior.* International Universities Press, New York, 1949.

Feldenkrais, Moshe, *The Elusive Obvious.* META Publications, Cupertino, Calif., 1981.

Fitt, Sally S., "Conditioning for Dancers: Investigating Some Assumptions," *Dance Research Journal,* 14/1 and 2, 1981–82, pp. 32–38.

Fitt, Sally S., "Identification of Some Conditions that Encourage Dance Injuries and Preventative Measures," in *American Alliance of Health, Physical Education, Recreation and Dance Research Consortium Papers.* Edited by Charles Corbin, 1(2), 1978, pp. 71–77.

Fitt, Sally S., Study of Laban's Full Efforts as They Reflect the Four Neuromuscular Excitation Patterns. UCLA Movement Behavior Laboratory. Unpublished, 1970.

Fitt, Sally S., "The Use of Observation Techniques for the Identification of Neuromuscular Excitation Patterns, *Dance Research Collage.* Edited by Rowe and Stodelle, Congress on Research in Dance (CORD), 1979, pp. 157–172.

Fitt, Sally S., The Validity and Inter-rater Reliability of Observation Techniques in Identifying the Neuromuscular Excitation Patterns. UCLA Doctorale Dissertation, 1975. The content of this work was later published as: Fitt, Sally S. "The use of observation techniques for the identification of neuromuscular excitation patterns." *Dance Research Collage.* Edited by Rowe and Stodelle, Congress on Research in Dance (CORD), 1979, pp. 157–172.

Fitt, Sally S., and Hanson, Deanna S., *Movement Behavior Programs for Young Children.* Unpublished, 1978.

Fuller, P.E., "An Identification of Common Injuries Sustained in Ballet and Modern Dance Activities." Texas Woman's University. Unpublished, 1975.

Francis, Carl, *Introduction to Human Anatomy,* 5th ed. C.V. Mosby, St. Louis, 1968.

Gardner, Ernest, *Fundamentals of Neurology,* 5th ed. W.B. Saunders, Philadelphia, 1968.

Gelabert, Raol, *Anatomy for Dancers,* Vols. I and II, *Dance Magazine,* 1964.

Granit, Ragnar, *Muscular Afferents and Motor Control.* John Wiley & Sons, New York, 1966.

Granit, Ragnar, *The Basis of Motor Control.* Academic Press, London, 1970.

Granit, R. and Pompeiano, O., *Reflexive Control of Posture and Movement.* Holland Biomedical Press, New York, 1979.

Gray, Henry, *Gray's Anatomy,* 15th ed. Bounty Books, New York, 1977.

Groves, Richard, and Camaione, David, *Concepts in Kinesiology.* W.B. Saunders, Philadelphia, 1975.

Haas, Robert, *Eat to Win: The Sports Nutrition Bible.* Rawson and Associates, New York, 1984.

Hall, Calvin S. and Lindzey, Gardner, *Theories of Personality,* 2nd ed. John Wiley & Sons, New York, 1970.

Hall, Hamilton, *The Back Doctor,* Berkley Books, New York, 1980.

Hamilton, W.G., "Tendonitis about the Ankle Joint in Classical Ballet Dancers," *American Journal of Sports Medicine,* 1977, 5(2), pp. 84–87.

Hanna, Thomas, "Dictionary definition of the word somatics." *Somatics,* 4(2), 1983, p. 1.

Hanna, Thomas, "Field of Somatics." *Somatics,* 1(1), August 1976, pp. 30–34.

Hinson, Marilyn, *Kinesiology.* Wm. C. Brown, Dubuque, 1977.

Hollinshead, W. Henry, *Functional Anatomy of the Limbs and Back.* W.B. Saunders, Philadelphia, 1976.

Howse, A.J.G., "Orthpaedists Aid Ballet," *Clinical Orthopaedics and Related Research,* 1972, 89, pp. 52–63.

Hunt, Valerie, "The Biological Organization of Man to Move," *Impulse,* 1968.

Hunt, Valerie, *Infinite Mind.* Malibu Publishing Company, PO Box 4234, Malibu, Calif. 90265, 1995.

Hunt, Valerie, "Movement Behavior: A Model for Action," *Quest,* Monograph II, Spring 1964, pp. 69–91.

Jacobson, Edmund, *Progressive Relaxation.* University of Chicago Press, Chicago, 1929.

Jencks, Beata, *Your Body: Biofeedback at Its Best.* Nelson Hall, Chicago, 1977.

Jensen, Clayne and Schultz, Gordon, *Applied Kinesiology.* McGraw-Hill, New York, 1970.

Johnson, Warren, *Science and Medicine of Exercise and Sports.* Harper & Row, New York, 1960.

Jones, Frank, *The Alexander Technique: Body Awareness in Action.* Schocken Books, New York, 1976.

Kapit, Wynn, and Elson, Lawrence, *The Anatomy Coloring Book.* Harper & Row, New York, 1977.

Karpovich, Peter, and Sinning, Wayne, *Physiology of Muscular Activity,* 7th ed. W.B. Saunders, Philadelphia, 1971.

Kelley, David L., *Kinesiology: Fundamentals of Motion Description.* Prentice-Hall, Englewood Cliffs, N.J., 1971.

Klafs, Carl, and Arnheim, Daniel, *Modern Principles of Athletic Training,* 3rd ed. C.V. Mosby, St. Louis, 1973.

Klein, Karl, *The Knee in Sports.* Jenkins, New York, 1969.

Knott, Margaret, and Voss, Dorothy, *Proprioceptive Neuromuscular Facilitation,* 2nd ed. Harper & Row, New York, 1956.

Kubisant, Tom, *Performing Your Best.* Life Enhancement Publications, Champaign, Ill., 1986.

Kulund, Daniel, *The Injured Athlete.* Lippincott, Philadelphia, 1982.

Laban, Rudolph, and Lawrence, F.C., *Effort.* MacDonald and Evans, London, 1947.

Lamb, David, *The Physiology of Exercise: Responses and Adaptations.* Macmillan Publishing Company, New York, 1978.

Laws, Kenneth, *The Physics of Dance.* Schirmer Books, New York, 1984.

Lejbov, E.B., and Rohlin, G.D., "Several Characteristics of the Skeleton of Ballet Artists," *Arkhiv Anatomii, Gistologii i Embriologii,* November 1967, 53, pp. 42–47.

Lockhart, R.D., Hamilton, G.F., and Fyfe, F.W., *Anatomy of the Human Body.* Lippincott, Philadelphia, 1959.

Logan, Gene, and McKinney, Wayne, *Kinesiology.* Wm. C. Brown, Dubuque, 1970.

Lowen, Alexander, *The Betrayal of the Body.* Collier, New York, 1967.

MacConaill, M.A., and Basmajian, J.V., *Muscles and Movements: A Basis for Human Kinesiology.* Williams & Wilkins, Baltimore, 1969.

Mathews, Donald, and Fox, Edward, *The Physiological Basis of Physical Education and Athletics,* 2nd ed. W.B. Saunders, Philadelphia, 1976.

Miller, E.H., Schneider, H.J., Bronson, J.J., and McLain, D., "A New Consideration in Athletic Injuries—The Classical Ballet Dancer," *Clinical Orthopaedics,* September 1975, 3, pp. 181–191.

Miller, William, *The Keys to Orthopaedic Anatomy.* Charles C. Thomas, Springfield, Ill., 1965.

Morehouse, Lawrence, and Miller, Augustus, *Physiology of Exercise,* 5th ed. C.V. Mosby, St. Louis, 1967.

National Association of Schools of Dance (NASD), "Handbook and Directory." Reston, Va., 1986.

O'Connell, Alice, and Gardner, Elizabeth, *Understanding the Scientific Bases of Human Movement.* Williams & Wilkins, Baltimore, 1972.

Pelipenko, V.I., "Specific Characteristics of the Development of the Foot Skeleton in Pupils of a Choreographic School," *Arkhiv Anatomii, Gistologii i Embriologii,* 1973, 64(6).

Rathbone, Josephine L., *Relaxation.* Columbia University Press, New York, 1943.

Rolf, Ida, *Rolfing, The Integration of Human Structures.* Harper & Row, New York, 1977.

Restack, Richard M., *The Brain*. Bantam Books, New York, 1985.

Rosen, Gerald, *The Relaxation Book*. Prentice-Hall, Englewood Cliffs, N.J., 1977.

Sammarco, James, *Clinics in Sports Medicine: Injuries to Dancers*. W.B. Saunders, Philadelphia, 1983.

Schneider, H.J., King, A.Y., Bronson, J.L., and Miller, E.H., "Stress Injuries and Developmental Change of Lower Extremities in Ballet Dancers," *Diagnostic Radiology*, 1974, 113(3), pp. 627–632.

Shaw, Janet J., "The Nature, Frequency and Patterns of Dance Injuries: A Survey of College Dance Students." Unpublished, University of Utah, 1977.

Sheldon, W.H., *Atlas of Men*, Harper & Row, New York, 1954.

Shephard, Roy J., *Alive Man! The Physiology of Physical Activity*. Charles C. Thomas, Springfield, Ill., 1972.

Simonson, Ernst, *Physiology of Work Capacity and Fatigue*. Charles C. Thomas, Springfield, Ill., 1971.

Smith, David S., *Muscle*. Academic Press, New York, 1972.

Sparger, Celia, *Anatomy and Ballet*, Second Edition. Adam and Charles Black, London, 1952.

Spence, Alexander, *Basic Human Anatomy*. Benjamin/Cummings Publishing Co., Menlo Park, Calif., 1982.

Sperry, R.W., "Lateral Specialization of Cerebral Function in the Surgically Separated Hemispheres," in F.J. McGuigan (ed.), *The Psychophysiology of Thinking*. Academic Press, New York and London, 1973.

Steindler, Arthur, *Kinesiology of the Human Body*. Charles C. Thomas, Springfield, Ill., 1955.

Strauss, R.H. (ed.), *Sports Medicine and Physiology*, W.B. Saunders, Philadelphia, 1979.

Sturman, Janet, "The Dancer Specific Conditioning Program on the New Concept Reformer." Unpublished M.F.A. Project Report, University of Utah, 1993. (To be published by the Joseph H. Pilates Foundation. For information, call 1-800-PILATES.)

Swazey, Judith P., *Reflexes and Motor Integration: Sherrington's Concept of Integrative Action*. Harvard University Press, Cambridge, 1969.

Sweigard, Lulu, *Human Movement Potential*. Harper & Row, New York, 1974.

Thie, John, *Touch for Health*. DeVorss & Co., Santa Monica, Calif., 1973.

Thompson, Clem, *Manual of Structural Kinesiology*, 9th ed. C.V. Mosby, St. Louis, 1981.

Todd, Mabel Ellsworth, *The Hidden You*. Dance Horizons, New York, 1953.

Todd, Mabel Ellsworth, *The Thinking Body*. Dance Horizons, New York, 1968.

Tye, Marian, "Some Factors Affecting Vertical Jump Height from First Position." University of Utah Master's thesis, 1982.

Vincent, L.M., *The Dancer's Book of Health*. Andrews and McNeel, New York, 1978.

Volkov, M.V., and Badnin, I.A., "Occupational Accidents in Ballet Performers and Their Prevention." *Ortopediva, Travmatologiva i Protezirovanive*, 1970, 31, pp. 57–61.

Volkov, M.V., Mironova, Z.S., and Badnin, I.A., "Injuries to Ligaments of the Talocrural Joint in Ballet Dancers and Their Management," *Ortopediva, Travmatologiva i Protezirovanive*, 1973, 34, pp. 1–6.

Washington, B.L., "Musculoskeletal Injuries in Theatrical Dancers: Site, Frequency, and Severity." *American Journal of Sports Medicine*, 1978, 6(2), pp. 75–98.

Wells, Katharine, and Luttgens, Kathryn, *Kinesiology: Scientific Basis of Human Motion*. W.B. Saunders, Philadelphia, 1976.

Wessel, Janet, and Macintyre, Christine, *Body Contouring and Conditioning Through Movement*. Allyn & Bacon, Boston, 1970.

White, John, and Fadiman, James, *Relax*. Confucian Press, New York, 1976.

Wittrock, M.C., et al., *The Human Brain*. Prentice-Hall, Englewood Cliffs, N.J., 1977.

Woodburne, Russell T., *Essentials of Human Anatomy*, 2nd ed. Oxford University Press, New York, 1961.

Contributors to the Second Edition

Jacque Lynn Bell

Jacque Lynn Bell is a professional choreographer, dancer, and teacher of dance technique and Alexander Technique. Her choreography has been performed in the United States, Canada, Europe, and the Far East, including works presented by the Royal Winnepeg Ballet of Cananda, Utah Repertory Dance Theatre, Company of Four, and Virginia Tanner's Children's Dance Theatre, as well as several university dance companies. She has served as artistic director for the Fairmount Dance Theatre in Cleveland, Ohio, as well as for the Teton Dance Festival in Jackson, Wyoming. She has been the recipient of grants and awards for choreography from BACA Downtown Cultural Center in New York; American College Dance Festival in Washington, D.C.; Ohio Arts Council; and the University of Utah. She has been a Movement Specialist for the National Endowment for the Arts since 1977. She holds an M.F.A. degree for choreography from the University of Utah and is a Certified Instructor of the Alexander Technique.

As well as teaching Alexander Technique privately, Jacque has taught Movement for Actors for the Theatre Department and the Alexander Technique for the Department of Modern Dance at the University of Utah. She continues to explore the teaching of dance technique using Alexander Technique as a basis.

Mary Bond

Mary Bond has a Master's Degree in dance from the University of California, Los Angeles. She trained with Dr. Ida P. Rolf and is a Certified Rolfer and Rolfing Movement teacher in private practice in Los Angeles. Her book, *Rolfing Movement Integration: A Self-Help Approach to Balancing the Body,* is available through Healing Arts Press, One Park Street, Rochester, VT 05767.

Bonnie Bainbridge Cohen

Bonnie Bainbridge Cohen has an extensive background in movement, including various dance styles, dance therapy, body work, martial arts, voice, and yoga. She received a B.S. in occupational therapy from Ohio State University in 1963 and has been certified as a Neurodevelopmental Therapist by Dr. and Mrs. Bobath in England, as a Laban Movement Analyst by the Laban/Bartinieff Institute of Movement Studies in New York, and as a Kestenberg Movement Profiler by Dr. Judith Kestenberg. Among her many teachers have been Erick Hawkins and Irmgard Bartinieff in dance; Marion Chace in dance therapy; André Bernard and Barbara Clark in Neuromuscular Re-education; Haruchika Noguchi, developer of *Katsugen Undo,* a method of engaging in automatic movement; Yogi Ramira in yoga; John Upledger, D.O., and Richard McDonald, D.O., in Craniosacral Therapy; Fritz Smith, M.D. and acupuncturist, in Zero Balancing; Sylus Engum and Herbert Doussant in voice; and Eido Roshi in Zen practice.

Bonnie has taught dance at numerous colleges and dance schools throughout the United States, including Hunter College and the Erick Hawkins School of Dance in New York, and the Naropa Institute in Boulder, Colorado. She has also taught kinesiology in the graduate dance therapy program at Antioch College in Keene, New Hampshire, and has been a guest teacher at Esalen Institute in Big Sur, California. She worked with movement and body work at the University of Amsterdam's Psychiatric Research Clinic in the Netherlands and helped to establish a school for occupational and physical therapists in Tokyo.

In 1973 in New York City, Bonnie founded The School for Body-Mind Centering, dedicated to exploration and teaching of movement based upon anatomical, physiological, psychological, and developmental principles. In 1976 she moved with her family to Amherst, Massachusetts, where she continued the school. The school for Body-Mind Centering has offered several practitioner and teacher certification programs, which have been attended by several hundred people in North and South America, Europe, Australia, New Zealand, and Asia.

Bonnie currently teaches, writes, and has a private practice working primarily with infants and toddlers with mild to severe developmental difficulties. She lives in Amherst with her husband and three children and travels extensively to teach throughout the United States, Canada, and Europe.

Peggy Hackney

Peggy Hackney is internationally recognized for her work in Laban Movement Analysis (LMA) and Bartenieff Fundamentals and helped found the Intensive LMA Certification Programs in New York City, Seattle, Salt Lake City, and Berlin. She holds a B.A. in psychology from Duke University and an M.F.A. in dance from Sarah Lawrence College. Ms. Hackney performed in New York City for 10 years before joining the Bill Evans Dance Company and touring the United States. She was on the faculty of the University of Washington for eleven years and has taught throughout the United States as well as in Europe. She teaches movement classes and does one-on-one work in Bartenieff Fundamentals in Seattle, as well as working in physical therapy clinics helping people facilitate their own healing through individualized movement programs. Peggy's book on her work in Bartenieff Fundamentals, *Making Connections,* is being published by Gordon and Breach. Other publications include her videotape *Discovering Your*

Expressive Body and *A Study Guide to Elementary Labanotation,* both distributed by Princeton Book Company.

Carol Lessinger

Carol Lessinger is a Certified Feldenkrais Practitioner, trained by Dr. Feldenkrais and his Israeli associates. She is in full-time private practice in Salt Lake City, Utah, and has taught Awareness Through Movement at the University of Utah in the Division of Continuing Education for sixteen years, and, more recently, in the Department of Modern Dance. Prior to moving to Utah, she developed the first "on site" creative movement program for preschoolers in Tallahassee, Florida. She performed, choreographed, and developed workshops as an Artist in the Schools in Leon County, Florida.

Pamela Matt

Pamela Matt studied modern dance technique with Merce Cunningham, Carolyn Brown, and Beverly Blossom. In the 1960s and 1970s, she was involved with the early development of Release Technique through her studies with Joan Skinner and performance collaborations with John Rolland and Nancy Udow. Pam earned her M.A. degree in dance at the University of Illinois. Concurrent with her program there, she began intensive private study with Barbara Clark, founding teacher in the field of Ideokinesiology. Published in 1993 and distributed by Contact Quarterly, Pamela's book, *A Kinesthetic Legacy: The Life and Works of Barbara Clark,* presents a biographical portrait of Miss Clark and an exposition of her body philosophy. Pamela has worked as a Movement Specialist with professional dancers in New York and in Sydney and Melbourne, Australia. She has conducted workshops in dance science for professional schools in the United States and Europe and has lectured for regional and national dance conferences and festivals. Pamela is currently Associate Professor of Dance at Arizona State University, where she teaches courses in Ideokinesis and dance kinesiology; at the time of this writing she was serving as Acting Chair of the Department.

Susan McLain

Susan McLain a native New Yorker, graduated from New York City's High School of the Performing Arts and later received her B.A. degree in dance education from Lehman College, CCNY. Susan danced professionally for more than ten years, performing with Pearl Lang, Diane Gray, and Larry Richardson, and for six years (1977–1982) was a Principal Dancer with the Martha Graham Dance Company. She has performed extensively throughout the world, and has performed in such theaters as the Frankfurt Opera House, Alice Tully Hall, Covent Garden, and the Metropolitan Opera House. She has been seen in the *Dance in America* series for public television in Martha Graham's "Clytemnestra," and in *Live at Wolf Trap* in "Seraphic Dialogue."

Susan's teaching experience includes private studios (Larry Richardson's Dance Gallery, Alvin Ailey's American Dance Center, the Martha Graham School of Contemporary Dance, Repertory Dance Theater of Utah, and others) and colleges and universities. She has been a guest artist at Florida State University, Arizona State University, University of Colorado, University of Utah, and many others. Susan trained in the Pilates Studio in New York during the years that she was dancing with the Graham Company. While living in Salt Lake City, she worked in a private studio teaching Pilates-based work and was on the faculty of the Department of Modern Dance at the University of Utah for eight years. Susan's choreography can be seen in the repertoires of Utah's Repertory Dance Theatre, Ririe-Woodbury Dance Company, and Performing Dance Company of the University of Utah. She received her M.F.A. degree in modern dance from the University of Utah in 1992. She currently is an Assistant Professor on the faculty of the Dance Department of California State University at Long Beach.

Madeleine Scott

Madeleine Scott holds an M.A. degree in dance from UCLA and received certification as a Laban Movement Analyst in 1988. Before beginning her teaching career, Madeleine danced professionally with DANCE/LA, Manual Alum Dance Company, and Douglas Nielsen Dance Company. Madeleine is currently Professor of Dance at Ohio University in Athens, Ohio, where she teaches dance technique, kinesiology for dancers, choreography, Laban Movement Analysis, and Bartenieff Fundamentals.

Index

Numbers in bold refer to captions and tables; n. following numbers refers to footnotes.

The Author

Sally Sevey Fitt holds a B.S. in physical education from Hamline University, and an M.S. in recreation and an Ed.D. from the University of California at Los Angeles. From 1966 to 1970, she served as teaching and research assistant to Dr. Valerie V. Hunt at UCLA, assisting in classes on dance kinesiology, movement behavior, and crosscultural analysis of expressive movement, and also working as research assistant in the Movement Behavior Laboratory. From 1970 to 1973, she served as Movement Specialist and Demonstration Teacher for the Early Childhood Unit at UCLA's University Elementary School. From 1972 to 1976, she taught dance kinesiology and pedagogy in the Dance Department at UCLA. In 1976, she moved to Salt Lake City, Utah, to take a position in the Modern Dance Department at the University of Utah, where she has taught dance kinesiology, movement behavior, pedagogy, and conditioning for dancers.

Sally is the author or co-author of numerous articles, chapters, and books dealing with dance kinesiology, movement behavior, conditioning, and health issues for dancers. She is presently Professor and Director of Graduate Studies in the Department of Modern Dance at the University of Utah, where she teaches dance kinesiology, movement behavior, conditioning for dancers, Pilates-based dancer-specific conditioning, teaching methods, graduate seminar classes, and research design.